P9-DVJ-720

123 B 2

PASADENA CITY COLLEGE
LIBRARY
PASADENA, CALIFORNIA

*Other books by Paul F. Boller, Jr.*

GEORGE WASHINGTON AND RELIGION

QUOTEMANSHIP: THE USE AND ABUSE OF QUOTATIONS
FOR POLEMICAL AND OTHER PURPOSES

AMERICAN THOUGHT IN TRANSITION: THE IMPACT OF
EVOLUTIONARY NATURALISM, 1865-1900

AMERICAN TRANSCENDENTALISM, 1830-1860: AN
INTELLECTUAL INQUIRY

# Freedom and Fate
# in
# American Thought

## From Edwards to Dewey

## PAUL F. BOLLER, JR.

SMU PRESS • DALLAS

© 1978   •   PAUL F. BOLLER, JR.

*Library of Congress Cataloging in Publication Data*

Boller, Paul F.
  Freedom and fate in American thought.

  (Bicentennial series in American studies ; 7)
  Bibliography: p.
  Includes index.
  1.  Liberty.   2.  Free will and determinism.
3.   Philosophy, American.   I.   Title.
B861.L52B64                    123                    78-5813
ISBN O-87074-169-1

*For*

BOB AND BARBARA

DOUG AND FERN

HARRY AND DORIS

WITHDRAWN

790363

WITHDRAWN

7903b8

# Contents

# Preface

FREEDOM IS PROBABLY America's favorite word, but there has always been a strong note of determinism, even fatalism, in American thought. This book examines the various ways in which nine prominent Americans from the eighteenth century to the twentieth have thought about freedom and necessity.

At the highest level of abstraction freedom (or liberty) has had three major definitions: self-realization, self-perfection, and self-determination. The self-realizationist holds that a person is free if circumstances are such that he is able to do as he pleases, that is, realize his desires, even though his desires are causally shaped. The self-perfectionist asserts that only if an individual has emancipated himself from his passions and prejudices and brought his will into harmony with reason or moral law can it be said that he is truly free. And the self-determinationist believes that freedom is a power which the individual possesses innately to initiate on his own acts of will which are to some extent unshaped by antecedent determining conditions. From this point of view, if an individual has an inherent power of causal initiative, his will (and therefore he) is said to be free.

William James thought that only the third definition of freedom was truly libertarian and that the other two, in denying freedom of the will, were at heart deterministic. But since self-realizationists and self-perfectionists sought to reconcile freedom and determinism by defining freedom either as absence of coercion or as emancipation from passion, he called them "soft determinists." He reserved the term "hard determinists" for people who frankly acknowledge that universal causal determinism makes freedom an illusion, and he saw little to distinguish them from fatalists. Strictly speaking, however, determinism and fatalism, though sometimes used synonymously, have different connotations. Determinism holds that the actions of human beings, though they are necessitated, do make a difference in the causal sequence, while fatalism stresses implacable (even capricious) destiny, no matter what human beings do. Determinism involves predictability as well as causality; it holds that everything that happens in the universe, including human actions, is in principle predictable, given knowledge of antecedent conditions and appropriate laws of nature. Fatalism says little more than that whatever happens had to happen.

The French language contains the word *liberté*, and the German language the word *Freiheit*. English, however, has two words, liberty and freedom, and they have slightly different shades of meaning. Liberty implies positive exercise of power (*liberty to* speak) and freedom connotes absence of constraint and restraint (*freedom from* fear). Liberty also tends to be used in legal and political contexts and freedom in philosophical and more general contexts. Some people contend that liberty is French, foolish, and frivolous, while freedom is English, solid, and sensible (if a bit dull); but we need not take this distinction seriously. For the two words are virtually indistinguishable in meaning, and they are used interchangeably by the American people as well as by the English. In *The Idea of Freedom*, an immensely useful compendium of definitions and dialectical exchanges, Mortimer Adler adds to the three most common definitions of freedom (or liberty) mentioned above two further ones: collective freedom, a variant of self-perfection, which involves the group rather than the individual; and political liberty, a derivative of self-realization, which emphasizes the removal of obstacles to political participation by individuals.

In the present volume, I examine in some detail the major attitudes toward liberty and necessity which prevailed in the United States from colonial times to our own day. But in order to avoid excessive abstractionism I have linked each of these attitudes to specific persons, beginning with Jonathan Edwards and ending with John Dewey. Each person treated here is therefore to some extent a representative figure, though what he said about freedom and necessity naturally bears something of the stamp of his own personality. I have been interested in popular thinking as well as in high thought; and I have picked for analysis men of action as well as men of ideas. I have also chosen people from different professions and walks of life and from different periods 'in our history in order to convey something of the richness and variety contained in American definitions of freedom and to show how the approach to freedom and causality has developed steadily in depth and subtlety since colonial days.

Except for Jonathan Edwards none of the thinkers examined here wrote a full-scale treatise on freedom, and it has been necessary to put together each thinker's philosophy of freedom somewhat as one assembles a jigsaw puzzle. It has been no small part of my task to make explicit underlying assumptions about freedom, to arrange scattered reflections on freedom and fate in some kind of logical order, and in general to systematize piecemeal thinking about freedom where it was possible to do so without distorting a thinker's basic position. My treatment of American philosophies of freedom, then, is interpretive as well as descriptive; and to support my interpretation of the central vision of each of the thinkers treated here I have made liberal use of quotations from their writings. While extensive consideration of the genesis of the ideas touched upon was not part of my purpose in this inquiry, I have discussed biographical details when I thought they cast light on a writer's thinking about freedom and determinism.

With the nine people treated in detail in this book, I have been interested in commonalities as well as particularities; but my emphasis has been on the latter. Jonathan Edwards's case against free will seems to me acutely argued, but I have stressed the weaknesses as well as the strengths of his position and have tried to see him through the eyes of his critics. I have presented Thomas Paine as the exponent of the natural-rights view of freedom in its most democratic form, but I have also tried to make explicit the close association between freedom and virtue which he took for granted and to take account of criticisms of the natural-rights philosophy after Paine's day. In Ralph Waldo Emerson's case, I have not only shown how he identified freedom primarily with virtue and rationality; I have also pointed out the tension in his thinking be-between freedom as rationality and freedom as civil liberty as well as the conflict between his deep-seated determinism and his belief in creative intuition. In the case of John C. Calhoun, I have concentrated on his rejection of natural rights and on his conception of liberty as a prerogative of a privileged minority and, departing from traditional interpretations, have regarded his thinking about freedom as social rather than individualistic in nature from almost the very beginning.

When it came to Frederick Douglass, I was interested in definitions of freedom and slavery by a person who knew both and also in his experiences as a slave which impelled him to escape to freedom. In addition, I wanted to place his opinions about freedom in the larger framework of his religious affirmations and examine the problems which he never really resolved in his own mind. Edward Bellamy is of course my prime example of an American who took a collectivistic view of freedom; but I have also discussed the psychological approach to freedom appearing in his early writings and contrasted his youthful doubts about human rationality with his later utopian hopes. The discussion of William James brings together the varied approaches to freedom which he took at different times in his life and points out that his empirical case for freedom as creative effort (with which I am sympathetic) might have been strengthened if he had been able, like Charles Peirce, to discard universal determinism in nature and if he had emphasized the inherent unpredictability of creative achievement.

Mark Twain's fatalistic opinions are of course well known to students of American thought. But his scattered pronouncements on freedom and fate have never been brought together, as I have done here, and confronted as a whole; nor have they been examined, as they should be, in the light of the newer view of science (represented by Charles S. Peirce), of which Twain remained quite unaware. In the final chapter on John Dewey I have looked upon Dewey's organic view of freedom as a kind of culmination and synthesis of the various tendencies in American thinking about freedom and fate since Edwards, but I also believe that while Dewey regarded himself as in some respects an indeterminist he failed to account satisfactorily for the dynamics of creativity. A brief epilogue deals with the major trends in thinking about freedom and fate in America in the 1960s and 1970s.

We are all metaphysicians. We all find ourselves on occasion extrapolating from what Dewey called the "warranted assertabilities" about human experience and speculating about our universe in its deepest reaches. My own feeling is that chance, novelty, creativity, and indeterminism as well as necessity, regularity, uniformity, and determinism play a real part in this world; and this conviction has undoubtedly shaped the pages that follow. Like James, I find distasteful Thomas H. Huxley's famous statement that "if some great Power would agree to make me always think what is true and do what is right, on condition of being turned into a sort of clock and wound up every morning before I got out of bed, I should instantly close with the offer." When behaviorist B. F. Skinner quoted Huxley's statement approvingly in *Beyond Freedom and Dignity*, Peter Caws, reviewing Skinner for the *New Republic* on October 16, 1971, counterposed it with a quotation from Kierkegaard's *Theses Attributable to Lessing*: "If God held all truth concealed in his right hand, and in his left hand the persistent striving for truth, and while warning me against eternal error, should say: Choose! I should humbly bow before his left hand, and say: 'Father, forgive! The pure truth is for Thee alone.'" Like Caws, I regard the Kierkegaard passage as more beautiful—and more human—than the Huxley quotation.

I would like to thank David Van Tassel of Case Western Reserve University and Douglas Sloan of Teachers College, Columbia University, for their helpful suggestions while I was working on this book. The late Louis Ruchames, my friend and colleague at the University of Massachusetts in Boston for many years, gave the manuscript an enormously helpful critical reading when it was in its early stages. And I profited from discussions of the book after completing the first draft with Timothy McCarthy, a friend of mine in the History Department at U.M.B. I am also grateful for the encouragement Allen Maxwell and Margaret Hartley, my good friends at the SMU Press, gave me while I was pursuing my inquiry into freedom; and I appreciate deeply the careful editorial work which Margaret Hartley and Charlotte Whaley performed on the book in its final stages. To the Houghton Library of Harvard University I am indebted for permission to quote from two of Emerson's unpublished sermons.

Several portions of this book have appeared previously in a quite different form as essays: "Thomas Paine and Natural Rights: A Reconsideration," *Social Science* 52 (Summer 1977): 67-72; "Emerson and Freedom," *Forum* 4 (Spring 1966): 4-14; "Calhoun on Liberty," *South Atlantic Quarterly* 66 (Summer 1967): 395-408; "Looking Backward and Forward with Edward Bellamy," *Politeia*, December, 1964, pp. 33-49; "Freedom in the Thought of William James," *American Quarterly* 16 (Summer 1964): 131-52; "Mark Twain's Credo: A Humorist's

Fatalistic View," *Southwest Review* 63 (Spring 1978): 150-63; and "Freedom in John Dewey's Philosophy of Education," *Teachers College Record* 79 (September 1977): 99-118.

PAUL F. BOLLER, JR.

*Texas Christian University*
*Fort Worth, Texas*
*April 10, 1978*

# Freedom and Fate in American Thought

ioners (and all men and women everywhere) to prostrate themselves before Him. God, he told them, created the world and continued to sustain it by his infinite power at every moment; he worked through secondary causes and uniform natural processes and yet interfered in his creation whenever he saw fit; he gave all men and women common grace with which to improve their natural abilities, but he also freely bestowed his supernatural grace on a chosen few so that they could possess the kind of faith in Christ that guaranteed them salvation. Edwards's God predestined both the rain and the prayers for rain. He was omniscient and omnipotent; he had foreknowledge of all that was to come because he had foreordained the course of events through all eternity. He had created the world for his own glory; and it was the duty of his creatures to reflect this glory back upon their Creator by continual acts of praise and worship both in and outside of the church. Edwards's impassioned conviction was that "the whole is *of* God, and *in* God, and *to* God, and God is the beginning, middle, and end in this affair."[4]

## CALVINISM AND ARMINIANISM

In Edwards's predestined scheme, there was no place for freedom of the will; men and women could never transcend life's causal network. Their fate lay in God's hands and their destiny was ineluctable; the hopes and fears of all their years were foreordained, not freely chosen, for the creature possessed no autonomy apart from the Creator. After his youthful conversion in college, Edwards never doubted the absolute sovereignty of God; nor did he ever waver thereafter in his belief that the profoundest truths about the human condition were embodied in the Calvinist theology which he had learned as a boy in a Puritan parsonage. In an age that was beginning to exalt humanity at the expense of God, Edwards felt impelled to defend the Calvinistic view of creation with every weapon, scriptural and secular, which he could wield. Above all, he insisted on the doctrine of original sin: the belief that because of Adam's sin in disobeying God all human beings were born weak, selfish, perverse, depraved, and corrupt, and fully deserving of the hatred and wrath of God and the eternal punishment which he reserved for unrepentant sinners. Edwards thought that empirical observation as well as scriptural text proved beyond all doubt the validity of the doctrine of total depravity. "It is evident by *experience*," he asserted, "that

*great* evil, both moral and natural, *abounds in the world*. It is manifest that great injustice, violence, treachery, perfidiousness, and extreme cruelty to the innocent, abound in this world; as well as [that] innumerable extreme sufferings, issuing fatally in destruction and death, are general all over the world in all ages.[5]

Even children, to Edwards, were "young vipers."[6] His belief in God's sovereignty and man's depravity led him to accept, and vigorously champion, all the other Calvinist doctrines: unconditional election (God arbitrarily chooses certain people for salvation regardless of their merits or good works); limited atonement (Christ died to save some, but not all, people); irresistible grace (people play no part in achieving salvation but passively receive God's saving grace); and the final perseverance of the saints (an individual who has received God's grace never falls from his regenerate state). There was no room for free will in any of this; the Calvinistic "Five Points" which Edwards upheld rested squarely on a belief in predestination.

As a champion of orthodoxy, Edwards feared the spread of Arminianism. Arminian ideas were "creeping into almost all parts of the land," he warned his Northampton congregation in 1750, "threatening the utter ruin of the credit of those doctrines which are the peculiar glory of the gospel, and the interests of vital piety."[7] The Arminians made a larger place for humanity in their scheme of salvation than the Calvinists did. They rejected what one of them called the "Quinquarticulars" because there was no place for human initiative in any of them. Human nature, they insisted, was a mixture of good and evil tendencies, not infallibly predetermined to do evil; and a conscientious individual might, by his own efforts, as well as with the help of God, achieve salvation.

By playing down God's arbitrary grace and stressing man's potentiality for good, Arminianism had the effect of elevating the status of human beings at the expense of the glory and sovereignty of God. No wonder Edwards, the God-obsessed, observed the spread of Arminianism with alarm. Arminian views had come to prevail in the Church of England by Edwards's time, and by mid-century they were beginning to assume some importance among educated people in New England, especially in eastern Massachusetts. To Edwards the drift of orthodox Congregationalists toward Arminianism was appalling. Any watering down of the doctrine of God's free grace was for him an open invitation to deism, atheism, and the destruction of Christianity. " 'Tis very true," he once wrote in a brief summary of his views on the relation between God and man, that God requires nothing of us as condition of eternal life but what is in our own power, and yet 'tis very true at the same time that it's an utter impossible thing that ever man should do what is necessary in order to salvation, nor do the least towards it, without the almighty operation of the Holy Spirit of God—yea, except everything be entirely wrought by the Spirit of God.[8]

Increasingly, Edwards came to believe that the heart of the controversy between Calvinism and what he called the "new fashionable divinity" lay in the question of free will.[9] Free will, he warned, introduced a "wild contingence" into the universe, and for all practical purposes it made God dependent upon man.[10] If man possessed free will, he exclaimed, God would have "to mend and patch up, as well as he could, his system, which originally was all very good . . . but was marred, broken and confounded by the free will of . . . men."[11] To combat Arminianism, Edwards decided it was absolutely necessary for him to demolish the pernicious doctrine of free will, once and for all, and to present an unassailable case for predestination. Only if the doctrine of free will were shown for the absurdity it was would America—and the world— be made safe for orthodox Christianity. In August, 1752, while serving as Congregational minister and missionary to the Indians in Stockbridge, Massachusetts, Edwards finally found time to turn full attention to a subject that had long concerned him. He spent about four and a half months writing what is probably his greatest work, and in 1754 it was published as *A Careful and Strict Inquiry into the Modern Prevailing Notions of the Freedom of the Will Which Is Supposed to be Essential to Moral Agency, Virtue and Vice, Reward and Punishment, Praise and Blame.*

Edwards's book was directed to Englishmen as well as to Americans. No American clergyman with Arminian leanings had, in fact, published a book, or even a pamphlet or sermon, on free will when Edwards planned his attack, and he was forced to look to England for his major targets. He found four: two Anglican clergymen (Daniel Whitby and Samuel Clarke), a dissenting minister (Isaac Watts), and a popular writer on Deism (Thomas Chubb).

Edwards's choice of targets was curious. Whitby and Clarke were generally Arminian in orientation, for they rejected the doctrine of total depravity; but neither of them believed exactly in freedom of the will as Edwards understood it. True, they used the term *free will* approvingly in their books, but they did so imprecisely, meaning by it man's freedom from an inherent bias toward evil. They did not, however, think of the will as an initiating first cause or as a self-moving and self-determining power of the mind, any more than Edwards did. Edwards found plenty of inconsistencies in Whitby and Clark, but this was not surprising, since they said many things inconsonant with a belief in free will which they did not really hold. It is hard to escape the conclusion that Edwards picked them for criticism because of their rejection of total depravity rather than for what they said about the human will.[12]

With his other two targets—Chubb and Watts—Edwards was on firmer ground. Though neither was an Arminian (Watts was a moderate Calvinist and Chubb closer to being a Unitarian or Deist than anything else), both of them were outspoken advocates of free will. Chubb boldly defined the will as a self-determining power of motion which enabled people to choose freely whether "to be either virtuous, or vicious, to be either wise-men or fools," and he insisted that whenever a person made a choice, he "had it in his power, and was at liberty to have chosen and done the contrary."[13] Watts agreed with Chubb in regarding the will as "a free & self-determining Power" which "must chuse of itself whether it will follow Reason or Appetite, Judgement or Passion." He also asserted that while the understanding often served as a "director or guide" to the will, the will itself could exert power over the understanding both by forcing it to dwell on one side of an argument rather than another and by making decisions when the understanding confronted similar alternatives and suspended choice.[14] Edwards was utterly outraged by such notions, and he thought they were the logical outcome of Arminian tinkering with Calvinism's "Quinquarticular Points."[15] He hoped his treatise would set people straight on these momentous matters.

## EDWARDS'S CASE AGAINST FREE WILL

Edwards's *Freedom of the Will* is divided into four sections: one defining his terms and setting forth his view of the mind, another dissecting what he took to be the Arminian conception of free will, a third discussing the question of freedom and responsibility, and a final section dealing with the problems of sin, necessity, and moral endeavor. Though Edwards quoted Scripture freely and referred to Calvinist doctrines from time to time, his analysis was in the main a secular one, resting on what he regarded as irrefutable logic and psychology and shaped by his study of John Locke. It also rested on the Newtonian principle that "nothing ever comes to pass without a cause."

In a sense Edwards assumed from the outset what he set out to prove. He defined cause as the "ground or reason" why any object or event was as it was rather than otherwise and took an almost Kantian view of causality. That "whatsoever begins to be" must have a cause, he declared, "seems to be the first dictate of the common and natural sense which God hath implanted in the minds of all mankind, and the main foundation of all our reasonings about the existence of things, past, present, or to come."[16] His insistence on universal causation (as an innate principle or propensity of the mind) ruled out any form of free will. So did his identification of reasons and causes and his failure to distinguish between causal explanations and reason-explanations (which cannot be dated) as philosophers do today.[17] Edwards did not deny, of course, that human volitions played an immense role in the shaping of events. The "changes and revolutions which come to pass in empires, kingdoms, and nations, and all societies," he said,

depend innumerable ways on the acts of men's wills; yea, on an innumerable multitude of millions of millions of volitions of mankind. Such is the state and course of things in the world of mankind, that one single event, which appears in itself exceeding inconsiderable, may in the progress and series of things, occasion a succession of the greatest and most important and extensive events; causing the state of mankind to be vastly different from what it would otherwise have been, for all succeeding generations.[18]

But he insisted that none of these volitions was free or unnecessitated.

The main point of Edwards's treatise was psychological. The mind, he said, possesses two faculties: the understanding (which perceives, judges, and reasons) and the will (which feels, desires, and chooses). Acts of volition are determined by motives; the will always acts in accordance with the strongest motive presented to the understanding. The strongest motive, in turn, is whatever object (or idea), "as it stands in the mind's view, suits it best, and pleases it most; and in that sense, is the greatest apparent good."[19] The nature of the object, the circumstances surrounding it, the perspective from which it is viewed, and the frame of mind (resulting from habit, experience, education, and temperamental bent) at the time of perception all play a part in determining what "the greatest apparent good" is for a person at any given moment. When the mind, in short, for whatever reasons, deems something desirable above all else, it at once chooses to act on that desire. Perception, motive, choice, and action follow one another in a continuous (and usually instantaneous) sequence. It seemed outrageous to Edwards that exponents of free will sought to introduce a spurious freedom of self-determination of the will into what he regarded as a necessary psychological sequence. The idea that on occasion we choose among conflicting motives by concentrating our attention on one of them, increasing its intensity, and thus causing it to prevail, was unthinkable in Edwards's psychology.

To strengthen his case against free will, Edwards came close at times to presenting a unitary view of the mind. He proposed, for one thing, that the word *determines* be dropped entirely from a consideration of what goes on in the mind. Instead of saying that the will is *determined* by the greatest apparent good, he said, it was more accurate to say that "the will always *is* as the greatest apparent good, or as what appears most agreeable," because "an appearing most agreeable or pleasing to the mind, and the mind's preferring and choosing, seem hardly to be properly and perfectly distinct."[20] Going even farther, Edwards occasionally suggests that the mind does not actually possess separate faculties or powers like the understanding and the will, but acts as a unit. From this point of view, the mind perceives, desires, reasons, and chooses, and then the individual acts.

But although Edwards stressed the close relationship between thought and action, he also insisted that thinking and acting are radically different in nature and require quite different categories of analysis. The word *acting*, Edwards said, applies only to men's external motions, never to internal consciousness. Properly speaking, there are no "acts" of will. An individual feels, thinks, and acts; his thinking determines his acting, and he may be called the author or cause of his external actions. But words like "cause" and "determine" are inappropriate for describing "acts" of will. So long as a person acts as he wishes, his action is voluntary. People who engage in voluntary action, said Edwards, are "self-directed, self-determined, and their wills are the cause of the motions of their bodies, and the external things that are done."[21] On the other hand, unless men act "voluntarily, and of choice, and the action be determined by their antecedent volition, it is no action or doing of theirs."[22] Edwards thought people confused voluntary action with the thinking process and thus opened a Pandora's box of free-will speculations.

Freedom, for Edwards, resided in external action, not in the will; it belonged to a person, not to some willing faculty supposedly possessed by the person's mind. "The plain and obvious meaning of the words 'freedom' and 'liberty,' in common speech," he declared, "is power, opportunity, or advantage, that anyone has, to do as he pleases. Or in other words, his being free from hindrance or impediment in the way of doing, or conducting in any respect, as he wills."[23] Edwards distinguished two major obstacles to freedom of action: (1) constraint—forcing a person to do something he does not want to do; and (2) restraint—preventing a person from acting as he wants to. If a person is neither constrained nor restrained in acting, then, according to Edwards, he is free. Freedom, he said, is "that power or opportunity for one to do and conduct as he will, or according to his choice." And he added: "Let the person come by his volition or choice how he will, yet, if he is able, and there is nothing in the way to hinder his pursuing and executing his will, the man is fully and perfectly free, according to the primary and common notion of freedom."[24] But Edwards had nothing further to say either here or elsewhere about the ramifications of the kind of freedom he was defining in his free-will treatise. He failed to explore either the forms such freedom could take (in speaking, writing, worshiping, and assembling for social purposes) or the social limits to the freedom of the individual to "do as he pleases." Edwards was so eager, moreover, to demonstrate that a person could have freedom without possessing free will that he failed to recognize the fact that the kind of freedom he was emphasizing had never ranked high with his Christian forebears. John Calvin regarded absence of external restraint as a paltry kind of freedom, scarcely deserving of the name, as compared to the freedom which the Christian experiences in union with Christ. So did John Winthrop. In a "little speech" on liberty before the General Court in July, 1645, Winthrop called the ability to do as we please a "natural corrupt liberty" which was "common to man with beasts and other creatures" and needed to be severely limited by the civil and ecclesiastical authorities. For the Christian, Winthrop explained, moral liberty, i.e., the liberty to do what is "good, just, and honest," which comes from faith in Christ, is the only liberty worth taking seriously.[25]

Like all Christians, Edwards undoubtedly shared Winthrop's preference for moral over natural liberty, agreed with him in believing that sin and error as well as circumstances keep people in bondage, and recognized the necessity of hemming in an individual's "natural corrupt liberty" by means of inner and outer restraints. Still, he said nothing directly about any of these matters in his treatise on free will. About all he did, and that in a footnote, was to quote Locke approvingly on the rational use of liberty:

Is it worth the name of freedom, to be at liberty to play the fool, and draw shame and misery upon a man's self? If to break loose from the conduct of reason, and to want that restraint of examination and judgment, that keeps us from doing or choosing the worse, be liberty, true liberty, mad men and fools are the only free men. Yet I think nobody would choose to be mad, for the sake of such liberty, but he that is mad already.[26]

Edwards, of course, had more use for liberty of fools and madmen than Locke or Winthrop did. But he was more concerned with exposing Arminian errors than with reiterating what seemed to him obvious truths. He was so exasperated by the concept of free will that he concentrated all his efforts on demolishing Arminian notions of freedom rather than outlining in detail alternative views of his own on the subject. His approach to freedom was therefore largely negative, and he neglected to say anything about the kind of positive freedom (rational and moral) that Winthrop and Locke were talking about.

He also totally ignored the question of religious liberty. There are no paeans to "soul liberty"—freedom of conscience and belief—in Edwards as there were in Roger Williams (also a predestinarian) a century earlier, and there is nothing in Edwards of Williams's impassioned conviction that a society without "soul yokes" would produce better believers than an authoritarian society. But neither is there any exaltation of moral over civil liberty in Edwards as there was in Winthrop. Edwards seemed to think that once the outrageous notion of free will was placed beyond the pale true religion would flourish as never before. He was single-mindedly bent on removing the restraints and constraints of faulty ideas of freedom from the minds of his fellow Christians, and only by implication can he be said to link freedom with either rationality or morality. His treatise makes essentially only one point: freedom lies in a person's actions, not in his will. What a person chooses (e.g., to accept or reject the doctrine of free will) is always necessitated, but if he can act on his choice he is free. There was no mention in Edwards's analysis of the bearing of mind or reason on freedom and he consequently ignored a number of possibilities: that one person's impediments may be another person's opportunities, that growing awareness enables people to overcome obstacles, and that there is a big difference, when it comes to freedom, between the unimpeded actions of a drunken (or brainwashed, hypnotized, or drugged) person and one whose mind is clear. Edwards sounded at times like an out-and-out behaviorist.

There is a further weakness in Edwards's view of freedom. When he defined freedom as the power or opportunity to act as one pleases without being restrained by any external obstacles, Edwards overlooked the fact that the situation which he describes as involving freedom is really a matter of chance. It is entirely accidental, that is to say, if, when a person starts to do something, there are no impediments to his action at that particular moment. But Edwards rejected chance as a factor in the universe as forcefully as he rejected free will. In Edwards's world, what Carl Jung called "synchronicity" (the internal connection between two seemingly unrelated events)[27] is apparently at work if the concrete situation in which a person chooses to act happens to be devoid of external obstacles to his action at the time. The "chance" situation giving the individual his freedom to act has, in short, been prearranged by God. God is the Great Synchronizer throughout creation. The presence or absence of obstacles when an individual is motivated to act is determined by God's predestined scheme. Edwards's freedom may not be the paltry freedom Calvin thought it was; it may not be a freedom at all. Like everything else it was predestined.

Edwards was better at attacking the Arminians than at making a convincing case for his own definition of freedom. He spent little space, in fact, on expounding his own views. Having paused for a moment to present an alternative to the Arminian view of freedom, he went on to confront the self-determinative notion of freedom head on and used all the logic, wit, and sarcasm he could muster to reduce it to mincemeat. His first argument was an *ad absurdum* one. If, as free-willers contend, the will freely chooses its volitions, said Edwards, then the choosing itself must be freely chosen by the will. But this lands us in infinite regress: for if I want something (free act of will), then I must choose to want it (another free act of will), and I must also decide to choose to want it (still another free act of will), and, further, I must freely will to decide to choose to want it (one more act of free will), and so on, *ad infinitum*. If exponents of free will attempt to terminate the endless chain of uncaused acts of will by placing a first cause at the beginning of the sequence, then, insisted Edwards, they have surrendered the case for free will. Edwards returned repeatedly to the infinite-regress argument throughout his treatise, and he thoroughly enjoyed restating it with numerous variations in order to make the idea of free will sound as silly as possible.

Edwards's second argument against free will concerned what some free-will advocates called "liberty of indifference." According to this concept, when the mind confronts two or more things that are equally desirable, it has no preference and suspends its choice. Whenever it pleases, however, according to the free-willers, the mind can make a choice among the equally attractive alternatives, without reason, motive, or preference. Such a choice emerges from indifference; it is uncaused, unmotivated—in a word, free. Edwards was exasperated by such reasoning. If the mind is indifferent, he exclaimed, it does not choose at all; choice is simply impossible without preference. The mind may indeed be indifferent about things presented to it and suspend its choice; but suspending choice is itself an act of volition and has motivations of its own. How ridiculous, cried Edwards, "to insist, that the soul chooses one thing before another, when at the very same instant it is perfectly indifferent with respect to each! This is the same thing as to say, the soul prefers one thing to another, at the very same time that it has no preference."[28]

What of the free-willer's contention that necessity was incompatible with responsibility and that if the will were not free people could be neither praised nor blamed for what they chose to do? Edwards spent over half of his treatise on this question; he regarded the problem of freedom and responsibility as a major one facing him. But he was convinced that it was the free-will position, not his own, which was inconsistent with moral responsibility. If volitions occur by pure chance (as they seemed to with free will), then, he pointed out, morality is absolutely excluded from men's choices. How, after all, can acts springing from indifference have either merit or demerit in them? What virtue is there in a person's choosing without motive? Furthermore, if people choose their actions out of pure indifference, of what use are moral precepts? Free will, Edwards insisted, made "all instructions, counsels, invitations, expostulations, and all arguments and persuasions whatsoever" a sheer waste of time.[29] A self-determining will, in short, was not subject to moral governance; it was completely unmoved by all inducements to shun evil and seek virtue. Edwards concluded that the views of free-will advocates "do evidently shut all virtue out of the world."[30] But Edwards, of course, believed emphatically that men's decisions—however they came to them—could be evaluated. The virtuousness and the viciousness in men's choices, he said repeatedly, lay in the quality of these choices, not in the origin or causes of the choices. "When a thing is *from* a man," he said, "in that sense, that it is from his will or choice, he is to blame for it, because his will is *in it:* so far as the will is *in it*, blame is *in it*, and no further."[31]

Edwards thought the relation between freedom and responsibility could be clarified if one made a careful distinction between "natural necessity" and what free-willers called "moral necessity." Natural necessity, involving natural causes, is clear enough. By a natural necessity, we say, men's bodies move downward if there is nothing to support them. But moral necessity (which, according to champions of free will, dictates men's choices if the will is not free) is less clear. Obviously, moral necessity involves moral causes, and (if we reject free will, as we should) we can say, if we like, that it is present in all acts of will. But what are we actually saying when we say that the will cannot act morally otherwise than as it does? We are stating a mere tautology. We are simply saying: we *can't* will what we won't; we *must* will what we want; we are *unable* to will what we don't want. Edwards, in short, rejected the possibility, suggested by Chubb, that people possess a power of contrary choice, i.e., the ability to choose differently in identical circumstances from the way they actually do. For this reason he saw no point in saying that willing was necessitated. To say that moral necessity was involved in acts of will, he thought, was merely to say that the will wills as it wills. Moral necessity means the presence of a certain inclination in the mind; moral inability means the absence of inclination. But putting it this way adds nothing to what we already know about acts of will. To talk about necessity and inability where volitions are concerned was, Edwards thought, to take concepts belonging to the natural world and apply them to an area where they are not appropriate.

With natural necessity, however, Edwards was very much concerned. Natural necessity, he acknowledged, was inconsistent with praise and blame. To the extent that natural necessity dictates what people do it deprives them of their freedom and hence of their responsibility. Natural necessity sometimes takes the form of external constraint: a person is forced to do good or evil against his will. In such cases he is not acting freely, and he can be neither praised nor blamed for what he does. Edwards thought the case was a little different when natural necessity took the form of external impediments to a man's acting as he wills. If the man wants to do good and external obstacles block his freedom of action, then, said Edwards, he is to be praised for his intention and excused for his inability to act on it. On the other hand, if he wants to commit a crime but is prevented by outside forces from doing it, he is to be condemned for his intention and given only a negative kind of credit for not having committed the crime.

But necessity, according to Edwards, does not come into play solely where external constraint or restraint are present; it might also be involved in the natural capacities, physical and intellectual, which an individual possesses. A man may be handicapped by "want of natural capacity or strength; either capacity of understanding, or external strength."[32] A person may not be strong enough or know enough to do good when the opportunity arises. If so, he is not blamed for failing to act. Natural inability, for Edwards, was entirely excusable. If doing certain good things is naturally impossible (through physical weakness or a defect of understanding) for a person, he is excused for not doing them. And if he has a natural difficulty (because of deficiencies in body or understanding) in performing certain meritorious acts, then he is excused to some extent for not doing better. On the other hand, if he has a natural tendency to do things that turn out to be good, he gets little praise, because natural propensity comes close to being natural necessity. But what if natural necessity (e.g., defect of understanding) prevents a person from comprehending the Quinquarticulars? Is he thereby excused? Edwards does not say. Apparently he did not think that his concessions to common sense when it came to natural necessity clashed with his predestinarian presuppositions.

The last part of *Freedom of the Will* stresses theology. Having explored all the logical ramifications of his position on freedom and necessity, Edwards felt obliged to relate it to the Christian religion. To show that necessity was compatible with praise and blame, for instance, he observed that "God necessarily acts justly and faithfully" and yet is worthy of our highest esteem.[33] Christ was also necessarily holy and yet praiseworthy; and Judas, though predestined to sin, was justly excoriated by all men. To bolster his case for necessitated volition, Edwards also pointed out that "there is no event, past, present, or to come, that God is ever uncertain of" and that his foreknowledge extends to acts of will of moral agents.[34] To the question of whether God's infallible prescience of men's choices makes him the author of sinful volitions, Edwards's response was that God was "the permitter, or not a hinderer of sin," which is quite different from being the author of sin.[35] There was a difference, in other words, between efficient causation and permissive causation. Just as the absence of the sun was the occasion, but not the cause, of darkness, Edwards went on to say, so God's withholding of his action and energy was the occasion but not the cause of sin. But Edwards's efforts to reconcile God and sin in a predestined world by distinguishing between efficient and permissive causation was probably the least convincing part of his analysis. "How sin came to be permitted is more than we can comprehend," said James Dana, a critic of Edwards, impatiently. "To say that it could not have been prevented is saying more than any one knows."[36] And why, furthermore, should God permit sin to flourish in the world? Edwards's answer was that God might let sin come to pass for good ends and that he might hate something (like the Crucifixion) and yet permit it to occur for wise (though mysterious) purposes of his own. "Is it not better," Edwards asked,

that the good and evil which happens [*sic*] in God's world, should be ordered, regulated, bounded and determined by the good pleasure of an infinitely wise Being . . . than to leave these things to fall out by chance, and to be determined by those causes which have no understanding or aim?[37]

Perhaps so. But, again, was not Edwards "saying more than any one knows"? And did not Edwards's reasoning make "intemperance, debauchery, oppression, murder, malice, envy, all the lusts of the flesh and spirit" indispensable to the good of the world and thus "perfectly agreeable" to God? "What obligations," exclaimed Dana sarcastically, "do mankind owe to drunkards and gluttons, to fornicators and adulterers, to the fraudulent and oppressors, to thieves and liars, and false swearers, to robbers and murderers. . . !"[38]

Dana certainly had a point. When it came to problems like these, Edwards simply begged the question. Predestination, he said time and again, was infinitely preferable to the "wild contingence" following from free will and an unstructured universe. The "all-wise determiner of all events," he insisted, knew what he was about when he allowed sin in the world.[39] Edwards was absolutely sure that under God's wise providence (but only under his providence) this world, with all its terrible shortcomings, was the best of all possible worlds. Predestination, it is clear, made bearable for Edwards (and countless others) the many intolerabilities of human existence by placing them in the context of a wider meaning and purpose.

But doesn't predestination make all moral endeavor useless? Why pray for rain (asked some critics of high Calvinism) if both the prayer and the rain have been decreed by God in the first place? Why strive to live a righteous life if the course of your life has been foreordained by God? Above all, why strive for salvation (as Edwards urged his congregations to do) when it is a matter of free grace and God has already chosen his saints and sinners? Why not take a moral holiday and let come what may? Edwards's response to questions like these—commonly regarded as crucial for predestination—was to turn the charge of inconsistency upon the questioner. If prior necessity makes all endeavors vain, said Edwards, it makes all nonendeavors vain also. The person who argues that in a predestined universe one might as well relax his efforts and seek a life of ease and pleasure is actually contradicting himself, according to Edwards; he goes

counter to the very principles he pretends to act upon: for he comes to a conclusion, and takes a course, *in order to an end*, even *his ease*, or the saving himself from trouble; he seeks something future, and uses means in order to a future thing, even in his drawing up that conclusion, that he will seek nothing, and use no means in order to anything future; he seeks his future ease, and the benefit and comfort of indolence.[40]

If predestination makes it illogical to choose a life of holiness, it makes it just as illogical to choose any other kind of life. Striving for eternal salvation is no more inconsistent with predestination than seeking earthly happiness, and it is surely wiser. God's will, after all, is partly secret, and the demands life makes on us are often incomprehensible. Still, God has revealed himself to man in part, and it is only the part of wisdom to try to follow his revealed will appearing in the Bible. And Scripture recommends "using means and taking pains," not a life of ease.[41]

Edwards emphatically rejected what he called "universal fatality."[42] Though he believed in predestination, he did not believe, as fatalists do, that all events are the direct result of supernatural influence or of abstract destiny, regardless of causal connection. He regarded himself as a necessitarian, not a fatalist; he thought that God worked through secondary causes (the laws of nature and natural processes) and that all actions were part of a chain of cause and effect. He denied that necessity made men "mere machines." Though man does not possess free will, said Edwards, he is

entirely, perfectly and unspeakably different from a mere machine, in that he has reason and understanding, and has a faculty of will, and so is capable of volition and choice; and in that, his will is guided by the dictates or views of his understanding; and in that his external actions and behavior, and in many respects also his thoughts, and the exercises of his mind, are subject to his will; so that he has liberty to act according to his choice, and do what he pleases; and by means of these things, is capable of moral habits and moral acts, such inclinations and actions as according to the common sense of mankind, are worthy of praise, esteem, love and reward; or on the contrary, of disesteem, detestation, indignation and punishment.[43]

On this view of human beings he rested his case against freedom of the will.

## THE CASE AGAINST EDWARDS: ABSOLUTE FATALITY

For more than a decade and a half there was no response of any consequence to Edwards's treatise. Jonathan Mayhew, Arminian minister in Boston, mentioned Edwards in a footnote appearing in a book of sermons published in 1755, but he regarded the free-will question as largely an exercise in futility.[44] Ebenezer Gay of Hingham announced his firm belief in "the Power of Self-Determination, of Freedom of Choice," but admitted that "the Manner of it's operating" was difficult to explain.[45] Henry Cummings of Billerica, another Arminian, dismissed Edwards's book as "nothing better than fatalism," but he did not attempt to come to grips with Edwards's analysis.[46] It was left to James Dana, Congregational minister in Wallingford, Connecticut, to make the first full-scale reply to Edwards in a book entitled *An Examination of the late Reverend President Edwards's "Enquiry on Freedom of the Will,"* published anonymously in Boston in 1770. Dana's book brought forth a defense of Edwards by Stephen West (*Essay on Moral Agency*, 1772), to which Dana responded in another critique of Edwards in 1773. Twenty years passed and then Samuel West, a New Bedford minister who had been studying the question since the 1770s, joined Dana in a lengthy attack on Edwards (*Essays on Liberty and Necessity*, first appearing in 1793 and then reissued with a second part added in 1795), to which Jonathan Edwards, Jr. responded in 1797 in *A Dissertation Concerning Liberty and Necessity*. The controversy over Edwards's book subsided at this point, though theologians in New England and elsewhere—Samuel Hopkins, Nathanael Emmons, Asa Burton, Nathaniel Taylor, Timothy Dwight, Charles Finney, Jeremiah Day, Albert T. Bledsoe, Edwards Park, and others—continued to thrash over Edwards's views on free will well into the nineteenth century. There were also sporadic replies to Edwards of an increasingly secular nature by interested laymen as late as the 1860s.[47]

The debate over Edwards's views, particularly in its early stages, was not especially illuminating. It was accompanied by confusion, misunderstanding, misrepresentation, and almost unbearable prolixity on all sides. Just as Edwards had misinterpreted the Arminian position on free will in his treatise, so the Arminians undertaking to answer him misunderstood some of the things he was trying to say and were not always clear as to what they were trying to say themselves. So long as the discussion was conducted within a strictly theological framework—with both Arminians and Calvinists taking for granted God's foreknowledge of all events—it was difficult to clarify the issues at stake between defenders of free will and champions of theological determinism. The Arminians were better at picking little holes in Edwards's position (and sounding out the unpleasant implications of his high Calvinism) than they were at describing alternative positions of their own with any precision. Yet out of the welter of charge and countercharge, doctrinal bickering, verbal hairsplitting, and copious scriptural citations, certain basic criticisms of Edwards's position did gradually become clear.

One of the prime criticisms of Edwards, interestingly, was that his stand on free will placed him squarely in the camp of freethinkers (and maybe, even, atheists) like Thomas Hobbes. Edwards denied that he had ever read Hobbes (though both Clarke and Whitby had mentioned him in books which Edwards attacked), but there is no question that his views on freedom were remarkably like those of the British philosopher. In *Of Liberty and Necessity* (1654), Hobbs declared that "the will itself, and each propension of a man during his deliberation, is as much necessitated, and depends on a sufficient cause, as any thing else whatsoever"; he also defined liberty as the *"absence of all the impediments to action that are not contained in the nature and intrinsical quality of the agent."*[48] And in *The Questions Concerning Liberty, Necessity, and Chance* (1656), he even referred to God's foreknowledge to uphold his belief in universal determinism: "It sufficeth me, that whatsoever was foreknown by God, was necessary: but all things were foreknown by God, and therefore all things were necessary."[49]

But it was Locke, not Hobbes, who shaped Edwards's approach to the free-will question. In a chapter entitled "Of Power" in his *Essay Concerning Human Understanding* (1690), Locke foreshadowed most of the basic points that Edwards made in his treatise on freedom of the will: he called attention to the absurdity of attributing liberty, which "is but a power," to the will, "which is also but a power"; showed how the notion of the will's determining itself could be transformed into an infinite series; insisted on a necessary connection between motive and will; attributed liberty to the person, not to his will, and defined it as the ability "to act or not to act, according as we shall choose or will."[50] But Edwards's analysis was no mere transcript of Locke's views. Where Locke had singled out "the most pressing uneasiness" as the determiner of the will, Edwards substituted "the greatest apparent good"; he also merged will and desire, which Locke had said could come into conflict, and denied that willing and desiring could ever run counter to each other. Unlike Locke, too, he made much of God's foreknowledge to uphold the case for determinism, and he linked his denial of free will with original sin.

Most secular philosophers in Edwards's day, however, supported their belief in universal determinism by referring, as Edwards did, to divine prescience. There is reason to believe, indeed, that modern scientific determinism had its roots in theological predestination and originated as a metaphysical affirmation rather than as a hypothetical presupposition to guide empirical or experimental research. Hobbes was not the only secular thinker in early modern times who thought God's prescience clinched the case for universal necessity. When the skeptic David Hume (whom Edwards did not read until after he had written his free-will treatise) discarded divine sovereignty and tried to explain causality on empirical rather than theological grounds, he found himself in deep trouble. Hume, like Edwards, identified "cause" with necessary connection between events and assumed, as Edwards did, that causality was universally operative; but he had great difficulty in finding satisfactory empirical evidence (which showed only that certain objects are constantly conjoined in experience) for his views. Yet his belief in universal necessity (apart from God and without empirical support) remained as firm as Edwards's, and Arminian critics liked to link Edwards with the Scottish skeptic as well as with Hobbes.[51]

But did the universal necessity which Edwards, as well as Hobbes and Hume, asserted mean a philosophy of fatalism? A second major criticism of Edwards was that his predestinarian theology landed him in a position of "absolute fatality" (Dana's term) which took the heart and soul out of Christian endeavor.[52] "And will not every man who embraces and acts consistently with this scheme, cast off all solicitude about his moral conduct. . . ?" queried Beach Newton in *A Preservative against the Doctrine of Fate* which he prepared for divinity students in 1770.[53] Some commentators on Edwards thought that the doctrines contained in *Freedom of the Will* led inexorably to the conclusion that "Whatever is, is, and cannot be otherwise, and could not have been otherwise" and obliterated all distinctions between good and evil, merit and demerit, praise and blame, truth and error.[54] Edwards had made a special point in his treatise of distinguishing his own necessitarianism from the views of the fatalists, but he left many of his readers unpersuaded. Edwards's critics doubted whether necessity and moral activism could be reconciled as smoothly as he thought they could; they could not help thinking that a completely necessitated universe reduced mankind to a "mere machine," for all Edwards's protestations to the contrary.

Years before Edwards composed his treatise, Benjamin Franklin published *A Dissertation on Liberty and Necessity* (1725) in which he commenced with assumptions similar to those of Edwards and presented an airtight case, so he thought, for what Edwards called "universal fatality" and what William James later called "hard determinism." Franklin's basic point was that if God is all-wise, all-good, and all-powerful and determines whatever happens (which was of course Edwards's belief), there can be no evil, no free will, and no morality in the universe. No evil, because nothing can happen in the universe without God's consent, and what he consents to must be good because he is good. No free will, because if man can do only what God arranges for him to do, he cannot choose freely. No morality, because if there is no free will, *"there can be neither Merit nor Demerit in Creatures"* and *"therefore every Creature must be equally esteem'd by the Creator."*[55] Since man is "a part of this great Machine, the Universe," Franklin went on to say, and "his regular Acting is requisite to the regular moving of the whole," it was fitting that all his choices and actions be governed by an all-wise Providence. It would have been absurd, said Franklin, for God to have peopled the world with free agents, for that would be just as if

an ingenious Artificer, having fram'd a curious Machine or Clock, and put its many intricate Wheels and Powers in such a Dependance on one another, that the whole might move in the most exact Order and Regularity, had nevertheless plac'd in it several other Wheels endu'd with an independent *Self-Motion*, but ignorant of the general Interest of the Clock; and these would every now and then be moving wrong, disordering the true Movement, and making continual Work for the Mender; which might better be prevented, by depriving them of that Power of Self-Motion, and placing them in a Dependance on the regular part of the Clock.[56]

Though Franklin, like Edwards, eliminated all "wild contingence" from the universe, he did not deny all freedom to man. He acknowledged that if liberty meant absence of impediments to action (as Edwards contended), then all our actions might be said to be the effects of liberty. But freedom of action, he observed, was closely related to necessity.

. . . it is a Liberty of the same Nature with the Fall of a heavy Body to the Ground; it has Liberty to fall, that is, it meets with nothing to hinder its Fall, but at the same Time, it is necessitated to fall, and has no Power or Liberty to remain suspended.[57]

But if a man was free the way a stone is free when it rolls down a hill and meets no obstacles, then the word *freedom* has no human content.

Franklin eventually abandoned his "hard determinism" as having "an ill tendency," and he came to believe in the "free agency" of man. In a piece called "On the Providence of God in the Government of the World," probably written in 1732, he reasoned that predestination and prayer were incompatible. God would be malicious, Franklin said, if he allowed people to pray in a world in which everything was foreordained. But God is good, not malevolent, and that means that things are not completely foreordained and that praying makes sense. Franklin finally decided that God permitted the laws of nature and the free agency of man to shape what happens in the world, but that on occasion, in order not to leave the rewarding of virtue and the punishing of evil entirely to chance, he "interferes by his particular Providence, and sets aside the events which would otherwise have been produc'd in the Course of Nature, or by the Free Agency of Men."[58] Franklin's certainly was not a very tidy solution to the problem; but it became fairly popular among religious people in America as predestination waned in influence.

Edwards was not acquainted with Franklin's essays on predestination and freedom, but he was thoroughly familiar with the line of reasoning taken in both of them. The argument for free agency contained in the second essay he of course regarded as Arminian nonsense leading to "blind contingence" in the world. But he was also irked by the belief (which appeared in Franklin's first essay) that necessitarianism reduced man to a "mere machine" and made human freedom an illusion. Though all of our actions are motivated, Edwards declared, we all know there is a vast difference between being coerced and being able to act voluntarily. Human beings, unlike machines, can behave freely—that is, they can act according to their choices and do what they please whenever circumstances are favorable, and this clearly means that they possess "liberty and agency." Edwards thought that critics of necessitarianism who talked about machines were trying to arouse the passions of people who have "too little capacity" to give the matter "serious and circumspect examination." But he scarcely did justice to the subject himself. He spent little space on the charge of mechanism in his free-will treatise and responded to it mainly by countercharging that Arminian free will produced "absolute blind contingence" in the world.[59] He did not seem to realize that the behavioral freedom he was defending also involved contingence: the coincidental conjunction of what people wanted to do and circumstances permitting them to do it.

Still, Edwards's case for the compatibility of necessity and voluntary action is, at least on one level, valid enough. Take, for example, the practical differences between what black slaves and free whites could do in Edwards's America. Slaves and freemen obviously differed in social status and in opportunities for self-fulfillment, even if one assumes, as Edwards did, that the motives of both were necessitated. And even the slave was no "mere machine." Though subject to external restraints which the freeman never experienced, the colonial slave, too, could act freely in realizing his necessitated desires and carrying out his motivated choices in certain crucial areas of his everyday life. Edwards was on firm ground, surely, in thinking of freedom (in one of its aspects) as the "power, opportunity, or advantage that anyone has, to do as he pleases." Entirely apart from the free-will and predestination question, Edwards's circumstantial freedom is unquestionably an empirical reality.

Edwards, though, reconciled predestination and voluntary action by interpreting the former, on the naturalistic level, as causal necessity. But the doctrine of predestination asserts more than causal necessity; it also holds that the "power, opportunity, or advantage" to do as one pleases is foreordained, not contingent on circumstances. It was this fact that led Edwards's critics to insist that the logic of predestination was fatalism. But with Edwards predestination was not a matter of logic; it was a matter of faith. And it was an animating, not a fatalistic, faith. Far from encouraging supine submission, predestination, as Edwards saw it, was an energizing doctrine which gave zest and sting to life. For if he regarded divine glory without predestination as inconceivable, he found it equally unthinkable for people to succumb to resignation when they recognized God's mighty predestinarian power. To Edwards, predestination meant that the universe was neatly structured, possessed unmistakable direction, and was shot through with divine purpose. In Edwards's teleologized universe, man lived in a theater of profound meaning and moral endeavor took on cosmic significance. God, Edwards never doubted, had assigned man an important part to play in the cosmic drama which He had planned, and it was man's duty—in fact, his privilege—to act out his part as best he could. He should strive to comprehend God's will, as it

had been revealed in part in the Bible; and he should put forth all the
efforts he could muster to live the life of righteousness prescribed by
God's holy word. In doing these things, he could take courage in the
knowledge that he was fulfilling the role marked out for him by his
sovereign God.

Edwards never denied that in the end eternal salvation, like worldly
success, would come to but a few, and that only God knew whom he had
elected for endless bliss and whom he had consigned to perdition. But
all men were sinners; and God's saving grace might come to any of them
regardless of their earthly station. Surely it was part of wisdom to try
to be at all times spiritually prepared for the momentous occasion when
God might infuse one with saving grace. Perhaps—who knows, except
God?—the very fact that a person worked hard to resist his sinful inclinations and live by God's revealed word was a sign that he was one of the
elect. Better still: perhaps when he at last fully and frankly and unre-
servedly comprehended his own utter worthlessness and incapacity and
acknowledged that only God himself could release him from bondage to
sin, he was experiencing God's grace. But of course it was God's will, not
his own, that was at work in all of this. Edwards repeatedly urged his
congregations to seek salvation by all appropriate means, and he even
suggested at times that such earnest seeking would be rewarded by God's
saving grace. This suggestion, however, clearly ran counter to his belief
in unconditional election. There was, in short, something tautological
about Edwards's predestinarian assertions. God, according to Edwards,
has decreed who is to be saved and who is to be damned; yet we were
to go about our business precisely as we would as if regeneration were
an open question and the option were ours. But whatever happened
would turn out to have been fated. For all of Edwards's protestations to
the contrary, his critics could not help thinking that this way of conceiving the matter logically made automata out of human beings.

## The Will as Causal Effort

The Arminians who tried to answer *Freedom of the Will* were by no
means Edwards's intellectual peers. The case they made for free will in
the course of criticizing Edwards was vague, hesitant, and somewhat
elusive; it lacked the logical rigor, clarity, and structure of Edwards's
exposition of the doctrine of universal necessity. Edwards's critics acknowledged their weaknesses as metaphysicians; and as they groped their way
through the thicket of definitions and counter-definitions that developed

during the controversy over free will, some of them came to feel (as Franklin eventually did) that excessive preoccupation with metaphysical niceties obfuscated more than it clarified the freedom-necessity question. Still, a positive case for some kind of internal freedom (if not precisely the freedom of the will over which Arminians and Edwardseans were ostensibly contending) did somehow slowly emerge from their endeavors to discover a mode of freedom in human beings more basic than mere absence of external restraint.

James Dana was convinced that introspection testified to the existence of an inner freedom in the human mind. "Let a man look into his breast," he exclaimed, "and he cannot but perceive inward freedom—*Inward* freedom—For if freedom be not in the mind, it is nowhere. And liberty in the mind implies *self-determination*."[60] Samuel West agreed: "We certainly feel ourselves agents—feel ourselves free, and accountable for our conduct—we feel ourselves capable of praise and blame." While Jonathan Edwards, Jr. protested that immediate consciousness revealed only volitions, not freedom, West went on to propose a threefold division of the mind (perceptions, propensions or inclinations, and the will) in which the will possessed the power of determining whether the mind should follow reason or inclination. He was neither clear nor convincing about any of this, but he did open up a fruitful line of analysis by suggesting that the idea of cause itself meant power, not necessary connection, that it had an internal origin, and that it came from our consciousness of exerting efforts and initiating mental and physical activities of our own.[61]

Once Edwards's critics began locating causal initiative in the mind, as West did, and conceiving of the will itself as involving effort, not choice, the road was open for the discovery of real alternatives to Edwards. Neither Dana nor West got very far along this road, but later commentators on Edwards went quite far in this direction. By the nineteenth century the debate over Edwards had taken a new form. Critics of Edwards like Henry P. Tappan and Rowland G. Hazard began talking about freedom of the mind, not about freedom of the will; and when they spoke of self-determination, they meant the mind's, not the will's, ability to shape itself. By this time, moreover, the will was no longer, as with Edwards, the realm of desires, inclinations, and choices; it was the arena of conscious effort (which Edwards had ignored). "When I wish to do anything," wrote Henry Tappan, Congregational clergyman-philosopher and first president of the University of Michigan, "I make an effort. . . ;

I make an effort to raise my arm, and I raise it. This effort is simply the volition."[62] Motives (in the form of rational or passional inducements) still existed in abundance; but they did not automatically necessitate choice and action. The mind, according to Rowland Hazard (a Rhode Island manufacturer who wrote extensively on free will and debated John Stuart Mill on the subject), takes various inducements to action under advisement, considers the future effects of any course of action it might adopt, formulates rules to guide it, and puts forth efforts to carry out its plans of action. In the deliberate intentions and conscious efforts involved in human actions lay authentic human freedom. The mind, viewed in this way, became a creative first cause, unfettered by past conditions, producing significant changes in the world of matter and motion.[63] As to divine prescience, Hazard said that God abstained from exerting his own power so that men might act freely and then adapted his own action to whatever occurred, like a master chess-player, so that he would not be "frustrated of His end."[64] (The idea that life was a chess-game with the outcome certain was slow in dying even among anti-Edwardseans.) In the 1880s, William James resumed discussion of the free-will question where Tappan and Hazard left off, and by discarding the closed universe of the religious and scientific determinists he was able to explore from a new perspective and with fresh insights the possibilities contained in the concept of the will as creative causal effort.

There was another possibility. In *Freedom of the Will*, Edwards suggested that instead of thinking of the mind as being subdivided into various faculties or powers, each of which performed a different function, it might be wiser to conceive of the mind as acting as a unit. For, obviously, if the mind did not possess separate faculties like the will and the understanding, there was no problem of freedom of the "will" to plague philosophers and theologians. Edwards himself did not adhere consistently to the unitary view in his treatise, and he thus failed to make the most of this promising line of inquiry. It was not until the late nineteenth century that John Dewey, with his organic philosophy of life, attempted to dispose of the free-will question, once and for all, by formulating a unitary and functional view of the human mind and body.

By Dewey's time, however, most Americans had long since ceased to concern themselves with what John Milton, in *Paradise Lost*, called "Providence, foreknowledge, will and fate,/ Fixed fate, free will, foreknowledge absolute." Could Edwards (like his God) have foreseen the twentieth-century indifference toward theology, he would have been sorely grieved and would have regarded it as the final upshot of Arminian notions circulating in America in his own day. But he would also have seen the hand of God in it as in everything else. When fatally stricken following inoculation against smallpox in March, 1758, shortly after becoming president of the College of New Jersey, Edwards was, according to the earliest editor of his works, perplexed for a while about God's "mysterious conduct" in calling him "to a public scene of action and influence" and then suddenly striking him down. But his perplexity was short-lived; he soon recognized the wisdom and goodness of God in "this surprising event," submitted calmly to the "Sovereign Disposal of Heaven," and departed this life filled with the joy of faith.[65]

# 2

# Thomas Paine and the
# Natural Right to Freedom

THOMAS PAINE blasted the "absurd and impious doctrine of predestination," asserted his firm belief in "free agency," and proclaimed the natural right of human beings throughout the world to freedom.[1] "I consider freedom as personal property," he announced; it is "inseparable from the man as a man."

Paine defined liberty as "the power to do everything that does not interfere with the rights of others" and slavery as "being subject to the will of another."[2] But "free agency" for Paine was not mere absence of restraint or constraint as it was for Jonathan Edwards; it contained more positive elements: the right of people to better themselves by their own efforts, to participate in social decisions involving their welfare and happiness, and to think, talk, and act freely with due respect for the rights of others. Paine praised Jean-Jacques Rousseau and the Abbé Raynal for their "sentiment in favor of liberty," but complained that they left people "in love with an object, without describing the means of possessing it."[3] Paine kept his eyes on the means. His lifelong concern was with social and political arrangements guaranteeing the freedom and happiness of people everywhere. He was anxious to see the natural-rights philosophy at work in the world, and his utopian dream was of a democratic society composed mainly of small farmers and artisans, freely exchanging their produce and enjoying equal rights, representative government, and economic plenty.

Paine was a militant rationalist who despised predestinarian theology. He never seriously pondered the free will question, however, and he was closer to Jonathan Edwards in some respects than he realized. Though he substituted a genial Deist God for Edwards's ineffable Jehovah, he tended to merge science and religion in his thinking as Edwards did. Science deals with processes and religion with purposes; but Paine, like Edwards, united the two by teleologizing the cosmos and finding moral values in the natural world. Freedom, for Paine, existed in a state of nature; it was a natural, not a social, right in origin. This meant that nature, not social circumstances, generated moral principles and that although circumstances might change, the principle of individual liberty remained permanently valid. Paine did not realize that the natural-rights view of freedom which he cherished, particularly with its individualistic emphasis, was a peculiarly Western creation and that it would have seemed "absurd and impious" (to use his own description of predestination) to the majority of people before modern times. It would also have seemed absurd (even impious) to most people in Asia, Africa, the Middle East, and other parts of the non-Western world in 1776, when Paine's friend Thomas Jefferson incorporated it into the Declaration of Independence. Partly under Paine's tutelage the natural-rights doctrine came in time to have a worldwide influence. But in the Western world itself, as science and religion drifted apart and the cosmos was progressively deteleologized, the idea that freedom was in any sense a natural right came to seem absurd (though not necessarily impious) to increasing numbers of educated people.

## FREEDOM AND NATURE

Paine's love of liberty may have come from his Quaker background. Son of a Quaker corset-maker in Thetford, England, Paine never joined the Society of Friends but always spoke of the Quakers (except for Quaker pacifists during the American Revolution) with affection. In *Age of Reason*, that powerful blast against organized religion, he singled out the Quakers as the only sect that had not engaged in persecution, praised their philanthropy, and said they were closer to "true Deism, in the moral and benign part thereof" than any other religious group.[4] But science, not religion, was Paine's major interest, though he would not have distinguished the two when it came to fundamentals. He adored

Newton as Edwards did; but where Edwards utilized Newtonianism to bolster Calvinism, Paine made it the basis of all his social and religious thinking. Conceiving of the universe, as all deistic Newtonians did, as an immense machine and of God, its creator, as a Great Mechanic, Paine saw unerring order and universal harmony at the heart of things and looked upon the laws governing the physical world as immutable, eternal, and beneficent. For Paine, moreover, as for all Deists, moral and social laws were just as uniform, unchanging, and beneficial as the physical laws which scientists like Newton had discovered. He dismissed with scorn the notion that abstract ideas and general principles were human contrivances with social purposes; he thought of them as truths of divine origin which were accessible to the reason of man if he but took thought.

Paine's natural world was orderly, disciplined, rational, and benign; the social institutions he saw about him were clumsy, irrational, disorderly, and oppressive. His plans for reform called for reproducing the harmony, order, and simplicity of nature in social relations. All that was necessary, he thought, was to liberate mankind from the excrescences of centuries of ignorance and superstition and to create opportunities for people to live together freely and easily according to the laws of nature which God had established for their benefit. Freedom, for Paine, meant doing what comes naturally; and that meant behaving sensibly, not foolishly. But he never adequately explained how in a Newtonian universe people came to behave so unnaturally. Nor did he ever face the problem of reconciling his belief in the free agency of man with his conviction that causal laws governed the moral as well as the natural world. And it never occurred to him that reality might be richer than thought, that nature might possess irregularities as well as regularities, and that the universe's deepest secrets might have to be approached poetically as well as mathematically.[5] His interests were mainly social and political, and he lacked even Franklin's passing interest in metaphysical problems. He was not a philosopher but a polemicist, though for the most part a highly principled one.

Paine had no Quaker humility about the validity of the principles he espoused. "What I write is pure nature," he averred, "and my pen and my soul have ever gone together."[6] He also boasted: "I scarcely ever quote; the reason is, I always think."[7] Though his thinking was shaped by the natural-rights philosophy well known to all educated and informed people in the West in the late eighteenth century, Paine thought his ideas came from acts of pure reason on his own part, and he sincerely believed that he was a "man of nature" ruminating about basic issues that no one else had pondered for centuries.[8] Actually, only in the rigorous consistency and boldness with which he carried certain principles to their logical conclusion can he be considered original. But the lucidity, precision, and assurance with which he expounded natural-rights ideas gave them wide currency, and his popular influence far outran his originality. He was probably the eighteenth-century's clearest exponent of freedom as a natural right. "I am a *farmer of thoughts,*" he told Henry Laurens in the spring of 1778, "and all the crops I raise I give away."[9]

## A PHILOSOPHY FOR THE AMERICAN REVOLUTION

Paine had not intended to become a farmer of thoughts, at least not political thoughts, when he came to America in 1774. He came to the New World looking for a career in science or teaching, but he soon took up journalism and quickly discovered he had a great gift for popularizing abstract ideas. When the American Revolution came, he thought he saw a "vast scene" opening in the thirteen colonies with momentous consequences for the freedom of humanity, and he at once joined the rebels.[10] In addition to contributing *Common Sense* and *The Crisis* to the American cause, he served in the Continental Army and also worked for the Continental Congress. After the Revolution he looked back with pride on the part he had played in helping to found "a New Empire raised on the principles of liberty and liberality."[11]

Paine devoted considerable energy to expounding the principles of liberty for which he thought the American Revolution was fought. He saw them as grounded in natural rights. "Natural rights," he said, "are those which appertain to man in right of his existence" and they "always imply *inherent liberty.*"[12] Each individual, according to Paine, echoing Locke, possessed a natural right (an "animal right," he once called it) to all the freedom necessary to preserve and protect himself, with due regard for the rights of others, and every society possessed a similar natural right. Natural rights were based on "justice and reason," not on "mere conquest, power or violence," and they were sacred, hereditary, and inalienable and appertained "to ALL, and not to any one more than to another."[13] Paine was vexed by the view that rights grow largely out of social experience, are prescriptive in nature, and rest on precedents, charters, acts of Parliament, and other conventions agreed upon by people in the recent and dim past. "The error," he said, of those who reason by precedents drawn from antiquity, respecting the rights of man, is that they do not go far enough into antiquity. They do not go the whole way. They stop in some of the intermediate stages of an hundred or a thousand years, and produce what was then done as a rule for the present day. This is no authority at all.[14]

Paine wanted to eliminate all the barriers between people and their natural rights which he thought had accumulated through long history and restore the pristine liberty and equality which he insisted all human beings had received from God at the moment of creation. "Every age and generation must be free to act for itself, *in all cases*, as the ages and generations which preceded it," he declared. "The vanity and presumption of governing beyond the grave, is the most ridiculous and insolent of all tyrannies." Circumstances in the world were continually changing, and people must be free to adjust to new conditions without being hamstrung by past precedents. It was the living, not the dead, who were to be accommodated. "I am contending for the rights of the *living*," he declared, "and against their being willed away, and controlled and contracted for, by the manuscript assumed authority of the dead."[15]

What were the rights of the living? They were all the rights which men possessed in a state of nature or, as Paine called it, a "state of natural liberty." Paine accepted the social-contract theory of government, popular in his day, in its most idealistic form and departed substantially from the philosophy of such celebrated contractarians as Hobbes and Locke in his emphasis on individual rights and democratic objectives. Hobbes, as C. B. Macpherson has shown, used the theory largely to demonstrate the necessity for a self-perpetuating sovereign to protect life and property and to enforce legal contracts in a possessive market society; and Locke, equally a champion of possessive individualism, placed major emphasis on a natural right to property prior to the establishment of civil society and government, defended the accumulation of property in the hands of a few, asserted that civil society and government were established by property-holders to protect their rights and interests, and excluded the unpropertied—the laboring classes and the poor—from full membership in political society.[16]

Unlike Hobbes and Locke, Paine, who came from a disfranchised class and had known poverty in England, was more concerned with human than with property rights (though he did not deny the inevitability of unequal property holdings in society) and his version of the social-contract theory reflected this concern. He based his philosophy on the historicity of the state of nature. In a state of nature antedating civil society, he said, each individual was "a Sovereign in his own natural right," and thus his own lawgiver.[17] He possessed intellectual rights: freedom of thought, conscience, and speech. He also possessed physical rights: the freedom to do whatever he pleased so long as he did not infringe on the rights of others. But equality of rights was not matched by equality of powers. Some people were stronger than others and better able to exercise their rights in a state of nature. And even the strongest people were not always able to do as they wished, for their natural powers always fell somewhat short of their natural wants. Because of the natural limitations on the powers of individuals, therefore, and because, in addition, people have a natural propensity for social life, the first settlers in any region quickly abandon the state of nature and form themselves into a society for mutual assistance and protection.

Paine had the highest regard for the social state. It was a kind of Garden of Eden, as he described it, minus the serpent. Only once removed from the state of nature, it retained most of the liberty belonging to man's natural state and required people to limit their freedom of action only to the extent needed for voluntary cooperation. In society, said Paine, "nearly the whole of the business is performed by the natural operation of the parts upon each other."[18] Natural to man because of his social sympathies, society "promotes our happiness *positively* by uniting our affections."[19] Paine thought that all the "great laws of society" were laws of nature and that people had only to consult their consciences to know what they were and act in accordance with them.[20] Conscience, not force, was the arbiter in man's social state.

And yet, somehow, the serpent slithered quietly into Paine's garden after all. The "impulses of conscience," he admitted, did not turn out to be "clear, uniform and irresistibly obeyed," and people did not remain "perfectly just to each other" in the social state.[21] Inevitably, after they overcome the first difficulties of settlement, people "begin to relax in their duty and attachment to one another" and commence encroaching on each other's natural rights. The result is that the weak find themselves at the mercy of the strong and no individual is powerful enough to feel completely secure against the depredations of his fellows.

At this point a restraining force must be added to that of conscience: government. Government for Paine was necessary "to supply the defect of moral virtue," and he took a low view of it (rather than of the human beings who required such a device). "Society in every state is a blessing," he declared, "but government, even in its best state, is but a necessary evil." Like dress, government is "the badge of lost innocence"; it is "a mode rendered necessary by the inability of moral virtue to govern the world."[22]

But there are governments and governments. Some are founded on force and fraud and others, for all their shortcomings, on reason and common consent. Paine could approve only of governments which emerged naturally from society and were based on voluntary agreement. In such cases, he said, "the *individuals themselves*, each in his own person and sovereign right, *entered into a compact with each other* to produce a government; and this is the only mode in which governments have a right to arise, and the only principle on which they have a right to exist."[23] The objectives of rational governments are freedom and security for all citizens, and to achieve them people must agree to surrender some of their natural rights in order to have their other rights better safeguarded.

Which class of natural rights are retained and which class surrendered? "The natural rights which [man] retains," said Paine, "are all those in which the *power* to execute is as perfect in the individual as the right itself."[24] In the first class are mainly the rights of the mind (forming and expressing opinions) and any others (not specified by Paine) "which can be fully exercised by the individual without the aid of exterior assistance; or in other words, rights of personal competency." Rights of the second class are "those of personal protection, of acquiring and possessing property, in the exercise of which the individual natural power is less than the natural right," and these are deposited in a common stock and entrusted to the safekeeping of government.[25] The individual gains rather than loses by the transaction; he exchanges natural rights involving security of person and property, which he is unable to enforce by himself, for civil rights backed by public force.

Paine placed great emphasis on the distinction between natural and civil rights. With respect to natural rights, he said repeatedly, we "act wholly in our own person"; with civil rights, "we agree not to do so, but act under the guarantee of society."[26] But since civil rights (or rights of compact) involve "the assistance or agency of other persons" and are enforced by government, the upshot is greater actual freedom for the individual than he possessed in a state of natural liberty.[27] Every civil right, Paine declared, had for its foundation some natural right preexisting in the individual. A man, for example, had a natural right to judge in his own cause; and so far as the right of the mind is concerned, he never surrenders it; but what availeth it him to judge, if he has not power to redress? He therefore deposits his right in the common stock of society, and takes the arm of society, of which he is a part, in preference and in addition to his own. Society grants him nothing. Every man is proprietor in society, and draws on the capital as a matter of right.[28]

A man also has a natural right to redress himself whenever he is injured. But he may not possess the power to do so; and even if he did, exercising that power might be harmful to society. "Therefore," said Paine, "the *civil* right of redressing himself by an appeal to public justice, which is the substitute, makes him stronger than the natural one, and less dangerous."[29] Civil rights, like natural rights, are equal for all citizens. "Every man," said Paine, "takes the arm of the law for his protection as more effectual than his own; and therefore every man has an equal right in the formation of the government, and of the laws by which he is to be governed and judged."[30] Paine thought these equal rights should be spelled out in written constitutions prepared by people entering into social contracts.

Though Paine acknowledged that exchanging some natural rights for civil rights represented a gain for the individual, he did not want people to yield to civil society any more of their individual rights than was absolutely necessary. He continually reminded his readers that individuals retained an important class of natural rights even after forming their government and that to compromise on any of these rights was to flirt with slavery.

First and foremost among the retained rights was freedom of thought. Paine wanted people to realize that this was their most precious right and that no one could deprive an individual of his freedom to think but himself. When men yield up the privilege of thinking for themselves, Paine warned, "the last shadow of liberty quits the horizon."[31] He also thought the truly free mind respected the right of others to opinions at variance with his own. "He who denies to another this right," he pointed out, "makes a slave of himself to his present opinion, because he precludes himself the right of changing it." He was insistent on the point. "My idea of supporting liberty of Conscience and the rights of Citizens," he told Thomas Walker, "is that of supporting those rights in *other people*, for if a man supports only his *own* rights for his *own sake*, he does no moral duty."[32]

Closely associated with freedom of thought was freedom of conscience in religious matters. "Religion," wrote Paine, "is a private affair between every man and his Maker" and it is "not otherwise an object of just laws than for the purpose of protecting the equal rights of all, however various their belief may be."[33] Like Roger Williams many years before him (though for quite different reasons), Paine was implacably opposed to what he called the "adulterous connection" of church and state; religious establishments, he said, produced superstition, ignorance, bigotry, inquisitions, heresy-hunts, and persecution.[34] "Of all the tyrannies that afflict mankind," he exclaimed, "tyranny in religion is the worst."[35] He called national churches "human inventions, set up to terrify and enslave mankind, and monopolize power and profit."[36]

Paine was irritated, however, by the idea of "toleration" in religion, which he thought missed the whole point of religious freedom. "Toleration, he said, "is not the *opposite* of intoleration, but is the *counterfeit* of it. Both are despotisms. The one assumes to itself the right of withholding liberty of conscience, and the other of granting it."[37] Paine had nothing but scorn for the English Toleration Act of 1689 because its authors assumed that liberty of conscience was theirs to give. "In America," he said loftily, "we consider the assumption of such power as a species of tyrannic ignorance, and do not *grant* liberty of conscience as a *favor* but *confirm* it as a *right*."[38] The "UNIVERSAL RIGHT OF CONSCIENCE" was Paine's most cherished right; without it, he did not think political freedom was possible.[39] Paine once said that spiritual freedom was the root of political freedom and that the two freedoms were so intimately related "that the one cannot be wounded without communicating an injury to the other."[40]

But if liberty of conscience was essential to political freedom, so was liberty of expression. Paine emphatically believed that freedom of speech was one of the natural rights of man always retained.[41] Every person, he said, should be free to publish his thoughts and opinions without fear of harassment. This was especially important in political matters. Freedom of criticism was indispensable to good government. "Every part of which a government is composed must be alike open to examination and investigation," said Paine; "and where this is not the case the country is not in a state of freedom; for it is only by the free and rational exercise of this right, that errors, impositions, and absurdities can be detected."[42] Paine always found utilitarian reasons as well as principled reasons for freedom.

If freedom of thought, conscience, and speech were inalienable rights,

so was the right to self-government. Every people, said Paine, "has at
all times an inherent, indefeasible right to abolish any form of government it finds inconvenient, and establish such as accords with its interests, disposition, and happiness."[43] The natural right to self-government
formed the basis for the social contract by which all truly free governments come into existence. "To ELECT, and to REJECT" public officials
was "the prerogative of a free people," according to Paine, and "the essence of liberty."[44] Representative government

has its origin in the natural and eternal rights of man; for whether a man
be his own lawgiver, as he would be in a state of nature; or whether he exercises his portion of legislative sovereignty in his own person, as might be
the case in small democracies where all could assemble for the formation of
the laws by which they were to be governed; or whether he exercises it in
the choice of persons to represent him in a national assembly of representatives, the origin of the right is the same in all cases.[45]

Popular sovereignty, in short, was essential to free government, "for
wherever the sovereignty is, there must the freedom be."[46] In a free community, the people mutually agreed upon their constitution and form of
government and went on to elect their public officials and hold them responsible for their policies.

Paine was unalterably opposed to property qualifications for voting.
He thought the right of suffrage belonged equally to all citizens and was
"inherent in the word liberty."[47] In a series of articles for the *Pennsylvania Gazette* in December, 1778, discussing Pennsylvania's new democratic constitution of 1776, he argued forcefully against placing restrictions on male suffrage. The imposition of property qualifications for voting, he warned, would bind and fetter political freedom and jeopardize
freedom in general. "Freedom must have all or none," he declared, "and
she must have them equally"; the "floor of Freedom is as level as water."
To tie suffrage to property, he said, was to "regulate freedom by fortune." But freedom was eternal while fortune was fickle and the two
"have no natural relation." Freedom "connects herself with man as God
made him, not as fortune altered him," and it was a kind of personal
property in itself, "inseparable from the man as a man." But property
qualifications for voting subjected the electorate to the fluctuations of
fortune. If the vote is "dangerous in the hands of the poor from ignorance," said Paine, "it is at least equally dangerous in the hands of the
rich from influence, and if taken from the former under the pretence of

safety, it must be taken from the latter for the same reason." His concluding advice to Pennsylvanians: *"Leave Freedom free."*[48]

Seventeen years later, in his *Dissertation on First Principles of Government* (1795), he was still arguing the case for universal manhood suffrage. Even a small property qualification, he said, "exhibits liberty in disgrace, by putting it in competition with accident and insignificance." And in one of his rare attempts at humor he asked this question:

When a broodmare shall fortunately produce a foal or a mule that, by being worth the sum in question, shall convey to its owner the right of voting, or by its death take it from him, in whom does the origin of such a right exist? Is it in the man, or in the mule?

Paine thought that making property (which could be acquired without merit and lost without crime) the criterion for political rights was disgraceful. He placed far less emphasis than Locke did on property rights, for he thought protecting people was more important than protecting property. He also viewed the wisdom, skill, and experience which a person acquired in life as the most valuable kind of property he possessed and thought it deserved as much protection as "exterior property" did. To make the latter the standard for voting was "a total departure from every moral principle of liberty, because it is attaching rights to mere matter, and making man the agent of that matter." When he wrote his articles for the *Pennsylvania Gazette* in 1778, Paine excluded indentured servants (and criminals) from the suffrage because he thought they had voluntarily "forfeited" their freedom during their period of service and he believed it was important for voters to be completely free agents. By 1795, however, when he wrote his *Dissertation on First Principles of Government*, he had come to believe that it was wrong to "disfranchise any class of men" since the right to vote was "the primary right by which other rights are protected."[49]

Paine thought that the representative (or republican) system of government was not only in accord with man's natural freedom but also "parallel with the order and immutable laws of nature." It was a law of nature, he said, that intelligence was independent of family or property and appeared unpredictably among all classes of people. It was absurd to try to fix the "heredityship" of wisdom as monarchical and aristocratic forms of government did; it would be just as sensible to try to make beauty hereditary. Wisdom, said Paine, was like a seedless plant:

It may be reared when it appears, but it cannot be voluntarily produced.

There is always a sufficiency somewhere in the general mass of society for all purposes; but with respect to the parts of society, it is continually changing its place. It rises in one to-day, in another to-morrow, and has most probably visited in rotation every family of the earth, and again withdrawn.[50]

Just as the republic of letters brings forward the best literary productions by encouraging talent wherever it may be, so representative government "is calculated to produce the wisest laws, by collecting wisdom where it can be found." But representative government does more than simply avail itself of wisdom wherever it can be found; by permitting all citizens to participate in politics it also stimulates the expression of wisdom which might otherwise go to waste. And it fosters an improvement in human nature by making unnecessary the habits of suspicion and distrust natural to monarchies. "If we wish to benefit our posterity," concluded Paine, "let us leave them liberty as a bequest."[51]

It was such a bequest that Paine thought the American Revolution was leaving future generations. He found it difficult to conceal his irritation when Abbé Raynal, in an essay appearing in September, 1782, suggested that the American Revolution originated in a dispute over whether Britain had a right to levy a slight tax on the colonies. In a lengthy response to the Abbé, Paine assured him that it was liberty, the nature of government, and the dignity of humanity, not a mere tax, that were at stake.[52] Like American Whigs generally, Paine thought the British king was an inveterate enemy of liberty and that his ministers had been working against colonial rights long before the Revolution. But he saw this as no matter for surprise; governments based on monarchy and hereditary succession were by their very nature inimical to liberty as a matter of principle. In fighting America, he said, Britain was in effect declaring war against the natural rights of all mankind. Independence would not only free the colonists from an absurd and oppressive system of government running contrary to the natural rights of man; it would also give them an opportunity to experiment with republican forms of government and to develop their country as an "asylum for the persecuted lovers of civil and religious liberty from *every part* of Europe."[53]

The downfall of kingly government in America, moreover, would be the prelude to its downfall elsewhere, and the triumph of liberty in America would pave the way for its victory elsewhere in the world. Paine was anxious to have the world know that the American cause was universal. He made the point repeatedly in *The Crisis*: America "has bravely put herself between Tyranny and Freedom"; "Had it not been for America, there had been no such thing as freedom left throughout the whole universe"; the American Revolution "has contributed more to enlighten the world, and diffuse a spirit of freedom and liberality among mankind, than any human event . . . that ever preceded it."[54]

In *Common Sense*, Paine called for "an open and determined DEC-LARATION FOR INDEPENDENCE" from Britain, and during the first part of 1776 his "sound doctrine and unanswerable reasoning," as George Washington noted with satisfaction, began "working a wonderful change" in the minds of many Americans.[55] The Declaration of Independence adopted by the Continental Congress on July 4, 1776, has been attributed to Paine by some of his admirers, though Paine himself put it this way: "I was myself among the first that proposed independence, and it was Mr. Jefferson who drew up the declaration of it."[56] But Jefferson's Declaration was a perfect reflection of Paine's own views. The philosophy of the first part of the document contained all of Paine's major ideas: an appeal to natural law, a statement of self-evident truths, an insistence on equal natural rights for all people, an assertion of the social-contract basis of government, and an announcement of the right of the people to alter or abolish governments which violated their natural rights. The inalienable rights which Jefferson singled out for emphasis—life, liberty, and pursuit of happiness—were also consonant with Paine's views of natural rights. Though he never mentioned pursuit of happiness as a basic right, he customarily linked freedom with happiness. And, like Jefferson, he tended to think of property (which Jefferson, departing from Locke, omitted in the Declaration) as a civil rather than natural right, since it could not exist without the protection of society and government.

What about Negro slavery? In an antislavery clause which Congress eliminated from the Declaration of Independence because of objections to it by delegates from South Carolina and Georgia, Jefferson excoriated the slave trade as "cruel war against human nature itself, violating its most sacred rights of life and liberty." As the owner of many slaves in Virginia, however, he said nothing in the clause about slaveholding itself (though he opposed it in principle), and he blamed the slave traffic entirely on the British king.

Paine went much farther in his opposition to slavery than Jefferson did; and, unlike Jefferson, he at no time in his life expressed doubts about the ability of black people. In an essay on "African Slavery in America" for the *Pennsylvania Journal and the Weekly Advertiser* on

March 8, 1775, he not only asserted the "natural, perfect right" of Negro slaves to claim freedom for themselves; he also went on to suggest that slaveowners be excluded from the fellowship of free men and to demand that colonial governments give all slaves brought to America their freedom and punish people who continued to hold them in bondage.[57] He even proposed legislation for giving black people economic assistance to tide them over after emancipation. Throughout the essay, he emphasized the irony of a situation in which the American colonists complained loudly about British efforts to reduce them to slavery while holding multitudes of blacks in bondage without any qualms. In a short piece for the *Pennsylvania Journal* on October 18, Paine went on to urge immediate action: "an act of continental legislation, which shall put a stop to the importation of Negroes for sale, soften the hard fate of those already here, and in time procure their freedom."[58] As clerk of the Pennsylvania assembly, Paine wrote the preamble to a law providing for the gradual emancipation of slaves in Pennsylvania (the first such legislative enactment in America) which was passed on March 1, 1780.[59]

Paine left the United States in 1787 and did not return until 1802. Once back in America, however, he continued his opposition to slavery. When French inhabitants of Louisiana petitioned Congress (shortly after the Louisiana purchase) for admission to the Union and for the right to continue importing slaves, Paine, in an indignant address to the petitioners in September, 1804, questioned the right of people who enslave other people to demand freedom for themselves. Writing President Jefferson the following year, Paine recalled a plan Jefferson had once outlined for setting aside land for emancipated blacks to settle on, and he urged congressional action to develop some such program in Louisiana. He also told Jefferson that the people of Liverpool were particularly active in the slave trade and responsible for sending many slaves to New Orleans, and he exclaimed: "Had I the command of the elements I would blast Liverpool with fire and brimstone. It is the Sodom and Gomorrah of brutality."[60]

Still, emancipation was never a major cause of Paine's. Though he abhorred slavery (and received much criticism in France for siding with the black rebels in Santo Domingo) he never wrote extensively on the subject after 1775 and never became actively involved in antislavery work. Nor did he do much for women's rights. He published two articles in 1775 pointing out that women were "adored and oppressed" everywhere, and he later became a friend of Mary Wollstonecraft. But there is no record of his participation in her campaign for the rights of women.[61]

## PAINE AND BURKE ON FREEDOM AND VIRTUE

Paine went to Europe in 1787, mainly to promote his plan for a single-arch bridge, and he intended to return the following year. But he was soon caught up in the swirl of events in France and he ended by remaining in Europe, shuttling, for a time, between Paris and London, until 1802. The outbreak of the French Revolution, Paine thought, opened up an opportunity to extend "the principles of liberty and fraternity through the greater part of Europe," and he felt duty-bound to remain on hand to contribute his services to the revolutionary cause.[62] In Paine's opinion, the French cause, like the earlier American cause, was the cause of all mankind and involved the freedom and rights of all men. "It is to the peculiar honor of France," he exclaimed in 1792, "that she now raises the standard of liberty for all nations; and in fighting her own battles, contends for the rights of all mankind."[63] Revolution meant republicanism to Paine: representative government based on the freely given consent of the people and dedicated to promoting the freedom and happiness of all citizens.

The French Revolution, from this point of view, did not altogether please Paine. In its initial stages, it was too conservative for a "sound Republican" like himself, particularly in retaining a hereditary executive in its first constitution; later on, the "execrable Reign of Terror" appalled him.[64] Still, he remained loyal to the French cause throughout (even though he spent ten months in prison during the Terror) and he never questioned that the Revolution, for all its excesses, had "laid the axe to the root of tyranny" and represented a gigantic advance for the "sacred *hereditary rights of man*" everywhere. "It is not because right principles have been violated," he reminded critics of the Revolution, "that they are to be abandoned."[65]

During the French Revolution, Paine did what he could to help: consulted with French leaders, served in the French National Assembly, and participated in constitution-making. Above all, he defended the principles of the Revolution in his forthright essays and pamphlets, and he tried to promote a republican revolution in England. When Edmund Burke published *Reflections on the Revolution in France* late in 1790, attacking French radicalism, Paine at once began converting an essay he was working on into a vigorous reply. The first part of *The Rights of Man*, his lengthy response, appeared early in 1791 and the second part in February, 1792. Paine's book was a forceful defense of the "principles of 1776 and 1789" and an aggressive assault on the British Constitution.[66] Enormously popular among English radicals (and much liked by Jefferson and his followers in America), *Rights of Man* was regarded as seditious in Britain and led to Paine's outlawry in December, 1792.

Paine's controversy with Burke centered chiefly on clashing views of government, but at issue also were definitions of freedom. For Burke, the freedom which natural-rights advocates like Paine emphasized was too abstracted from circumstances to be meaningful as a guide. More than that, the elevation of freedom from external restraints into a principle of universal moral worth was, in Burke's view, both misleading and dangerous. "The effect of liberty to individuals," he said, "is, that they may do what they please: We ought to see what it will please them to do, before we risque congratulations."[67] Proclaiming his own devotion to "a manly, moral, regulated liberty," Burke posed this question for champions of the natural right of all men to freedom:

Is it because liberty in the abstract may be classed among the blessings of mankind, that I am seriously to felicitate a madman, who has escaped from the protecting restraint and wholesome darkness of his cell, on his restoration to the enjoyment of light and liberty? Am I to congratulate an highwayman and murderer, who has broke prison, upon the recovery of his natural rights?

The appeal to liberty in the abstract pleases the mind and warms the heart, Burke acknowledged; but, he exclaimed,

what is liberty without wisdom, and without virtue? It is the greatest of all possible evils; for it is folly, vice, and madness, without tuition or restraint. Those who know what virtuous liberty is, cannot bear to see it disgraced by incapable heads, on account of their having high-sounding words in their mouths.[68]

In *Rights of Man*, Paine did not respond directly to Burke's animadversions on the natural-rights view of liberty. He probably did not feel obliged to. For one thing, Burke's remarks on freedom formed only a small part of *Reflections*. For another, Paine took it for granted that freedom and virtue were closely linked, and he rarely went out of his way to say so. The nature to which he appealed when talking about the natural right of freedom was, after all, disciplined and orderly, not wild and woolly. Burke's point about "virtuous liberty" was obvious to him; and he was anxious to say other things about freedom which were customarily overlooked by the traditionalists. Where Burke and other exponents of government by tradition went wrong, he thought, was in failing to recognize that social institutions permitting freedom of expression advanced, rather than retarded, the development of virtue and wisdom in individuals. The restraints of repressive institutions like monarchy, hereditary nobility, and the established church, he said time and again, kept people in an emotional fog and prevented them from developing their moral and rational faculties properly. Virtue was possible only under conditions of freedom. Writing the British Home Secretary in June, 1972, regarding prosecution of *Rights of Man,* Paine made the point that in a free society like that of the United States the authorities did not need to worry about the behavior of citizens. "This is a government that has nothing to fear," he said of the U.S. government.

It needs no proclamations to deter people from writing and reading. It needs no political superstition to support it; it was by encouraging discussion and rendering the press free upon all subjects of government, that the principles of government became understood in America, and the people are now enjoying the present blessings under it. You hear of no riots, tumults, and disorders in that country; because there exists no cause to produce them. Those things are never the effect of freedom, but of restraint, oppression, and excessive taxation.[69]

Paine was, in fact, no more tolerant of license than Burke (or Winthrop). In January, 1776, in an appendix to *Common Sense,* he had warned the American people about growing lawlessness. "The present state of America," he wrote with concern,

is truly alarming to every man who is capable of reflection. Without law, without government, without any other mode of power than what is founded on, and granted by, courtesy. . . . Our present condition is, Legislation without law; wisdom without a plan; a constitution without a name. . . . The property of no man is secure in the present unbraced system of things. The mind of the multitude is left at random, and seeing no fixed object before them, they pursue such as fancy or opinion presents. Nothing is criminal; there is no such thing as treason; wherefore, every one thinks himself at liberty to act as he pleases.[70]

Forgetting the idyllic picture of the state of natural liberty which he had painted in the first part of his pamphlet, Paine went on in his appendix

to *Common Sense* to sketch a plan of government for the ᵤ
He was, in fact, forever outlining constitutions, sketchin₃
government, and inventing political devices. It is true that his ₚ
for unicameral assemblies and his failure to provide for a bala
power, as a safeguard for liberty, in his systems of government evᵤ
considerable criticism from people like John Adams. Still, in the 178ᵤ
he joined nationalists like Alexander Hamilton and Robert Morris in
calling for a stronger central government and despite some reservations
supported the U.S. Constitution.

Freedom, Paine once observed, "connects herself with man as God
made him . . . and continues with him while he continues to be just and
civil."[71] Freedom, in other words, flourished only under conditions of
justice and civility. Paine's faith in human rationality in free societies
was undoubtedly excessive. But he did not want freedom for madmen
and highwaymen any more than Burke (or Locke and Edwards) did.
He simply thought that free societies produced fewer madmen and highwaymen than repressive societies did. As to the French Revolution, he
did not deny in *Rights of Man* that there had been atrocities in the early
stages of the upheaval, though remarkably few, he thought, given the
brutality of the *ancien régime*. But he explained the cruelty displayed by
the French masses, not as an inevitable accompaniment of their newfound freedom, but as a result of the training in cruelty which they had
received under the terroristic rule of the old regime. "It is over the lowest
class of mankind that government by terror is intended to operate," he
observed in *Rights of Man*,

and it is on them that it operates to the worst effect. They have sense enough
to feel they are the objects aimed at; and they inflict in their turn the examples of terror they have been instructed to practise. . . . In the com-
mencement of a revolution, those men are rather the followers of the *camp*
than of the *standard* of liberty, and have yet to be instructed how to reverence it.[72]

Paine thought the principles animating the French Revolution would
eventually eliminate the brutalities inherited from the old order. But he
warned French leaders in 1793 that the principles of "liberty and
humanity" were inseparable and that neglect of moral principles would
"injure the character of the Revolution and discourage the progress of
liberty all over the world." Paine, to be sure, wasn't always true himself
to his high principles. After the Terror he had high hopes for Napoleon

Bonaparte and tended to gloss over the dictatorial nature of Napoleon's rule. He also failed to see that the ideals of liberty he cherished had deep roots in British experience and that a French invasion of England, which he eagerly promoted when Napoleon was in power, would have seriously damaged that liberty, not advanced it. And yet his lapses were remarkably few considering his long and stormy career. Time and again he showed real courage, principle, and compassion in difficult situations. He argued and voted against the execution of Louis XVI in the French National Convention when it was not easy to do so. He also helped two British Tories, who loathed his ideas, escape the guillotine. And he pointed out to French leaders that an

avidity to punish is always dangerous to liberty. It leads men to stretch, to misinterpret, and to misapply even the best of laws. He that would make his own liberty secure must guard even his enemy from oppression; for if he violates this duty he establishes a precedent that will reach to himself.

But Paine thought that conservatives as well as revolutionaries could misuse liberty. When he returned to the United States in 1802, he was shocked by the outrageous attacks of the Federalists on his friend Jefferson, and he warned the American people that *"those who abuse liberty when they possess it would abuse power could they obtain it."*[73]

Like Burke, Paine believed that people must learn to use their freedom wisely. All human beings of course deserved it as a natural right; exercising that right in society, however, was not automatic. The achievement of freedom in practice required vigorous efforts on the part of people. It could not be handed to them on a golden platter; it must be striven for, and the harder the struggle, the more glorious the triumph. "Those who expect to reap the blessings of freedom," Paine told Americans during the Revolutionary War, "must, like men, undergo the fatigues of supporting it."[74] Paine had grave reservations, as we have seen, about granting the French inhabitants of Louisiana immediate self-government. "You are arriving at freedom," he told them, "by the easiest means that any people ever enjoyed it; without contest, without expense, and even without any contrivance of your own." Paine wanted Congress to establish a provisional government for Louisiana and postpone statehood until the people there had gained experience in governing themselves at the municipal level. He assured the Louisianans that "in proportion as you become initiated into the principles and practise of the representative system of government, of which you have yet had no experi-

ence, you will participate more and finally be partakers of the whole."
To support his recommendation for delay, Paine appealed to his own
experience in the French Revolution:

You see what mischief ensued in France by the possession of power before
they understood principles. They earned liberty in words, but not in fact.
The writer of this was in France through the whole of the Revolution, and
knows the truth of what he speaks; for after endeavoring to give it principle,
he had nearly fallen a victim to its rage.

As to the petition of the Louisianans, Paine said he had no objection
to "the principles of liberty it contains, considered in the abstract. The
error lies in the misapplication of them, and in assuming a ground they
have not a right to stand upon."[75] The sentiment could have been Burke's.

Yet the differences between Burke and Paine were profound. Paine's
contempt for royalty, nobility, and privilege was complete; his preference for an open society with equal opportunities and wide freedom of
expression was overpowering. In his revulsion against the limits and
bounds of the old order, he came close at times to thinking in almost
purely laissez faire terms. "It is the fault of all the governments in the
old world," he once told Americans, "that they GOVERN TOO MUCH."[76]
He wanted every man to be able to "pursue his occupation, and enjoy
the fruits of his labor, and the produce of his property, in peace and
safety," without governmental interference. He opposed paper money,
price controls, and artificial restrictions on private enterprise, commercial expansion, and economic development. He also favored abolishing
laws limiting workmen's wages. "Why not leave them as free to make
their own bargains, as the law-makers are to let them farms and houses?"
he asked. "Personal labor is all the property they have. Why is that little,
and the freedom they enjoy, to be infringed?" He also favored free trade
among nations, for he thought that removing restrictions on the free
flowing of international trade would mightily advance the cause of world
peace and prosperity. He regarded war ("the *lo here!* and the *lo there!*
that amuses and cheats the multitude") as one of the greatest enemies
of freedom.[77] Like most people, though, he approved of some wars and
tended to distrust people who did not share his approval.

But despite his fear of despotic governments, Paine was too sensitive
to the plight of the European masses to think that the negative freedom
of laissez-faire individualism was adequate to insure them their equal
rights. In *The Rights of Man*, he balanced his laissez-faire recommenda-

tions with proposals for an ambitious program of state aid to the poor, the young, and the elderly, not as a favor, but as a matter of right. In *Agrarian Justice*, his last pamphlet, published in the winter of 1795-96, he even presented a quasi-socialist view of property. The earth in its natural and uncultivated state, he said, was the common property of the human race, and only the improvements made on it could be regarded as the individual property of the cultivator. From this it followed that every proprietor of cultivated land owed the community a ground-rent covering the natural (as opposed to the improved) value of the land. Paine then went on to take a social view of all property. "Personal property," he said, "is the *effect of society*; and it is as impossible for an individual to acquire personal property without the aid of society, as it is for him to make land originally." His deduction: the socially created value contained in private property belonged to the community.[78]

## THE NATURAL-RIGHTS PHILOSOPHY AND ITS CRITICS

After the publication of *The Rights of Man*, a veritable hailstorm of critical books, articles, and pamphlets descended on Paine, and he was charged with everything ranging from ignorance, mendacity, and vulgarity on the one hand to recklessness, demagoguery, and downright anarchism on the other. Even people who sympathized in part with his views were offended by his loud strictures on the British system of government. But critics of "this American rifle-man," as one British writer called him, mainly followed Burke: they emphasized the natural inequalities of men and the need for various orders and degrees in society; pointed out that systems of government, like languages, were products of gradual growth, not of abstract principles; and defended the British Constitution, with its hereditary monarchy and nobility and established church, as having produced "a Happy state of Law and Liberty" for the British people.

As to freedom, most of Paine's critics thought that his paeans to popular liberty opened the watergates to corruption, license, disorder, and anarchy. Paine's preference, exclaimed one critic, was for "*Mob Government*," which "leaves people *free* to do all the mischief they please, and only restrains them from doing good.—It sets the passions and vices of mankind at liberty, and controls only their virtues." Even John Quincy Adams, who shared Paine's belief in natural rights (though not his enthusiasm for the French Revolution) warned that his passion for abstract freedom led him to overlook the important part that established institutions played in safeguarding liberty. Yet until Paine published *Age of*

*Reason*, with its harsh criticisms of orthodox Christianity, in 1794, and made a vituperative attack on George Washington in 1796, he remained generally popular in the United States and his statement of natural rights continued to be influential with many Americans.[79]

During the period of the American Revolution, the natural-rights philosophy was firmly enshrined in the American democratic faith, and its catchwords—individual freedom, inalienable rights, consent of the governed—became common currency among Americans in the years that followed. After Paine's death in 1809, however, the idea of natural rights began to come under sharp attack from southern apologists for slavery like John C. Calhoun. Calhoun borrowed from Burke in making his case against natural rights, but he also attempted to define liberty within the American constitutional framework in such a way as to exclude the black man. But abolitionists like Frederick Douglass continued to invoke the doctrine of natural rights in their crusade against chattel slavery; and during the Civil War Abraham Lincoln, though departing to some extent from orthodox natural-rights doctrine, singled out government by consent and universal freedom as the heart of the American experiment in politics.

After the war, however, natural rights received another vigorous assault at the hands of Social Darwinists like William Graham Sumner. Natural-rights views of freedom, Sumner conceded, may have been enormously useful in the struggle to throw off the restraints and restrictions of medieval feudalism; in the modern world, however, their usefulness had long since passed and they could no longer be regarded as anything but sentimental myths. It was necessary, now, he said, to take a more realistic view of the human condition and face the hard facts of life: that nature was harsh and demanding, not benign; that inequality, not equality, was man's natural birthright; that human rights were achieved by civilization, not bestowed by nature; and that liberty was won only by a toilsome struggle involving knowledge, discipline, and responsible action on the part of individuals.

The historical view of the origin of human rights which Sumner took came generally to prevail among social thinkers in America in the twentieth century, and increasingly the state of nature, social contract, and natural rights were written off as illusory fictions. At the same time, there was a tendency among social historians to dismiss natural rights as mere rationalizations or ideological covers for the needs and aspirations of the rising commercial classes in western Europe in the seventeenth and eighteenth centuries.[80] People like Paine, under this view, were spokesmen for the middle classes in their revolt against the landed aristocracy; and when they talked about freedom as a natural right they were thinking primarily of opportunities for profitable enterprise on the part of bankers, businessmen, and traders. But natural rights, as we have seen, meant much more to Paine than economic enterprise, and he espoused social programs for the working classes and the poor that were marked departures from the spirit of Locke's possessive individualism. He would have had no sympathy with the utilization of natural rights by American conservatives in the Gilded Age to support corporate privilege.

Despite twentieth-century criticisms of social-contract theory, the fact had to be faced that the American Revolution had been fought in the name of natural rights and the American Constitution and Bill of Rights shaped in part by the belief in liberty as an inalienable right. It was also a fact that throughout American history minority groups—abolitionists, feminists, Populists, trade-unionists, democratic socialists—seeking to expand their opportunities within the American system, had regularly appealed to the natural-rights philosophy of the Declaration of Independence to justify their stand. Even radicals (though not of course serious Marxists) appealed to natural rights. In the 1960s, the Black Panthers included phrases from the Declaration of Independence in the preamble to the constitution of their organization, and historian Staughton Lynd traced his radical philosophy to the natural-rights sentiments of revolutionists like Paine and abolitionists like William Lloyd Garrison.[81]

Were all of these reformers victims of a "delusion and superstition," as Sumner characterized natural rights? And was the American republic itself founded on what he called an "exploded myth"? American historians found the question difficult to answer. Carl Becker said that the question of the truth of the natural-rights philosophy, which he found historically superficial and psychologically naïve, was meaningless; the historian was concerned only with the fact that it had inspired American patriots in their struggle for independence. Clinton Rossiter took a somewhat similar line. Conceding that the natural-rights philosophy overlooked such realities as groups, classes, and power elites, Rossiter stressed the fact that for American revolutionists natural-rights doctrine was an earnest faith, not an ordered theory, and that as such it was one of the most noble and influential of all political philosophies in human history. Charles Beard took the view that rights rested at bottom on morals rather than on anything physical nature guarantees human being and

that natural-rights concepts could best be understood by transposing them
into moral rights. Anybody could assert or claim a moral right, he went
on to say, and whenever enough people joined in upholding the assertion
or claim and thus won respect for it from society and government, that
right became an actuality. But since all rights rested on the moral standards of the community and nation, he added, concepts of rights changed
as the habits, sentiments, and practices of the community changed.[82]

That human rights embodied in the habits, beliefs, and practices of
a community are the product of gradual development over a long period
of time is undeniable. But it is also true that the development of rights
depends heavily on the creative efforts of individuals like Paine who discover new possibilities for human relationships, take the trouble to assert
claims (to use Beard's language), and work hard to win support for
them from other people. It seems true, further, that there must be some
sort of transcendent standards, like natural rights, by which to judge prevailing norms in a community and justify the individual who departs
from accepted use and wont and engages in promising innovative action.
The "individual" apart from his society is doubtless an abstraction, even
a fiction; but so is "society" considered apart from the individuals com-
posing it. The natural-rights theory may have slighted the social nature
of human rights, but it was correct in calling attention to the importance
of some degree of individual autonomy to the growth of civilization.
Natural rights from this point of view are those enabling individuals to
develop their natural vitalities (which emerge independently of political
society) freely and fruitfully. To thwart or distort an individual's natural
growth along unique lines is, on this theory, contrary to nature. A child,
for example, born with extraordinary musical gifts into a family that was
implacably hostile to musical endeavor in a community rigidly insistent
on absolute obedience to parental commands would surely have a "natural
right," it would seem, to seek ways of expressing his musical talents in
defiance of parental and community authority. In this sense, the individual
who searches for appropriate outlets in his environment for his natural
energies may be said to be exercising his natural right to freedom.

John Dewey thought there was some validity in the contention of
natural-rights advocates that the individual possessed freedom prior to
the establishment of social and political organization. "A certain natural
freedom is possessed by men," he said.

That is to say, in some respects harmony exists between a man's energies

undings such that the latter support and execute his purposes.
is free; without such a basic natural support, conscious contriv-
lation, administration, and deliberate human institution of social
: cannot take place. In this sense natural freedom is prior to po-
om and is its condition.

But this kind of freedom, Dewey hastened to add, depended on accident.
The natural environment might or might not be compatible with an
individual's energies at any given moment, and unless people agreed to
work together in regularizing their relations with nature they would be
entirely at the mercy of their surroundings. In arriving at conscious agree-
ments to "supplement and in some degree supplant freedom of action
which is the gift of nature," individuals have to make some concessions.
"They must consent to curtailment of some natural liberties in order that
any of them may be rendered secure and enduring. They must, in short,
enter into organization with other human beings."[83] Paine would not have
dissented from this view of the matter. He was fascinated by the problem of devising social and political arrangements by which people regu-
larized their relations with each other and with nature. He insisted only
that they fulfill, not stifle, the individual's natural right to free expression. He would have liked Richard Taylor's way of putting it in *Freedom,
Anarchy, and the Law* (1973): freedom is a gift of nature, that is, an
individual is by nature his own sovereign power and governs his conduct
to some extent by his will; the ultimate justification for government is
the expansion and enhancement of this freedom; and when people voluntarily submit to the authority of the state, they do so in the belief that
their "freedom or sovereignty is not thereby cancelled or compromised,
but strengthened."[84]

For a time, when Paine was in Europe in the years following the
achievement of American independence, he was disturbed by reports
(from Jeffersonians) that attachment to the principles of the American
Revolution was declining in the new nation. But on his return to America
in 1802, he was reassured to learn that, with his friend Jefferson as President, "a spark from the altar of *Seventy-six*, unextinguished and unex-
tinguishable through the long night of error, is again lighting up, in every
part of the Union, the genuine name of rational liberty."[85] Still, what if
America should fail? What if she eventually went the way of all other
nations? Only once did Paine contemplate such a possibility, and he
found it too melancholy a thought to hold for long. "When we contemplate the fall of empires and the extinction of nations of the ancient

world," he mused, "we see but little to excite our regret than the moul-
dering ruins of pompous palaces, magnificent monuments, lofty pyra-
mids, and walls and towers of the most costly workmanship." But with
America it was different. If America should fail, he said,

the subject for contemplative sorrow will be infinitely greater than crum-
bling brass or marble can inspire. It will not then be said, here stood a temple of vast antiquity, here rose a Babel of invisible height, or there a pal-
ace of sumptuous extravagance; but here, ah painful thought! the noblest
work of human wisdom, the grandest scene of human glory, the fair cause
of freedom rose and fell![86]

But Paine was convinced that America and the cause of individual freedom would never fall.

# 3

# Ralph Waldo Emerson's
# Transcendental View

AS A YOUNG MAN Ralph Waldo Emerson was anxious to be free: to
transcend the conventional wisdom of his time and place and live an
autonomous life. It was no easy task. Unlike Paine, he was troubled by
the free-will question. Son of a Unitarian minister, with generations of
Calvinist clergymen in his family background, he was pondering questions like these at nineteen:

How shall he reconcile his freedom with that eternal necessary chain of cause
and consequence which binds him and Nature down to an irreversible decree? How shall he reconcile his freedom with that prophetic omniscience
which beheld his end long before the infant entered on the world?

It would be a bold man, he decided, who undertook to answer beyond a
doubt such perplexing questions.[1] But he was determined to try. He read
Edwards on free will and copied passages on liberty and necessity from
famous philosophers into a book of quotations which he began compiling
in 1824.[2] And after becoming a Unitarian minister in 1826, he continued to explore the question of freedom in his Sunday sermons.[3] "When
we say we are free," he told one congregation, "we rest on a conviction
that is too mighty for reason and must stand whether reason can sanction
it or not." In all of our actions, he went on to say, we feel that we may

do or forbear if we wish; we also feel that we may be "unquestioned masters of our purposes."[4]

Being master of his own purposes was a matter of some urgency for young Emerson. He had entered the ministry (after studying at Harvard) with misgivings The scholarly side of a Unitarian clergyman's life was appealing to Emerson, and he found some outlet for his creative energies in preparing sermons. But the pastoral duties—sick calls, Bible classes, public prayers—were irksome, and the work of the church as a whole seemed unchallenging. Unitarianism, Emerson concluded, was "corpse-cold"; it lacked heart and soul.[5] "And without soul," he wrote in his journal, "the freedom of our Unitarianism here becomes cold, barren, & odious."[6] The church, he acknowledged, did permit him a great deal of liberty, but it was not nearly enough. He needed unbounded freedom to delve into the innermost recesses of the human heart, send his mind soaring across the universe's vast spaces and aeons of time, and then to say what he thought and felt about things with absolute honesty and without regard for the prevailing opinions of his own or any other day.

When, in September, 1832, Emerson finally told the Second Church in Boston that he intended to resign his pastorate, he singled out his conscientious inability to administer the ordinance of the Lord's Supper as the immediate reason for his decision. The real reason was deeper: the clerical profession, even in so liberal a church as the Unitarian, simply did not permit him to be his own master. Freedom, he told his congregation, was the essence of Christianity; its object was to make people good and wise, and its institutions should be as flexible as the wants of men. But the forms of the church (of which the Lord's Supper was typical) were too rigid for his own wants. "It is my desire," he announced, "to do nothing which I cannot do with my whole heart." And he added simply: "Having said this, I have said all."[7]

## SELF-RELIANCE AND CREATIVE INSPIRATION

Emerson felt considerable relief when the Second Church granted him dismission in October. "I walk firmly toward a peace & a freedom which I plainly see before me albeit afar," he assured his brother William, and he went on to mention projects of "action, literature, philosophy" that were sprouting in his mind. There was even the possibility of a new magazine in which he could express his own individuality.[8] After a trip to Europe, where he met Samuel Taylor Coleridge and Thomas Carlyle (whose break with the "sensational philosophy" of the British empiricists

had already attracted his fascinated attention), Emerson took to the lecture platform and launched his new career as lecturer, essayist, poet,
philosopher, and editor. By this time his revolt against the "corpse-cold"
rationalism of Unitarianism was complete and he had worked out the
basic foundations for an "intuitional philosophy" which soon came to
be called Transcendentalism. Basic to this philosophy was Coleridge's
distinction between Reason (intuitive grasp of universal truths) and
Understanding (empirical observation and inductive generalization).
"Reason," Emerson explained in a letter to his brother,

is the highest faculty of the soul—what we mean often by the soul itself; it
never *reasons*, never proves; it simply perceives; it is vision. The Understanding toils all the time, compares, contrives, adds, argues, near-sighted but
strong-sighted, dwelling in the present, the expedient, the customary. Beasts
have some understanding but no Reason. Reason is potentially perfect in
every man—Understanding in very different degrees of strength. . . . Religion,
Poetry, Honor belong to the Reason; to the real, the absolute.[9]

Intuition (Reason), in short, was the Transcendental road to freedom.
If a person took seriously the sudden insights, spontaneous fancies, and
unorthodox notions welling up in his consciousness, he could, Emerson
decided, free himself from the rigidities and conventionalities of his society and develop authentic moral and intellectual autonomy. During
the next few years he transcendentalized with mounting excitement. In
his paeans to Reason, he tended to slight at this point the role of critical
reflection in creative activity; but his own journals and notebooks showed
that he carefully worked over many of his own intuitive insights before
presenting them to the public. In September, 1836, he published his little
azure-colored pamphlet, *Nature*, a beautifully organized statement of the
Transcendental world-view; in August, 1837, he gave his Phi Beta Kappa
oration on "The American Scholar" in which he took a Transcendental
view of literature and scholarship; in July, 1838, he delivered his Divinity School Address at Harvard, in which he transcendentalized Christianity and brought the wrath of Unitarian conservatives down on his head;
and in July, 1840, he saw the first issue of the short-lived *Dial*, which
he helped edit, come from the press.

Occasionally Emerson felt glad to the brink of fear over his new-
won freedom. "It is awful," he exclaimed at one point, "to look into the
mind of man & see how free we are. . . . Outside, among your fellows,
among strangers, you must preserve appearances, a hundred things you

cannot do; but inside, the terrible freedom!" But freedom was mainly exhilarating: "Good it is to grow familiar with your own thoughts & not shun to speak them."[10] In a burst of euphoria after leaving the church and finding his true vocation, Emerson plumbed the depths of his Transcendental consciousness and reported his findings with the zest and triumph of a man who has sighted a new land. Emerson's imaginative insights, like those of any creative thinker, were unquestionably a major source of novelty and originality in his Transcendental vision and in the expression of that vision. Still, like all intuitions, Emerson's sprang from his deepest needs, interests, and experiences, and the Transcendental world which he portrayed was by no means entirely new. Much of what he announced to the world after departing from the ministry had been implicit in his sermons, and his Transcendentalism was permeated with the idealism of his Puritan ancestors raised to the highest pitch and shorn of all theological trappings. Emerson's pronouncements from the Unitarian pulpit had been, in fact, a remarkable prevision of his utterances as a Transcendental philosopher. Though the language of the sermons had been mostly plain and unadorned and lacked the exalted tone and stunning imagery of his Transcendental declarations, the major themes were all there in embryo: the insistence on individual character, self-truth, and integrity; the importance of finding one's vocation in life and developing one's God-given talents to the utmost; the elevation of intuitive insight over logical analysis as the way to the deepest truths; the belief that spiritual laws govern both nature and humanity and that a "Vast Mind" is immanent in all natural and moral processes; and the conviction that freedom in its highest reaches is moral and rational in nature and transcends the empirical world of particulars.

Having found his vocation as literary artist and Transcendental philosopher, Emerson at last felt he was unquestioned master of his own purposes, and he was anxious to share his experience with others. He had decided that freedom was grounded in self-trust, and he spent the rest of his life preaching what he had learned to his countrymen. "Free should the scholar be,—free and brave," he told the Phi Beta Kappa students at Harvard. "Free even to the definition of freedom, 'without any hindrance that does not arise out of his own constitution.'"[11] But if Emerson's basic message to the world was self-reliant freedom, he regarded this kind of freedom as inseparable from a Transcendental angle of vision. To be free, he said repeatedly, an individual must transcend his time and place and assert his independence of society's customs, tra-

ditions, and habits of thought when it seemed to him that they were
founded on compromise and expediency (the Understanding) rather
than on moral principle (the Reason). He once told an inquirer that "if
he wished at any time to know what the Transcendentalists believed, he
might simply omit what in his own mind he added from the tradition, and
the rest would be Transcendentalism."[12]

Emerson's traditionless Transcendental Man was remarkably like
Paine's traditionless Natural Man in basic wisdom and decency, and
though far less interested in politics, he was equally forthright in his
social dissent. "Society everywhere," Emerson complained, "is in con-
spiracy against the manhood of its members" and its favorite virtue is
conformity.[13] Hence:

A man comes now into the world a slave. He comes saddled with twenty or
forty centuries. Asia has arrearages and Egypt arrearages; not to mention all
the subsequent history of Europe and America. But he is not his own man, but
the hapless bondman of Time, with these continents and aeons of prejudice
to carry on his back. It is now grown so bad that he cannot carry the mountain any longer and be a man. There must be a revolution. Let the revolution
come, and let one come breathing free into the earth to walk by hope alone.
It were a new world, and perhaps the ideal would seem possible, but now it
seems to me they are cheated out of themselves and live on another's sleeve.[14]

The Transcendentalist, according to Emerson, refuses to live on someone
else's sleeve; he follows his own instincts, and if this brings him into
conflict with church and state, then so much the worse for those institutions. "Acquiescence in the establishment," Emerson insisted, indicated
lack of self-esteem.[15] "Whoso would be a man, must be a nonconform-
ist. . . . Nothing is at last sacred but the integrity of your own mind."[16]
For: "The height, the deity of man is to be self-sustained, to need no
gift, no foreign force." Emerson admitted that the Transcendentalists

are not good citizens, not good members of society; unwillingly they bear
their part of the public and private burdens; they do not willingly share in
the public charities, in the public religious rites, in the enterprises of education, of missions foreign and domestic, in the abolition of the slave-trade, or
in the temperance society. They do not even like to vote.[17]

But this was because they refused to surrender their intellectual independence to organized enterprises of any kind, even to those established
for worthy purposes. Nor would they bow to the authority of the printed

word. "Some books leave us free," Emerson observed, "and some books make us free," but most books do not even merit a scholar's idle times.[18] As for friendship: "I do . . . with my friends as I do with my books. I would have them where I can find them, but I seldom use them. We must have society on our own terms, and admit or exclude it on the slightest cause."[19]

Such aloofness surely risked offending one's associates. "Yes," Emerson admitted, "but I cannot sell my liberty and my power, to save their sensibility." The important thing was to maintain one's godlike independence.[20] Even the Transcendental philosophy itself, Emerson feared, faced the danger, after its ideas became familiar, of hardening into an orthodoxy which would be inimical to independent thinking. "It is only as a man puts off all foreign support and stands alone," he said,

that I see him to be strong and to prevail. . . . He who knows that power is inborn, that he is weak only because he has looked for good out of him, and elsewhere, and, so perceiving, throws himself unhesitatingly on his thought, instantly rights himself, stands in the erect position, commands his limbs, works miracles.[21]

The struggle for Transcendental autonomy was difficult and unending. Still, Emerson advised, "If you cannot be free, be as free as you can."[22]

To the doubting and hesitant, Emerson promised that a vast creative power and tremendous self-assurance followed from the achievement of Transcendental freedom. "With the exercise of self-trust," he assured his countrymen, "new powers shall appear": intellectual insight, moral strength, aesthetic distinction, heroic endeavor. "Every man is a new method and distributes things anew," insisted Emerson. "The power which resides in him is new in nature, and none but he knows what that is which he can do, nor does he know until he has tried. . . . The eye was placed where one ray should fall, that it might testify of that particular ray."[23] Emerson had at length discovered his own particular ray, and he was convinced that every person must do the same if he was to live freely and wisely. Finding one's proper vocation in life was the key to self-reliant freedom. "Every man," Emerson said, "has this call of the power to do something unique, and no man has any other call." Until a person comes to know what his special talents and interests are, he remains a prisoner of circumstances and his life is pinched, mean, and precarious. But with the discovery of his unique mission in life and the determination to follow it through, he enters on the road to freedom. "There is one direction in which all space is open to him," said Emerson. "He has faculties silently inviting him thither to endless exertion. He is like a ship in a river; he runs against obstructions on every side but one; on that side all obstruction is taken away and he sweeps serenely over God's depths into an infinite sea."[24]

By doing his own work a person unfolds himself, grows naturally, and expresses the force and meaning residing within him. He comes to possess "soul" and wins universal respect. "Who has more soul than I masters me . . . ," said Emerson. "Who has less I rule with like facility." Emerson wanted Americans to do their thing, that is, choose the vocation which was proper for them. "But do your thing," he said, "and I shall know you. Do your work, and your work shall reinforce yourself."[25] And perhaps in time the self-reliant individual might even become absolute master of his circumstances and bend events to his will.

## EMERSON AND FREE WILL

In exalting the creative power which he thought lay dormant in all people, Emerson sometimes talked as if he believed in freedom of the will. He described Americans as "free-willers," contrasted "American free will" with Asian passivity, and declared that "nothing is free but the will of man."[26] But he was not using the expression *free will* with any more precision than had Jonathan Edwards's targets, Daniel Whitby and Samuel Clarke. He was simply emphasizing the activistic nature of American culture and its rejection of the doctrine of meek submission to blind fate.

In one poem, it is true, he gave the impression that he believed in freedom in some absolute sense. "When Duty whispers low, *Thou must*," he wrote, "The youth replies, *I can*."[27] Here he seems to be echoing Kant's view that "ought implies can" and that moral obligation presupposes the freedom to act out of duty even if one wills to do otherwise. But Emerson did not really believe people possessed this kind of categorical freedom, and he did not subscribe to the doctrine of free will any more than Edwards did. Indeed, it was impossible for him to do so, given the basic assumptions of his Transcendental faith. Attributing the power of causal initiative to the human will meant rending the seamless web of things and introducing ambiguities and accidents into the universe which were utterly at variance with the monistic angle of vision from which he observed creation. Free will placed human life at the mercy of the whims of individuals, shattered the majestic universal laws which Emerson saw everywhere at work, delivered the universe over to "the blank and shapeless agency of Chance," and substituted disorder and anarchy for unity and uniformity.[28] Emerson's fear and distrust of the idea of chance was as powerful as Edwards's. As a young man he confided to his journal what was to be a lifelong view:

He who believes that Chance created the Universe, and may shortly demolish it, that he is himself here only by a lucky accident, and that no unseen Mind has measured his progress or appointed his end, must often, in his dark hours of weariness or distress feel that he is alone and sink under the disgust of his uncomfortable solitude. It is a desolate belief which converts into a wilderness the great and blooming garden of nature; which, by depriving things & beings of object & utility, deprives them of the very principles of beauty. . . . But add to this Universe an Omniscient Governor and you have infused a soul into the mighty mass. . . . You feel at once *secure*. . . . The march of events which was loose and fortuitous, becomes dignified and divine.[29]

As an adult Emerson delighted in transmuting coincidence into causality. "I read today a horrid story of murder," he wrote in his journal in 1838; "it fills one with glooms, bludgeons & gibbets: then it turns out to be a systematic longsought accurately-measured revenge: instantly the gloom clears up; for in a degree the light of law & of cause & effect shines in."[30]

Emerson never dreamed while he was writing these words that scientists like James Clerk Maxwell would soon begin to undermine the Newtonian determinism on which he (and Edwards and Paine) founded so much of their philosophy. Maxwell, British physicist who studied the dynamics of gases, found it useful to discard mechanical causation for a statistical approach to the behaviour of large numbers of gas molecules based on the theory of probability, and he was fully aware of the philosophical implications of what he was doing. "If the actual history of Science had been different," he noted, "and if the scientific doctrines most familiar to us had been those which must be expressed in this way, it is possible that we might have considered the existence of a certain kind of contingency a self-evident truth, and treated the doctrine of philosophical necessity as a mere sophism."[31]

Emerson learned something about statistical laws in his later years; but he remained, like most of his contemporaries, a good Newtonian. From the beginning to the end of his adventure of ideas he exalted "sublime Necessity" over "Chance and Fortune" and he associated the latter with the doctrine of free will. "If we thought," he once exclaimed, "men were free in the sense that in a single exception one fantastical will could prevail over the law of things, it were all one as if a child's hand could pull down the sun. If in the least particular one could derange the order of nature,—who would accept the gift of life?"[32] Not Emerson, certainly. "If we had not confidence," he said, "that the Law provided for every exigency, that not an impulse of absolute freedom could exist, we should rush by suicide out of the door of this staggering Temple."[33] For Emerson there was no discontinuity in creation. "There is no chance and no anarchy in the universe," he declared. "All is system and gradation."[34] He firmly denied that there was "a weak or a cracked link" in the chain joining things together.[35] "We are persuaded," he said, "that a thread runs through all things: all worlds are strung on it, as beads; and men, and events, and life, come to us only because of that thread: they pass and repass only that we may know the direction and continuity of that line."[36] Emerson's insistence that there was a "strict connection between every pulse-beat and the principle of being" clearly ruled out a belief in freedom of the will.[37]

The insistence on the "Godhead of man" also excluded free will from Emerson's philosophy.[38] The heart of Emersonianism was its belief that a divine energy (variously referred to as God, Over-Soul, Universal Spirit, Supreme Mind, Universal Power, and Universal Consciousness) dwelt within nature and humanity and objectified itself in the laws of the mind and in laws of nature. "Man," said Emerson, "is a stream whose source is hidden. Our being is descending into us from we know not whence. . . . I am constrained every moment to acknowledge a higher origin for events than the will I call mine."[39]

Like Coleridge and other English Romantics, Emerson was keenly aware of the importance of unconscious mentation in creative endeavor, and he looked upon the "Unconscious" as the source of intuitive insight and artistic inspiration. But he regarded creativity as divinely inspired; "the Unconscious," he said, "is ever the act of God himself."[40] He was endlessly insistent on the point: all creative acts are in the last analysis acts of God. Poet, dramatist, artist, philosopher, scientist, and man of action alike draw their inspiration from the "superincumbent spirit"; they are "vessels filled with the divine overflowings, enriched by the circulations of omniscience and omnipresence."[41] The individual will, far from possessing any original power of its own, is largely an obstacle to creativity. By its tendency to become absorbed in the private, selfish, and particular, and by its consequent blindness to universal truth, goodness, and beauty, it serves to check the influx of the divine mind into our minds and prevents true health and greatness.[42]

To him who, by God's grace, has seen that by being a mere tunnel or pipe through which the divine Will flows, he becomes great, and becomes a Man,—the future wears an eternal smile, and the flight of time is no longer dreadful. . . . I am willing . . . to be as passive to the great forces I acknowledge as is the thermometer or the clock, and quite part with all will as superfluous.[43]

The will, in short, is not only unfree; it is also largely an encumbrance. Self-reliance, Emerson's basic message to the world, resolved itself into God-reliance. Dependence on the Universal Spirit was the only way a person could achieve freedom from stifling traditions and hidebound conventions. Novelty and divinity were firmly linked in Emersonian Transcendentalism, and creativity was associated with passivity.

Emerson's view of creativity was in some respects unexceptionable. Many artists (and scientists, too) have stressed the importance of receptivity as a condition of creative endeavor. Ideas came "like a foreign guest" to Goethe; they sprang forth "like the free children of God." For Nietzsche (a great admirer of Emerson), thoughts "flashed out like lightning" and "quite without volition." And for Mozart: "*Whence* and *how* they come, I know not; nor can I force them." Twentieth-century analysts (like Freud), it is true, have tended to regard the creative act as ultimately inexplicable, but George Bernard Shaw came close to Emerson's view of the matter when he declared that a writer was "an instrument in the grip of Creative Evolution." For Emerson the creative person was "a mere tunnel or pipe" through which divine energy flowed whenever he opened himself to its reception.[44]

To the question of why some minds are open to divine illumination and others are not, Emerson had no answer. "There is the incoming or the receding of God," he declared: "that is all we can affirm; and we can show neither how nor why."

If you say, "the acceptance of the vision is also the act of God:"—I shall not seek to penetrate the mystery, I admit the force of what you say. If you ask, "How can any rules be given for the attainment of gifts so sublime?" I shall only remark that the solicitations of this spirit, so long as there is life, are never forborne. Tenderly, tenderly, they woo and court us from every object in nature, from every fact in life, from every thought in the mind. The one condition coupled with the gift of truth is its use.[45]

Emersonianism was a kind of secularized Edwardseanism. Edwards's saving grace became creative inspiration in Emerson's philosophy, and the striving for salvation became a search for intellectual and artistic independence. Emerson's autonomous individual, moreover, resembled Edwards's elect; he achieved his status only by the grace of God.

Nevertheless, Emerson's conviction that the creative energies animating man and nature were essentially divine did not mean that he was a fatalist. Like Edwards, Emerson carefully distinguished between a necessary and meaningful connection between events and an arbitrary arrangement of things by blind fate. Belief in brute fate or destiny was intolerable to Emerson, for he regarded it as rank superstition, on a level with the childish belief that spilling salt or reciting the Lord's Prayer backward brought penalties, "nowise grounded in the nature of the thing, but on an arbitrary will." The fatalist, Emerson pointed out, thought that events were controlled by "a law not adapted to man" which "holds on its way to the end, serving him if his wishes chance to lie in the same course, crushing him if his wishes lie contrary to it, and heedless whether it serves or crushes him." The Transcendentalist believed, on the contrary, that by taking thought human beings could apprehend the grand laws governing creation and utilize them for their own purposes. To be a fatalist was to believe that an immense whim was at work in the world and that all human endeavor was ultimately pointless. To be a Transcendentalist was to believe that by getting in tune with the infinite the individual could release the immense creative power within him in order to shape the world. Emerson criticized Goethe (whom he otherwise admired) for accepting the base doctrine of fate. Goethe's poetry, as a result, he said, was

external, the gilding of the chain, the mitigation of his fate; but the Muse never assays those thunder-tones which cause to vibrate the sun and the moon, which dissipate by dreadful melody all this iron network of circumstance, and abolish the old heavens and the old earth before the free will or Godhead of man.[46]

It was the divinity within man, Emerson insisted, that enabled him to rise above the iron network of circumstances and cause the sun and moon to vibrate. Transcendental freedom made man superior to fate; it liberated his spirit from tyrannical circumstances.

## TRANSCENDENTAL FREEDOM AND SOCIAL REFORM

But freedom was not purely spiritual for Emerson. He recognized that it had an objective as well as a subjective dimension that was important to human beings. Though he considered the emancipation of the individual spirit from the tyranny of circumstances to be Transcendentalism's chief objective, he also realized that if Transcendentalism was to flourish it was necesary to have social arrangements permitting people to seek opportunities for creative expression. Emerson was, in short, a civil libertarian, like Paine, and when Rufus Choate dismissed the natural-rights ideas of the Declaration of Independence as "glittering generalities," he reacted as Paine would have: "Say, rather, GLITTERING UBIQUITIES!"[47] Emerson regarded civil liberty (freedom of speech, press, religion, and association) as essential to civilization, and he seems at one time to have contemplated writing a paper discussing its origin and development in history.[48] He wrote approvingly about the longings for civil freedom of seventeenth-century English and American Puritans, acclaimed the Quaker George Fox as a lover of liberty, celebrated Elijah Lovejoy as a martyr for the rights of free speech and opinion, and, in *English Traits* (1856), praised the British for their contributions to the development of civil liberties. He also wrote at length about John Milton's heroic fight for civil, ecclesiastical, literary, and domestic liberty.[49]

The most outrageous violation of civil freedom in Emerson's day lay of course in the institution of Negro slavery. In journals which he kept as an undergraduate at Harvard, Emerson first took up the question of "whether any individual has a right to deprive any other individual of freedom without his consent; or whether he may continue to withhold the freedom which another hath taken away?" After considering the arguments on behalf of slavery in some detail (even to the extent of toying with the idea that blacks were somehow inherently inferior to whites), Emerson decided: "To establish by whatever specious argumentation the perfect expediency of the worst institution on earth is *prima facie* an assault upon Reason and Common Sense. No ingenious sophistry can ever reconcile the unperverted mind to the pardon of *Slavery*." Since he was also wrestling with the problem of free will at this time, he added that one must oppose slavery whether he believes in free will or not:

It is an old dispute which is not now and never will be totally at rest, whether the human mind be or be not a free agent. And the assertor of either side must be scandalized by the bare naming of the theory that man may impose servitude on his brother. For if he is himself free, and it offends the attributes of God to have him otherwise, it is manifestly a bold stroke of impiety to wrest the same liberty from his fellow. And if he is not free, then his inhuman barbarity ascends to derive its origin from the author of all necessity.[50]

It was inconceivable to Emerson, as it was later to Lincoln, that a just God could sanction human bondage. And yet until the 1840s he remained largely aloof from the abolitionist movement.

Emerson's attitude toward abolitionism (particularly in the years when he was expounding the principles of Transcendental self-reliance with the greatest urgency) was the same as his attitude toward all social-reform movements. He sympathized generally with their objectives, but he did not feel that his own gifts lay in the field of political and social action. "Each man has his own vocation," he explained. "The talent is the call."[51] Emerson's vocation, as he had learned from hard experience, was that of poet and prophet, not minister or reformer; and for him to expend his energies in social action would be to circumscribe the free expression of his own unique God-given talents. Obedience to one's own genius, he insisted, "is the only liberating influence. . . . Only by obedience to his genius, only by the freest activity in the way constitutional to him, does an angel seem to arise before a man and lead him by the hand out of all the wards of the prison."[52] He explained his position frankly to humanitarian reformers: "More than our good-will we may not be able to give. We have our own affairs, our own genius, which chains each to his proper work. We cannot give our life to the cause of the debtor, or the slave, or the pauper, as another is doing."[53] Emerson's initial lukewarmness to such reforms as abolitionism also grew out of his fear that affiliation with an organized cause would lead to loss of intellectual independence.

Each "cause" as it is called,—say Abolition, Temperance, say Calvinism, or Unitarianism,—becomes speedily a little shop, where the article, let it have been at first never so subtle and ethereal, is now made up into portable and convenient cakes, and retailed in small quantities to suit purchasers.[54]

Emerson was resolved not to become an Organization Man, no matter how praiseworthy the organization.

The chief reason, however, for Emerson's reluctance to associate himself with reform movements was his conviction that true reform came from within an individual and not from alterations in the individual's outer environment. No change of circumstances, he declared, could repair a defect of character. The French Revolution, from which so much was expected by men of good will, failed in the end, Emerson asserted, because it wrought no change in the hearts of men; social advance, he thought, was the effect, not the cause of moral improvement.[55] The kind of freedom for which reformers were struggling—emancipation from artificial restrictions imposed by society on its members—seemed to Emerson to be merely a negative freedom. An individual may achieve freedom of this kind and yet be woefully lacking in courageous self-reliance. For Emerson, nothing was "more disgusting than the crowing about liberty by slaves, as most men are, and the flippant mistaking for freedom of some paper preamble like a Declaration of Independence or the statute right to vote, by those who have never dared to think or to act."[56] Conversely, an individual may be in chains and yet within his heart may achieve a genuine spiritual autonomy lacking to the freeman. "Is an iron handcuff so immutable a bond?" Emerson once asked. It was possible, he thought, for a slave with high principles to have "a freedom which makes his master's freedom a slavery."[57] In his "Lecture on the Times" (1841), Emerson was blunt, even brutal, in expressing his irritation with reforms directly solely toward removing obstacles from people's freedom of action:

The Reformers affirm the inward life, but they do not trust it, but use outward and vulgar means. They do not rely on precisely that strength which wins me to their cause; not on love, not on principle, but on men, on multitudes, on circumstances, on money, on party; that is, on fear, on wrath, and pride.

As for the slavery question:

This denouncing philanthropist is himself a slaveholder in every word and look. Does he free me? Does he cheer me? He is the state of Georgia, or Alabama, with their sanguinary slave-laws, walking here on our northeastern shores . . . how trivial seem the contests of the abolitionist, whilst he aims merely at the circumstance of the slave. Give the slave the least element of religious sentiment, and he is no slave; you are the slave; he not only in his humility feels his superiority, feels that much deplored condition of his to be a fading trifle, but he makes you feel it too. He is the master. The exag-

geration which our young people make of his wrongs, characterizes themselves. What are no trifles to them, they naturally think are no trifles to
Pompey.[58]

The most that Emerson would promise was to refrain from ridiculing
the work of reformers and from throwing stumbling blocks in their way,
as the popular press was doing. That oppressive social conditions degrade
the human spirit (as Paine realized) and militate against the kind of
high-minded self-reliance that he sought to foster in people was a premise which Emerson was not prepared at this point to concede. Nor did
it seem to occur to him that his chilling words might be as effective stumbling blocks in the way of the antislavery movement as those of openly
hostile organs of opinion and influence. As a self-reliant Transcendentalist, Emerson felt obliged to remain steadfastly true to his own genius.
He would not move, he announced, until he had the highest command:
and the organized antislavery movement did not, in his opinion, proceed
from the highest command. The abolitionists, in fact, he once remarked
in the 1830s, were a little crazy, like phrenologists and all men and
women of one idea, and they should be treated tenderly but not taken too
seriously.[59] One freed the slaves, apparently, by giving them Epictetus to
read.

Emerson was in time to modify his attitude toward reform, and the
time eventually came when he not only abandoned his lofty condescension toward abolitionism but also became deeply involved personally in
the antislavery struggle. But during the early years of his career as poet,
essayist, and lecturer, when he was seeking most earnestly to effect a
Transcendental revolution in the hearts of people, he could not help regarding the freedom sought by reformers as a limited, possibly even dangerous, freedom. Like Winthrop and Burke, he had the feeling that if
people had too much freedom to do as they pleased, they would behave
outrageously. In *English Traits*, he spoke with irritation of the "pursy
man" who "means by freedom the right to do as he pleases, and does
wrong in order to feel his freedom, and makes a conscience of persisting
in it." There was a far nobler freedom than the freedom to do as one
wished (which could degenerate into license), and Emerson believed it
was his mission to preach this kind of freedom. It was the freedom which
an individual possesses when he emancipates himself from enslavement
to selfish motives and coarse appetites and allows himself to be animated
by the highest principles of truth and righteousness. Moral freedom stood

first with Emerson, as it had with Puritans like John Winthrop two centuries earlier. Like Winthrop, he placed the positive freedom to do "the good, the just, and the honest" far above the negative liberty to do as one pleased without external restraint.[60]

In his ministerial days, Emerson had had a great deal to say about the freedom that comes from virtuous conduct. Self-direction and self-command, he told one congregation in 1828, consist of freeing oneself from the yoke of vulgar sensibility, mad passion, and frivolous impulse and placing one's appetites under the control of reason.[61] True freedom, he explained to another congregation in 1829, is identical with virtue. "Our prejudices, our fears, our affections," he said, "entangle us & abridge our liberty." The greedy man, the glutton, the timeserver, the timid conformist, the braggart, and the vengeful person are all prisoners of their passions and dwell in thralldom, not in liberty. No person can be wholly free, Emerson acknowledged, but all virtuous action is a perpetual approximation to true freedom.[62] Vice is slavery, Emerson announced in a sermon on "Freedom" in 1831, and goodness is liberty. Goodness redeems the will from slavery to fear, interest, and passion, and enables the individual to choose to do what he knows is right. The free person follows moral law, not as a servant, but as a son: out of love and in a spirit of adoption. "Where the spirit of the Lord is," said Emerson, quoting 2 Cor. 3:17, "there is liberty." "And ye shall know the truth," he liked to say (John 8:32), "and the truth shall make you free."[63]

After becoming a Transcendentalist, Emerson continued to believe that liberty came from within the individual and that it was associated with the perception of truth and goodness. "The soul raised over passion," he said, "beholds identity and eternal causation, perceives the self-existence of Truth and Right, and calms itself with knowing that all things go well."[64] He admitted the apparent paradox: it was "a voluntary obedience, a necessitated freedom" that he was calling for. What he wanted was *freedom from* one's "lower self," which holds one in servitude to particulars, and willing *submission to* one's "higher self," which apprehends universal laws. "Liberty," he said,

is never cheap. It is made difficult, because freedom is the accomplishment and perfectness of man. . . . Therefore mountains of difficulty must be surmounted, stern trials met, wiles of seduction, dangers, healed by a quarantine of calamities to measure his strength before he dare say, I am free.[65]

Viewed in this light, Transcendental freedom, self-reliance, God-reliance, and virtue became interchangeable terms in Emerson's philosophy. "I am free to speak the truth," exclaimed Emerson. "I am free to do justly. I am not free to lie, and I wish to break every yoke all over the world which hinders my brother from acting after his best thought."[66] When a person realizes that there is "no liberty but his invincible will to do right," he declared, "— then certain aids and allies will promptly appear: for the constitution of the Universe is on his side."[67] Emerson never doubted that his teleologized universe was always on the side of the free individual, but he insisted that a person was free only when he pierced through the illusory appearances of things to the moral order underneath and voluntarily submitted to its laws.

The positive freedom which Emerson celebrated has never been popular with the American people. While most Americans acknowledged, as Paine did, that the exercise of freedom must be accompanied by ethical restraints, they have tended to be wary of identifying freedom with mastery of one's lower self or with conformity to higher law. They have been particularly on guard when exponents of positive freedom have contemptuously dismissed absence of coercion on the individual as a negative and inferior form of freedom. Virtue is one thing, they have argued, and freedom another; why confuse important issues by identifying the two? Winthrop, they have felt, was seeking justification for authoritarian controls over people when he exalted positive over negative liberty; and John Cotton was doing the same when he told Roger Williams that "soul liberty" might lead a person to sin against his own conscience and destroy his freedom to accept God's will. As for the contention of Jonathan Boucher, Tory clergyman, at the time of the American Revolution, that since "liberty consists in subserviency to law," people in America could find true liberty only in submission to the King, most Americans simply refused to take him seriously.[68]

Still, Emerson was surely right in contending that servitude to narrow and selfish impulses can drastically limit an individual's autonomy and that submerging one's self-regarding tendencies in a larger and more generous view can multiply the possibilities of personal growth and liberation. Emerson, fortunately, did not think of positive freedom all of the time in isolation from negative freedom; he was as devoted in his own way to natural rights as Paine was. Nor of course did it ever enter his mind to identify his "higher freedom" with state, church, or a collective social authority of some kind as modern authoritarians, appropriating the language but not the substance of liberty, have done. He came increasingly to realize, moreover, the importance of civil liberties to the kind of moral autonomy he cherished for the individual and to insist on the indispensability of outer to inner freedom and the interaction and continuity between the two.

## FREEDOM AND FATE

In the salad days of Transcendentalism, Emerson preached the doctrine of self-reliant freedom and moral perfection with vigor and confidence and expressed scorn for people who thought that circumstances could overpower the individual. "You think me the child of my circumstances," he declared loftily: "I make my circumstances."[69] A person, he said, should "carry himself in the presence of all opposition as if every thing were titular and ephemeral but he."[70] If he consulted his inner gifts and asserted himself boldly, he would make the need felt which he could supply, create the taste by which he would be enjoyed, and provoke the wants to which he could minister.[71] In *Nature* (1836), Emerson announced that the free man could perform miracles:

... he can reduce under his will, not only particular events, but great classes, nay the whole series of events, and so conform all facts to his character. Nature is thoroughly mediate. It is made to serve. It receives the dominion of man as meekly as the ass on which the Saviour rode. It offers all its kingdoms to man as the raw material which he may mould into what is useful. . . . More and more, with every thought, does his kingdom stretch over things, until the world becomes, at last, only a realized will,—the double of the man.[72]

With the passing of time, however, Emerson became less sanguine in his hopes for humanity. He began wondering whether it was as easy as he had once thought it was for a person to build his own world, and he became increasingly impressed by the implacabilities, recalcitrancies, even sheer perversities, that the individual encounters in his daily living. Not that he weakened in his Transcendental faith. He remained serenely optimistic about things in general to the end of his days. Nevertheless, he came gradually to temper his optimism with a harder, tougher view of the world and with an acknowledgment of the limits and bounds which circumstances place on individual autonomy. Though he never abandoned his belief that the creative individual could work miracles, he became more and more impressed with the power of circumstances to block and frustrate his wishes and designs. There was, he decided, a "stupendous antagonism" between the power of the individual and the power of circumstances. Freedom and necessity were locked in endless battle.[73] In an essay on "Fate" which he placed first in a book of essays on *The Conduct of Life* (1860), Emerson admitted frankly: "Once we thought positive power was all. Now we learn that negative power, or circumstance, is half. Nature is the tyrannous circumstance."[74]

Emerson's essay on fate represented his mature thought about the great themes that had occupied his attention since his college days. If it centered around the concept of fate (by which he meant causal necessity, not arbitrary destiny), it also dealt with man's resistance to fate and spelled out in greater detail than ever before what freedom at its most glorious meant to Emerson. In the first part of the essay, Emerson discussed with unsparing severity the power of fate (which he defined variously as "irresistible dictation," "immovable limitations," and "laws of the world") over human life. But he made it clear that he intended to affirm liberty as well as necessity and to show how "necessity does comport with liberty."[75] His emphasis in the first portion of the essay on the inescapability of necessity in human affairs has been interpreted as an abandonment, or at least as a serious attenuation, of the doctrine of self-reliance which he had been preaching so exuberantly twenty years earlier. But, at the deepest level, there is nothing in the essay that is incompatible with what he had proclaimed in his early essay on "Self-Reliance." Self-reliance, as we have seen, never meant free will to Emerson; from the beginning, it had involved absolute dependence on the Universal Spirit or Divine Reason permeating the universe. He now preferred to speak of blessed unity, beautiful necessity, and beneficent tendency rather than of God or Over-Soul, but his point was what it had always been: there is a divine energy giving order, purpose, and direction to creation. "The universe is all chemistry," he told Caroline Sturgis Tappan in July, 1853, but "a magnificent *Whence or Whereto*" makes "mountains of rubbish reflect the morning sun & the evening star."[76]

The mood of Emerson's essay on fate, it is true, is more somber than the mood of his earliest essays, though there had always been a note of austerity in everything he said. The American people, he observed at the outset, must overcome their superficial optimism and face the "odious facts" of life with honesty and courage.[77] Nature, he exclaimed, in a passage that would have bewildered Paine, is no sentimentalist,—does not cosset or pamper us. We must see that the world is rough and surly, and will not mind drowning a man or a woman, but swallows your ship like a grain of dust. The cold, inconsiderate of persons, tingles your blood, benumbs your feet, freezes a man like an apple. The diseases, the elements, fortune, gravity, lightning, respect no persons. The way of Providence is a little rude. . . . Providence has a wild, rough incalculable road to its end, and it is of no use to try to whitewash its huge, mixed instrumentalities, or to dress up that terrific benefactor in a clean shirt and white neckcloth of a student in divinity.[78]

Though Emerson was convinced that there was an ultimate beneficent tendency at work in creation, he also believed that it was weak and cowardly to close one's eyes to the fact that the individual was often sacrificed to the ongoing meliorative processes of the universe. With unrelenting harshness, he traced the power of fate (i.e., the inexorable laws of nature) in the universe. On every side human beings were hemmed in by tyrannical circumstances: their hereditary endowments, for good or ill, were irrevocable and the calamities of life—famine, typhus, frost, war, and suicide—statistically calculable. Even progress in civilization did not free people from fate. "If we are brute and barbarous," said Emerson, "the fate takes a brute and dreadful shape. As we refine, our checks become finer. If we rise to spiritual culture, the antagonism takes a spiritual form. . . . The limitations refine as the soul purifies, but the ring of necessity is always perched at the top."[79]

And yet, having asserted the immensity of fate, Emerson went on to reject firmly the attitude of supine resignation. In a universe governed by implacable necessity, there does, in a meaningful sense, exist a place for human freedom. It is the freedom that comes from insight into the nature of things. "Intellect annuls Fate," declared Emerson. "So far as a man thinks, he is free." "The revelation of Thought takes man out of servitude into freedom. . . . The day of days, the great day of the feast of life, is that in which the inward eye opens to the Unity in things, to the omnipresence of law:—sees that what is must be and ought to be, or is the best." Fate, then, was "a name for facts not yet passed under the fire of thought; for causes which are unpenetrated" and penetrating these causes means assuming some measure of control over them.[80] The "first step into thought," said Emerson, "lifts this mountain of necessity."[81] Thought "composes and decomposes" nature and enables people to transcend their circumstances: "Once we were stepping a little this way and a little that way; now we are as men in a balloon, and do not think so much of the point we have left, or the point we would make, as of the liberty and glory of the way."[82]

Freedom, in short, comes from a knowledge of fate—that is, from an awareness of what we can and cannot do in a world governed by uniform physical and moral laws. If we come to understand the laws governing phenomena, Emerson insisted, we can utilize these laws for our own benefit and escape bondage to particulars. Steam, for example, was once "the devil we dreaded." But eventually it occurred to scientists that "where was power was not devil, but was God" and that steam could be utilized for the benefit of mankind. Ignorance of the workings of natural forces means bondage to these forces; knowledge brings power, and with power comes freedom. "Just as much intellect as you add, so much organic power." Water, for example,

drowns ship and sailor like a grain of dust. But learn to swim, trim your bark, and the wave which drowned it will be cloven by it and carry it like its own foam, a plume and a power. The cold is inconsiderate of persons, tingles your blood, freezes a man like a dew-drop. But learn to skate, and the ice will give you a graceful, sweet and poetic motion. . . .

The annual slaughter from typhus far exceeds that of war; but right drainage destroys typhus. The plague in the sea-service from scurvy is healed by lemon juice and other diets portable or procurable; the depopulation by cholera and small-pox is ended by drainage and vaccination; and every other pest is not less in the chain of cause and effect, and may be fought off.[83]

But an awareness of nature's necessities by itself was not enough, according to Emerson, to generate freedom. With such awareness must go a recognition of the beneficence of the forces regulating the universe and a willing accommodation to them. There was a moral as well as a rational dimension to freedom as insight. Emerson's intuitive Reason included moral sentiment as well as rational penetration. "If thought makes us free," he said, "so does the moral sentiment"; with "the perception of truth is joined the desire that it shall prevail." Rational insight by itself is unproductive; moral affection without knowledge is ineffectual. There must be a fusion of insight and affection to generate energy of will. When man comes to understand, say, the nature of steam, he realizes that it is not a blind, senseless force, alien to humanity, but that it works for the good of the whole. And his recognition of its power for good, together with the "desire that it shall prevail," galvanizes him into harnessing it for his own uses, thereby transmuting necessity into opportunity. His affirmation that "what is must be and ought to be, or is the best" (an act of the moral sentiment) is an essential condition for his acquisition of power over nature and hence for freedom. "Whoever has had the experience of the moral sentiment," declared Emerson, "cannot choose but believe in unlimited power."[84]

Emerson's universe was thoroughly moral. Knowledge and morality had from the beginning been inextricably linked in his thought. "The axioms of physics," he said, "translate the laws of ethics." Such laws as "the whole is greater than its part" and "reaction is equal to action" had an ethical as well as physical meaning for Emerson. Moral law, he affirmed, "lies at the centre of nature and radiates to the circumference. It is the pith and marrow of every substance, every relation, and every process. All things with which we deal, preach to us."[85] His famous law of compensation, which held that every good action was inevitably rewarded and every evil act somehow subsequently punished, was a manifestation of necessity in morals corresponding to necessity in nature. Fundamentally, the laws of ethics and the laws of science were the same, he thought (somewhat as Paine had believed), since both were grounded in the divine energy animating the universe. He therefore united moral affirmation with rational insight in the act of freedom, and thereby showed his Christian training. What John Winthrop and other Christians called "the liberty whereby Christ made us free" became with Emerson the harmonizing of our individual wills with the universal moral laws governing the universe. But Emerson was closer in his point of view to modern secularists than to Christians like Winthrop. Twentieth-century philosopher Sidney Hook put it very much as Emerson did when he asserted:

Freedom of the mind implies an acceptance of what knowledge reveals concerning the necessary order of things. This acceptance is not the resignation of one who, baffled and bewildered in a world too complex for his wits, represses his instincts and desires in severe asceticism. . . . It is an acceptance that is at the same time an affirmation—an affirmation of the world's necessity—an affirmation which leaves the mind sane and unperturbed by illusion and anguish. . . . When joy is consequent upon the complete understanding of necessity then freedom is intensified.[86]

The freedom, then, that Emerson extolled involved not only knowledge of necessity but also joyous assent to its reign in man and nature. "He who sees through the design," he said, "presides over it, and must will that which must be."[87] For by his insight into the moral necessity inherent in the structure of things and the harmonization of his will with that necessity, he lifts himself out of slavery to the petty, finite, and transient in life into the realm of universal law in which he achieves authentic spiritual freedom. The last lesson in life, according to Emerson, was

a voluntary obedience, a necessitated freedom. Man is made of the same atoms as the world is, he shares the same impressions, predispositions and destiny. When his mind is illuminated, when his heart is kind, he throws himself joyfully into the sublime order, and does, with knowledge, what the stones do by structure.[88]

Emerson ended his essay on fate with a paean to the "Blessed Unity" which "holds nature and souls in perfect solution, and compels every atom" to serve a universal end.

Let us build altars to the Beautiful Necessity, which secures that all is made of one piece. . . . Let us build to the Beautiful Necessity, which makes man brave in believing that he cannot shun a danger that is appointed, nor incur one that is not; to the Necessity which rudely or softly educates him to the perception that there are no contingencies; that Law rules throughout existence; a Law which is not intelligent but intelligence;—not personal nor impersonal—it disdains words and passes understanding; it dissolves persons; it vivifies nature; yet solicits the pure in heart to draw on all its omnipotence.[89]

Only the pure in heart, Emerson believed, ever achieve real freedom. Before the pure in heart "opens liberty,—the Better, the Best."[90] It is the liberty that the moral person attains when he frees himself from a narrowly selfish and parochial view of things, perceives the glorious laws governing the cosmos, and reverently wills to act in accordance with these laws. Compared to the moral autonomy possessed by the spiritually enlightened individual, the circumstantial freedom from external restraints which occupied the attention of humanitarian reformers seemed to Emerson a mere trifle. And so he ended *Conduct of Life*, as he had ended *Nature*, with an impassioned plea for people to pierce through the cloud of illusions surrounding them to the spiritual realities beneath and bring their lives into harmony with them. But it was not clear whether he thought that an individual's rational and moral insights were freely achieved or mere passive expressions of the "high *Whence & Whither*" which he believed propelled all creation. Probably the latter.

Like Edwards, who urged predestined people to choose salvation as their destiny, Emerson tended to call for creative efforts on the part of people whose free will he denied.[91] To the end he was unable to free himself from the moral determinism which his monistic philosophy imposed on him. Yet the inconsistency between his plea for novelty, originality, and creativity on the part of the individual and his underlying determinism seems never to have bothered him.

## CIVIL LIBERTY AND MORAL FREEDOM

Emerson never abandoned his belief that the freedom achieved by moral and intellectual insight stood highest in the hierarchy of human values. Nevertheless, as the agitation over slavery gained momentum in the 1840s, he began to take a friendlier view of the work of the abolitionists. Was the freedom they were trying to advance really so trifling a thing? As time passed he came less and less to think so. During the 1840s, his sympathy for the antislavery cause increased steadily and with it his respect for the kind of freedom championed by the abolitionists.

Emerson had always opposed slavery. But at the height of his Transcendental fervor he had believed that if the high principles he was preaching won acceptance the problem of slavery would take care of itself. Now he was no longer sure. Perhaps the "semi-barbarous nations" of the South would never become enlightened without the work of the abolitionists. In 1844 he began participating in the annual West Indies Emancipation meetings held on August 11 by the Massachusetts Anti-Slavery Society, and at these gatherings he began hailing the abolitionists as the party of freedom. The enactment of the Fugitive Slave Law in 1850 turned him once for all toward abolitionism. Could a man who was forced to comply with this law, he asked himself, ever achieve genuine moral freedom? Emerson was certain that he could not. Slavery for blacks, he finally decided, meant slavery for whites as well. The idea, which he had voiced in the 1830s, that a slave might possess an internal freedom lacking to the master no longer seemed adequate. With the passage of the Fugitive Slave Act, Emerson felt obliged to descend from his Transcendental heights and make common cause with the abolitionists. "I will not obey it, by God," he thundered when the Fugitive Slave Act became law.[92]

In an address to the citizens of Concord in May, 1851, Emerson voiced his utter revulsion against a law which required inhabitants of free states to send people who had run the gauntlet of a thousand miles for their freedom back into slavery. "The popular assumption that all men loved freedom," he said angrily, had turned out to be "hollow American brag; only persons who were known and tried benefactors are found standing for freedom" in the slavery crisis.[93] The temporizing attitude in Congress of Edward Everett, who had been a hero of his youth, made him wonder whether all of his former professor's apostrophes to freedom were mere claptrap. But his contempt for Daniel Webster for helping bring about the passage of the Fugitive Slave Act knew no bounds. "The word *liberty* in the mouth of Mr. Webster," he wrote in his journal, "sounds like the word *love* in the mouth of a courtezan." Webster, in his opinion, had helped bring the state of Massachusetts down to the cannibal level, and people like Everett who supported Webster's position revealed that they had little real love of liberty.[94]

In a lecture in New York City on March 7, 1854, the fourth anniversary of Webster's famous speech supporting the Compromise of 1850, Emerson spoke in glowing terms about the kind of external freedom for which he had formerly had only a qualified admiration. "I never felt the check on my free speech and action," he said candidly, "until, the other day, when Mr. Webster, by his personal influence, brought the Fugitive Slave Law on the country." The liberty which Webster had betrayed now seemed to Emerson to be "an accurate index, in men and nations, of general progress. The theory of personal liberty must always appeal to the most refined communities and to the men of rarest perception and of delicate moral sense." The world, in fact, existed, Emerson declared, "to teach the science of liberty, which begins with liberty from fear" and he urged his listeners to do what they could to make good the cause of freedom.[95] In January, 1860, he made a speech at Salem praising John Brown as "the founder of liberty in Kansas," and in June he spoke in Boston on abolitionist Theodore Parker's great service to freedom.[96] When the Civil War came, he looked on it as a momentous contest between slavery and freedom in which "one army will stand for Slavery pure; the other for Freedom pure." With the elimination of slavery by war, the United States, he was convinced, was destined to enter a new era in which freedom of thought, religion, speech, and suffrage would flourish.[97] By this time Emerson had come to cherish the kind of freedom which Paine celebrated almost as much as the Transcendental freedom of the inner spirit.

And yet, even after becoming actively involved in the struggle for emancipation of the blacks, Emerson never forgot what his primary purpose in life was. "I waked at night," he wrote in his journal in 1852,

and bemoaned myself, because I had not thrown myself into this deplorable
question of Slavery, which seems to want nothing so much as a few assured
voices. But then, in hours of sanity, I recover myself, and say, "God must
govern his own world, and knows his way out of this pit, without my deser-
tion of my post, which has none to guard it but me. I have quite other slaves
to free than those negroes, to wit, imprisoned spirits, imprisoned thoughts,
far back in the brain of man,—far retired in the heaven of invention, and
which, important to the republic of Man, have no watchman, or lover, or
defender, but I.[98]

Social reform, he recognized, was essential to the building of a better
civilization. But the production of art, literature, science, religion, and
philosophy was the highest purpose of civilized life, and for the artist to
abandon his own work for the task of social reconstruction was, for Emerson, to betray the very cause of civilization. There was a "heroism of
scholars," he told students at Tufts College, after the Civil War began,
as well as a "heroism of soldiers."[99]

In the end, then, despite his commitment to the antislavery cause,
it was the "free air of thought" that Emerson valued above all else. For
him, the "absolute illumination we call Reason, and thereby true liber
ty" was man's noblest achievement.[100] Emerson was gradually persuaded
that civil freedom was an indispensable condition for the development of
true liberty in the hearts of men. At the same time he continued to believe that civil freedom by itself was insufficient for the progress of humanity. The "foundations of civil liberty," he insisted, lay in "the deep
convictions of love and right."[101] Authentic freedom, in Emerson's philosophy, was inseparable from wisdom and virtue. For if a society based
on fear and force rather than on civil freedom could hardly hope to produce wise and virtuous citizens, a society lacking roots in wisdom and
goodness could scarcely be expected to produce citizens who would exercise their freedom intelligently and creatively. If, after the 1830s, Emerson learned something of importance about freedom, he also had something of importance to teach about it. He learned to place a high value
on individual freedom from external coercion, which he had once regarded as merely selfish, negative, and inferior. He also learned that it could
not be taken for granted and that it must be continuously defended by
all real lovers of liberty. At the same time he had an important point to
make (which the post-Appomattox generation lost sight of): civil liberty

must be accompanied by rational and moral freedom if it is to be meaningful and enduring. Emerson never really solved the free-will problem, and to the end he remained a determinist who grounded his Transcendental freedom in Universal Spirit. Yet his insights (necessitated or not) were considerable. He came to realize that freedom was many-sided, that it had an objective as well as a subjective dimension, and that it involved social action as well as rational understanding and moral autonomy. In a final synthesis of his thinking about freedom he reached the conclusion that the hopes of civilization rested on an indissoluble union of civil liberty, intellectual achievement, and moral character.

# 4

# John C. Calhoun on
# Liberty as Privilege

ONE OF THE MOST FAMOUS confrontations in American history took place between President Andrew Jackson and Vice-President John C. Calhoun, at a Jefferson birthday dinner in Washington on April 13, 1830. When it came time for the President to propose a toast, Jackson, determined to meet head-on the nullificationist threat within the Democratic party, stood up, faced the vice-president, and, looking him straight in the eye, thundered: "Our Federal Union—it must be preserved." While the banqueters watched breathlessly, Calhoun, his hand trembling, proposed firmly in his turn: "The Union—next to our liberty the most dear."[1]

Liberty was one of Calhoun's favorite words, and it is not surprising that one of his biographers declared: "With Milton he was ready to say, 'Where liberty dwells, there is my country.' "[2] But Calhoun's liberty had little in common with Milton's; it was in fact quite compatible with slavery. For Calhoun liberty was not a natural right possessed by every individual; it was a social privilege, and it was reserved for peoples and groups he regarded as superior. Twentieth-century scholars have been wide of the mark when they called the South Carolinian a "strong individualist," described him as "the most articulate and influential exponent of the individualistic tradition," and said of him: "Human liberty, the dream of the free individual, was the vision that beckoned and urged him on."³ He was not an individualist, and he regarded the natural-rights philosophy as both false and dangerous because of its individualistic emphasis.

### CALHOUN'S CONCEPT OF LIBERTY

Though he rejected natural rights, Calhoun placed liberty, as he conceived of it, high in his hierarchy of values. "With me," he once told the Senate, "the liberty of the country is all in all. If this be preserved, every thing will be preserved, but if lost, all will be lost."⁴ From his earliest days in public life on the eve of the War of 1812 until his last days during the sectional crisis following the Mexican War, Calhoun looked upon liberty as his primary guide for public policy. His letters, reports, and speeches were filled with the catchphrases of freedom: blessings of liberty, personal liberty, free country, free people, the liberties of mankind. A campaign biography appearing in 1843 (prepared in great part by Calhoun himself) reports that when Calhoun was only nine his father taught him that the best government was one which allowed the most individual liberty compatible with social order and tranquillity and that "the improvements in political science would be found to consist in throwing off many of the restraints then imposed by law, and deemed necessary to organized society."⁵ Calhoun's father voted against ratification of the U.S. Constitution on the ground that it permitted outsiders to levy taxes on the people of South Carolina. Unlike his father, Calhoun was a lifelong champion of the Constitution, but only because he thought that, properly interpreted, it represented the fundamental basis for liberty in the American system.

Calhoun defined liberty the way Locke (whom he studied as a young man) and Edwards did: as absence of external obstacles to voluntary action. But despite the Scotch-Irish Presbyterian background and his experience as an undergraduate at Calvinist Yale, he at no time in his life evinced any interest in the free-will question. Nor was he ever much interested in the Lockean liberty of individual action that Paine and Emerson thought was so important. From almost the beginning of his public career Calhoun tended to regard the notion of an individual as apart from his society as a foolish and even dangerous fiction. The southern states, he said time and again, were aggregates of communities, not of individuals, and the United States itself was an aggregate of states. This meant that individual liberty was intimately linked with the liberty

of the community (nation, section, state) and was always subordinate
to it where vital issues were at stake. Denouncing proposals to keep
states without antislavery constitutions out of the Union, Calhoun angrily
told the Senate on February 19, 1847:

It is proposed, from a vague, indefinite, erroneous, and most dangerous conception of *private individual liberty*, to override this *great common liberty*
which the people have of framing their own constitution! Sir, the right of
framing self-government on the part of individuals is not near so easily to
be established by any course of reasoning, as the right of a community or a
State to self-government. And yet, Sir, there are men of such delicate feelings on the subject of liberty—men who cannot possibly bear what they call
slavery in one section of the country . . .—that they are ready to strike down
the *higher right of a community* to govern themselves, in order to maintain
the *absolute right of individuals*, in every possible condition to govern
themselves![6]

Calhoun simply did not believe in "the absolute right of individuals" to
govern themselves. He put the "great common liberty"—the right of a
political community to sovereignty, independence, security, and material
well-being—far above the rights and liberties of individuals. He was no
Hegelian; but he came close at times to dissolving the freedom of individuals in that of the collectivity. The great common liberty, he said
repeatedly, was the *sine qua non* for whatever liberties people making
up the community possessed and thus a "higher right" which might
necessitate restrictions on liberty for individual citizens. Calhoun's inclination, throughout his career, was to relate every important public issue
with which he was concerned to its bearing on liberty conceived in this
fashion. Like the Founding Fathers, Calhoun once said, his first reaction
when questions of magnitude came before him was to ask: "Is it constitutional?" "Is it consistent with our free, popular institutions?" "How
is it to affect our liberty?"[7] But he never meant individual freedom to
take precedence over communal liberty. It was misleading and, in fact,
downright irresponsible, he thought, to look upon liberty as an "absolute
right of individuals." He was never at heart a real individualist, and he
was not much attracted to Paine's philosophy even in his younger Jeffersonian days. He loved liberty, but he was not a civil libertarian.

## LIBERTY AND UNION

Calhoun began his career as a vigorous nationalist, and for a number
of years he usually had the United States as a whole in mind when he

thought of liberty. He regarded the American Revolution as a glorious struggle for freedom from British oppression, and he wanted the American people to show the world that they not only "inherited that liberty which our Fathers gave us" but also possessed "the will & power to maintain it."[8] Entering Congress as a Representative from South Carolina in 1811, he at once joined the "War Hawks" who were clamoring for war with Britain because of her violations of American maritime rights and began talking about "the second struggle for our liberty."[9] From the outset he preferred military to economic measures against the British, and he criticized the "restrictive system" (cessation of trade with Britain and France as a means of forcing them to respect American neutral rights) as contrary to American principles of liberty. Said he:

To say to the most trading . . . people on earth, you shall not trade . . . does not suit the genius of our people. . . . Our government is founded on freedom and hates coercion. To make the restrictive system effectual requires the most arbitrary laws. . . . The peculiar geography of our country, added to the liberty of its government, greatly encreases [sic] the difficulty [of enforcing the system].[10]

When Congress declared war in June, 1812, Calhoun hailed the conflict with Britain as "the war of the Revolution revived" and exclaimed that "we are again struggling for our liberty and independence."[11] He thought the War of 1812 involved two major issues, both having to do with freedom: British interference with American neutral rights at sea and the impressment of American sailors into the British navy. It was, in short, a "war for Free Trade and Sailors' Rights."[12] In taking on Britain, Calhoun declared, the United States was fighting for both "the noble end of the liberty of the seas" and "the liberty of our sailors and their redemption from slavery."[13] But since "life and liberty are more estimable than ships & goods," he said, the impressment of American seamen was a more urgent issue than the commercial injuries which Britain was inflicting on the United States.[14] In speech after speech in Congress he pictured the plight of impressed seamen ("victims of barbarity"; "doomed to an ignominious and slavish bondage"; "at the mercy of every insignificant drunken midshipman") to underscore his point that it was "our duty, most sacredly our duty, to protect the life and liberty of our citizens against foreign oppression."[15]

With his fervent conviction of the righteousness of the American cause, Calhoun found it difficult to be patient with opposition to the war (chiefly by New England Federalists) or with criticisms of measures taken for its prosecution. He warned against "factious opposition" (that "bane of freedom") to the war measures of the Madison administration and declared that the evil of factionalism

is deeply rooted in the constitution of all free governments, and is the principal cause of their weakness and destruction. It has but one remedy, the virtue and intelligence of the people—it behooves them as they value the blessings of their freedom, not to permit themselves to be drawn into the vortex of party rage. For if by such opposition the firmest government should prove incompetent to maintain the rights of the nation against foreign aggression, they will find realized the truth of the assertion that government is protection, and that it cannot exist where it fails of this great and primary object. The authors of the weakness are commonly the first to take advantage of it, and to turn it to the destruction of liberty.[16]

Calhoun conceded that fair and moderate (and therefore presumably ineffectual) criticism of official policy ought to be respected at all times, but he denied that the Constitution authorized the "dangerous and vicious species" of opposition which he was condemning:

He called on those who made the claim to so extravagant a power to point out the article of that instrument which would warrant such a construction. Will they cite that which establishes the liberty of speech here? Its object was far different; and it furnishes not the shadow of such a power. Will they rely on its general spirit? It knows no object but the general good, and must for ever condemn all factious opposition to measures emanating from its own authority. It is then not authorized either by the letter or the spirit of the Constitution. If then our opponents have the right, it is because it is not expressly forbidden. In this sense there is no limitation to their constitutional rights. A right might be thus derived to violate the whole decalogue.[17]

Calhoun proposed no Alien and Sedition Acts to silence critics of the Madison administration, but it is clear that he did not favor allowing much leeway for the exercise of free speech when he thought the national interest was concerned. As always, he placed the "great common liberty" of the people, as he conceived it, over that of the individual. During the War of 1812, it was the nation which he had in mind when he spoke of the people; later on, it was to be his section and state. In each case, however, the liberty of the community took precedence over (because Calhoun deemed it the *sine qua non* for) individual freedom.

Calhoun rejoiced that "nationality of feeling" eventually triumphed over sectional spirit during the war with Britain, and his fond hope after the war was that this national spirit would continue to prevail undiminished.[18] Since he thought the peace established by the Treaty of Ghent in 1815 would only be temporary and that a renewal of hostilities was inevitable, he was anxious for the Unted States to build up her national strength after the war in anticipation of future clashes with Britain. He called for a bigger navy, a better system of fortifications throughout the country, more military academies like West Point, and a stronger army. Proposing a peacetime draft, he had this to say:

All free nations of antiquity entrusted the defence of the country, not to the dregs of society, but to the body of citizens; hence that heroism which modern times may admire but cannot equal. I know that I utter truths unpleasant to those who wish to enjoy liberty without making the efforts necessary to secure it. Her favor is never won by the cowardly, the vicious or indolent. It has been said by some physicians that life is a forced state; the same may be said of freedom. It requires efforts; it presupposes mental and moral qualities of a high order to be generally diffused in the society where it exists. It mainly stands on the faithful discharge of two great duties which every citizen of proper age owes the republic; a wise and virtuous exercise of the right of suffrage; and a prompt and brave defence of the country in the hour of danger.[19]

Liberty, in short, was a communal achievement and depended on the vigorous exertions of citizens for its existence. But Calhoun's case for freedom through military power attracted no converts, and his military proposals were rejected by Congress. With his economic program for strengthening the nation after the war, however, he was more successful.

Calhoun warmly supported—indeed, was a leading sponsor of—three measures combining to make up a program of economic nationalism after the war: a national bank, a protective tariff, and federal aid for internal improvements. These measures, he thought, would strengthen the Union; in his opinion, "the *liberty* and the *union* of this country were inseparably united!"[20] A national bank would straighten out the mess into which the currency had fallen during the war, a protective tariff would stimulate American manufacturing, and the construction of roads and canals binding different sections of the country together would help to "counteract every tendency to disunion" and bolster up "a form of government at once combining liberty and strength." As to the constitutionality of the last measure, Calhoun announced flatly that he was "no advocate for refined arguments on the Constitution. The instrument was not intended as a thesis for the logician to exercise his ingenuity on."[21] President Madison thought otherwise, however, and though accepting the bank and the tariff, vetoed Calhoun's bill for internal improvements.

From 1817 to 1824 Calhoun served as secretary of war in James Monroe's cabinet. During these years he continued to press plans for combining liberty and strength in the American system, but he failed to persuade Congress to adopt his military and public-works proposals. Secretary of State John Quincy Adams praised Calhoun at this time for being "above all sectional and factious prejudice" and for having "no petty scruples about constructive powers and state rights."[22] Relations between Adams and Calhoun began deteriorating in 1823, however, as the two men maneuvered for support for the presidential nomination; and in 1825, when Adams became President and Calhoun vice-president, an open rupture quickly followed. The immediate occasion was Calhoun's failure, as president of the Senate, to call John Randolph of Virginia to order for making offensive remarks about the Adams administration. During the spring and summer of 1826, Adams resorted to the newspapers under the name of "Patrick Henry" to criticize Calhoun's inaction, and Calhoun responded under the name of "Onslow." Calhoun's main point, repeated with numerous variations, was that Adams's views were "dangerous to our liberty" because they called for the vice-president to restrict freedom of debate in the Senate. Freedom of debate, declared Calhoun loftily,

ranks first, even before the liberty of the press, the trial by jury, the rights of conscience, and the writ of habeas corpus, in the estimation of those who are capable of forming a correct estimate of the value of freedom, and the best means of preserving it. Against this palladium of liberty your blows are aimed. . . . If you should succeed in establishing the points you labor, that the Vice-President holds a power over the freedom of debate, under the right of preserving order, beyond the will of control of the Senate, and that, consequently, he alone is responsible for what might be considered an undue exercise of the freedom of speech in debate, a solid foundation would be laid, from which, in time, this great barrier against despotic power would be battered down.[23]

It is ironic that the man who wrote this plea for free speech had denounced "factious opposition" in 1812 and was, a few years later, to propose excluding abolitionist petitions from the Senate because they touched off discussions of slavery; while Adams, whom he accused of subverting the right of free discussion, later fought valiantly against a "gag rule" on the reception of antislavery petitions in the House of Representatives. If, as some people have thought, Calhoun was primarily an opportunist, he was never more so than on this occasion. For all of his impassioned rhetoric in 1826 about free speech, a sincere dedication to the right of free discussion simply cannot be considered to have been one of his strong points.[24]

While he was vice-president, Calhoun began abandoning his nationalistic principles and moving into the camp of the states' righters. It was the protective tariff (which South Carolina, and hence Calhoun, came to believe was deleterious to staple-producing regions like the South) which precipitated the change, but in due course he reversed himself on just about every issue of importance. Liberty continued to be his touchstone, but it was now liberty of section and state, rather than of nation, that was his prime concern. Individual liberty, he now decided, depended mainly on local liberty, and the greatest threat to local liberty came, not from disunion, but from what might be called over-union. The feeling of nationality in which he had exulted after the War of 1812, he now came to feel, was an implacable foe of local and regional and hence of individual liberty.

In *South Carolina Exposition and Protest,* which he prepared for the South Carolina legislature in 1828, Calhoun called the protective tariff "unconstitutional, unequal, and oppressive, and calculated to . . . destroy the liberty of the country." Describing in minute detail the adverse effects of the tariff on the economy of the South, *Exposition* contained all the major themes of Calhoun's newly worked-out philosophy of government: the compact theory of the Union, the doctrine of nullification, the primacy of the reserved powers of the states over the delegated powers of the federal government, the perils of unchecked majority rule, and the necessity of penetrating the political facade to the economic realities underneath to discern the ultimate determinants of public policy. If he had one overarching theme, it was that liberty in the United States was secure only so long as the power of the federal government was checked by an "equal antagonist power" on the part of the states comprising the Union.[25] Calhoun spent his remaining years elaborating on these themes orally and in writing.

When South Carolina, in 1832, attempted to nullify the high tariffs enacted by Congress, Calhoun of course sided with his state, characterizing the nullification crisis as a momentous struggle between "power and liberty—power on the side of the North, and liberty on the side of the South."[26] Though he supported the compromise tariff by which the dispute was settled, his breach with Jackson, who made it clear he would use force, if necessary, to compel South Carolina to obey the law, was irreparable. Now in the Senate, Calhoun joined the Whigs in inveighing against executive tyranny; there was little that Jackson could say or do during the remainder of his presidency that Calhoun did not interpret as an insidious effort "to choke and stifle the voice of American liberty."[27] But he was bitterly opposed to the tariff-bank-public-works program of the Whigs, which he had once supported. Increasingly, he became an apparent apostle of laissez-faire liberty in its purest form; just about every action of the federal government, he declared, represented a drain on productive labor in the country because it diverted men from useful private pursuits to the "unproductive employment" of government.[28]

Like Adam Smith, Calhoun made one reference to an "invisible hand" which he thought regulated a laissez-faire economy; but he went much farther than Smith in calling for a diminution of government activity.[29] The American people, he said, should realize that "a cheap and simple Government" was "indispensable to the preservation of their institutions and liberty."[30] He wanted the number of federal officials drastically reduced, called for a total separation between government and banking, and proposed that public lands in the newer states be turned over to state authorities for administration and disposal. Summarizing his views in the Senate in August, 1842, he announced that on the banner of his party were inscribed the words: "FREE TRADE; LOW DUTIES; NO DEBT; SEPARATION FROM BANKS; ECONOMY; RETRENCHMENT; and STRICT ADHERENCE TO THE CONSTITUTION."[31] But he omitted one crucial word: slavery. By the mid-thirties, slavery was beginning to replace economic issues as Calhoun's major preoccupation. The Negro, it was clear, was to be forever totally excluded from any share in the laissez-faire liberty about which Calhoun talked with such feeling in Congress. Calhoun never dreamed of applying the principles of laissez-faire individualism to the southern economy.

There was a direct link in Calhoun's mind, however, between laissez-faire and slavery when it came to national affairs. Since an energetic federal government was likely to put states' rights, and thus slavery, in jeopardy, Calhoun got into the habit of objecting to most bills (even minor ones, like appropriating money to purchase the Madison manuscripts) calling for federal action or the expenditure of federal money. He wanted to reduce federal activity to a minimum, he said, and federal policy to a "wise and masterly inactivity."[32] When Jackson called for action by Congress in December, 1835, to exclude abolitionist literature from the federal mails, Calhoun suggested a state-rights alternative: legislation requiring federal postal officials to cooperate with local officials in keeping such material from being delivered in states where it was proscribed by law. His plan, unlike Jackson's, he said, did not violate the free-speech and free-press guarantees of the First Amendment, which restricts Congress, not the states. It was preposterous, Calhoun insisted, to regard state laws prohibiting "the introduction and circulation of papers calculated to excite insurrection" as violating liberty of the press. He accompanied his restrictive proposals with professions of undiminished devotion to the First Amendment freedoms.[33] In the opinion of one critic, however, anyone who thought that muzzling the press promoted liberty or that "LIBERTY and SLAVERY can be advocated in the same breath" did not know the meaning of despotism.[34]

In addition to trying to restrict the distribution of abolitionist literature, Calhoun also tried to limit the discussion of slavery in Congress. In March, 1836, he urged the Senate not to receive antislavery petitions any more because they tended to "agitate and distract the country, and to endanger the Union itself." Under "our free and popular system," he explained, the right of petition was "among the least of all our political rights."[35] The right to hold slaves, it was clear, was coming to supersede all other rights in Calhoun's philosophy. The Senate adopted neither of Calhoun's recommendations for stilling abolitionism, but Calhoun did not relax his efforts on behalf of slavery. By 1837, he was saying that slavery was "a good—a positive good" and proposing resolutions designed to protect it from the abolitionists. "Never before," he said,

has the black race of Central Africa, from the dawn of history to the present day, attained a condition so civilized and so improved, not only physically, but morally and intellectually. It came among us in a low, degraded, and savage condition, and in the course of a few generations it has grown up under the fostering care of our institutions, reviled as they have been, to its present comparatively civilized condition. This, with the rapid increase of numbers, is conclusive proof of the general happiness of the race, in spite of all the exaggerated tales to the contrary.[36]

While defending slavery in this fashion as a kind of gigantic charitable institution, Calhoun continued to regard himself as "a firm and unflinching friend of the Union." But he was adamant on one point: slavery and the Union stood and fell together.[37]

In his later years Calhoun ceased to be a "War Hawk." He came to realize that war, the most powerful centralizing force in human affairs, and state rights are utterly antithetical, and he no longer shrugged off "the danger of standing armies to our liberties" as he had once done.[38] He refused to vote for war with Mexico in May, 1845, and during the conflict he repeatedly urged that steps be taken for ending it as speedily as possible. He feared that the United States might embark on a gigantic war of conquest leading to a fearsome increase of power in the federal government and to the incorporation of alien peoples, "so little qualified for free and popular government," into the Union.[39] He also foresaw a fierce struggle between North and South over the disposition of territories acquired in the war. When the sectional crisis came after the war, as he expected, he supported the Compromise of 1850 by which North and South reached a temporary accommodation. But he did not think the northern states had made enough concessions to the South, and shortly before his death he remarked that it was "difficult to see how two people so different and hostile can exist together in one common Union."[40] When he died at the end of March, 1850, Senator Thomas Hart Benton mused: "He is not dead, sir; he is not dead. There may be no vitality in his body. But there's plenty in his doctrines."[41]

## DISQUISITION ON LIBERTY AND GOVERNMENT

Calhoun's doctrines are contained in two treatises which he completed shortly before his death: *Disquisition on Government* and *A Discourse on the Constitution and Government of the United States*. (John Stuart Mill had a high regard for the former.[42]) Most of the ideas in these treatises he had been expounding in one form or another since the late 1830s in speeches in the Senate and elsewhere. Previously, however, he had presented his views in piecemeal fashion; now he was attempting to bring them together into a unified system. The *Disquisition on Government*, in particular, represents a major effort on his part (unusual for an American politician) at sustained thinking about fundamentals of human nature and government. Ultimately, to be sure, Calhoun hoped by his analysis to erect an unassailable case for slavery and minority rule, and in this respect his doctrines have had a retarding effect on the kind of freedom Paine and Emerson sought for America. But Calhoun had unusual analytical gifts; and, driven as he was to discover intellectually compelling foundations for his prejudices, he probed more deeply into the springs of human action and the nature of government than most of his American contemporaries. In so doing he inevitably raised incisive questions about liberty.

Fundamental to Calhoun's philosophy was his emphatic rejection of the concept of a state of nature antedating society and government, in which men lived in freedom and equality without the restraints of organized institutions. Occasionally, it is true, in his earlier years, Calhoun used the language of natural rights. In 1831, for example, he declared that "in a state of nature, no man has a right to govern another without his consent."[43] But, as we have seen, Calhoun had never regarded it as particularly fruitful to think of an individual apart from his social group; and by the 1840s he had concluded that the state of nature was a "mere hypothetical truism" which, taken literally, was "the most false and dangerous of all political errors."[44] In June, 1848, he declared that the statement in the Declaration of Independence that "all men are created equal" had produced a train of "poisonous fruits." Among other things, it had led Jefferson to

take an utterly false view of the subordinate relation of the black to the white race in the South; and to hold, in consequence, that the latter, though utterly unqualified to possess liberty, were as fully entitled to both liberty and equality as the former; and that to deprive them of it was both unjust and immoral. To this error, his proposition to exclude slavery from the territory northwest of Ohio may be traced,—and to that the ordinance of 1787, and through it the deep and dangerous agitation which now threatens to ingulf . . . our political institutions, and involve the country in countless woes.[45]

It was the need to defend slavery which led Calhoun to repudiate the Jeffersonian faith on which he had been reared. In its place he erected a system of thought in which the state of nature, natural rights, and the social contract had no place and in which liberty was reconciled with slavery.

Calhoun began his *Disquisition* by insisting that man is a social being who never lives isolated and apart from his fellowmen. But man has selfish as well as social feelings, and these are so powerful that they would produce conflict, violence, and anarchy unless checked by government. Government is therefore as necessary to society as society is to man; it is rooted in "the law of our nature." "Like breathing," wrote

Calhoun, "it is not permitted to depend on our volition. Necessity will force it on all communities in some form or another." But government, though part of man's natural state, is fraught with grave dangers. It is administered by human beings, and since self regarding instincts are stronger in most people than social propensities, public officials will be irresistibly tempted to abuse their powers. Government must be strong enough to protect society from internal disorder and external aggression, but its powers must be restrained in some fashion to prevent the persons exercising them from oppressing the rest of the community. "Power," said Calhoun, "can only be resisted by power,—and tendency by tendency."[46]

Only a constitution safeguarding liberty can check the power of government; but while society and government are necessary and natural to man (and thus of divine ordination), not matters of choice, a constitution is a "contrivance of man."[47] An effective constitutional government contains devices which enable people to resist the abuse of power by their rulers. The right of suffrage is one of these devices; it is indispensable to constitutional government. With access to the ballot, citizens can be expected to look after their own selfish interests at election time and vote despotic officials out of office.

Calhoun, like Paine, located sovereignty in the people. The "essence of our liberty," he once told Congress, is that "Congress is responsible to the people immediately."[48] But he detached popular sovereignty from the natural-rights-social-contract philosophy with which Paine and most Americans associated it and proposed another basis for it: the practical, realistic efforts of men to check the abuse of governmental authority. The right to vote, basic to popular rule, was for Calhoun not a natural right; it was a civil right developed by the people (especially the British and the Americans) out of long experience to restrain their rulers. It was a countervailing power designed to safeguard liberty from governmental oppression.

But liberty itself, according to Calhoun, was not a natural right; like the suffrage, it was a civil right created by the people out of social experience. Calhoun, like Burke (whom he admired), denied that all men are born free and equal possessing inalienable rights like liberty. Infants, he said, are not born free; they are subject to their parents, guardians, and to older people generally; and only gradually, as they develop into mature, responsible persons, do they acquire the civil and political rights prevailing in their society. Human rights are never natural; they are always conventional or customary rights existing within and inseparable from the social order. Every right which individuals possess is the product of long history and is based on social utility; it has proven itself to be conducive to the welfare of the community as a whole.

But if Calhoun thought the ultimate sanction for individual rights was societal welfare, he also thought that the needs of society dictated an unequal enjoyment of these rights by different members of the community. Some people, he said, are superior, mentally and morally, and it benefits society to have them exercise certain rights freely; but other people are inferior in natural endowments, and it would detract from the well-being of society to bestow any rights on them.

Calhoun favored giving people he regarded as superior preferential rights and privileges. In every society, he maintained, there are gifted individuals who are eager to improve themselves; the "desire of individuals to better their condition" is the fountainhead of social advance.[49] By improving themselves, these people at the same time benefit the community, and it is society's obvious interest to see to it that they have liberty to get ahead in life and security in the possession of the fruits of their exertions. Calhoun regarded individual liberty and private property as necessary inducements to individual enterprise and therefore indispensable to social progress. But private property, like liberty and the suffrage, is an acquired, not a natural, right; it is justified by its contribution to the material welfare of society. Since individuals differ in native ability, health, strength, and ambition, and some accumulate more worldly goods than others, the protection of private property means the maintenance of inequality in property holdings. But economic inequality is natural and proper and should be upheld by government. The same is true of liberty. Calhoun regarded inequality in the enjoyment of liberty as both necessary and desirable.

The question of who gets liberty and how much liberty he gets was for Calhoun the great problem of government. Government must be strong enough to protect society against internal and external dangers, but it must also permit enough liberty for people with ability to get ahead in life. Calhoun wanted able individuals to have as much freedom as possible, consonant with law and order, to better their condition, and he came to favor laissez-faire on the federal level. But he did not think it was possible to lay down any hard and fast rules regarding the proper balancing of liberty and authority. Societies vary considerably in intelligence, historical experience, and social and economic circumstances, and what is possible in one community may be neither possible nor desirable in another. Some communities, Calhoun pointed out,

require a far greater amount of power than others to protect them against anarchy and external dangers; and, of course, the sphere of liberty in such must be proportionally contracted. The causes calculated to enlarge the one and contract the other are numerous and varied. Some are physical—such as open and exposed frontiers surrounded by powerful and hostile neighbors. Others are moral—such as the different degrees of intelligence, patriotism, and virtue among the mass of the community, and their experience and proficiency in the art of self-government. Of these, the moral are by far the most influential. A community may possess all the necessary moral qualifications in so high a degree as to be capable of self-government under the most adverse circumstances, while, on the other hand, another may be so sunk in ignorance and vice as to be incapable of forming a conception of liberty or of living, even when most favored by circumstances, under any other than an absolute and despotic government.[50]

Calhoun insisted that no people could possess for long more liberty than that to which they were fairly entitled. If people lack the character and training to exercise their liberties wisely, they will probably descend into license and anarchy. Genuine liberty depends on virtue and enlightenment, and if people show little promise of being able to behave decently, it is absurd to grant them liberty. Liberty, in short, is

a reward to be earned, not a blessing to be gratuitously lavished on all alike —a reward reserved for the intelligent, the patriotic, the virtuous and deserving, and not a boon to be bestowed on people too ignorant, degraded, and vicious to be capable either of appreciating or of enjoying it.[51]

Like Calhoun, Paine, as we have seen, linked liberty with virtue and thought it had to be earned. Unlike Calhoun, though, he insisted that all human beings, including blacks, had a right to earn it.

Needless to say, Calhoun, as a white supremacist, thought that the Negro lacked the requisite capacity for freedom and that his natural inferiority, physical, mental, and moral, justified all the restraints imposed on him by the institution of slavery. Calhoun made extensive use of the Census of 1840 (despite its proven errors) in order to show that the free black in the North was far worse off in every respect than the Southern slave because he did not know what to do with his freedom. In the free states, Calhoun contended, the blacks had "invariably sunk into vice and pauperism, accompanied by the bodily and mental afflictions incident hereto—deafness, blindness, insanity and idiocy—to a degree without example." But in the South, where the states "retained the ancient relation" between the races, the blacks had "improved greatly in every respect—in number, comfort, intelligence, and morals."[52] Abolishing slavery, he warned, would not "raise the inferior race to the condition of freemen," but rather would "deprive the negro of the guardian care of his owner, subject to all the depression and oppression belonging to his inferior condition." It would also lead to "deadly strife between the two races" and eventually a "war of races" throughout the Western hemisphere.[53]

By means of slavery, the South, Calhoun was convinced, had achieved a proper balance between liberty and authority: it extended liberty to those worthy of it (whites) and withheld it from the undeserving (blacks). It was a fair, just, stable, and contented society, in Calhoun's opinion, and he wanted to keep it free from outside interference. The South's major problem, as he saw it, was to protect its "constitutional liberty," that is, its freedom under the U.S. Constitution to order its internal affairs as it saw fit.[54] Since the South was part of a Union in which majority rule prevailed at the federal level, Calhoun was naturally alert to threats to the South's "constitutional liberty" posed by majority rule and anxious to suggest devices by which the southern states might retain their freedom within the American system to preserve slavery. In *Disquisition*, therefore, Calhoun had something quite specific in mind: the desire to safeguard the liberty of the southern slaveowner (not that of Negro, Indian, or poor white) against any majority that threatened to interfere with his way of life. But he discussed the question throughout in only the most general terms, and his *Disquisition* has been regarded as an astute analysis of the dangers to individual liberty and minority rule presented by representative institutions in general.[55] It is so, however, only if the liberties of all individuals and the rights of all minorities and not just of a privileged few are taken into account.

In *Disquisition*, Calhoun emphasized a fact he thought most Americans were prone to overlook: elected rulers have just as selfish an interest in abusing their power as hereditary rulers have. Abuse of authority was just as real a possibility in a representative system of government, he thought, as under a despotic form of government. Calhoun saw four specific dangers to liberty in general (though he was thinking primarily of the slaveholder's liberty) developing out of the operation of representative government in the United States.

There was, first, the danger coming from political parties, representing different interests in the country, which grow up of necessity in connection with representative institutions. Political parties inevitably take a partial view of the public welfare; they seek their own selfish ends and neglect the common good. Increasingly, the spoils system, Calhoun thought, was coming to dominate American politics; and the greed for obtaining the "honors and emoluments" of office, rather than public service, was becoming the primary motivation of party politics.[56] Party leaders were willing to go to any lengths to win elections and capture the spoils of office; and once they won control of government, there was little likelihood that they would treat the rights and liberties of those out of office with any tender regard. Calhoun believed that party contests in the United States were degenerating into naked battle for power and pelf, devoid of all principle, and that a precipitous decline in both public and private morality was following as a natural consequence. He also warned against the growth of party discipline and the centralization of party organization in the hands of a few leaders, necessitated by the desire for victory at the polls, as menaces to liberty. Calhoun never proposed abolishing political parties in the United States, but he did suggest abandoning presidential nominating conventions and returning to the indirect method of choosing Presidents, as provided in the Constitution, as one solution to the threat to American liberty posed by the party system.

A second threat to liberty, connected with the first, was the steady proliferation of officials under the federal government. Government officials, even in minor positions, tend naturally to abuse their powers, Calhoun declared, and the more of them there are, the less secure is liberty. Calhoun was convinced that the number of offices under the federal government was increasing at an alarming rate, and during the 1830s and 1840s he repeatedly urged that federal activities be curtailed in order to reduce the bureaucratic threat to liberty.

In the third place, Calhoun was concerned by the ease which government in a representative system falls under the sway of special interests and is utilized to favor some groups at the expense of others. Tariff and banking measures were prime examples for Calhoun of special-interest legislation which artificially builds up privileged economic groups at the expense of everyone else. Calhoun came to believe that an alliance between government and private interests (especially banking and excluding, of course, slavery) was more dangerous to liberty than an alliance between church and state. No Jacksonian Democrat was more fervent than Calhoun (after Jackson left the White House) in denouncing the "monied power" and the whole Hamiltonian philosophy of economic privilege, at least so far as the federal government was concerned. "Can that be favorable to liberty," asked he, "which concentrates the money power, and places it under the control of a few powerful and wealthy individuals?"[57]

Finally, Calhoun feared the abuse of power by the American press. He did concede that a free press might be of great service in informing and educating voters in a representative system, but he also pointed out that the impulse to selfishness motivated newspaper-owners as much as everyone else and that they tended to shape public opinion for their own devious purposes. In Calhoun's opinion, American newspapers had become the organs of special interests, and they sought to advance these interests rather than the good of the country. In no serious respect, concluded Calhoun, could newspapers be depended on to provide people with fair, honest, and impartial information and thus act as effective brakes on the abuse of authority under popular government.

Overshadowing political parties, government bureaucracy, special-interest legislation, and a "kept" press as threats to liberty in the American system was majority rule, of which the other four were merely symptoms. Calhoun feared the operation of unchecked majority rule above all other threats to liberty. In his early days, it is true, he had scoffed at the idea that "all the misfortunes and miseries of free States originated in the blunders and follies of majorities"; but this was during the War of 1812, when he was defending the wisdom of the majority in supporting the war with England.[58] By the 1830s he had become critical of majority rule. He thought the inevitable tendency of governments based on the will of the numerical majority, without "constitutional check or limitation of power" was to "faction, corruption, anarchy, and despotism."[59]

Quite simply, Calhoun did not believe in the wisdom of the majority of people: "We make a great mistake," he told the Senate on January 4, 1848, "in supposing all people are capable of self-government."[60] Though he supported the suffrage and on occasion conceded the desirability of some measure of majority rule in the American system, his preference was for leadership by a social and economic elite. Unlike Paine, he equated property with wisdom and virtue; the "wealthy and intelligent," he said, should be leaders and protectors of the "poor and ignorant." Men of means, according to Calhoun, were likely to be educated and enlightened, and their independent wealth freed them from the pressures of the marketplace and enabled them to take a disinterested, public-spirited view of social issues.[61] The majority of men, by contrast, could not be expected to take a rational view of the public good; hard-pressed economically, they were always selfish and short sighted in outlook. The great danger in representative government, Calhoun thought, was that the numerical majority would gain control of government and then resort to unjust oppression and selfish exploitation of the civilized minority. The most difficult problem facing popular governments in general and the American government in particular was that of protecting the liberty and property of the minority against the encroachments of the majority.

Calhoun attempted to ground his political analysis in economic realities. Societies, he said, naturally split into diverse economic interests and groupings. The larger the society, the more numerous the variety of interests and the harder it is to insure that the laws impose equal burdens and benefits on all of them. If no single economic interest constitutes a majority by itself, the less dissimilar interests will unite on what they have in common until they form a majority, win control of government, and place minority interests at their mercy. Calhoun, with the United States in mind, said that geographical contiguity was one of the strongest factors binding different interests together, that political parties tended to be sectional parties, and that majority oppression tended to be sectional oppression. Calhoun was thinking of the South in all of this; majority rule, he thought, was placing both the liberty and the property of the South, a minority section in the Union, in grave jeopardy. He regarded it as absolutely essential to the survival of the Union that the American constitutional system be revised in such a way as to compel the various interests and sections of the country to be fair and just to one another (and especially to the South).

Calhoun's solution was what he called the "concurrent majority." In any genuinely representative government, he said, the numerical majority must be replaced or supplemented at strategic points by the concurrent majority. The numerical majority considers only numbers; the concurrent majority takes interests (or sections) into account. Under the concurrent majority, the powers of government are so divided and distributed that interest (and section) has an effective part in making laws as well as the right to veto legislation deemed injurious to its welfare. The concurring majority, said Calhoun, is "the only solid foundation for constitutional liberty."[62] In such a system the southern states, a minority in the Union, would have the power to block federal measures (tariff, banking, public-works, and, above all, antislavery measures) which were regarded as hostile to their liberty and disruptive of their social order.

Calhoun proposed vesting the power of the federal executive in two officers, one elected by the North and one by the South, as one possible way of introducing the concurrent voice into the American system. Under this plan, the approval of both presidents would be required for the validity of all congressional legislation. Calhoun denied that the concurrent majority would lead to deadlock in government on the federal level; on the contrary, he said, it would produce mutual consideration, tolerance, and forbearance on the part of the different interests and sections of the country toward one another. By a kind of high-level log-rolling, one section would support measures desired by the other section in order to win approval for measures of its own; the ruling principle would be compromise and good will. Since each section would be protected against unfair treatment by the other, people in both sections, feeling their liberty secure, would develop great love for and loyalty to the country as a whole and sincere dedication to the general welfare. The consequences would be almost Utopian: the expansion of individual liberty, the advance of material welfare, and the enhancement of public and private morals. Calhoun did not consider the possibility that the old Adam in man (with which he began his *Disquisition*) would find ways of perverting this system as he had all other systems of government. By concurring in one another's selfishness, Calhoun seemed to think, men would become unselfish.

Calhoun believed that a proper understanding of the concept of sovereignty was just as crucial to a solution of the liberty-authority problem as was a firm grasp of the nature of majority rule. Before Calhoun, most Americans thought the United States had a divided sovereignty. In *Federalist* No. 39, for example, James Madison said that the federal government was supreme in some areas and state governments were supreme in others. Calhoun at first accepted this view of sovereignty and then came to view it with abhorrence. Sovereignty, the highest power in a community, he finally decided, simply could not be divided without being destroyed. By its very nature sovereignty was indivisible; it was impossible for there to be two or more sovereigns in the same community. To speak of half a sovereignty, he said, was as ridiculous as to speak of half a square or half a triangle. (He was not willing to concede the federal government even half a sovereignty.) A sovereign might, to be sure, delegate the exercise of its powers to agents; but it could never surrender its sovereignty without annihilating itself.

In the United States, Calhoun came to insist, sovereignty rested with the people of the several states. It was they who framed state constitutions and established state governments to be their agents in the exercise of their sovereign powers. It was also they who entered into a "compact" at Philadelphia in 1787 to establish a federal government (or general government, as Calhoun habitually called it) as their joint agent for common purposes. In drawing up the U.S. Constitution, the delegates in Philadelphia did not surrender the sovereignty of the people of the several states whom they represented; they simply delegated the exercise of some of the people's power to a joint agent (delegated powers) and retained for the people of the states crucial reserved powers over which the federal government had no jurisdiction. It followed that if the federal government unlawfully encroached upon the reserved rights of any state in the Union, that state had the "constitutional liberty" to assert its sovereignty and resist Federal action.[63] Calhoun proposed that the aggrieved state call a special convention, elected by the people, to decide whether the federal act in question violated its reserved rights as guaranteed by the Tenth Amendment to the Constitution. If the act was deemed unconstitutional, the convention was then to proclaim it null and void and of no force within the borders of the state.

Calhoun regarded nullification (or interposition, as he preferred to call it) as a power implicitly reserved to the states in the Constitution, providing them with a check on unauthorized action by their agent, the federal government, and he insisted that it was indispensable to the liberty of the states. He did not, however, look upon it as an irrevocable act. After a state had interposed its authority to nullify a federal law, it was still possible, he explained, to frame an amendment granting the disputed power to the federal government and then, if three-fourths of the states ratified the amendment, the nullifying state would be obliged in good faith to accept the new federal power. Nevertheless, if the state thought that the amendment was inconsistent with the purposes for which the Constitution had been framed, it was free to secede from the Union.

The sovereign states, in other words, possessed a right of secession as well as a right of nullification. But nullification was quite different in character from secession, for it was a means of preserving the Union in its original character. Calhoun regarded nullification as a safeguard against "consolidation" of all power in the federal government and thus a guarantee of liberty. He also insisted that his views were based on "the doctrines of '98" (the Virginian and Kentucky Resolutions) and thus had the high authority of Jefferson and Madison.[64] In 1835, however, Madison called nullification an "absurdity . . . in its naked and suicidal form" and said that in adopting the Constitution the states had given up parts of their sovereignty and retained other parts.[65]

## LIBERTY AND SLAVERY

In *Disquisition* and *Discourse on the Constitution*, Calhoun said almost nothing about slavery directly. His propensity, even in Senate speeches, was to talk in abstract terms, and he was, not surprisingly, charged by contemporaries with being too "metaphysical."[66] Calhoun's powers of logical analysis, given his premises, were indeed of a high order, but they frequently led him to prefer scoring a point to coming to grips with an issue. His *Discourse*, in particular, resembles an interminably involved scholastic exercise in logic-chopping, full of brilliant reasoning but utterly remote from the realities of American life. In all of Calhoun's lofty ruminations on society and government there was an unstated but fundamental premise: the indispensability of slavery to American civilization. The Union, he thought, could endure only half slave and half free. At the heart of his philosophy, shaping all that he thought and said about liberty, was an unshakable belief in racial inequality. Calhoun was not exceptional in believing the black man inferior to the white; in varying degrees most whites in Calhoun's day believed this. But that slavery followed logically from this assumption as the proper status for the Negro seemed a preposterous deduction for increasing numbers of whites in Europe and America after the eighteenth century.

Unlike many southerners before 1830, Calhoun is never known to have favored working for a gradual end to slavery. In a speech in Congress in 1816, it is true, he referred to the slave trade as an "odious traffic" and in 1820 he supported the Missouri Compromise delimiting slavery.[67] But he came to regret the Missouri Compromise and by the mid-1830s he was praising slavery as an unqualified good. When he talked, as he did ceaselessly, about protecting the liberty of the minority against the tyranny of the majority, he was never thinking of the Negro, the most abused, exploited, and helpless minority in Calhoun's America. In Calhoun's system the black was to have no rights of nullification, concurrence, or secession to defend himself against oppression. Calhoun may have been quite right about human nature: people may be incurably self-centered, and it may be society's primary task to find ways of keeping the human lust for power and pelf in check. But what was Calhoun's whole philosophy itself but an elaborate, self-interested effort to justify the abuse of power by the dominant majority in his own state and section over a defenseless minority?

Calhoun's philosophy of inequality included whites as well as blacks, for there were large qualifications on his respect even for people of his own race. Though he accepted popular sovereignty in principle and sometimes referred to the United States as a "constitutional democracy," he actually had little faith in the competency of the majority of white people.[68] In justifying slavery in the South, Calhoun was led (partly, no doubt, for polemical reasons) to sketch a theory of society in which the majority of people everywhere, regardless of color, are always kept in a distinctly subordinate status. There has "never yet existed," he declared, "a wealthy and civilized society in which one portion of the community did not, in point of fact, live on the labor of the other."[69] Social progress, in his view, comes about only by exploitation; the advance of civilization has always depended on the exploitation of the many by the few. In every community, he said, there is a master class which appropriates a sizable share of the fruits of the labor of working people for its own use. By exploiting the laboring classes, members of the master class achieve an economic security which frees them from manual labor and provides them with the wealth and leisure to cultivate the civilized arts and engage in public service. This is just as true in the North, where capital exploits labor, he said, as in the South; and he attempted to win the support of northern businessmen for slavery by arguing that the equalitarian natural-rights views of the abolitionists, when spread among the lower classes, were as threatening to the property rights of northern capitalists as to those of southern planters.

In some respects, though the point can be overstated (Calhoun's economic analysis is very broad and sketchy and full of simplisms), Calhoun was saying what Karl Marx was saying, though Calhoun, of course, favored exploitation of the workers by the nonproducing classes, while Marx wanted them to revolt. Calhoun thought that rule by a superior elite was necessary for social, economic, and intellectual progress in every society. In the end, he wanted more than a concurrent voice for his privileged minority; he was asking for domination. In Calhoun, concern for "the great common liberty" of the nation had given way to a concern for the liberty of section and state and finally to preoccupation with the liberty of the aristocratic few. Like George Fitzhugh, he had come to believe that liberty was "the privilege of the few—not the right of the many."[70] He refused to entertain Paine's idea that liberty was a privilege which people of all races and classes had a right to achieve.

Abraham Lincoln readily saw the catch in Calhoun's view of liberty. "We all declare for liberty," he observed in a speech on April 18, 1864,

but in using the same *word* we do not all mean the same *thing*. With some the word liberty may mean for each man to do as he pleases with himself, and the product of his labor; while with others the same word may mean for some men to do as they please with other men, and the product of other men's labor.[71]

For Lincoln, the liberty which Calhoun came to celebrate was in reality tyranny; it was the liberty of the wolf to plunder the sheep. But the Declaration of Independence, on which Calhoun poured so much scorn, repudiated this kind of liberty; it "gave promise," said Lincoln, "that in due time the weights should be lifted from the shoulders of all men, and that *all* should have an equal chance."[72] Lincoln looked upon this promise as the central idea of American politics. He tended to view liberty and equality as twentieth-century liberal democrats do: not as natural rights existing as actual facts in a past state of nature, but as worthy moral ideals to be endlessly striven for in the present and future; and he thought that apologists for slavery, in rejecting these ideals, rejected the very meaning of American civilization.

In his later years Calhoun said that he wanted the United States to return to what it had been in its pristine purity in 1789. But he would have had to go farther back than that to find what he wanted, for, like Lincoln, most of the founders of the Republic regarded liberty as a promise for all rather than as a privilege for a few. Though Calhoun regarded himself as a conservative, he died, as William E. Dodd has written, "the greatest reactionary of his time."[73] And though his view of liberty as an achievement of the social process rather than as a gift of nature places him closer to contemporary thought than Jefferson and Paine, the uses he made of this insight make his philosophy relevant to authoritarians in the contemporary world rather than to lovers of individual liberty. Calhoun talked continually about liberty, but it was his "sweet land of slavery" that he came finally to prize most highly. His motto, at the end, should have been: "The Union—next to our Slavery, the most dear."

# 5

# Frederick Douglass on
# Bondage and Freedom

FREDERICK DOUGLASS was offended by the imprecision with which
northern reformers talked about slavery. Even the most humane whites,
he complained, used the word slavery carelessly. Temperance advocates
called excessive drinking slavery, women's-rights advocates said that being deprived of the vote was slavery, and labor leaders described conditions among white workingmen as slavery. Douglass thought that
using the terrible word in this way detracted from its true horror, and
he proposed giving a more precise definition. "Slavery in the United
States," he announced in 1846, "is the granting of that power by which
one man exercises and enforces a right of property in the body and soul
of another." It meant physical brutality: floggings, scourgings, brand-
ings, and chainings. It also involved psychological cruelty: contempt for
the slave's intellect and denial of his moral personality. Douglass admitted there were exceptions: some masters kind toward their slaves and
some slaves able, through efforts of their own and through sheer good
luck, to escape the worst effects of the slave system. But the intention of
slavery, he insisted, and its general effect was to corrode the mind and
heart of the black. By turning a human being into a piece of property,
he said, it "makes deliberate and constant war upon human nature itself,
robs the slave of personality, cuts him off from the human family,

and sinks him below even the brute. It leaves nothing standing to tell the world that here was a man and a brother."[1]

Freedom, by contrast, meant dignity, self-reliance, and moral responsibility. It meant, Douglass declared, the possibility of choosing a vocation and working at it with pride and zest. It also meant continual growth in knowledge, virtue, and social concern. There was nothing lawless about freedom; it was closely linked with character. Nor was there anything easy about it; it required hard work to achieve and determined efforts to retain. For Douglass, *"Freedom, Industry, Virtue and Intelligence"* were all of a piece, as they were for Emerson, and it was slavery's denial of a person's right to moral and intellectual development that chiefly made it an abomination. From the beginning, Douglass confessed, his own unhappiness as a slave had been "less physical than mental"; it was *"slavery,* not its mere *incidents"* that he had come to hate. "The thought of being only a creature of the *present* and the *past* troubled me," he declared, "and I longed to have a *future*—a future with hope in it. To be shut up entirely to the past and present is to the soul, whose life and happiness is unceasing progress, what the prison is to the body—a blight and a mildew.[2]

Of the economics of slavery Douglass had almost nothing to say at any time in his life. He would have been surprised to learn that southern plantations were more efficient than northern farms (according to a recent controversial study) and that slaves ate more and better food than the population of the United States as a whole, but it would not have changed his attitude toward slavery an iota.[3] For when he became an abolitionist leader he sternly rejected economic arguments as a basis for the antislavery crusade (such as the argument that slavery improverished the states and communities where it was established) and insisted that slavery was purely a moral issue. The true basis for opposition to slavery, he declared, was the fact that

the slave is a man, clothed by the eternal God with the full dignity of manhood—a being of moral and intellectual powers, rights, duties, and responsibilities, and that to enslave him, to make of him, as slavery must, a beast of burden, strip him of his rights, shut against him the golden gates of knowledge . . . and doom him to unending slavery, is a most atrocious and revolting crime against nature and nature's God. . . . All else is weak, and standing alone is worthless.[4]

## From Bondage to Freedom

It was impossible for Douglass to avoid melodrama when recalling his first moments on free soil. "I felt as one might feel upon escape from a den of hungry lions," he declared. "I was a FREEMAN, and the voice of peace and joy thrilled my blood." For years, he told friends in later years, he had felt as if he were dragging a heavy chain around with him, all the while knowing that he "was not only a slave, but a slave for life." But after escaping from Maryland and reaching New York City safely in September, 1838, he experienced unspeakable joy at the thought that the chains were gone. "A new world had opened upon me," he said of his first day in the North. "If life is more than breath, and the 'quick round of blood,' I lived more in one day than a year of my slave life. It was a time of joyous excitement which words can but tamely describe."⁵

But Douglass's joy was mingled with fear. There were perils, he recalled, as well as opportunities for him in the free states. There was the terrible danger of being caught and sent back into slavery. There was the problem of subsistence: "I was indeed free—from slavery, but free from food and shelter as well."⁶ There was the overpowering loneliness and insecurity which he experienced in a new and strange environment. There was also the dismay he felt when he first encountered race prejudice in the North. Douglass quickly learned that there were many whites in the North who despised black people and that there were even northerners who favored slavery and hated abolitionists as much as southern slaveholders did. Before long he decided he had gained only nominal freedom, not full liberation, when he reached free soil, and that for American blacks there were narrow limits to freedom as a living reality in the North as well as in the South. No one could describe more vividly than Douglass what it was like to be a slave; but no one could write more feelingly about the precarious position of the free black in America. Despite his insistence on strict definitions, there were, he discovered, degrees of freedom for blacks in America as well as degrees of slavery.

Freedom became Douglass's absorbing passion: the kind of universal freedom to which Paine had dedicated his life. Douglass fought racial discrimination in the North as well as slavery in the South, insisted on his right to mingle publicly with whites, protested when railroad conductors and hotel clerks denied him equal facilities, and worked for desegregation of the schools in Rochester, New York, where he settled in 1847. On one occasion it took several trainmen to remove him from a railroad coach reserved for whites, and the seats to which he was clinging were torn loose during the altercation. Douglass came to believe that slavery and racial prejudice enthralled whites as well as blacks and that no white could be truly free in America while blacks were oppressed and enslaved. His great vision as an abolitionist leader was to end slavery of all kinds and degrees for all people. He dedicated his life as a free man to transforming nominal freedom into authentic freedom for all blacks, for all Americans, and finally for all people everywhere.

It would be rash to generalize with assurance about why some slaves, like Douglass, sought to escape to freedom and others did not. Not all fugitives who reached the free states or Canada recorded their experiences, and those who attempted to escape and failed left no records. Moreover, there is no way of estimating the numbers of those who had serious intentions of fleeing but no opportunities. The obstacles were enormous; ignorance of geography by itself was enough to make the effort to escape futile, and the brutal punishment awaiting the captured fugitive also operated as a deterrent. Nor was it easy to tear oneself away from family and friends. Douglass thought that thousands of blacks would have escaped from slavery "but for the strong cords of affection that bind them to their families, relatives and friends." It was easier, of course, to escape from border states like Maryland and cities like Baltimore where Douglass lived. But even in the Deep South there were hundreds, perhaps thousands, of slaves who because of cruel abuse escaped temporarily by leaving the plantation and hiding out in nearby woods and swamps for days or even weeks at a time.

Solomon Northrup, a free black who was kidnapped in 1841 and kept in slavery until 1853, believed that every slave, even the most ignorant, was keenly aware of the difference between his status and that of the whites and yearned for freedom. At the same time he acknowledged that he encountered slaves who seemed reasonably content, or at least resigned to their condition, if the master was decent, and some who even betrayed fugitives to slaveowners. Northrup attributed the latter to the degradation that slavery produced in people, and Henry Bibb, a Kentucky slave who reached free soil, called slavery "the graveyard of the mind."[8]

Among those who escaped the graveyard and later published detailed narratives (about eighty full-length autobiographies before the Civil War) explaining what led them to risk their lives for freedom, certain elements do appear time and again: unusually cruel treatment by masters; promises of freedom (by self-purchase or in the wills of owners) betrayed; awareness of the fact that other slaves had succeeded in escaping; the prospect of being separated from family and loved ones by sale to another owner; fear of being sent into the Deep South; knowledge of the possibilities for self-fulfillment under conditions of freedom gained from learning to read and write. Douglass always emphasized the last element in his own case. It was the sheer good luck of becoming literate, he said, that kept the ideal of freedom steadily before him, even in his darkest moments, and persuaded him to risk the perils of trying to escape.

Douglass was born in Maryland, sometime around 1817, the son of a white father and a slave mother, and escaped to New York in 1838 when he was about twenty-one. In 1845 he published his *Narrative of the Life of Frederick Douglass,* and it was immediately recognized as one of the finest slave narratives to appear in the United States. Ten years later he expanded it into *My Bondage and My Freedom,* containing material about his life as a freeman, and in 1881 he published the first edition of *Life and Times of Frederick Douglass,* in which he discussed his activities during and after the Civil War. In all of these books he attempted to account for the genesis of his desire to escape from slavery and to trace the development of the spirit of freedom in him amid conditions of servitude. In retrospect, he was struck by the amount of sheer accident that shaped the course of his life as a slave, but he also concluded that the acquisition of literacy had been crucial in his own case and that some degree of informed intelligence was indispensable to the nourishing of freedom in the hearts of men.

Knowledge of the cruelty of slavery came early. Though as a slave-boy on the Lloyd plantation in eastern Maryland Douglass was left free, in his earliest years, to fish, swim, and roam about pretty much as he pleased, he also became aware of the cruel whippings, forced separations of families, and economic deprivation that were a part of slavery. Two episodes in particular had a searing effect on the boy: seeing the bloody and scarred body of a female cousin who had been beaten by a drunken overseer and witnessing the flogging of Aunt Esther, a pretty young slave girl, who had visited her lover against her master's orders. These incidents, Douglass thought, looking back, first made him reflect on his own status as a slave and wonder why some people were slaves and others masters.

Another incident powerfully affecting the boy was the escape of Aunt Jennie and Uncle Noah to freedom in the North. He had already talked to slaves who remembered being forcibly brought to America from

Africa or who had parents stolen in Africa, and the knowledge, he said, made him realize that slavery was a crime, not a decree of God. But the success of his relatives in escaping servitude was, Douglass believed, "the first fact that made me seriously think of escape for myself." He was only seven or eight at the time, but already, "in spirit and purpose, a fugitive from slavery."⁹ After that, Douglass recalled, he became increasingly resentful of the mistreatment he received, the hunger and cold he suffered, the terrible stories of cruelty he heard, and the outrages he personally observed.

Douglass's first big break came in 1825 when he was sent to Baltimore to live as a houseboy in the family of Hugh Auld and take care of Auld's little boy Tommy. A city slave, Douglass discovered, was somewhat better off than a plantation slave; he was better fed and clothed, subject to fewer whippings, and allowed to "hire out" his own time if he developed a skill. Douglass, like other city slaves, developed considerable autonomy in Baltimore, where he learned to calk and began making contracts of his own for work in the shipyards, paying Auld part of the earnings. In Auld's wife ("Miss Sopha"), moreover, he found for a time something like a mother. Mrs. Auld took a kindly interest in the boy's welfare and at his request began teaching him how to read. It was a major turning point in his life; without literacy, Douglass always believed, he would never have persisted in his determination to escape from slavery. But when Hugh Auld found out what was going on, he reprimanded his wife severely; reading, he raged, would unfit the boy to be a slave. But his intervention came too late. "Very well," decided Douglass, "knowledge unfits a child to be a slave"; it must be "the direct pathway from slavery to freedom." Auld's determination to keep him in ignorance, Douglass wrote many years later, "only rendered me the more resolute to seek intelligence," and he continued studying secretly on his own.¹⁰

With the help of young white playmates Douglass eventually mastered Noah Webster's spelling book, and he went on to devour *The Columbian Orator*, a popular schoolbook on "the ornamental and useful art of eloquence" which he heard the boys talk about and which he purchased for fifty cents. First published in Boston in 1797 and edited by Caleb Bingham, Boston educator and pioneer textbook writer, the *Columbian Orator* contains famous speeches, sermons, and poems by ancient and modern figures, including Socrates, Cicero, Cato, Washington, Pitt, and Timothy Dwight, and it exudes old-fashioned patriotism, self-help moralism, love of individual liberty, deep religiosity, and fervent antislavery sentiment in about equal measure.

The book undoubtedly had a profound effect on young Douglass. Years later he remembered the fiery speeches it contained on liberty and human rights by men like Philip Sheridan and Charles James Fox, and he also recalled reading and rereading a dialogue about human bondage between a master and his slave in which the master is consistently outargued throughout. In the latter selection, the master insists that it is the order of Providence that one man be subservient to another, and the slave retorts that Providence "has also given me legs to escape." The slave (who had been kidnapped and sold into slavery) also explains why he cannot feel any gratitude for the master's kindness to him and tells him that it is "impossible to make one, who has felt the value of freedom, acquiesce in being a slave." In the end, the master decides to free the slave, and the latter then voluntarily agrees to become his servant.

The *Columbian Orator* contains several other selections that must have impressed the boy: a piece on justice to the Indians, a debate on whether Anglo-Americans are as talented as Europeans, and, above all, a two-act play, "Slaves in Barbary," which is filled with ironies. In the play, which Douglass probably read with wry fascination, whites, not blacks, are the slaves; one cruel southern slaveholder is himself sold to the highest bidder (so that misery will "teach him, what he never could learn in affluence, the lesson of humanity") and put under the charge of his former black slave. Douglass later called the *Columbian Orator* a "noble acquisition," and he absorbed its lessons thoroughly.[11]

He also began reading Baltimore newspapers about this time, and in them he learned something about the activities of the northern abolitionists. To develop his writing skills, he used Tommy Auld's copybooks when the family was away; he also stayed up late at night when everyone else was asleep, copying passages from the Bible and the Methodist hymnbook for practice. Hugh Auld was quite right: Douglass's growing knowledge made him increasingly dissatisfied with his life as a slave. "I was wretched and gloomy beyond my ability to describe," Douglass wrote years later. "This everlasting thinking distressed and tormented me, and yet there was no getting rid of this subject of my thoughts. Liberty, as the inestimable birthright of every man, converted every object into an assertor of this right."[12]

In 1833 Douglass became the slave of Thomas Auld, Hugh's brother,

and was transferred to St. Michael's, a village about forty miles from
Baltimore. His growing independence soon became apparent, however,
and his new master resolved to break his spirit, once and for all. Early
in 1834 he hired Douglass out to Edward Covey, a professional slave-
breaker, who deliberately subdued recalcitrant slaves by overwork and
weekly floggings. Under Covey, Douglass felt that he reached the nadir
of his existence. "If at any one time of my life, more than another, I
was made to drink the bitterest dregs of slavery," he wrote later,

that time was during the first six months of my stay with this man Covey.
We worked all weathers. It was never too hot, or too cold; it could never
rain, blow, snow, or hail too hard for us to work in the field. Work, work,
work, was scarcely more the order of the day than of the night. The longest
days were too short for him, and the shortest nights were too long for him.
I was somewhat unmanageable at the first, but a few months of this discipline tamed me. Mr. Covey succeeded in *breaking* me—in body, soul, and
spirit. My natural elasticity was crushed; my intelligence languished; the
disposition to read departed, the cheerful spark that lingered about my eye
died out; the dark night of slavery closed in on me, and behold a man
transformed to a brute!

On Sundays, when he did not have to work, Douglass remembered lying
under a tree all day in a stupor, only rousing himself occasionally to
gaze at the ships on Cheaspeake Bay and cry out for freedom. Finally,
in desperation, he decided on resistance, and the next time Covey began
beating him he fought back and ended by giving the slave-breaker a
good thrashing. Covey never laid a finger on him again; he was afraid
that people might find out that he was unable to whip a boy of sixteen.
Looking back on the episode, Douglass viewed his resistance to Covey
as another major turning point in his life; it "rekindled in my breast
the smouldering embers of liberty" and "revived a sense of my own
manhood," he decided. "I had reached the point at which I was *not
afraid to die*. This spirit made me a freeman in *fact*, though I still remained a slave in *form*. When a slave cannot be flogged, he is more
than half free."[13]

   In January, 1834, Auld hired Douglass out as a field hand to
William Freeland, a planter who, in contrast to previous masters, had
some sense of justice and feelings of common humanity. But though
Douglass's situation improved with Freeland, his dissatisfaction mounted
steadily. The better a slave's lot, he concluded, the less resigned he is
to slavery. At least, this was his own experience. "Beat and cuff the

slave," wrote Douglass, "keep him hungry and spiritless, and he will follow the chain of his master like a dog, but feed and clothe him well, work him moderately and surround him with physical comfort, and dreams of freedom will intrude." As he was fond of telling people in later years: "Give him a bad master and he aspires to a good master; give him a good master, and he wishes to become his own master."[14] After an unsuccessful attempt to get away in 1836, Douglass finally made good his escape to freedom in September, 1838, by borrowing a free black sailor's protection papers and boarding a train for New York. Eventually he settled in New Bedford, Massachusetts, did odd jobs as a laborer, began reading the *Liberator*, heard William Lloyd Garrison lecture, and started attending antislavery meetings. His pride and joy at being his own master were enormous.

In 1841 Douglass became an agent for the Massachusetts Anti-Slavery Society, and for the next ten years he was closely associated with Garrison and the "moral suasion" wing of the antislavery movement. His education, he used to tell people, came from "Massachusetts Abolition University: Mr. Garrison, President."[15] He accepted Garrison's view that the way to fight slavery was to convince people of the enormity of the crime of holding people in bondage and thus lead them to demand its immediate abolition. He also shared for a time Garrison's belief that abolitionists ought not to form their own political party, that the U.S. Constitution was a slaveholder's document, and that the free states ought to dissolve their union with the slave states.

In company with other abolition leaders, black and white, Douglass toured New England and the Midwest giving speeches describing his experiences as a slave. His commanding appearance, his melodious voice, and his wit and irony made him one of the most effective of all the abolitionist lecturers. He developed such articulateness as a speaker, in fact, that people came to doubt that he had ever been a slave. To dispel such doubts he decided to write an account of his life as a slave, and during the winter of 1844-45 he worked on his *Narrative*, naming names, places, dates, and precise events. Publication of the book in March, 1845, placed his freedom in jeopardy and his friends advised him to go abroad for his safety. In May, 1845, he sailed for England. He spent nineteen happy months touring the British Isles and winning support for the cause of abolition. While he was in England his British friends raised money which enabled them to purchase his freedom from Hugh Auld late in 1846.

Douglass's experience abroad was important to him. In the British Isles he felt that he was experiencing real rather than nominal freedom for the first time in his life. He was impressed by the absence of prejudice and discrimination in Britain and by the ease with which he could go anywhere he wanted to, do anything he chose to, and associate with anyone he pleased. "I find myself not treated as a *color*, but as a *man*," he exclaimed shortly after reaching Britain.[16] He could not help contrasting the freedom he experienced in England with the discrimination he encountered in the United States. "Instead of a democratic government, I am under a monarchical government," he wrote Garrison from Belfast in January, 1846. "Instead of the bright blue sky of America, I am covered with the soft grey fog of the Emerald Isle. I breathe, and lo! the chattel becomes a man."[17] There might be aristocracies in England, but at least they weren't based on skin color. Monarchical freedom, he told Garrison, was surely preferable to republican slavery; "things are better than names. I prefer the substance to the shadow."[18] From Scotland he wrote: "I feel myself almost a new man—freedom has given me new life."[19] Paine would have been astonished by the ironic way things had turned out.

In a farewell speech in London on March 30, 1847, just before leaving for the United States, Douglass tried to convey to the British people something of what his life in England had meant to him personally. He came to England, he told them, accustomed to being excluded from museums, lyceums, athenaeums, theaters, literary and scientific institutions, and from public places of every description, but in London he was able to pass through them all—colosseums, museums, art galleries, the House of Commons, and even the House of Lords—without molestation. "I say that I have here, within the last nineteen months," he cried, "for the first time in my life, known what it was to enjoy liberty."[20]

Three months before coming to England, he recalled, he had been thrown out of a church because of his color. When planning his trip abroad, he boarded several steamships, but on all of them he was driven out of the cabin and "all the respectable parts of the ship" onto the forward deck among horses and cattle. Just before leaving Boston, "the cradle of liberty," he was kicked out of an omnibus because he was a black. "The people of the United States," he thundered, "are the boldest in their pretensions to freedom, and the loudest in their profession of love of liberty; yet no nation upon the face of the globe can exhibit a statute-book so full of all that is cruel, malicious, and infernal, as the

American code of laws."[21] But "I came to this land—how greatly changed!" he exclaimed; he came to England a slave and was leaving it a freeman.[22]

Douglass could have remained in England, but he knew that his life lay with fellow blacks in America and that it was his duty to return and continue the fight against slavery. He sailed for the United States in April, 1847, and shortly after his arrival settled in Rochester, New York, founded the *North Star* (which became *Frederick Douglass' Paper* in 1851), and continued his abolitionist work in print as well as on platform. He established his newspaper, against the advice of Garrison and other abolitionists, partly because he thought blacks should strike a blow against slavery and caste "on their own hook" and partly because he was anxious to prove to timid blacks and scornful whites that an ex-slave could manage a newspaper enterprise successfully. Freedom, he told his fellow blacks, required strenuous efforts: ". . . OUR ELEVATION AS A RACE, IS ALMOST WHOLLY DEPENDENT UPON OUR OWN EXERTIONS." The "open sesame" for the American Negro was "action! action!! action!!"[23]

## DOUGLASS AS ABOLITIONIST

In presenting the case for emancipation in lectures and in the *North Star*, Douglass, like his associates in the antislavery movement, appealed continually to the natural-rights philosophy of the Declaration of Independence. Like Paine, Douglass believed that man's right to liberty was self-evident and that the desire to act on this right was the deepest and strongest of all man's desires. Man's right to freedom, he declared in December, 1850,

existed in the very idea of man's creation. It was *his* even before he comprehended it. He was created in it, endowed with it, and it can never be taken from him. No laws, statutes, no compacts, no compromises, no constitutions, can abrogate or destroy it. It is beyond the reach of the strongest earthly arm, and smiles at the ravings of tyrants from its hiding place in the bosom of God. Men may hinder its exercise, they may act in disregard of it, they are even permitted to war against it; but they fight against heaven and their career must be short, for Eternal Providence will speedily vindicate the right.[24]

Like all abolitionists, Douglass deeply revered the Declaration of Independence as a "watchword of Freedom."[25] But he was tempted to turn it to the wall, he said, because its "glorious universal truths" were so shamelessly violated in practice.[26] On July 5, 1852 (New York blacks substituted July 5 for July 4 as state emancipation day), Douglass gave a speech on "The Meaning of July Fourth for the Negro" in Rochester. Addressing white Americans, he exclaimed: "The Fourth [of] July is *yours*, not *mine*. *You* may rejoice, *I* must mourn." Then turning to the blacks, he asked: "What, to the American slave, is your 4th of July?" His answer:

a day that reveals to him, more than all other days in the year, the gross injustice and cruelty to which he is the constant victim. To him, your celebration is a sham; your boasted liberty, an unholy license; your national greatness, swelling vanity; your sounds of rejoicing are empty and heartless; your denunciation of tyrants, brass fronted impudence; your shouts of liberty and equality, hollow mockery; your prayers and hymns, your sermons and thanksgivings, with all your religious parade and solemnity, are, to Him, mere bombast, fraud, deception, impiety, and hypocrisy—a thin veil to cover up crimes which would disgrace a nation of savages. There is not a nation on the earth guilty of practices more shocking and bloody than are the people of the United States, at this very hour.[27]

Douglass was outraged that people could denounce tyranny in Russia and Austria and invite victims of oppression abroad to seek refuge in America and yet uphold oppression in the American South and show no sympathy for fugitives from southern tyranny. "You are all on fire at the mention of liberty for France or for Ireland," he said bitterly, "but are as cold as an iceberg at the thought of liberty for the enslaved of America."[28] Douglass implored American whites to take their Declaration of Independence seriously. There were principles in it, he exclaimed, "which would release every slave in the world and prepare the earth for a millennium of righteousness and peace."[29]

What about the belief that blacks were unfit for freedom? While Douglass was proclaiming equal rights, Samuel Morton, George Gliddon, Josiah Nott, and other American anthropologists were trying to amass evidence for the diverse origins of the races of man and for the assertion that blacks were inferior, physically and mentally, to whites. In a speech on "The Claims of the Negro Ethnologically Considered" at Western Reserve College on July 12, 1854, Douglass presented a powerful critique of scientific racial determinism in the United States. He pointed out, in the first place, that scientists were by no means in agreement on the origin of man and that many of them rejected the polygenic theory,

held that mankind was one species, and insisted that the different races
had a common ancestor. In the second place, Douglass pointed out that
the polygenists were not objective scientists but prejudiced whites, convinced of their own racial superiority and anxious to provide a rationale
for slavery. In the third place, Douglass, who had done considerable reading on the subject, ridiculed the efforts of Morton and his colleagues to
explain away the fact that the ancient Egyptians, whose remarkable cultural achievements they could hardly deny, were dark in complexion and
possessed other Negroid physical traits. To Douglass it was just as sensible to deny the affinity of American whites to Englishmen as to deny the
affinity between Negro and Egyptian, and he quoted at length from historical sources to demonstrate that there was a direct relationship between the two. For himself, Douglass found any alternative to the mono-
genic theory of man unconvincing. He had no doubts about the unity of
mankind in one species. Blacks, he said, "are a part of the human family,
and are descended from a common ancestry, with the rest of mankind."
Did not the Bible itself declare that "God has made of one blood all nations of men for to dwell upon all the face of the earth?" And did not
James C. Prichard, the distinguished British ethnologist, conclude in *The
Natural History of Man* (1843), after a thorough study of the question,
that the similarities among the races of men far exceeded the differences
and that "all human races are of one species and one family"?[30]

Douglass was in many respects an environmentalist. Though convinced, like all abolitionists, that the eradication of evil necessitated
changing the hearts of men, he was also impressed, as Paine had been,
by the power of social conditions to shape human behavior. "A man's
character," he said, "always takes its hue, more or less, from the form
and color of things about him."[31] Far less than Emerson was he inclined
to stress the self-sufficiency of the autonomous individual. "A man is
worked upon by what *he* works on," he declared. "He may carve out his
circumstances, but his circumstances will carve him out as well."[32] Southern slaves for the most part lived degraded lives, he observed, but it was
wrong to think that this was their natural state. Blacks, he said repeatedly, had as great a potentiality for intellectual and moral development as
any other members of the human species. "I utterly deny, that we are
originally, or naturally, or practically, or in any way, or in any important
sense, inferior to anybody on this globe."[33] What apologists for slavery
did, he thought, was to attribute the evils flowing from the slave system
—ignorance and moral depravity—to the inherent character of the vic-

tims of slavery. By locating the crimes produced by slavery in the black man rather than in the institution of slavery, where it belonged, they were able to utilize the terrible fruits of slavery as justification for the monstrous system itself. "Take any race you please," said Douglass in a speech in Boston on February 12, 1862,

French, English, Irish, or Scotch, subject them to slavery for ages—regard and treat them everywhere, every way, as property, as having no rights which other men are required to respect.—Let them be loaded with chains, scarred with the whip, branded with hot irons, sold in the market, kept in ignorance, by force of law and by common usage, and I venture to say that the same doubt would spring up concerning either of them, which now confronts the Negro.[34]

In Ireland, which he visited in 1845, he was struck by the similarity of people living in the poorer districts to plantation slaves: "The open, un-educated mouth—the long, gaunt arm—the badly formed foot and ankle —the shuffling gait—the retreating forehead and vacant expression— and, their petty quarrels and fights—all reminded me of the plantation, and my own cruelly abused people."[35]

Douglass noted that oppressors always justified their exploitation of other people by calling them inferior. When Russia wanted to conquer the Ottoman Empire, she said the Turks were an inferior race; and when England sought justification for oppressing Ireland, she said the Celts were inferior. In the same fashion, people exploiting Jews, Indians, and Mexicans rationalized their behavior by looking down on these people. But Douglass's favorite example was the Anglo-Saxon himself. Even the proud Anglo-Saxon was at one time virtually a slave.

It is only about six centuries since the blue-eyed and fair-haired Anglo-Saxons were considered inferior by the haughty Normans, who once trampled upon them. If you read the history of the Norman Conquest, you will find that this proud Anglo-Saxon was once looked upon as of coarser clay than his Norman master, and might be found in the highways and byways of old England laboring with a brass collar on his neck, and the name of his master marked upon it.

No more than the Anglo-Saxon serf was the American slave naturally inferior. He was simply what social conditions made him.

Douglass never doubted at any time in his life that the black man's possibilities were as great as the white man's. Like all men, he said in speech after speech, blacks possessed a natural right to freedom and self-development. This right was of course not absolute. "All admit," said Douglass, "that the right to enjoy *liberty* largely depends upon the use made of that liberty" and that society must intervene whenever people abuse liberty "by invading the liberties of their fellows" through irresponsible or criminal behavior. But he insisted that blacks were just as capable as whites of learning to use their freedom wisely. And he regarded the "intelligent and upright free man of color" as "an unanswerable argument in favor of liberty, and a killing condemnation of American slavery."[36]

Douglass viewed slavery from a theological as well as from a natural-rights point of view. Like most abolitionists, he regarded slavery as a sin in the eyes of God as well as a violation of the principles of the Declaration of Independence. Though not a church member and though highly critical of organized religion for its complicity in slavery, Douglass was deeply religious and made frequent allusions to the Bible in his public addresses. We live, Douglass was continually saying (like Emerson), in a moral universe, governed by divine laws which people violate at their peril. According to the laws of God, all human beings are spiritually equal, members of a common family with a common destiny. "In the sight of the Most High . . . ," Douglass declared, "we stand upon a common and equal footing. With Him, there is neither Jew nor Gentile, barbarian nor Scythian. He is no respecter of persons, and hath made of one blood all nations for to dwell upon all the face of the earth."[37] God, said Douglass, "causes His sun to shine alike upon the black and the white—and the elements of nature to respond to the wants of all His creatures."[38] The Negro, like the white, "bears the seal of manhood" on his brow "from the hand of the living God" and possesses "an immortal soul, illuminated by intellect."[39] Douglass, like other abolitionist leaders, was anxious to establish a conviction among Americans that slavery was a monstrous sin, a crime against nature and nature's God, and a transgression against the laws of eternal justice. "Slavery has NO RIGHTS," he exclaimed impatiently in the *North Star* in February, 1850.

It is a foul and damning outrage upon all rights, and has no right to exist anywhere, in or out of the territories. "The earth is the Lord's" and "righteousness" should "cover it", and he who concedes any part of it to the introduction of slavery, is an enemy of God, an invader of his dominion, and a rebel against his government.

Douglass believed that the source of slavery and oppression lay in "the pride, the power, and the avarice of man," and like all abolitionists he sought a revolution in the hearts of men and conformity to the highest moral principles.[40] Rebellion against God, he warned, brought dire punishment, and the American people would pay a heavy penalty some day if they persisted in depriving the black of his freedom in contravention of God's law.

Douglass was no better at explaining the presence of evils like slavery in his moral universe that Paine had been. As a slave boy, he recalled, he found it difficult to reconcile the goodness of God with the enslavement of black people. But he finally decided that it was "not *God*, but *man*, that afforded the true explanation of the existence of slavery" and that "what man can make, man can unmake." At this point, he said, the "appalling darkness faded away, and I was master of the subject." While he never really explained to his own satisfaction why a benevolent Creator permitted slavery to flourish, he did come as a boy to believe firmly in the efficacy of human endeavor and to look with impatience on pious slaves who thought God required them to accept their lot with meekness and humility. And upon achieving freedom for himself, he dedicated his life to "unmaking" slavery for others and to encouraging his fellow blacks to prove their fitness for freedom by hard work and exemplary behavior. But he linked human effort closely with the causal moral laws by which he thought God governed creation. In an editorial in *Douglass' Monthly* shortly after the outbreak of the Civil War, in which he called on abolitionists to redouble their efforts, Douglass pointed out that

effects do evermore flow from causes, and are in exact accordance with them in meagerness or in magnitude. We may not always be able to comprehend the form and power of causes, or the extent of their operation by attending exclusively to them; but we know that plenty comes not of idleness, that figs are not gathered of thistles, nor grapes of thorns.

The Protestant Ethic—the doctrine, emphasized by the *Columbian Orator*, that God helps those who help themselves—was prominent in Douglass's thinking as it was in that of most of his associates in the abolitionist movement. But there was also a predestinarian note in his outlook. He was firmly convinced that slavery, being a loathsome evil, was destined by God's will to die and that slave owners and apologists for slavery were blind not to recognize that fact. The laws determining the destinies of nations and individuals were eternal, he said; slavery, which violated these laws, was doomed to extinction; and those guilty of complicity in slavery were headed toward inevitable disaster.

Douglass recognized that chance as well as human endeavor and moral law shaped history, and he was fully aware of the crucial importance of accidents in shaping his own and other people's lives. Nevertheless, he tended to feel that "there was something more intelligent than *chance*, and something more certain than luck" involved in the apparent accidents and seeming coincidences which he observed in the lives of human beings, and he came to accept the doctrine of the "special interposition of Divine Providence" in human affairs. Thus he reached a kind of balance in his thinking between human agency, moral causation, and Providential interposition which enabled him to fight the good fight with hope and determination even when things looked bleakest, because he was confident that "all the Divine powers of the universe are on the side of freedom and progress." In joyous moments (such as when Lincoln issued the Emancipation Proclamation) he even expressed faith in "the millennium—the final perfection of the [human] race." God predestines good to triumph and evil to fail, he came to believe, by helping those who help themselves and hurting those who hurt others. His views came to resemble those of Benjamin Franklin, who also believed that the free agency of man and the laws of nature shaped the course of human events but that on occasion God intervened to make sure that the rewarding of virtue and the punishing of evil were not left to chance.[41]

One of the inexorable laws on which Douglass counted was that law that "we shall reap what we sow." American whites, he declared, were already paying dearly for breaking God's laws. The enslavement of blacks, he thought, had had an adverse effect on the freedom of whites throughout the nation. In the South, perpetuating slavery required the suppression of antislavery sentiments among whites, and this meant discouraging freedom of thought and restricting freedom of speech. Calhoun himself was a victim of slavery.

How completely has slavery triumphed over the mind of this strong man! It holds full, complete, and absolute control in his mind; so much so, that seeing it, he cannot and does not desire to see anything else than slavery. The right of speech, the freedom of the press, the liberty of assembling, and the right of petition, have in his judgment no rightful existence in the Constitution of the United States.[42]

But the assault on freedom had been carried to the nonslaveholding states as well, and in the North friends of the South and enemies of the blacks were trampling on the right of petition, suppressing free discussion, fettering the press, gagging the pulpit, and terrorizing, even murdering, spokesmen for emancipation. Douglass continually emphasized the intimate connection between slavery for blacks and the suppression of free speech for whites. "Liberty," he said,

is meaningless where the right to utter one's thoughts and opinions has ceased to exist. That, of all rights, is the dread of tyrants. It is the right which they first of all strike down. They know its power. Thrones, dominions, principalities, and powers, founded in injustice and wrong, are sure to tremble, if men are allowed to reason of righteousness . . . and of a judgment to come in their presence.[43]

Douglass once said that if freedom of speech were permitted to flourish in the South for five years it would bring an end to the slave system.[44]

Douglass was so devoted to the principle of free speech that he was unwilling to deny it even to his enemies. During the Civil War he opposed the suppression of freedom of speech for Copperheads; he agreed with Jefferson, he said, in believing that error could be safely tolerated where reason was free to combat it.[45] His devotion to freedom, moreover, led him to support other struggles for human rights besides emancipation of his fellow blacks. He was a warm supporter of women's rights and participated in the convention for equal rights held in Seneca Falls, New York, in July, 1848. And though he admired Britain, he sympathized with the Irish; he identified himself, he said, with the poor and wretched everywhere, for "the cause of humanity is one the world over."[46] As he told Garrison:

I am the advocate of civil and religious liberty, all over the globe, and wherever tyranny exists, I am the foe of the tyrant; wherever oppression shows itself, I am the foe of the oppressor; wherever slavery rears its head, I am the enemy of the system, or the institution, call it by what name you will. I am the friend of liberty in every clime, class and color.[47]

Garrison, a moral universalist himself, heartily approved of his young co-worker's sentiments.

During his first few years as an abolitionist, Douglass was thoroughly Garrisonian. He viewed the U.S. Constitution as a slaveholder's document, accepted moral power, not political action, as the way to fight

slavery, and favored separation of the free states from the slave states
and dissolution of the Union. There were three clauses in the Constitution which Garrisonians like Douglass thought made it inimical to
freedom: the clause empowering the President to call out the armed
forces to suppress domestic insurrections, which seemed to be directed
against slave uprisings; the fugitive-slave clause, which Douglass called
"one of the most deadly enactments against the natural rights of man"
ever made; and the clause setting forth the "federal ratio" by which
slaves were counted as three-fifths of freemen in allotting representation
in Congress.[48] "The foundation of this government—the great Constitution itself—is nothing more than a compromise with man-stealers,"
wrote Douglass in May, 1847, and he said he would welcome an end
to the Union because under it "lie the prostrate forms of three millions
with whom I am identified."[49] He also said he would rather have his
right hand wither than cast a ballot under such a proslavery Constitution.[50] By 1849, however, he was beginning to modify his views. Under
the influence of Gerrit Smith and other political activists in the abolitionist movement, he was coming to believe that the Constitution,
properly interpreted, could be regarded as an antislavery document. The
word *slave*, he noted, appeared nowhere in the Constitution, and if the
document were to fall from the sky onto a land unfamiliar with slavery,
the people there would never dream there was anything in it sanctioning
human bondage. Douglass announced his change of mind at a meeting
of the American Anti-Slavery Society in Syracuse, New York, in May,
1851, and his relations with Garrison, already strained, soon came to a
final end.

Douglass "abolitionized" the U.S. Constitution by singling out clauses
in it which he thought were clearly incompatible with slavery. The
preamble to the Constitution, for one thing, began with the words, "We
the People"; not white people, not rich people, not privileged people,
Douglass emphasized, but all the people, white and black, rich and poor,
great and small, who lived in the United States. For another, the basic
purposes of the Union announced in the preamble (defense, welfare,
tranquillity, justice, and liberty) were all obviously inconsistent with
slavery and favorable to freedom. In the main body of the Constitution,
moreover, there were a number of provisions which Douglass thought
categorically ruled out slavery: the clause prohibiting bills of attainder;
the clause guaranteeing every person the right to a trial by jury; the
clause insuring every person the writ of habeas corpus; the clause stat-

ing that "no person shall be deprived of liberty without due process of law"; the clause specifying that "the right of the people to be secure in their persons shall not be violated"; and, finally, the clause asserting that "the United States shall guarantee to every State in this Union a republican form of government." All of these clauses, Douglass maintained, made slavery unconstitutional and imposed a duty on Congress to abolish it everywhere in the land. The Constitution was a charter of freedom, like the Declaration of Independence, not a slaveholder's document.[51]

Having given the Constitution an abolitionist reading, Douglass went on to reverse himself about the Union. Dissolving the Union, he now believed, would help, not hinder, slavery, for it would leave southern slaveholders free to manage the slaves as they pleased without any interference from the North. Douglass now favored drawing the bonds of Union more tightly in order to increase the power and influence of the free states in the Union and enable them to throw their weight more effectively against slavery in the South. Douglass also came to favor political action; he became active in the Liberty party, took an interest in the Free Soil party, and later supported the Republican party.[52]

As time passed, however, Douglass had growing doubts about whether either moral suasion or political action would be sufficient to bring an end to slavery. Sojourner Truth was upset when she heard him suggest that perhaps force was necessary to end the curse of slavery. "Frederick," she asked at one point, "is God dead?" "No," replied Douglass, "and because God is not dead slavery can only end in blood."[53] But though he helped fugitive slaves to escape, defended forcible resistance to slave-catchers, and said he would welcome a slave insurrection in the South, Douglass did not himself engage in force. He admired John Brown but refused to join in Brown's plan to raid Harpers Ferry in 1859, because, he said, his abolitionist work did not extend to attacking arsenals of the U.S. government. "The tools to those that can use them," he declared; his own tools were educational and political.[54]

## THE CIVIL WAR AND EMANCIPATION

When the Civil War came, Douglass was anxious to make it a war of liberation. His slogan was "carry the war to Africa," and he insisted that fighting slaveholders required emancipating slaves.[55] By freeing the slaves and enlisting blacks in the army, he said, the Union would win the enthusiastic support of four million blacks in fighting the Confederacy and thus hasten victory. *"The south says that the Union must die that slavery may live,"* he declared in July, 1862. *"The north must yet be brought to say, slavery shall die that the Union may live."*[56]

Douglass worked hard to abolitionize the war. Not only did he urge the Union government to make emancipation its major objective; he also put unremitting pressure on the Union army to accept black volunteers. After resistance to admitting blacks into the army gave way, Douglass toured the country encouraging Negro enlistments, and he also put pressure on the government to place black soldiers on an equality with white soldiers in matters of pay, promotions, and treatment as prisoners of war. When the Emancipation Proclamation was announced, Douglass greeted it with joy. Though disappointed by its perfunctory wording, he hailed it as a major step toward abolitionizing the war. "We are all liberated. . . . The black man is liberated, the brave men now fighting the battles of their country against rebels and traitors are now liberated, and may strike with all their might." Ever the hopeful idealist, Douglass thought the Proclamation was an advance in freedom for all men everywhere. "It is a mighty event for the bondman," he declared, "but it is a still mightier event for the nation at large, and mighty as it is for both, the slave and the nation, it is still mightier when viewed in its relation to the cause of truth and justice throughout the world."[57]

But though he was gratified by the Emancipation Proclamation and by the growing enlistment of blacks in the Union army, Douglass was disheartened by the lingering of old prejudices among northern whites. He was especially dismayed by the renewal of the campaign to colonize emancipated blacks in Africa or in other parts of the world. Douglass had opposed colonization from the very beginning of his career as an abolitionist. He held that it was just as logical to send whites back to Europe as to send blacks to Africa. American blacks, he told Montgomery Blair in September, 1862, "are Americans by birth and education, and have a preference for American institutions as against those of any other country."[58] Douglass insisted that the "native land of the American Negro is America. His bones, his muscle, his sinews, are all American. His ancestors for two hundred and seventy years have lived and laboured and died, on American soil, and millions of his posterity have inherited Caucasian blood."[59] Colonization was a "twin sister" of slavery as far as Douglass was concerned.[60] "But why, oh why!" he lamented, "may not men of different races inhabit in peace and happiness

this vast and wealthy country? . . . What is it in the American branch
of the Anglo-Saxon race which renders it incapable of tolerating the
presence of any people in the country different from themselves?"[61]
When Lincoln advised some black leaders who conferred with him in
the White House to support colonization, Douglass castigated the President as arrogant, hypocritical, and contemptuous of Negroes.[62]

Toward Lincoln Douglass had mixed feelings. There were qualities
in Lincoln's character and personality which he found enormously appealing; he also gave Lincoln generous praise whenever he thought his
policies were advancing the cause of freedom. On the other hand, he
could not contain his impatience with the President's reluctance to
abolitionize the war and his willingness to compromise, in the early war
years, on issues Douglass regarded as crucial to the struggle for freedom.

There was much to deplore in Lincoln: the low priority he gave
emancipation at first; his excessive concern for the loyalty of the border
slave states; his solicitude for conservative white opinion in the North;
his revocation of orders by some of the Union generals freeing slaves
escaping to Union lines; his slowness to accept blacks in the Union army;
and his support of colonization schemes. Long after the war was over,
Douglass still had not forgiven Lincoln for his procrastination on
emancipation. In a speech at the unveiling of the freedmen's monument
to Lincoln in Washington on April 14, 1876, Douglass frankly told
his mixed audience (which included President Grant):

He was preeminently the white man's President, entirely devoted to the welfare of white men. He was ready and willing at any time during the
first years of his administration to deny, postpone, and sacrifice the rights of
humanity in the colored people to promote the welfare of the white people
of this country. . . . The race to which we belong were not the special objects of his consideration. . . . First, midst, and last, you and yours were the
objects of his deepest affection and his most earnest solicitude. You are the
children of Abraham Lincoln. We are at best only his step-children; children
by adoption, children by forces of circumstances and necessity.[63]

But Douglass recognized that there was another side to Lincoln:
despite his slowness, the cause of freedom did somehow advance steadily
during his administration. Under Lincoln's "wise and beneficent rule,"
Douglass pointed out, some 200,000 blacks enlisted in the armed forces
to fight for liberty and Union. Under Lincoln, the internal slave trade
was abolished and slavery was eliminated in the District of Columbia.

Under Lincoln, the law was enforced for the first time against the foreign slave trade and the first slave-trader was hanged "like any other pirate or murderer." Under Lincoln came the Thirteenth Amendment to the Constitution, ending slavery for all time in the American republic. Under Lincoln, diplomatic recognition was first extended to the black republic of Haiti (the "special object of slaveholding aversion and horror") and the Haitian minister was cordially welcomed by the President in Washington.[64] From Douglass's point of view, Lincoln had moved slowly during the war; but he had moved swiftly, Douglass admitted, by the standards of most northern whites.

Douglass met Lincoln on three occasions during the war, and each time he was impressed by his simple, natural friendliness and his freedom from all pomp and ceremony. Douglass's respect for Lincoln's fairness, honesty, and wisdom increased with each encounter, and he came to believe that Lincoln was profoundly committed to the cause of freedom. He was especially struck by Lincoln's entire lack of pretentiousness and condescension. "Mr. Lincoln was not only a great President," Douglass concluded, "but a *great man*—too great to be small in anything. In his company I was never in any way reminded of my humble origin, or of my unpopular color."[65] In all his interviews with Lincoln, Douglass said, he was

impressed with his entire freedom from popular prejudice against the colored race. He was the first great man that I talked with in the United States freely, who in no single instance reminded me of the difference between himself and myself, of the difference in color, and I thought that all the more remarkable because he came from a state where there were black laws.[66]

Long before Union victory was in sight, Douglass was giving thought to the question of what to do with the slave after emancipation. His initial impulse was to recommend laissez-faire liberty, pure and simple, as a postwar policy. In an article on "What Shall Be Done with the Slaves If Emancipated?" for *Douglass' Monthly* in January, 1862, he told white Americans:

Our answer is, do nothing with them; mind your business, and let them mind theirs. Your *doing* with them is their greatest misfortune. They have been undone by your doings, and all they now ask, and really have need of at your hands, is just to let them alone. They suffer by every interference, and succeed best by being let alone.

Douglass went on to say that whenever whites wanted to do anything for blacks, it usually meant depriving them of some right, power, or privilege for which they themselves would die rather than give it up. Perhaps, then, the best policy would be simply to let the freedman alone and "mind your own business." But he explained what this entailed:

If you see him plowing in the open field, leveling the forest, at work with a spade, a rake, a hoe, a pick-axe, or a bill—let him alone; he has a right to work. If you see him on his way to school, with spelling book, geography and arithmetic in his hands—let him alone. Don't shut the door in his face, nor bolt your gates against him; he has a right to learn—let him alone. Don't pass laws to degrade him. If he has a ballot in his hand, and is on his way to the ballot-box to deposit his vote for the man whom [sic] he thinks will most justly and wisely administer the Government which has the power of life and death over him, as well as others—let him *alone*; his right of choice as much deserves respect and protection as your own. If you see him on his way to the church, exercising religious liberty in accordance with this or that religious persuasion—let him alone.—Don't meddle with him, nor trouble yourselves with any question as to what shall be done with him.[67]

Laissez-faire, in short, meant removing all obstacles to the Negro's full citizenship. Douglass recognized, to be sure, that the ex-slave needed more than this to adjust to his new situation, and after the war he wanted Congress to adopt measures enabling the freedom to purchase land on easy terms. Still, he never wavered in his belief that the eradication of all the restraints of discriminatory laws and practices would go a long way toward transforming the black from a slave into a freeman. Laissez-faire toward the blacks, as Douglass conceived it, was not an end in itself but a necessary condition for black citizenship. And citizenship included the right to vote as well as the right to enjoy all the civil rights which American whites enjoyed. Douglass placed special emphasis on Negro suffrage. The ballot, he said, was "essential to the freedom of the freedman" because it was "the only measure which could prevent him from being thrust back into slavery."[68] Like Paine, Douglass thought the right to vote was indispensable to political freedom because in a representative system it was the one great power on which all other individual rights rested. The liberties of Americans, he said, rested on the ballot-box, the jury-box, and the cartridge-box, and the Negro must have all three in order to "guard, protect, and maintain his liberty" as a citizen.[69]

Douglass wanted more than equal rights for blacks. He also wanted to see the wall of separation between blacks and whites crumble after the Civil War. A thorough assimilationist whose second wife was white, he had a great vision of racial brotherhood in America. "I expect," he told W. J. Wilson jauntily in August, 1865,

to see the colored people of this country, enjoying the same freedom, voting at the same ballot-box, using the same cartridge-box, going to the same schools, attending the same churches, travelling in the same street cars, in the same railroad cars, on the same steam-boats, proud of the same country, fighting the same foe, and enjoying the same peace and all its advantages.[70]

He was by turns hopeful and despondent as he observed the march of events in the postwar era. At times he thought southerners were making "wondrous progress in their ideas of freedom," that "a new dispensation of justice, kindness, and human brotherhood" was dawning in the nation at large, and that victory in the Negro's struggle for freedom, "if not complete," was "at least assured."[71] On other occasions he was plunged into despair as he observed the "reactionary tendencies of public opinion against the black man" and a decline in the "sentiment that gave us a reconstructed Union on a basis of liberty for all people."[72] By 1872 he was remonstrating with Congress for not enforcing the Fourteenth and Fifteenth Amendments to the Constitution guaranteeing the Negro his civil rights.[73] By 1881 he was puzzling over the persistence of "The Color Line" in America for the *North American Review*, denying that it was either natural or inevitable and suggesting that it had something to do with economic status.[74] By 1883 he was accusing the Supreme Court of having hauled down the "flag of liberty" when it invalidated the Civil Rights Act of 1875.[75]

As time passed, it became increasingly difficult to be sanguine about the future; but Douglass did his best. He kept hoping that the Republican party would "cease its backsliding" and resume its old character as the "party of progress, justice, and freedom."[76] Occupying the position of elder statesman among American blacks during his last years, Douglass seemed to think that his work for the Republican party was in some fashion helpful to the people of his race and that his own good standing with Republican officials was a sign of good will by a great party toward the Negro and a promise of things to come. At election time he dutifully took to the stump and denounced Democrats and rallied black votes for the party. His disappointment with Republican leaders for their declining interest in his people mounted steadily, but he tried to stifle his

doubts, hoped for the best, remained a party regular, and opposed both
the Liberal Republican revolt against Grant in 1872 and the Mugwump
revolt against James G. Blaine in 1884. He even supported Republican
plans for expansion abroad, arguing that with the achievement of emancipation, the extension of American power and influence overseas could
only be beneficent.

He was rewarded for his party services by appointments as assistant
secretary of a commission to sound out Santo Domingo on annexation
(which he favored) in 1871, as marshal of the District of Columbia
in 1877, as recorder of deeds for the District in 1881, and as minister
to Haiti in 1889. But at the same time he was receiving these honors,
he was asked by Republican leaders to stay away from a National Loyal-
ist convention in Philadelphia in 1866 (to which he had been elected
as the only black); he was excluded from the dining room of a government vessel on which the Santo Domingo commissioners were traveling; he was omitted from the guest list when the commissioners dined
with President Grant on returning from Santo Domingo; he was not
invited to attend presidential receptions as district marshal (as previous
marshals had) in order to introduce guests at White House state occasions; and when he sailed to Haiti as U.S. minister, the captain of the
ship refused to eat at the same table with him.

Douglass chafed under these slights and humiliations, but in the
last edition of *Life and Times of Frederick Douglass,* appearing in 1892,
he tried to minimize or explain away the neglect and indifference with
which he had been treated by Presidents to whom he had been so loyal.
Still, he could not down the feeling that the best part of his life had
ended at Appomattox.[77] In the last edition of his autobiography he included nostalgic accounts of revisits to the places of his boyhood, and
he even described a reunion with his former master Thomas Auld.

Though times looked increasingly bleak for American blacks in the
1880s and 1890s, Douglass did not lose heart; and he was too fundamentally religious ever to become cynical. He never abandoned his deep
faith in universal freedom or his feeling that somehow things would
improve for his people in God's good time. His belief that all human
beings, regardless of race, sex, or social condition, possessed a natural
right to freedom had, he thought, the support of "all the invisible forces
of the moral government of the universe."[78] Freedom was indivisible
in Douglass's universe, and the other side of the coin was universal
slavery. "No man," he continued to say to the end, "can put a chain

about the ankle of his fellow-man, without at last finding the other end
of it about his own neck."[79] It helped, at any rate, to keep the faith if
one reminded himself from time to time that there would eventually be
a day of reckoning for those who betrayed the faith.

Occasionally the old fire returned and Douglass lashed out against
the enemies of black freedom with the magnificent scorn and wrath of
the young abolitionist. Returning from a tour of the South in March,
1888, shocked by conditions among Negro sharecroppers and convinced
that perhaps "so-called emancipation" had been a stupendous fraud
after all, Douglass made a biting speech in Washington in which he
blistered the federal government for abandoning the black, ignoring his
rights, and leaving him a "deserted, a defrauded, a swindled, and an
outcast man—in law, free; in fact, a slave."[80] His last essay, published
in June, 1894, was a vigorous attack on lynching, economic exploitation
of the blacks, and efforts to deprive them of the vote in the South.[81]

Shortly before his death following a heart attack while attending a
meeting of the National Council of Women in Washington in February,
1895, Douglass was interviewed by a Negro student in Providence,
Rhode Island. "What have you to say to a young Negro just starting
out?" the young man asked. "What should he do?" And Douglass is
said to have exclaimed: "Agitate! Agitate! Agitate!"[82] Even in his last
book he had turned aside for a moment from apologies for the shabby
behavior of American Presidents to remark that many Republicans
"found it much more agreeable to talk of the principles of liberty as
glittering generalities, than to reduce those principles to practice."[83] At
another point, he also suddenly burst out with an opinion he had expressed many times in the old abolitionist days: "Nowhere in the world
are the worth and dignity of manhood more exalted in speech and press
than they are here, and nowhere is manhood pure and simple more
despised than here."[84] And to his beloved fellow countrymen, most of
whom still shared his teleological view of the universe, he gave this
final warning:

The lesson of all the ages upon this point is, that a wrong done to one man
is a wrong done to all men. It may not be felt at the moment, and the evil
may be long delayed, but so long as there is a moral government of the
universe, so sure as there is a God of the universe, so sure will the harvest
of evil come.[85]

# 6

# Edward Bellamy's
# Collectivistic Freedom

EDWARD BELLAMY WAS UNUSUAL for his day: he thought freedom was a collective rather than an individual undertaking, and he regarded the American tradition of personal salvation and individual enterprise in which he was reared as out of place in an age of corporate organization. "We nationalists," he wrote in 1893, "are not trying to work out our individual salvation, but the weal of all, and no man is a true nationalist who even wishes to be saved unless all the rest are. A slight amendment in the condition of the mass of men is preferable to elysium attained by the few."[1] The doctrine of the elect was outmoded, he insisted, in both religion and economics. But it took him some years to shuck off the doctrine himself. And although he eventually became famous as a utopian reformer, his initial revolt was in religion rather than in economics. Bellamy came to think that both Calvinism and capitalism were major enemies of freedom, but when he was young liberating himself from Calvinist imperatives seemed a matter of special urgency.

## UP FROM CALVINISM

That Bellamy's revolt came in religion first is not surprising. His boyhood was something like Jonathan Edwards's. Son of a Baptist minister in Chicopee Falls, Massachusetts, he attended two services on Sunday, went to Sunday school, participated in family devotions, said prayers every night before retiring, and believed that "he was a grievous sinner, accursed from God with whom he must make peace or suffer the most terrible consequences." Unlike Edwards, he drifted rapidly away from the orthodoxy of his home after a short-lived conversion at fourteen, and by his early twenties he had discarded the faith of his fathers and was trying to work out a religion of humanity which would be free of the fear, guilt, and anxiety produced by the Calvinist consciousness.[2]

Bellamy's revolt against Calvinism was thoroughgoing; he rejected its psychology as well as its theology. Too much conscience, he decided, was as harmful as "actual depravity"; Calvinism's "sick conscientiousness" encouraged selfishness, not brotherly love, for it made people too absorbed in their own feelings of guilt to relate creatively to other people. The puritanical restraints of Calvinism also struck him as life-denying, and he came to deplore the false modesty, hypocrisy, and prudishness produced by efforts of pious people to suppress man's emotional life. "For God's sake," he exclaimed, "off with these interminable veils and petticoats wherewith ages of prudes have covered the antique strength and ruggedness of man's true nature. Let us for God's sake get at the truth and have done with our ahs and ohs and qualms and queries."[3]

Bellamy never seriously considered entering his father's profession, as Edwards did, even during the days of his conversion. He wanted to be a soldier. But after failing the physical examination at West Point he tried law briefly, and then took up journalism. As editorial writer and book reviewer for the *Springfield Union* and other newspapers he began to develop a social conscience. A trip to Europe with a wealthy cousin first opened his eyes to "the existence and urgency of the social problem," and his newspaper work familiarized him with the leading issues of the day: political corruption, the Granger movement, immigration, child labor, tenements, conditions among factory workers, and women's rights. He came to be moved by social injustice as much as by religious tyranny, and he was increasingly convinced that industrial capitalism was a "social barbarism" based on oppression and violating the plainest principles of equity.[4]

In an address before the Chicopee Falls Village Lyceum in the early 1870s, Bellamy warned that an aristocracy of wealth was coming to dominate the nation, and he called for a fairer division of the burdens and pleasures of life and a more equitable distribution of the fruits of labor. "I only ask," he said, "that none labor beyond measure that others may be idle, that there be no more masters and no more slaves among men. Is this too much? . . . Not so, for nothing that is just can be impossible."[5]

Poor health forced him to leave the *Union* in 1877 and take a trip to Hawaii with his brother. On his return he became a free-lance writer. During the next two years he published three novels and seven short stories. He continued to be interested in political and economic problems, but his earliest fiction concentrated mainly on psychological rather than social themes. Only *The Duke of Stockbridge* (1879), dealing with Shays' Rebellion, revealed any of his serious interest in social issues. Apparently Bellamy had to come to grips with the burden of the past, especially the Calvinist heritage, before tackling the burden of the present. The past meant slavery: anxiety, guilt, melancholy, and a sense of failure. Bellamy knew all of these in abundance until he finally found his "*great work*" in life as a writer and reformer. The future meant freedom: rising above one's petty individuality, with all its fears and frustrations, and dedicating oneself to the cause of humanity. "Forward, not backward, is the law of life and work," Bellamy insisted; but it was necessary, he thought, for people to free themselves from the "mind-paralyzing worship of the past" before they could move ahead.[6]

## THE DEAD HAND OF THE PAST

A French critic, with *Looking Backward* in mind, once referred to Bellamy as the "Jules Verne of socialism"; if he had been acquainted with Bellamy's earlier writings he might have called him the "Jules Verne of psychology".[7] For Bellamy's imaginative ventures into the workings of a society freed from social and economic oppression were preceded by fanciful probings into the workings of a human psyche released from the intolerable burden of past memories. "Ghosts of the future are the only sort worth heeding," says young Henry in "The Old Folks' Party" (1876), one of Bellamy's first short stories. "Apparitions of things past are a very unpractical sort of demonology, in my opinion, compared with apparitions of things to come."[8] It was the interplay between apparitions of things past and things to come in the life-history of the individual that formed the major theme of Bellamy's earliest short stories and novels. In "The Old Folks' Party," a group of young people experiment with a masquerade party in which they attempt to

act out their roles as they conceive themselves to be fifty years hence.
They are startled, somewhat frightened, by the apparent disparity between their actual selves at twenty and their assumed identities at
seventy, and one of them concludes that "there are half a dozen of each
one of us, or a dozen if you please, one in fact for each epoch of life, and
each slightly or almost wholly different from the others. Each one of
these epochs is foreign and inconceivable to the others, as ourselves at
seventy now are to us."[9]

The idea that the life of an individual consists of a succession of
separate and distinct personalities continued to fascinate Bellamy, and in
a story entitled "Lost," published in 1877, he carried it one step farther.
A young American visiting Bonn becomes engaged to a German girl,
but upon his return to the United States he promptly forgets all about
her. Seven years later he is suddenly overwhelmed by guilt for having
deserted her and returns to Germany determined to make amends. When,
after a frantic search, he finally locates her, he discovers that she has
become an entirely different person from the girl he had jilted. Long
since happily married, she is now stout, jolly, and matronly, with scarcely
any recollection of their former relationship. It is impossible for him
to atone for his heartless behavior, he learns, because the girl whom he
offended no longer exists; nor, for that matter, does the callous young
man who mistreated her exist any longer. Both have become quite new
identities and it dawns on him that

amends were never possible, nor can men ever make atonement; for, ere the
debt is paid, the atonement made, one who is not the sufferer stands to receive it; while on the other hand, the one who atones is not the offender,
but one who comes after loathing his offense and himself incapable of it.
The dead must bury their dead.[10]

But most people, Bellamy suggests, are denied the insight of the sensible
young man; they go through life plagued by the memory of their past
mistakes. Their consciences are hopelessly Calvinistic.

In his first major novel, *Dr. Heidenhoff's Process* (1880), Bellamy
not only explored the destructive effects of guilt feelings on the human
personality but also, speaking through the "mental physiologist" Dr.
Heidenhoff, argued that "these black devils of evil memories" are without either intellectual or moral justification.[11] "What is past," he insists,
"is eternally past," and only fools pride themselves on their past virtues

or tortue themselves over their past misdeeds.[12] "Memory," asserts Dr. Heidenhoff,

is the principle of moral degeneration. Remembered sin is the most utterly diabolical influence in the universe. It invariably either debauches or martyrizes men and women, accordingly as it renders them desperate and hardened, or makes them a prey to undying grief and self-contempt. When I consider that more sin is the only anodyne for sin, and that the only way to cure the ache of conscience is to harden it, I marvel that even so many as do, essay the bitter and hopeless way of repentance and reform. In the main, the pangs of conscience, so vaunted by some, do most certainly drive ten people deeper into sin where they bring one back to virtue.[13]

In *Dr. Heidenhoff's Process*, Madeline Brand is Bellamy's example of a victim of evil memories. A young lady with an impeccable reputation in her little village, she enters into a liaison with the town clerk, and when she is abandoned she flees to Boston in despair. The efforts of Henry Burr, a former suitor (who is willing to forgive and forget and whose offer of marriage she listessly accepts), to console her prove unavailing. The memory of her disgrace totally incapacitates her for living: "She no longer thought of herself in the present tense, still less the future."[14] One morning, however, she discovers that she has fallen in love with Henry and she is momentarily restored to health. Then memory lays "its icy finger on her heart" and she is plunged into still deeper remorse for having dared even for an instant to be happy.[15] Hearing of a "thought-extirpation" process being developed by Dr. Heidenhoff, whereby it may be possible "to extract a specific recollection from the memory as readily as a dentist pulls a tooth," the distraught Madeline seeks the doctor's assistance in hope of achieving peace of mind.[16] Dr. Heidenhoff feels obliged to defend his mode of treatment morally before accepting Madeline as a patient. "I say," he tells the couple, quite un-Calvinistically,

that there is no such thing as moral responsibility for past acts, no such thing as real justice in punishing them, for the reason that human beings are not stationary existences, but changing, growing, incessantly progressive organisms, which in no two moments are the same. Therefore justice, whose only possible mode of proceeding is to punish in present time for what is done in past time, must always punish a person more or less similar to, but never identical with, the one who committed the offense, and therein must be no justice . . . . The difference between the past and present selves of the same individual is so great as to make them different persons for all moral purposes.[17]

Dr. Heidenhoff acknowledges that society must punish crimes as a matter of social expediency, but he insists that the rationale for punishment is deterrence, not justice, for the present bears no moral responsibility for the past. When individuals come to experience sincere regret for an act which they have committed, he says, they have thereby repented of that act; and, according to every theory of moral accountability, their repentance balances the moral account for them. Yet the nature of our culture is such that recollection of the past misdeed continues to torment sensitive souls like Madeline, and their moral recovery is incomplete. By erasing this memory from their minds, therefore, the doctor's "thought-extirpation" process simply completes physically what has already been accomplished morally. Ministers and moralists "tell the penitent he is forgiven," the doctor points out, but they leave him a prisoner of his disagreeable memory. Dr. Heidenhoff offers the penitent genuine freedom from the past and the opportunity of resuming an unconstricted and useful life in the present. "I free him from his sin," says the doctor. "Remorse and shame and wan regret have wielded their cruel sceptres over human lives, from the beginning until now. Seated within the mysterious labyrinths of the brain, they have deemed their sway secure, but the lightning of science has reached them on their thrones and set their bondmen free."[18]

Madeline is eventually given a form of electric-shock treatment by the doctor and, with the obliteration of the unpleasant memory from her consciousness, is restored to full emotional health. The novel ends, however, with Henry's awakening from a dream, and it turns out that Dr. Heidenhoff and his electrotherapy were only figments of Henry's imagination. Henry then learns the cruel truth: Madeline, unwilling to let him "pick up from the gutter a soiled rose," has taken her life.[19] The past, as ever in a Puritanic culture, has devoured the present.

In *Miss Ludington's Sister* (1884), subtitled "A Romance of Immortality," Bellamy experimented once more with his notion that an individual is composed of a multiplicity of successive personalities—infancy, childhood, youth, maturity, and old age—and suggested the possiblility that each of these personalities, upon dying, becomes immortal. Young Paul falls madly in love with a portrait of his aging cousin, Ida Ludington, made when she was only seventeen. Coming to believe in the immortality of past selves, he seeks the assistance of a spiritualistic medium in calling forth Miss Ludington's former youthful self from the spirit world. He is preposterously successful: not only does the young spirit appear to him at a séance but, what is more, she is eventually "materialized" and goes to live with her wealthy "sister" on the latter's lavish estate. (Bellamy may not have been a great writer, a European critic remarked, but at least the subject matter of his fiction was never hackneyed.)[20] When Paul reveals his profound devotion and proposes marriage, however, the young woman flees in shame (as did so many of Bellamy's heroines) to the anonymity of the big city. The materialization has, of course, been a hoax, contrived by the impecunious medium to get her niece into the well-to-do Ludington household. But it is impossible for the niece, having fallen in love with Paul, to continue the deception, and in the end she confesses everything. But Miss Ludington and Paul (who are as un-Calvinistic as Dr. Heidenhoff) readily forgive her:

> Their habit of distinguishing between the successive phases of an individual life as distinct persons, made it impossible for them to take any other view of the matter.
> In their eyes the past was good or bad for itself, and the present good or bad for itself, and an evil past could no more shadow a virtuous present than a virtuous present could retroact to brighten or redeem an ugly past. It is the soul that repents which is ennobled by repentance. The soul that did the deed repented of is past forgiving. There was no affectation on the part of Paul or Miss Ludington of ignoring the fraud which Ida [the niece] had practised, or pretending to forget it. This was not necessary out of any consideration for her feelings, for they did not hold that it was she who was guilty of that fraud, but another person.[21]

Since Miss Ludington's young "sister," unlike Madeline Brand, comes to recognize the disparateness of the past and the present, it is possible for her to throw off her sense of guilt and reenter the society of the living as a free and creative person. In the end she and Paul are happily married and Miss Ludington, an aged spinster who had been obsessed by memories of her own lost youthful beauty, also decides to break with the past and start living in the present. She muses:

> It is very strange to see people who dread death always looking forward for it instead of backward. In their fear of dying they quite forget that they have died already many times. It is the most foolish of all things to imagine

that by prolonging the career of the individual, death is kept at bay. The present self must die in any case by the inevitable process of time, whether the body be kept in repair for later selves or not. The death of the body is but the end of the daily dying that makes up earthly life.[22]

It is not necessary, surely, to assume that Bellamy held a literal belief in the curious doctrine of multiple identities presented here. His major interest was in dramatizing in a new form his favorite theme that the past is dead and gone and it is the present that matters.

In his rebellion against the tyranny of the past, Bellamy even toyed with the idea that humanity's fatal taint lay in the fact that *homo sapiens* was endowed with a faculty of memory rather than with a faculty of foresight. In one of his last stories, "The Blindman's World" (1886), a professor of astronomy visits Mars in a dream and encounters a race of creatures who, because they have foreknowledge of their individual careers on Mars, despise the past and live wholly in the present and the future. Earth people, one of the Martians tells the professor, are indeed pitiable, blindfolded creatures; all their knowledge, affections, and interests are rooted in the past, and as they grow older their memories become increasingly precious possessions which they are reluctant to give up in death. "The accumulated treasures of memory," he says,

which you relinquish so painfully in death, we count no loss at all. Our minds being fed wholly from the future, we think and feel only as we anticipate; and so, as the dying man's future contracts, there is less and less about which he can occupy his thoughts. His interest in life diminishes as the ideas which it suggests grow fewer, till at the last death finds him with his mind a *tabula rasa*, as with you at birth. In a word, his concern with life is reduced to a vanishing point before he is called on to give it up. In dying he leaves nothing behind.[23]

Not only does the faculty of foresight make death easy to accept; it also makes life supremely happy. With foreknowledge, Martians look forward to moments of happiness—love, friendship, personal achievement—with eager anticipation instead of backward on them with regret, as people on earth do because they did not realize at the time how happy they were. Since Martians know what the future will bring them, moreover, they experience neither hope nor fear; everyone knows his individual destiny, and there is no rivalry, emulation, or competition on Mars. Remorse and regret are unheard of. Impressed by life among the Martians, the narrator of the story concludes:

The lack of foresight among the human faculties, a lack I had scarcely thought of before, now impresses me, ever more deeply, as a fact out of harmony with the rest of our nature, belying its promise,—a moral mutilation, a deprivation so arbitrary and unaccountable. The spectacle of a race doomed to walk backward, beholding only what has gone by, assured only of what is past and dead, comes over me from time to time with a sadly fantastical effect which I cannot describe. I dream of a world where love always wears a smile, where the partings are as tearless as our meetings, and death is king no more.[24]

Bellamy's fantasy obviously rested on two highly questionable assumptions: that the future his Martians foresaw was charted with precision, and that knowledge of the future would not affect people's behavior in such a way as to alter that future. (Bertrand Russell made similar assumptions when he, like Bellamy, speculated in one of his books about "a set of beings who know the whole future with absolute certainty."[25]) But Bellamy, who had thrown off his boyhood Calvinism, didn't really think the future was predestined; he simply wanted people to thrust aside the dead hand of the past (which seemed "postdestined") so they could gain some control over the future.

The dream of a world emancipated from servitude to the past dominated Bellamy's entire writing career. Nevertheless, he was interested in social as well as psychological problems, and he became increasingly convinced that the two were intimately related. In the beginning, when he was struggling against Calvinistic imperatives himself, Bellamy seems to have believed that freedom comes largely from within the individual and that it involves breaking the chains imposed upon one's spirit by the past-obsessed conscience. But his European experience and his growing familiarity as a journalist with the conflicts and tensions of a rapidly industrializing America led him to the conclusion that human freedom was primarily a matter of equitable social and economic arrangements and that social freedom was an indispensable condition for the flowering of spiritual freedom. He was ready at this point to turn from psychological to social fantasy, and the stage was prepared for the composition of *Looking Backward, 2000-1887*.

Bellamy began writing *Looking Backward* late in 1886 as "a mere literary fantasy, a fairy tale of social felicity."[26] But as he proceeded, his mounting passion for social justice came to the foreground and he ended by sketching a complete outline for social reconstruction which he regarded with the utmost seriousness. The publication of the novel in

January, 1888, made him famous overnight, and from that time until his death in 1898 he was absorbed in the affairs of the Nationalist movement, which grew up in the late 1880s and sought to socialize the American economy according to Bellamy's principles.

In his last novel, *Equality* (1897), a sequel to *Looking Backward*, Bellamy replied at length to the major objections to his proposals raised by critics. He never returned to psychological fiction. "It would indeed be a delight to me to revert to those psychologic studies and speculations which were the themes of my earlier writings," he admitted to Horace Scudder. "But since my eyes have been opened to the evils and faults of our social state and I have begun to cherish a clear hope of things better, I simply 'can't get my consent' to write or think of anything else."[27] He devoted his remaining years to lecturing on the principles of Nationalism and writing essays on the subject for the *Nationalist* and the *New Nation* (which he founded), organs of the Nationalist movement, and for popular magazines. In his later writings, as in *Looking Backward*, he was anxious to convince the American people that drastic social change could come about without force and violence, without class conflict and hatred, and without militant hostility to religion. He also wanted to demonstrate that liberty and equality, time-honored American watchwords, were not antithetical concepts, as the Social Darwinists of his age contended, but were intimately united.

### LIBERTY AND EQUALITY IN BELLAMY'S UTOPIA

William Graham Sumner, speaking probably for the majority of middle-class Americans during the Gilded Age, laid it down as a rule that liberty and equality were absolutely incompatible. "Let it be understood," he announced, "that we cannot go outside of this alternative: liberty, inequality, survival of the fittest; not-liberty, equality, survival of the unfittest. The former carries society forward and favors all its best members; the latter carries society downward and favors all its worst members."[28] If the state, Sumner declared, attempts to equalize conditions among its citizens through welfare measures, it destroys the liberty, and thus the incentive, of ambitious individuals who wish to get ahead of their fellows, deprives society of their enterprising talents, and ends by reducing the nation to a state of economic stagnation. For Sumner, the only progressive system was the competitive-capitalist system. By guaranteeing freedom of competition for profit and by securing private-property rights, the capitalist state, according to Sumner, insures

that the ablest individuals rise to the top and the incompetent fall by
the wayside. Social and economic inequality is necessary, he insisted, to
both individual liberty and social progress.

Bellamy sharply challenged Sumner's Social Darwinist views. Not
only did he insist that liberty and equality were compatible; he also insisted that without equality there could be no true liberty. The industrial
commonwealth which he portrayed in *Looking Backward* and for which
he crusaded during his last years was founded on the principle of
economic equality. In his novel, public capitalism or Nationalism
(Bellamy carefully avoided the word *socialism* because of its pejorative
connotations for most Americans) was to replace private capitalism by
means of a bloodless revolution at the end of the nineteenth century,
and a "Republic of the Golden Rule" was to take the place of the dog-
eat-dog American Republic of the Gilded Age. In Bellamy's utopian
society, which Julian West, a rich young Bostonian, awakens from a
long sleep to discover in the year 2000, every citizen, including women,
serves in a national industrial army in various capacities between the
ages of twenty-one and forty-five, receives for his services credit tickets,
throughout his entire lifetime, amounting to around $4,000 a year in
value, and, in addition, is provided with innumerable free health, education, and welfare benefits by the nation. The industrial army, Julian
learns, consists of three grades of private soldiers and a hierarchy of
officers composed of lieutenants, captains (foremen), and lieutenant-
generals (department chiefs). At the head is a General-in-Chief (President of the United States), elected by citizens who have completed their
twenty-one-year tour of duty, and a council of economic advisers made
up of the chiefs of the ten great departments supervising the economy.
All officers, including the President, must have started as privates and
worked their way up through the ranks.

In Utopia 2000 A.D. the profit motive has been outlawed, and in
its place public service, prestige, and power have become the main in-
centives to economic endeavor. According to Bellamy, the first motive
("the sense of honorable and moral obligation to do one's duty" for
one's country and one's fellowman) would increase steadily in importance in a system based on justice and fair play for all. The second
motive (the "love of approbation, the desire to be well thought of, and
to be admired by one's fellow men and women") was for Bellamy the
most powerful, constant, and universal of human motives. He arranged
for it to be stimulated by medals, honors, prizes, and promotions for

meritorious service in the industrial army. And the third motive ("the desire of power, authority, and public station, the wish to lead and direct instead of being led and directed") would, he thought, spur people on to work hard in order to advance in rank in the national army. Two motives important for capitalism—fear of poverty and desire for inordinate wealth—have no place in Bellamy's utopia.[29]

In its efforts to increase production and facilitate the distribution of goods, the administration managing the economy makes every effort to develop each citizen's natural aptitudes and to permit him to choose the occupation for which he is best fitted and which he most enjoys. Under a program of national planning, made possible by total mobilization of the country's economic resources, the uncertainties, wastes, and periodic crises, as well as the inequities, of nineteenth-century capitalism have vanished. An economy of scarcity gives way to an economy of abundance in which all citizens share equally. The United States becomes an astonishingly affluent society (with radios, air cars, concrete highways, air conditioning, and electrical tractors) and health, harmony, and happiness reign among its citizens. Since no one misbehaves any more, the problem of the sickly conscience, which had once bothered Bellamy, is implicitly solved. In a sermon which Julian, for a small credit-card fee, hears over an ingenious telephonic device, Rev. Mr. Barton declares proudly: "Humanity's ancient dream of liberty, equality, fraternity, mocked by so many ages, at last was realized."[30] But how much liberty, Julian asks Dr. Leete, his mentor in the new society, actually coexists with so much equality and fraternity?

Dr. Leete assures Julian that individual dignity and freedom are held in highest regard in the cooperative commonwealth and that "there is far less interference of any sort with personal liberty nowadays" than there was in Julian's society.[31] There is, first of all, the freedom of everyone from care which Nationalism insures by means of generous equal incomes and numerous free public services. The new nation has become "a universal insurance company for the purpose of assuring all its members against want, oppression, accident, or disability of whatever sort."[32]

Next, there is the freedom of each individual to select the vocation which appeals most to him and for which he has special talents. Before entering the service at twenty-one, people have a chance to discover their interests and aptitudes in school. Then, upon joining the industrial army, they spend the first three years performing common labor and becoming familiar with the wide variety of occupations from which they will select their life's work. At the end of this initial period, each person chooses his vocation (agricultural, mechanical, professional) and enrolls in the school offering the appropriate training. Upon completing the required courses he launches on his career; and he has until the age of thirty to make his final choice.

In addition to being free from care and free to work at what they enjoy, citizens in the new republic are also free to utilize their credit-tickets in any way they please. They may spend them on consumer's goods; or they may decide to pool some of their credits and found a newspaper, organize a church, publish a book, or produce a play. The government prints the newspaper, publishes the book, furnishes buildings and equipment, and gives released time from industrial service for all voluntary activities of this kind (in return for credit-card fees), but it scrupulously avoids censorship or control in any form.

Finally, upon retirement from the industrial army at forty-five citizens are completely "enfranchised from discipline and control" and can spend their time (and credits) freely in leisure pursuits of their own choosing; they can, in fact, if they so wish, retire at reduced pay at the age of thirty-three.[33] The upshot: within the industrial army, as well as outside of it, the system of Nationalism is "elastic enough to give free play to every instinct of human nature which does not aim at dominating others or living on the fruit of other's labor."[34] Women share in the newfound freedom and prosperity along with men, though they serve in separate military units, headed by officers of their own choosing. (The blacks were also segregated. Bellamy's utopia was not exactly the millennium to which Frederick Douglass looked forward.)

One thing is compulsory in the new economic democracy: work. The requirement that each citizen serve the nation for a fixed period in the industrial army is mandatory and inescapable. The motto is "from all equally; to all equally"; there must be an equal term of service (except for the physically handicapped) in return for equal maintenance. As Dr. Leete candidly expresses it:

. . . to speak of service being compulsory would be a weak way to state its absolute inevitableness. Our entire social order is so wholly based upon and deduced from it that if it were conceivable that a man could escape it, he would be left with no possible way to provide for his existence. He would have excluded himself from the world, cut himself off from his kind, in a word, committed suicide.[36]

Nevertheless, he explains, service in the army "is regarded as so absolutely natural and reasonable that the idea of its being compulsory has ceased to be thought of."[37] Amid conditions of equality, security, and abundance, the natural nobility of human nature—which is essentially "good, not bad, . . . generous, not selfish, pitiful, not cruel, sympathetic, not arrogant"—has been enabled to flower.[38] As a consequence, the Nationalist order "depends in no particular upon legislation, but is entirely voluntary, the logical outcome of the operation of human nature under rational conditions."[39] Julian is readily persuaded by the good doctor. Critics of *Looking Backward* had serious reservations.

Some of the criticisms of Bellamy's book were manifestly unfair: the charge, for example, of ultramilitarism. Bellamy, it is true, like William James, was impressed by the fact that military service may nourish such qualities as courage, honor, self-sacrifice, and heroism that are often lacking in peacetime existence. But like James he hated war and sought a moral equivalent for it. There were no armies and navies in his utopian world, and his industrial army was, in a way, a kind of gigantic peace corps. Other criticisms were more to the point, particularly the observation that a twenty-four-year period of service in a militarily organized unit, with its inevitable *mentalité hierarchique*, was scarcely conducive to the kind of original thinking and independence of mind that makes for a dynamic social order.

The favorite point made by critics of Bellamy's utopian scheme was, however, that human nature was basically selfish, not noble, and that under conditions of enforced equality the worst fears of the Social Darwinists would be realized. "All the qualities of human nature remain as of old," J. W. Roberts declared in his anti-utopia, *Looking Within* (1893). "There is no improvement. Passions are just as strong; ambitions are just as grasping; popularity is craved as greatly as ever; the 'master-passion' still rules the human breast. Nothing is changed but law and custom. Idleness and inclination promote vice and crime."[40] The fruits of Nationalism for Roberts were the killing off of "emulation, skill, personal enterprise" and the emergence of "*a vast system of slavery*" in which there was neither freedom nor abundance.[41] Conrad Wilbrandt made essentially the same point in *Mr. East's Experiences in Mr. Bellamy's World* (1891): under Nationalism, man had become a slave with "no free will, free decision, free movement," and the system itself was producing economic ruin.[42] And in *A Sequel to Looking Backward; or, Looking Further Forward* (1891), Richard Michaelis depicted the officers

commanding the industrial army as a tight little oligarchy exercising
despotic power over the draftees, giving easy jobs, good records, and
rapid promotions to their relatives and friends and to those currying
their favor and treating with ruthless brutality those incurring their
disfavor. "Whoever dares to openly oppose the ruling spirits," declares
one of the characters in Michaelis's novel, "may be sure that all the
wrath and all the unpleasantness at the command of the administration
will be piled upon him and his relations and friends."[43] The result is a
system characterized by "favouritism, corruption, servility, and, suppression of opponents."[44]

Bellamy seems to have been surprised, even wounded, by the nature
of the criticisms directed at his book. As thoroughly devoted as Thomas
Paine had been to such primary liberties as freedom of speech, religion,
press, and expression and political suffrage, he had taken pains to make
clear in his novel that these liberties remained undiminished in his
utopian commonwealth and that Nationalism represented an extension
of freedom from the political to the economic realm. His response to
critics, in speeches to the Nationalist clubs and in articles for the
*Nationalist* and the *New Nation*, was in part a *tu quoque*: those most
concerned about freedom in the collectivist economy which he advocated
were entirely silent about the "sordid bondage" which the majority of
people experienced under the prevailing system of monopolistic capitalism.[45] But he also undertook a more positive defense of his position.
"Always except this precious liberty of loafing," he wrote,

I am quite unable to understand what liberties the nationalist plan of industrial organization curtails. Assuming that it is right to require a man
to work, is it a loss of liberty to guarantee him the opportunity to work at
what he likes best and can do best? Is it tyranny to insure him promotion,
leadership and honor in precise proportion to his achievement? Is it a
curtailment of his liberty to make him absolutely free of dependence upon
the favor of any individual or community for his livelihood by giving him
the constitutional pledge of the nation for it? Is it oppressive to guarantee
him against loss of income in old age, and absolute security as to the welfare
of his wife and children after he is gone? If to do all these things for a man
means to take away his liberties and tyrannize over him, we had better get
a new dictionary for the definitions in the old ones are evidently all wrong.[46]

How, then, did Bellamy himself define liberty? And how did he view
the relationship between liberty and equality, the "Cain and Abel of
politics" for so many of his critics? In his last book, *Equality*, published

a year before his death, Bellamy examined these questions with some care. Cast in the form of a novel like *Looking Backward*, but with even less of a story line, *Equality* consists largely of a series of long-winded conversations between Julian West, Dr. Leete, and the doctor's daughter Edith (with whom Julian's romance understandably grinds to a halt), in which the principles of Nationalism are defended vigorously against the strictures of its critics. For Bellamy, authentic freedom rested on two conditions: first, the absence of external constraints (and Bellamy was of course thinking primarily of economic constraints) on the individual and his ability to choose between alternatives; and second, the presence of opportunities for the individual to develop his native talents and find expression for them in work and in play. From Bellamy's point of view, the American system in the late nineteenth century was woefully lacking in both kinds of freedom for the majority of citizens. And the absence of these freedoms he linked directly with the prevalence of glaring inequalities inherent in the capitalist mode of organizing the economy. Reversing Sumner's dictum, he asserted in effect that non-liberty was the inevitable accompaniment of inequality and that only equality ensured real liberty for the majority of people.

There was, in the first place, Bellamy argued, the non-liberty resulting from inequality of power in American society in the Gilded Age. The concentration of the means of production in the hands of a few great capitalists (and Bellamy expected this concentration to increase as the trustification of the economy continued) meant that a small minority of individuals monopolized economic power and that the large majority of Americans were without any share in this power. Possession of power, obviously, brings with it the means of asserting control over one's fellows; and the natural consequence of inequality of economic power in the United States was that a few individuals exercised almost complete and totally irresponsible dominion over the masses of people. In such a situation, the masses of people could scarcely be said to be free; they lived in a state of virtual slavery, Dr. Leete insists, to the "possessing class."[47] The "liberty of economic initiative by the individual," so fondly celebrated by Social Darwinists, was not a reality for most people.[48] As Julian, looking back on his own period, obligingly concedes: "Capital had practically monopolized all economic opportunities by that time; there was no opening in business enterprise for those without large capital save by some extraordinary fortune."[49] A society in which only a handful of people actually possessed freedom in the economic sense insisted on by the Social Darwinists could hardly be described as a free society even by Sumner's philosophy.

But inequality of power not only deprived most Americans of the liberty of economic initiative; it also made them completely and helplessly dependent on the masters of capital for their jobs and hence for their very existence. "What is liberty?" asks Dr. Leete. "How can men be free who must ask the right to labor and to live from their fellow-men and seek their bread from the hands of others?"[50] The pressure of want drove people in Julian's day to accept work on any terms dictated by their employers. The "coercion of economic need," says Dr. Leete, created a situation in which the majority of people "accepted servitude to the possessing class and became their serfs on condition of receiving the means of subsistence."[51] For the much-vaunted concept of freedom of contract—"the voluntary, unconstrained agreement of the laborer with the employer as to terms of his employment"—Dr. Leete has only scorn:

What hypocrisy could have been so brazen as that pretense when, as a matter of fact, every contract made between the capitalist who had bread and could keep it and the laborer who must have it or die would have been declared void, if fairly judged, even under your laws as a contract made under duress of hunger, cold, and nakedness, nothing less than the threat of death! If you own the things men must have, you own the men who must have them.[52]

Abject dependence for their livelihood on the monopolizers of economic power, Bellamy believed, deprived the majority of people in the Gilded Age of any real freedom. They were economically coerced, not free. There was no range of economic alternatives available to them from which they might freely choose. As a result, industrial slavery, Dr. Leete tells Julian, had replaced chattel slavery after the Civil War. "Slavery exists," he says,

where there is a compulsory using of men by other men for the benefit of the users. I think we are quite agreed that the poor man in your day worked for the rich only because his necessities compelled him to. . . . With the mass of workers the compulsion of necessity was of the sharpest kind. The chattel slave had the choice between working for his master and the lash. The wage-earner chose between laboring for an employer or starving. . . . It was a difference between the direct exercise of coercion . . . and an indirect coercion by which the same industrial result was obtained.[53]

The chattel slave, in fact, Dr. Leete continues (arguing along lines reminiscent of proslavery apologetics before the Civil War), was in many respects "a more dignified and heroic figure than the hireling of your day who called himself a free worker."[54] The antebellum slaveowner, out of self-interest, usually saw to it that the slave and his family were adequately taken care of and well treated; but the captain of industry had no such concern for the welfare of his employees. If they became incapacitated for work or perished from malnutrition, disease, or industrial accident, he could easily replace them from the vast hordes of unemployed willing and eager to secure employment under any conditions he laid down. The upshot of inequality of power, Dr. Leete concludes, was "to reduce almost the total human race to a state of degrading bondage to their fellows."[55]

Nationalism was designed to emancipate the human race from economic duress. It provided full employment, equal and generous remuneration, cradle-to-grave security regardless of condition, and permitted each citizen to select and prepare himself for the kind of work which was most appealing to him. The only inequalities in power remaining under Nationalism were those incident to rank and responsibility in the industrial army; but any talented and ambitious individual, willing to put forth his best efforts, could rise as fast and as far in the army as he wished. Under Nationalism, in sum, a responsible democracy of power superseded the irresponsible aristocracy of power prevailing under monopoly capitalism.

But inequality of power, according to Bellamy, was only one source of nonliberty in capitalist society. Inequality of wealth, and hence of access to the things that wealth commands, was an additional means of depriving the vast majority of people of freedom. Freedom for Bellamy meant more than simply absence of domination by one's fellowmen; it also involved the availability of opportunities for personal self-development and self-expression. An individual was free, Bellamy declared, only to the extent that he had a chance to make the best use of his natural powers, physical, mental, and spiritual, and to contribute in his own unique way to the civilization of which he was a part. But the inequality of circumstances, and therefore of opportunities, resulting from maldistribution of wealth shut most people off from the possibility of achieving this kind of freedom during the Gilded Age. Subject to ill health and disease by his squalid living conditions, unable to afford proper health and medical services, denied by his poverty adequate vocational and educational training which would nourish and bring to fruition his natural faculties and interests, and the wretched victim of the fears and anxieties growing out of economic deprivation and uncertainty, the average American under capitalism remained physically and intellectually stunted in growth. He was the unhappy prisoner of his circumstances.

Because he sought to provide everyone with free opportunities for development by equalizing individual incomes, Bellamy was accused of wanting to destroy individuality and reduce all people to a dead level of uniformity. It is a disgrace in Bellamy's utopia, Mrs. Leete tells Julian in *Squinting Sideways*, a parody of *Looking Backward*, "to be above or below the normal in anything."[56] But Bellamy indignantly denied the charge. "I am a Nationalist," he told Henry George, one of his critics, "because I am an individualist."[57] He was acutely sensitive to individual differences and anxious to preserve them in the new order. No more than his critics did he believe that human beings were equal in their natural capacities; he recognized the physical and mental inequalities bequeathed to individuals by nature and, in fact, welcomed them. What he sought was the natural and unhampered expression of these basic differences among people; and this, he asserted, required the eradication of artificial differences among individuals following from the inequitable distribution of wealth and the creating of circumstances in which fair opportunities for everyone made the realization of these natural differences a genuine possibility. The "fullest liberty," he thought, was "a medium in which the natural is sure at last to rise and survive, and the artificial to sink and disappear.[58] Bellamy's view was like Paine's in this respect, though Paine, unlike Bellamy, did not want governments to govern too much.

The economic equality which Bellamy sponsored in his Nationalist program was to be "the level standing ground, the even floor, on which the new order proposed to range all alike, that they might be known for what they were, and all their natural inequalities be brought fully out." In the Nationalist utopia, equal incomes, collective provision for health and welfare services available to all citizens, and equal access to educational facilities eliminated the false and unnatural inequalities existing in societies based on sensational extremes of wealth and circumstances. From the introduction of Nationalism, Dr. Leete declares, "dates the first full and clear revelation of the natural and inherent varieties in human endowments."[59] Equality, Julian is told, "creates an atmosphere which kills imitation, and is pregnant with originality, for every one acts out himself, having nothing to gain by imitating anyone else."[60] By making everyone secure economically, moreover, Nationalism fosters boldness of mind and spirit. It transforms the "cowardly time-serving, abject" individual of capitalist society into a free and independent-minded citizen who is "absolute lord of himself and answerable for his opinions, speech, and conduct to his own conscience only."[61] Under conditions of economic freedom, as Bellamy has defined it, the political liberties formally guaranteed by the U.S. Constitution, as well as the free expression of individual differences, would become, for the first time, living realities for all Americans. "Liberty," Dr. Leete assures Julian, "is the first and last word of our civilization."[62]

Bellamy thought that women would make special gains under conditions of economic equality. In capitalist society, he believed, women were little better than slaves. They labored under a triple yoke: subjection to class rule of the rich (along with the mass of men); humiliating dependence on men for economic support and the necessity to place themselves in the marriage market if they were to survive; and slavish conformity to the artificial and repressive standards of behavior which nineteenth-century society expected of all women. Woman's life was "soul-stifling and mind-stunting" under capitalism; the "slave code" by which she lived enfeebled her body, cramped her mind, and crushed her spirit.[63] "It seems to us," Dr. Leete muses to Julian,

that women were more than any other class the victim of your civilization. There is something which, even at this distance of time, penetrates one with pathos in the spectacle of their ennuied, undeveloped lives, stunted at marriage, their narrow horizon, bounded so often, physically, by the four walls of the home, and morally by a petty circle of petty interests.[64]

Bellamy believed that making one person dependent on another for the means of support was morally shocking as well as indefensible in any rational society. "What would become of personal liberty and dignity under such an arrangement?" he has Dr. Leete ask Julian.

I am aware that you called yourselves free in the nineteenth century. The meaning of the word could not then, however, have been what it is at present, or you certainly would not have applied it to a society of which nearly every member was in a position of galling personal dependence upon others as to the very means of life, the poor upon the rich, or employed upon employer, women upon men, children upon parents.[65]

The first condition of ethical action in any relation, Dr. Leete reminds Julian, is freedom of the actor. But since women, because of their economic dependence, were not free agents, the relations between the sexes under capitalism, despite all the rigid rules and regulations and emphasis on the sanctity of the marriage contract, were in no sense truly ethical. It was impossible, he insists, for societies based on economic inequality to have free, healthy, natural, and fundamentally moral relations between men and women. Even the women's-rights movement missed the point. It failed to see that the root of sexual bondage was the same as the root of industrial bondage: unequal distribution of economic power. The feminists, Bellamy lamented, squandered their energies in seeking the right to vote and superficial changes in property and divorce laws rather than the basic changes in society which would bring about the real emancipation of women.[66]

Under Nationalism, women's liberation becomes a reality. Equal schooling, equal social and political rights, equal opportunities for careers, and equal incomes bring to an end woman's age-old subservience to men. The new woman discards the bustles, corsets, and long, tight skirts which once hampered her physical development and adopts trousers as the most natural and convenient mode of dress. She gives up the sedentary and semi-invalid existence which so many nineteenth-century women lived, takes up athletics, lives an active life in the wide social world, and becomes healthy, vigorous, and more physically attractive than ever before. She becomes a full member of the industrial army, leaving it only when maternal duties claim her, and works in all the trades, occupations, and professions at which men are found. She is no longer a household slave, for new inventions plus cooperative methods of housekeeping have lifted the burden of household chores. Most important of all, with economic independence she is no longer a "sexual slave"; she bestows her love freely and honestly on whom she will and bears children only if she wants to.[67]

Dr. Leete regards the "frankness and unconstraint" characterizing sexual relations under Nationalism as one of its greatest achievements. "The sexes," he reports, "now meet with the ease of perfect equals, suitors to each other for nothing but love."[68] Marriages no longer mean "incarceration" for women; they are "matches of pure love."[69] The result is a kind of Darwinian sexual selection by which the best types attract each other, marry, and transmit their qualities to their descendants. The new sexual freedom also produces automatic population control, since

economic coercion no longer forces women to marry and become "involuntary mothers."[70] Natonalism, in short, is "women's Declaration of
Independence."[71] It gives "free mothers to the race—free not merely from
physical but from moral and intellectual fetters."[72]

## COLLECTIVE MORAL FREEDOM

Bellamy was called a rank materialist for his emphasis on economic
security and abundance. "It is certainly a new idea in the world," com-
mented one critic of *Looking Backward*, "that virtue is the child of comfort."[73] Bellamy was understandably enraged by such criticism, and it
surely fell wide of the mark. Economic well-being he regarded simply
as the necessary foundation for moral and spiritual development, not
as an end in itself. His ultimate quest in *Looking Backward* was the
same as it had been in *Dr. Heidenhoff's Process*: genuine freedom for
the human spirit. His impassioned dream was the liberation of humanity
from the shackles (psychological, social, and economic) of the past in
order that it might enter freely upon the endless search for full expression in the present and in the future: in sports and recreation, in art,
music, and literature, in the pursuit of knowledge, in religion, and in
love and friendship. As Mr. Barton, the clergyman in *Looking Backward*,
explains in his sermon:

The solution of the problem of physical maintenance . . . so far from seeming to us an ultimate attainment, appears but as preliminary to anything
like real human progress. We have but relieved ourselves of an impertinent
and needless harassment which hindered our ancestors from undertaking the
real ends of existence. . . . The enfranchisement of humanity . . . from
mental and physical absorption in working and scheming for the mere bodily
necessities, may be regarded as a species of second birth of the race. . . .
Since then, humanity has entered on a new phase of spiritual development,
an evolution of the higher faculties, the very existence of which in human
nature our ancestors scarcely suspected. . . . The betterment of mankind
from generation to generation, physically, mentally, morally, is recognized as
the one great object supremely worthy of effort and of sacrifice. We believe
the race for the first time to have entered on the realization of God's ideal
of it.[74]

Though Bellamy had long since broken with organized religion, he made
the supreme goal of his utopia a spiritual one: an ever closer relation to
the universal spirit which, like Emerson, he believed pervaded creation,
joined all men and women in a world-wide community, and made them

at one with the universe. "The priestly idea," Mr. Barton goes on to say,

that the past was diviner than the present, that God was behind the race,
gave place to the belief that we should look forward and not backward for
inspiration, and that the present and the future promised a fuller and more
certain knowledge concerning the soul and God than any the past had
attained.[75]

For Bellamy, spiritual freedom and moral perfection came from looking
forward rather than backward. It was this very spirituality in Bellamy's
thought that for a time attracted the Theosophists, with their doctrine of
human brotherhood, to the Nationalist movement.[76]

Bellamy's freedom was a collective enterprise. No person could be
free, according to Nationalism, unless all people were free. Bellamy was
not a Marxist, but he clearly shared the Communist Manifesto's sentiments in favor of "an association, in which the free development of *each*
is the condition for the free development of *all*." He wanted to see the
principle of individual freedom universalized and conditions for its realization equalized. The kind of freedom he envisaged obviously required
drastic social reconstruction: the elimination of class distinctions, the removal of economic want and insecurity, and the eradication of all arbitrary domination of one person over another. But social ownership of the
means of production and distribution was not an end in itself; it was
merely the necessary foundation for spiritual freedom: the liberation of
the individual from absorption in his own finite, limited, and parochial
interests and the merging of his individual energies with those of his
fellowmen.

Political liberty, Bellamy once wrote, was of little account unless
the soul was free from bondage to selfishness. The new society which he
sketched would, he believed, free people from bondage to narrow self-
interest and bring to fruition the spirit of love, sympathy, generosity, and
brotherhood that lay dormant in all people. Social salvation, in short,
would bring about individual redemption. Bellamy advocated a "religion
of solidarity," which he defined as an "impassioned sense of the solidarity
of humanity and of man with God."[77] Such a religion, he was continually
asserting, was the truest Christianity; "it is the religion Christ taught,"
he said. It is Christ's doctrine of the duty of loving one's neighbor as
oneself applied to the reorganization of industry.[78] "Liberty, equality, and
fraternity," he declared, were "nothing less than the practical meaning
and content of Christ's religion."[79]

Was human nature in fact perfectible in this fashion? Bellamy had not always thought so. In an entry in one of his notebooks which he made after breaking away from his Calvinist background, he reflected with fascination on what he called the "charm of wickedness." It is "wickedness for its own sake," he wrote,

that is considered by some inexplicable. Its true explanation, to my mind, is found in the gratification of the instinct of liberty, the passion for freedom, which is popularly reckoned a by no means discreditable or undesirable feeling. To break laws without the least regard to their quality, just because they are laws, to defy and overlook restraint just because it is restraint, these are among the most ineradicable instincts of human nature. They gratify that passion for freedom whose active form is a revolt against all restraint, without reference to the wisdom acknowledged by ourselves of the course into which it would force us. We may indeed recognize that course as ideally most desirable, it may be the one we had made up our minds to follow, and yet so soon as we find ourselves guided and constrained thereto we instantly rebel and, leaping the fences, take to the fields. There we taste the sweets of liberty. The pleasure of sin is the sense of freedom; this gives its flavor to stolen fruit, a flavor so wild, racy, penetrating, that no sauce on earth equals it. With it the root and herb of the law-breaker have a zest that no ragout of virtue can ever possess.[80]

In building his utopian commonwealth many years later, however, Bellamy made no place for the wayward and unruly "passion for freedom" which when he was a young man he had regarded as inborn. John Winthrop would have approved of Bellamy's exclusion of this kind of freedom from his community. But one wonders how Henry Thoreau would have fared in Utopia 2000 A.D. He would probably have jumped into Walden Pond, though it, too, would have been nationalized.

Unlike Calvinistic Puritans, Bellamy thought that our "natural corrupt liberties" (as Winthrop called them) would disappear in the right kind of social order; he neither allowed elbowroom for them in his commonwealth nor contemplated authoritarian controls (as Winthrop did) to keep them in hand. He also seemed to think that tragedy would never interrupt the smooth operations of his utopian society and that such human universals as pain, sorrow, suffering, and death (which were much on his mind as a young man) would have no effects on the attitudes and behavior of the people living in it. As an adult, Bellamy himself could live courageously, even nobly (once he discovered a cause in which to immerse his individuality) with pain and suffering (his health became

increasingly wretched before he died at forty-eight), and he assumed
that other people could too. He failed to recognize that there are few
heroes or saints in any society (least of all those who think of themselves as such) and that people, even in the best of communities, tend
to seek outlets for the inescapable frustrations of life in their relations
with other people. Idealistic reformers are not notably easier to get along
with than other people.

It is surely a safe rule to assume, as the Founding Fathers did, that
human nature will probably be no better under a new system than it
was under the old one, though it is also necessary, surely, to hope for
more than this. Alexander Hamilton was probably right in thinking that
it was a piece of egregious folly to base one's plans for the future on
"speculations of lasting tranquillity."[81] Bellamy placed too much faith in
wholesale reconstruction; like most utopians, he offered solutions to the
problems of the world he knew without realizing that every solution
engenders new problems of its own and that some solutions turn out to
be far greater problems themselves than the difficulties they were designed to meet. Twentieth-century lovers of liberty have become too
familiar with utopia-turned-dystopia in both fancy and fact not to have
grave misgivings about an industrial army as a solution to modern industrial problems.

Bellamy, who once admitted his "deep-seated aversion to change,"
had too much faith in what he called the "heavenly quality of con-
stancy," and he ignored the possibilities of economic diversity in his
socialistic utopia: individual or family ownership for small enterprises,
cooperative ownership by workers for medium-sized enterprises, and some
form of social ownership for large-scale enterprises.[82] He also dismissed
too hastily at first the possibilities of piecemeal reform of concrete evils,
with its emphasis on trial and error, probability, and provisionality rather
than on absolute certainty and finality. The method of trial and error,
which has had such enormous success in the natural sciences, is of course
far more compatible with freedom of thought, expression, discussion, and
debate than is the utopian method.

Still, for all the shortcomings of his utopianism, Bellamy's social
criticism was acute, his analysis of the liberty-equality equation illuminating, and his efforts to combine individual liberty (frequently dis-
paraged by modern socialists) with collective freedom worthy of respect.
All men are created unequal as to their natural endowments, Bellamy
recognized; but only when the artificial inequalities and false distinctions

rooted in inherited circumstances and opportunities are eliminated can
the inequalities of character and intellect have full and free expression.
"A society," as R. H. Tawney put it,

is free in so far, and only in so far, as, within the limits set by nature,
knowledge and resources, its institutions and policies are such as to enable
all its members to grow to their full stature, to do their duty as they see it,
and—since liberty should not be too austere—to have their fling when they
feel like it. In so far as the opportunity to lead a life worthy of human
beings is needlessly confined to a minority, not a few of the conditions
applauded as freedom would more properly be denounced as privilege.
Action which causes such opportunities to be more widely shared is, therefore, twice blessed. It not only subtracts from inequality, but adds to
freedom.[83]

Bellamy presented the American people with a vision: the vision of
a society in which liberty and equality were in a fair balance for all
citizens. It was, to be sure, a utopian vision and thus forever impossible
of fulfillment, but no doubt some such vision is indispensable for any
kind of democratic reform. Bellamy kept his utopian vision to the end
despite the precipitous decline of the Nationalist movement after a
promising beginning in the late 1880s and early 1890s. But he seems
with the passage of time to have become less rigid in his plans for human
betterment. He was friendly toward all reform groups, came to support
the piecemeal reform proposals—municipal ownership of public utilities,
nationalization of railroads, telephones, and telegraph, creation of a
parcel post system, direct election of senators, the merit system in civil
service, income and inheritance taxes—which his Nationalist followers
put forward, and he also took a serious interest in Populism. "We confess," he wrote in an article on "The Piece-Meal Process" for the *New
Nation*, "we have very little respect for social reformers who are so
anxious to do everything in general that they do nothing in particular."[84]
He emphatically denied, moreover, that he regarded his utopia as a final
and fixed goal or that he thought it represented the last stage of history.
He was tinkering with it to the end. In his last days, when he was asked
whether he considered the social state portrayed in *Equality* as the ultimate goal of human progress, he exclaimed: "Oh no; it is only the
beginning. When we get there we shall find a whole infinity beyond."[85]

# 7

# William James on
# Freedom as Creative Effort

IN AN AGE in which scientific determinism was practically *de rigueur*
for Western intellectuals, William James chose to champion freedom
of the will. His first act of free will, he said, was to believe in free will.
Free will for James centered in the individual's power to shape his own
character and destiny to some extent, and it entailed a certain degree
of chance, novelty, and indeterminism in human experience. James
acknowledged that freedom in this sense was a possibility, not a certainty.
But this was also true of determinism. Both were postulates about the
world; and when scientific and moral postulates clashed and objective
proof was lacking, he said, the only course was voluntary choice between them. Science, he insisted, "must be constantly reminded that
her purposes are not the only purposes, and that the order of uniform
causation which she has use for, and is therefore right in postulating,
may be enveloped in a wider order, on which she has no claims at all."[1]

James was impatient with people who claimed that freedom and
determinism were easily reconciled. Determinists who defined freedom
as acting without external restraint (as Edwards did) or as acting
rightly or in acquiescence in the law of the whole (as Emerson did)
were, he thought, evading the real issues at stake between freedom and
determinism. He was especially vexed by philosophers who harmonized

liberty and necessity by defining freedom as "recognition of necessity" or
"bondage to the highest," and he called them "soft determinists."[2] (A
"hard determinist" was an out-and-out necessitarian like Franklin when
he wrote his *Dissertation on Liberty and Necessity*.) He was outraged
by Thomas Huxley's announcement that

if some great Power would agree to make me always think what is true and
do what is right on condition of being turned into a sort of clock and wound
up every morning before I got out of bed, I should instantly close with the
offer. The only freedom I care about is the freedom to do right; the freedom
to do wrong I am ready to part with on the cheapest terms to any one who
will take it of me.[3]

James was repelled by the notion of clockwork freedom, and he insisted
that the "ridiculous 'freedom to do right' " was a sham freedom depriving
the individual of any real autonomy. He also thought it tended to resolve
itself into the freedom to do as Huxley or any other deterministic philosopher thought was right and represented more certitude about what was
right and wrong in this immense universe of ours than was warranted.
"After all," he exclaimed, "what accounts do the nethermost bounds of
the universe owe to me? By what insatiate conceit and lust of intellectual
despotism do I arrogate the right to know their secrets, and from my
philosophic throne to play the only airs they shall march to, as if I were
the Lord's annointed?"[4] In James's universe there were uncharted paths,
ambiguous possibilities, perpetual novelties, and creative efforts by individuals which it was impossible for deterministic systematizers (even
so ambitious a system-builder as Hegel) to encompass in their monistic
nets. In such a universe individual freedom meant something far more
profound than mere absence of outward restraint or bondage to the
highest.

James, in short, was anxious to take a new look at the old question
of freedom of the will. The question of the will's initiative was one of
the livest of all issues for him, and he made it his earliest and latest concern. "It is in fact," he declared, "the pivotal question of metaphysics, the
very hinge on which our picture of the world shall swing from material-
ism, fatalism, monism, towards spiritualism, freedom, pluralism,—or
else the other way."[5] Insisting that not all the juice had been squeezed
out of the free-will problem, he returned to it time and again. Even when
hiking in the Adirondacks he would frequently stretch himself out on
the ground on the top of a mountain and say to his friends: "Now bring

on the free will question."[6] In varying forms, freedom as individual self-determination formed an integral part of his psychology, his ethics, his social thought, and his metaphysics.

### FREE WILL AND THE EFFICACY OF CONSCIOUSNESS

The origin of James's preoccupation with the free-will question was, as he freely acknowledged, deeply personal. Shortly after taking his medical degree at Harvard in June, 1869, when he was twenty-eight, James entered a period of ill health and nervous depression which lasted, on and off, until about 1872. During this period he suffered an acute sense of moral impotence and a waning of the will to live. In the depths of his despair he wondered "how other people could live, how I myself had ever lived, so unconscious of that pit of insecurity beneath the surface of life."[7] His crisis was intellectual as well as emotional in nature. "I'm swamped in an empirical philosophy"—he wrote a friend in the early stages of his melancholia. "I feel that we are nature through and through, that we are *wholly* conditioned, that not a wiggle of our will happens save as the result of physical laws."[8] Desperately he sought for a view of the human situation which would release him from the emotional and intellectual "bind" in which he felt himself imprisoned and which would enable him to overcome the paralysis of action that gripped him. At some point during these years he experienced the severe attack of panic fear which he later described anonymously in *The Varieties of Religious Experience* (1902) in the course of a discussion of the "sick soul":

Whilst in this state of philosophic pessimism and general depression of spirits about my prospects, I went one evening into a dressing-room in the twilight to procure some article that was there; when suddenly there fell upon me without any warning, just as if it came out of the darkness, a horrible fear of my own existence. Simultaneously there arose in my mind the image of an epileptic patient whom I had seen in the asylum, a black-haired youth with greenish skin, entirely idiotic, who used to sit all day on one of the benches, or rather shelves against the wall, with his knees drawn up against his chin, and the coarse gray undershirt, which was his only garment, drawn over them inclosing his entire figure. He sat there like a sort of sculptured Egyptian cat or Peruvian mummy, moving nothing but his black eyes and looking absolutely non-human. This image and my fear entered into a species of combination with each other. *That shape am I*, I felt, potentially. Nothing that I possess can defend me against that fate, if the hour for it should strike for me as it struck for him. There was such a horror of him, and such a perception of my own merely momentary discrepancy from him, that it was if something hitherto solid within my breast gave way entirely, and I became a mass of quivering fear. After this the universe was changed for me altogether. I awoke morning after morning with a horrible dread at the pit of my stomach, and with a sense of the insecurity of life that I never knew before, and that I have never felt since.[9]

In his morbid identification of himself with the young patient who was little more than a machine, James was, it is perhaps not fanciful to suggest, confronting the issue of mechanical determinism versus freedom of the will in its most dramatic form.

James emerged from his years of despondency with a deep-seated belief in freedom of the will which no amount of scientific determinism was ever afterward able to shatter. It was the French philosopher Charles Renouvier who pointed the way for him. "I think that yesterday was a crisis in my life," James wrote in one of his notebooks on April 30, 1870.

I finished the first part of Renouvier's second "Essais" and see no reason why his definition of Free Will—"the sustaining of a thought *because I choose to* when I might have other thoughts"—need be the definition of an illusion. At any rate, I will assume . . . that it is no illusion. My first act of free will shall be to believe in free will. . . . Hitherto, when I have felt like taking a free initiative, like daring to act originally, without carefully waiting for the contemplation of the external world to determine all for me, suicide seemed the most manly form to put my daring into; now, I will go a step further with my will, not only act with it, but believe as well; believe in my individual reality and creative power. My belief, to be sure, *can't* be optimistic—but I will posit life (the real, the good) in the self-governing *resistance* of the ego to the world. Life shall [be built in] doing and suffering and creating.[10]

James's father, who had undergone a similar spiritual "vastation" (to use the Swedenborgian term which he himself used) in his own young manhood, was delighted by the eventual reappearance of his son's normally energetic and buoyant spirit. "I was afraid of interfering with it," he wrote Henry, Jr., after an animated visit from William,

or possibly checking it, but I ventured to ask what specially in his opinion had promoted the change. He said several things: the reading of Renouvier (specially his vindication of the freedom of the will) and Wordsworth, whom he has been feeding upon now for a good while; but especially his having given up the notion that all mental disorder required to have a physical basis. This had become perfectly untrue to him. He saw that the mind did act irrespectively of material coercion, and could be dealt with therefore at first-hand, and this was health to his bones.[11]

James's mind always creatively transformed whatever it touched; and although Renouvier's view of freedom became the foundation for much of his thinking, the uses he made of it were peculiarly his own, as Renouvier, who later translated essays of James into French, unhesitatingly acknowledged.

In his first major work, *Principles of Psychology*, appearing in 1890 (important parts had been published as separate articles during the preceding decade and more), James devoted several sections to the specific subject of free will. The entire book, however, emphasized the causal efficacy of the human consciousness and represents a sharp break with the traditional British empiricist view of the mind as a *tabula rasa* passively receiving simple and discrete sense impressions from the external environment and combining them into complex ideas by the mechanical laws of association. For James, nourished in Darwinian evolution as a medical student, the mind was an active, interested, and selective agency of human adaptation and survival. It was teleological in character—that is, it pursued ends (practical, moral, aesthetic, and theoretic) and chose means for the achievement of these ends.

James by no means slighted the organic basis of human mentality; he devoted long introductory sections of both *Principles of Psychology* and *Psychology: Briefer Course*, a shorter version of his work which appeared in 1892, to physiological data. Mental phenomena, he acknowledged, are indeed conditioned by bodily processes. On the other hand, mental states themselves effect bodily changes; and James laid it down as a general rule that no mental modification ever occurs which is not accompanied or followed by a bodily change. Emotions and bodily changes were, he thought, so closely related that it was possible to say that we feel sorry because we cry, angry because we strike, and afraid because we tremble, and not the other way around.

Before launching into an extended analysis of the nature and functions of human consciousness, James felt obliged to dispose of the "automaton theory" of man, then being put forward by Thomas Huxley and other naturalistically inclined writers. According to this theory, man was a "conscious automaton," that is, a mere bundle of nervous reflexes whose mental acts were explicable in purely physiological terms. Hence:

If we knew thoroughly the nervous system of Shakespeare, and as thoroughly all his environing conditions, we should be able to show why at a certain period of his life his hand came to trace on certain sheets of paper those crabbed little black marks which we for shortness' sake call the manuscript of Hamlet. We should understand the rationale of every erasure and alteration therein, and we should understand all this without in the slightest degree acknowledging the existence of thoughts in Shakespeare's mind.[12]

To James, this view of man (similar to that put forth in 1971 in behaviorist B. F. Skinner's *Beyond Freedom and Dignity*) seemed utterly irrational. "It is to my mind," he declared, "quite inconceivable that consciousness should have *nothing to do* with a business which it so faithfully attends."[13] The distribution of consciousness among living organisms, he argued, points to its utility and efficaciousness. The higher we rise in the animal kingdom, he noted, the more complex and intense the consciousness; that of man obviously exceeds that of the oyster.

From this point of view it seems an organ, superadded to the other organs which maintain the animal in the struggle for existence; and the presumption of course is that it helps him in some way in the struggle, just as they do. But it cannot help him without being in some way efficacious and influencing the course of his bodily history. If now it could be shown in what way consciousness *might* help him, and if, moreover, the defects of his other organs . . . are such as to make them need just the kind of help that consciousness would bring provided it *were* efficacious; why, then the plausible inference would be that it came just *because* of its efficacy—in other words, its efficacy would be inductively proved.[14]

The efficacy of consciousness James found in the fact that consciousness is at all times primarily a *selecting* agency:

Whether we take it in the lowest sphere of sense, or in the highest intellection, we find it always doing one thing, choosing one out of several of the materials so presented to its notice, emphasizing and accentuating that and suppressing as far as possible all the rest. The item emphasized is always in close connection with some *interest* felt by consciousness to be paramount at the time.[15]

The insistence that consciousness selects for special attention, in accordance with its varied interests, certain items from its experience and ignores or suppresses all the rest forms the major theme of James's psychology. Whether he is discussing sensation, perception, conception,

and memory, or, indeed, ethics, aesthetics, science, and philosophy, James
never fails to remark on the selective industry of the human mind. From
the lowest to the highest levels of intellection, the mind attends to some
features of its experience which seize its interest to the exclusion of all
the rest. The mind is thus

at every stage, a theater of simultaneous possibilities. Consciousness consists
in the comparison of these with each other, the selection of some, and the
suppression of the rest by the reinforcing and inhibiting agency of attention. The highest and most elaborated mental products are filtered from the
data chosen by the faculty next beneath, out of the mass offered by the faculty below that, which mass in turn was sifted from a still larger amount
of yet simpler material, and so on. The mind, in short, works on the data it
receives very much as a sculptor works on his block of stone. In a sense
the statue stood there from eternity. But there were a thousand different ones
beside it, and the sculptor alone is to thank for having extricated this one
from the rest. Just so the world of each of us, howsoever different our several
views of it may be, all lay embedded in the primordial chaos of sensations,
which gave the mere *matter* to the thought of all of us indifferently. We
may, if we like, by our reasonings unwind things back to that black and
white jointless continuity of space and moving clouds of swarming atoms
which science calls the only real world. But all the while the world *we* feel
and live in will be that which our ancestors and we, by slowly cumulative
strokes of choice, have extricated out of this, like sculptors, by simply rejecting certain portions of the given stuff. Other sculptors, other statues from
the same stone! Other minds, other worlds from the same monotonous and
inexpressive chaos! My world is but one in a million alike embedded, alike
real to those who may abstract them. How different must be the worlds in
the consciousness of ant, cuttle-fish, or crab![16]

James's impatience with the dogmatic temper of certain philosophical
rationalists and scientific materialists grew out of their failure to realize
that they were singling out for special emphasis certain aspects of reality
and neglecting all the rest. But reality overflows our conceptual bounds,
James thought, and "ever not quite" was his favorite admonition to anyone generalizing about human experience.

James's analysis of consciousness does not, of course, argue directly
for freedom of the human will, though it clearly parts company with the
crasser forms of scientific determinism. James accepted without question
the Darwinian view that human consciousness, with all its rich proliferation of interests and activities, was a product of countless spontaneous
variations, selected by natural forces for their survival value in the long

course of evolutionary development. It should be emphasized, moreover, that James's primary objective was to help make of psychology a natural science; and this meant attempting to formulate, on the basis of empirical data, a series of regular, uniform laws which would illuminate human behavior. His careful attention, throughout *Principles of Psychology*, to organic processes (especially in his theory of the emotions) makes him sound at times (in a curious reversal of roles) like a rank materialist in comparison with Freud; and it should be no matter for surprise that he is sometimes regarded as the father of both behaviorist and experimental psychology in the United States. But he would have regarded as ridiculous John B. Watson's denial, in *Behaviorism* (1924), that there is such a thing as conscious experience; and he would probably have enjoyed Freud's remark to Max Eastman in the 1920s: "Perhaps you're a behaviorist. According to your John B. Watson consciousness doesn't exist. But that's just silly. That's nonsense. Consciousness exists quite obviously and everywhere—except perhaps in America."[17]

For all of his emphasis on physiological and experimental data, however, James was ever ready to tackle broad ethical and philosophical problems where he thought it appropriate. These, after all, were also surely relevant to an understanding of human nature. If, in part, *Principles of Psychology* was unmistakably behavioristic, it was also, in part, profoundly moral. (Portions of the chapter on "Habit" might even be regarded as moralistic.)

In his chapter on "Attention," James confronts the question of free will directly for the first time. "*My experience*," he declares at the outset, "*is what I agreed to attend to*." Attention, whether sensorial or intellectual, is for James in large measure passive and automatic; it is reflex, effortless, the product of habit. Comes a stimulus, in the form of a sensory object or an ideal representation, and our reaction is immediate and involuntary. But attention is also in part active and voluntary; it may involve deliberate effort on our part. The question of free will, in James's opinion, hinges on the question of whether the effort which we exert in cases of voluntary attention is only a resultant of the sensory or mental stimulus presented to our consciousness or whether it is an active and spiritual force, spontaneous and unpredictable in advance, which we ourselves in some fashion contribute to the existing situation. We experience a feeling of effort particularly when there is a conflict of interests in our minds and when we succeed in focusing our attention on (and thus acting upon) the more difficult of the two ideas.

We think, for example, of a cigarette for the thirtieth time in the day (Idea A) and we simultaneously recall what we have read about lung cancer and emphysema in the newspaper (Idea B). Nicotine addicts that we are, it is only with an effort approaching the heroic that we concentrate our attention on Idea B, drop Idea A out of our consciousness, and end by abstaining from a smoke. James admitted frankly that even in such cases the expenditure of effort which we feel may be a mere "inert accompaniment" of the deliberative process and "not the active element which it seems."[19] Our abstention from smoking may be explicable in purely mechanical terms: Idea B triumphed because the associative processes which it called up in our minds were stronger than those evoked by Idea A. But the effort to attend, James suggests, may, in fact, be an "original, psychic force." If that were so:

It would deepen and prolong the stay in consciousness of innumerable ideas which else would fade more quickly away. The delay thus gained might not be more than a second in duration—but that second might be *critical*; for in the constant rising and falling of considerations in the mind, where two associated systems of them are nearly in equilibrium, it is often a matter of but a second more or less of attention at the outset, whether one system shall gain force to occupy the field and develop itself, and exclude the other, or be excluded itself by the other. When developed, it may make us act; and that act may seal our doom. . . . The whole drama of the voluntary life hinges on the amount of attention, slightly more or slightly less, which rival motor ideas may receive. But the whole feeling of reality, the whole sting and excitement of our voluntary life, depends on our sense that in it things are *really being decided* from one moment to another, and that it is not the dull rattling off of a chain that was forged innumerable ages ago. This appearance, which makes life and history tingle with such a tragic zest, *may* not be an illusion. As we grant to the advocate of the mechanical theory that it may be one, so he must grant to us that it may *not*.[20]

In his long chapter on the will, toward the end of *Principles of Psychology*, James resumed his analysis of the free-will problem, elaborating on the points which he had made in his discussion of attention and concentrating more directly on moral decisions. Effort of attention, he insisted, was the *"essential phenomenon of will."*[21] Accordingly:

*The essential achievement of the will, in short, when it is most "voluntary", is to* ATTEND *to a difficult object and hold it fast before the mind.* The so-doing *is* the *fiat*; and it is a mere physiological incident that when the object is thus attended to, immediate motor consequences should ensue.[22]

Whenever we are faced with a struggle between our moral ideals and our instinctive or habitual propensities, our decision for the former is invariably accompanied by effort.

Now our spontaneous way of conceiving the effort, under all these circumstances, is as an active force adding its strength to that of the motives which ultimately prevail. When outer forces impinge upon a body, we say that the resultant motion is in the line of least resistance, or of greatest traction. But it is a curious fact that our spontaneous language never speaks of volition with effort in this way. Of course if we proceed *a priori* and define the line of least resistance as the line which is followed, the physical law must also hold good in the mental sphere. But we *feel*, in all hard cases of volition, as if the line taken, when the rarer and more ideal motives prevail, were the line of greater resistance, and as if the line of coarser motivation were the more pervious and easy one, even at the very moment when we refused to follow it.[23]

James reduced the relation between propensity (P), ideal impulse (I), and effort (E) to the following equation:

$$I \ per \ se < P$$
$$I + E > P$$

The question of fact in the free-will controversy thus resolves itself into the question of whether E forms an integral part of I or whether its duration and intensity are adventitious and indeterminate in advance. Having reached this point in his analysis, James concluded that the question could not be solved by empirical psychology. After a certain amount of effort has been given to an idea, it is impossible, by any methods or measurements available to science, to determine whether more or less effort might have been put forth in any given case. James ended by accepting the causal initiative of human consciousness (in the sense in which he had defined it in *Principles*) as a reality, but he did so for ethical reasons. Since objective proof was lacking (and probably always would be) in the dispute between determinism and free will, it was possible, he said, to decide between the two only by an act of voluntary choice. For James, then, freedom was a moral postulate: the postulate (somewhat like Kant's) that "*what ought to be can be and that bad acts cannot be fated, but that good ones must be possible in their place.*" And if the will is in fact undetermined in certain respects, he added, it is only appropriate that belief in its freedom should be voluntarily chosen as an alternative to the deterministic postulate.

Freedom's first deed should be to affirm itself. We ought never to hope for any other method of getting at the truth if indeterminism be a fact. Doubt of this particular truth will therefore probably be open to us to the end of time, and the utmost that a believer in free-will can *ever* do will be to show that the deterministic arguments are not coercive. That they are seductive, I am the last to deny, nor do I deny that effort may be needed to keep the faith in freedom, when they press upon it, upright in the mind.[24]

But James's faith in freedom increased as he developed his radical empiricism. More and more he found himself emphasizing the evidence for freedom in the stream of consciousness itself. In our direct, immediate experience of moral effort and creative endeavor, he came to insist, we see causal initiative actually at work: "Sustaining, persevering, striving, paying with effort as we go, hanging on, and finally achieving our intention—this *is* action, this *is* effectuation in the only shape in which, by a pure experience-philosophy, the whereabouts of it anywhere can be discussed. Here is creation in its first intention, here is causality at work."[25] And causality at work in human consciousness meant freedom. The causality so dear to the heart of scientific determinists originated, according to James, in perceptual experience. Its conceptualization came later and its application to the physical world had an anthropomorphic tinge. The rationalist's causation was with James the empiricist's freedom.

## THE DILEMMA OF DETERMINISM

But James sought rational as well as empirical evidence for freedom. His most sustained argument for free will is contained in an essay entitled "The Dilemma of Determinism" (1884), to which he referred readers of *Principles* for a more complete exposition of his views. The argument in this essay was partly metaphysical and partly ethical in nature, and it centered primarily around the problem of evil. James began by insisting that both determinism and indeterminism were postulates about the universe and that neither rests on any incontrovertible evidence of an external sort. Both satisfy, in divergent ways, the human need to "cast the world into a more rational shape in our minds than the shape into which it is thrown there by the crude order of our experience." Determinism is monistic in its conception of things. It

professes that those parts of the universe already laid down absolutely appoint and decree what the other parts shall be. The future has no ambiguous possibilities hidden in its womb; the part we call the present is compatible with

only one totality. Any other future complement than the one fixed from
eternity is impossible. The whole is in each and every part, and welds it with
the rest into an absolute unity, an iron block, in which there can be no
equivocation or shadow of turning.

Indeterminism, by contrast, is a pluralistic hypothesis. It

says that the parts have a certain amount of loose play on one another, so
that the laying down of one of them does not necessarily determine what
the others shall be. It admits that possibilities may be in excess of actualities, and that things not yet revealed to our knowledge may really in themselves be ambiguous. Of two alternative futures which we can conceive, both
may now be really possible; and the one becomes impossible only at the very
moment when the other excludes it by becoming real itself. Indeterminism
thus denies the world to be one unbending unit of fact. It says there is a
certain pluralism in it; and, so saying, it corroborates our ordinary unsophisti-
cated view of things. To that view, actualities seem to float in a wider sea of
possibilities, from out of which they are chosen; and, *somewhere*, indeterminism says, such possibilities exist, and form a part of truth.[26]

The point at issue between the two, then, relates to the existence of
possibilities in the universe. When a volition has occurred, the determinist
says that no other volition could possibly have occurred in its place. The
indeterminist, however, says that another volition might have occurred;
he believes both in the reality of alternative possibilities in the past and
in the ambiguity of future human volitions. According to the indeterminist view, chance is a real factor in human experience; there is a
loose play of alternative possibilities ever present in the lives of people,
and human volitions have a way of escaping the network of deterministic
formulations. The determinist of course rules out chance (as James conceived it) from the course of events.

Having drawn the battle lines in this fashion, James next proceeded
to launch into a lengthy analytical dissection of the deterministic position
in an endeavor to impale it on the horns of a dilemma. A brutal murder,
let's say, occurs in our neighborhood. Our instinctive reaction is to express
a "judgment of regret" over its occurrence. According to determinism,
however, the murder was a necessary part of the structure of things; it
couldn't *not* have happened. But what kind of universe is it, James asks,
in which such appalling events as this murder (and, let us add, Hitler's
gas chambers) are necessitated to happen? Surely, says James, we must
descend, as we contemplate the nature of things, into a profound pes-

simism. The only deterministic escape from pessimism (and James admits candidly that he has nothing to say to those satisfied with a Schopen-
hauerian pessimism) is to abandon judgments of regret and make the
assumption that a certain amount of evil is a necessary condition of the
higher good. If we could view things from the broadest of all perspectives, in other words, we would realize that this is, despite all its shortcomings, the "best of all possible worlds."

But the transformation of deterministic pessimism into deterministic
optimism, James points out, lands us in a logical predicament. If our
judgments of regret are wrong because they are pessimistic in implying
that what ought to be was impossible, then presumably they should be
replaced by judgments of approval for whatever happens. But from the
deterministic point of view, our judgments of regret are themselves
necessitated, and nothing else can possibly be in their place. Thus we
reach a kind of logical seesaw: evil cannot be regarded as in some sense
good without our regrets being wrong; and our regrets are not justifiable
unless evil is regarded as bad. But both regrets (whether justifiable or
not) and evils (whether regretted or assimilated into a larger good) are
foredoomed, in any case; and the monistic determinist, for all his eager-
ness to see the totality of things as coherent and rational, ends with a
universe at least as fundamentally irrational as that of the pluralistic
indeterminist.

There is, however, one way, James suggests, for the deterministic
optimist to extricate himself from his logical difficulties and to proclaim
both the evils and the regrets "*all* good together."[27] It is the way of
gnosticism or subjectivism. The necessitated evils which we erroneously
regret may be good and our error in regretting them may also be good
if we regard the universe primarily "as a contrivance for deepening the
theoretic consciousness of what goodness and evil in their intrinsic na-
tures are."[28] Taken in this way, the universe exists not to challenge us
to do battle for good against evil but to enlighten, entertain, even thrill
us as spectators by its dramatic richness and diversity. Subjectivism, in
short, "makes the goose-flesh the murder excites in me a sufficient reason of the perpetration of the crime" and transforms life from a
"tragic reality into an insincere melodramatic exhibition" with subjective
illumination as its primary purpose.[29] James cites Emile Zola and Ernest
Renan as typical representatives of the subjectivistic philosophy:

Both are athirst for the facts of life, and both think the facts of human sensibility to be of all facts the most worthy of attention. Both agree, moreover, that sensibility seems to be there for no higher purpose—certainly not, as the Philistines say, for the sake of bringing mere outward rights to pass and frustrating outward wrongs. One dwells on the sensibilities for their energy, the other for their sweetness; one speaks with a voice of bronze, the other with that of an Aeolian harp; one ruggedly ignores the distinction of good and evil, the other plays the coquette between the craven unmanliness of his Philosophic Dialogues and the butterfly optimism of his Souvenirs de Jeunesse.[30]

James the moralist has obviously stepped in at this point. It was impossible for him to take seriously a universe in which the moral struggle was not meaningful. Conduct, not sensibility, was the "ultimate fact for our recognition."[31] James (who was a liberal democrat, an impassioned Dreyfusard, and a fervent anti-imperialist) proposed what he elsewhere called "meliorism" as an alternative to the optimistic or pessimistic ways of conceiving the world. There were real objective goods to be championed, he insisted, and real evils to be resisted in the universe. The fight for the better must perpetually go on, even though we frequently meet defeat and even though the ultimate outcome of things remains ever uncertain. But, in James's view, there is point to the moral effort only if we can believe that how we act is not mechanically predetermined but grows out of free choices made by us from alternative possibilities.

What interest, zest, or excitement can there be in achieving the right way, unless we are enabled to feel that the wrong way is also a possible and natural way,—nay, more a menacing and an imminent way? And what sense can there be in condemning ourselves for taking the wrong way, unless we need have done nothing of the sort, unless the right way was open to us as well? I cannot understand the willingness to act, no matter how we feel, without the belief that acts are really good and bad. I cannot understand the belief that an act is bad, without regret at its happening. I cannot understand regret without the admission of real, genuine possibilities in the world. Only *then* is it other than a mockery to feel, after we have failed to do our best, that an irreparable opportunity is gone from the universe, the loss of which it must forever after mourn.[32]

In defending free will in this fashion on moral grounds, James took pains to make it clear that he was not suggesting that "absolute accidents," completely irrelevant to the rest of the world, ever take place. Human behavior, he insisted, was no more capricious and chaotic for the indeterminist than for the determinist. The futures presenting them-

selves to our choice "spring equally from the soil of the past" and once
our choice is made it "interdigitates" with phenomena already there "in
the completest and most continuous manner."[33] The psychologist, said
James, quite properly neglects free will in his search for behavioral laws,
for although an act of free choice "might be morally and historically
momentous, yet, if considered dynamically, it would be an operation
amongst those physiological infinitesimals which calculation must forever neglect." Hence: "Psychology will be Psychology, and Science Science, as much as ever (as much and no more) in this world, whether
free-will be true in it or not." But science's purposes, James added, are
not the only human purposes; there are ethical and aesthetic purposes as
well as scientific ones, and the concept of uniform causation which seems
useful in science may be out of place elsewhere. The indeterminist, in
short, is by no means hostile to science; he only insists that when it comes
to ethics some room be made for freedom. He simply contends that "of
alternatives that really *tempt* our will more than one is really possible."[35] James thus carefully circumscribed the area of volitional freedom; at the same time he believed that the uses to which it was put were
crucial both in the development of individual character and in the
shaping of society.

## THE INDIVIDUAL AND SOCIETY

Societies, like individuals, according to James, also have ambiguous
possibilities of development. Social evolution, he maintained, was not
directed by inevitable laws of history; it was the product of "the accumulated influences of individuals, of their examples, their initiatives, and
their decisions."[36] But these influences are largely matters of chance;
thus indeterminism is to be found in history, and the future is always
partly open and in some measure unpredictable. James was thinking
particularly of the impact of exceptional individuals on the course of
history, and in an essay on "Great Men and Their Environment" (1880)
he vigorously defended the Great Man theory of history. His chief target
was Herbert Spencer, who had announced that the great man

must be classed with all other phenomena in the society that gave him birth
as a product of its antecedents. Along with the whole generation of which
he forms a minute part, along with its institutions, language, knowledge,
manners, and its multitudinous arts and appliances, he is a *resultant*. . . . The
genesis of the great man depends on the long series of complex influences

which has produced the race in which he appears, and the social state into which that race has slowly grown. . . . Before he can remake his society, his society must make him. All those changes of which he is the proximate initiator have their chief causes in the generation he descended from. If there is to be anything like a real explanation of those changes, it must be sought in that aggregate of conditions out of which both he and they have arisen.[37]

But, complained James, to say that the changes wrought by Voltaire, for example, in French thought were the resultant of "that aggregate of conditions" out of which both Voltaire and French society had emerged was no more enlightening than to say that I slipped on the ice in front of my house today because the earth detached itself from the sun ages ago. In the largest sense, to be sure, the birth of the earth (together with everything that happened after its birth) was a necessary condition of my existing at all. But it was certainly not a sufficient condition of my fall on the ice. And if, in my preoccupation with "aggregate conditions" (the origin of life, the discovery of America, World War I, the Cold War, etc., etc.), I neglect to sprinkle sand on the sidewalk, thus risking further falls, even Spencer would scarcely judge my behavior as rational. To explain great men and their influences in terms of "aggregate conditions" was like explaining them in terms of Fate, Destiny, or Hegel's Absolute. It contained the "enormous emptiness" of abstract propositions which explain everything in general but nothing in particular.[38] James was determined that the individual should not be swallowed up in the vague and impersonal generalizations of Spencerian sociology.

James's major argument for the decisive role of individuals in history, however, rested on a view of social evolution deriving from Darwin. In accounting for evolutionary development, Darwin saw that there were two different cycles of operation in nature: tendencies toward spontaneous variations in living organisms (physiological cycle) and natural selection acting to preserve or destroy these variations (environmental cycle). Each cycle proceeds independently of the other according to its own fixed laws; the interaction between the two is a matter of accidental "timing" and what results, therefore, is a matter of chance. James regarded the great man as a "spontaneous variation"; society may accept or reject his offerings, but if it accepts them, then his genius will have a fermentative effect, modifying the environment in "entirely original and peculiar ways."[39] Shakespeare, for instance, was not the product of sociological pressures. He was a unique human variant (the product, to be sure, of physiological forces) who chanced to appear at Stratford-upon-Avon in 1564. If he had died in infancy, James asks facetiously, does Spencer think that social forces would have brought forth a substitute at Stratford-atte-Bowe? Similarly with other geniuses in art, literature, science, religion, and politics: their appearance, from society's point of view, was a matter of accident, entirely unpredictable in advance. But their impact on history was far-reaching. "Would England," asks James,

have to-day the "imperial" ideal which she now has, if a certain boy named Bob Clive had shot himself, as he tried to do, at Madras? Would she be the drifting raft she is now in European affairs if a Frederick the Great had inherited her throne instead of a Victoria, and if Messrs. Bentham, Mill, Cobden, and Bright had all been born in Prussia? . . . Had Bismarck died in his cradle, the Germans would still be satisfied with appearing to themselves as a race of spectacled *Gelehrten* and political herbivora, and to the French as *ces bons*, or *ces naifs, Allemands*. Bismark's will showed them, to their own great astonishment, that they could play a far livelier game. . . . The lesson will not be forgotten.[40]

The most a social analyst can ever predict, said James, is that "*if a genius* of a certain sort show the way, society will be sure to follow."[41]

James acknowledged that the indeterminism he was expounding was not complete. The genius of exceptional persons had to fit the "receptivities of the moment" if it was to be influential.[42] A man may be born at the wrong time. Peter the Hermit would be committed to a mental institution in the twentieth century. John Stuart Mill would have lived in obscurity in the tenth century. Cromwell and Napoleon needed their revolutions and Grant his Civil War. Even here, though, James declared that what makes a certain genius incompatible with his society "is usually the fact that some previous genius of a different strain has warped the community away from the sphere of his possible effectiveness."[43] After Newton, no Ptolemy; after Voltaire, no Peter the Hermit. James did recognize that the social environment, by its educative influences, "remodels" the great man and directs his interests and activities "to some degree."[44] But he clung firmly to his main point: human genius cannot be created by society; it always appears unexpectedly, and if the timing is right, social evolution will move in new directions.

In the last part of his essay James examined the function of the environment in mental progress, and for the first time he made certain concessions to the environmental point of view. A "vast part of our mental furniture," he admitted, does derive from the order of "outer relations" which we experience.[45] Our memories, habits, conceptions, interests, and even the reasons why our consciousness attends to one thing rather than to another are indubitably shaped by our external surroundings. Nevertheless, James contended that environmental influences are paramount only in "the lower strata of the mind . . . the sphere of its least evolved functions." When we come to "those mental departments which are the highest" in man, however, we see that

the new conceptions, emotions, and active tendencies which evolve are originally produced in the shape of random images, fancies, accidental out-births of spontaneous variation in the functional activity of the excessively instable human brain, which the outer environment simply confirms or refutes, adopts or rejects, preserves or destroys.

This was especially true, James thought, of superior minds:

Instead of thoughts of concrete things patiently following one another in a beaten track of habitual suggestion, we have the most abrupt cross-cuts and transitions from one idea to another, the most rarefied abstractions and discriminations, the most unheard-of combinations of elements, the subtlest associations of analogy; in a word, we seem suddenly introduced into a caldron of ideas, where everything is fizzling and bobbing about in a state of bewildering activity, where partnerships can be joined or loosened in an instant, treadmill routine is unknown, and the unexpected seems the only law. According to the idiosyncrasy of the individual, the scintillations will have one character or another. They will be sallies of wit and humor; they will be flashes of poetry and eloquence; they will be constructions of dramatic fiction or of mechanical device, logical or philosophic abstractions, business projects, or scientific hypotheses, with trains of experimental consequences based thereon; they will be musical sounds, or images of plastic beauty or picturesqueness, or visions of moral harmony. But, whatever their differences may be, they will all agree in this,—that their genesis is sudden and, as it were, spontaneous.[46]

In responding to criticisms of his Great Man theory, James broadened his thesis to some extent, in passing, to take account of the contributions of all individuals, no matter how humble, to social change. "There is very little difference between one man and another," he declared; "but what little there is, *is very important*." Each individual is in some respects unique and he may add his bit, however small, to social change. And by recognizing the significance of unusually gifted individuals in history,

"each one of us," he concluded, "may best fortify and inspire what creative energy may lie in his own soul."[47] Here, as elsewhere, the instinctive
democrat in James modified the aristocratic elements in his thinking and
enabled him to avoid Carlylean extremes.

One does not have to be an economic determinist to recognize that
James overstated his thesis. Not only did he overlook the effects of
social events like the rise of capitalism, the industrial revolution, and
the great wars on historical development; he also failed to take note of
the way natural events (like the Black Death in fourteenth-century
Europe) can affect the course of history. Grant Allen, who thought
James exaggerated the role of unusual people in history, was probably
right in contending that even if Clive had shot himself, circumstances
in England at the time would have encouraged "another and equally
unscrupulous Bob Clive" to steal Bengal all the same. Still, it must be
remembered that James was reacting to the excesses of social analysts
in his own day who talked about applying scientific determinism to history and discovering necessary laws of social development that made
individual efforts practically superfluous. Scientist-historian John W.
Draper's views were typical of the "scientific" school of history:

As the Astronomer, from recorded facts, deduces the laws under which the
celestial bodies move, and then applies them with unerring certainty to the
prophesying of future events, so may the Historian, who relies on the im-
mutability of Nature, predict the inevitable course through which a nation
must pass.

Few historians take Draper seriously today. James seems far closer
to the truth. For all of James's slighting of environmental factors, it is
safe to say that contemporary historical thought is closer to his outlook
than it is to the nineteenth century's scientific-law school of history
which he was criticizing. "That history is made by men and women,"
wrote Sidney Hook (who agreed only in part with James) in *The Hero
in History* (1943), "is no longer denied except by some theologians
and mystical metaphysicians." In the twentieth century, which has seen
"event-making men" (to use Hook's phrase) like Lenin, Stalin, Hitler,
and Mao shape the course of history, there seems to be considerable
agreement among empirically minded analysts that outstanding individuals have made a crucial difference in political and economic development. And when it comes to science and the arts, the influence of

exceptional people like Einstein, Picasso, and Stravinsky in their respective fields seems decisive.[48]

But if James was right in rejecting monistic determinism in history, he was not entirely clear at this point as to the relationship between the kind of indeterminism he located in history and the indeterminism he talked about when discussing human volitions. His social indeterminism, that is to say, seems to have no direct bearing on the question of free will. There was no connection, apparently, in James's thought, between the individual's choice between moral alternatives, which involves casual initiative, and the creative energies of exceptional individuals, which result from "spontaneous variations in the functional activity of the excessively instable human brain." One involves freely willed effort; the other is an "accidental out-birth" from the stream of consciousness.

Some years later, James began clarifying his views in this area. As he began to take account of the conscious effort involved in creative work he began stressing its similarity to moral striving and linking it, along with the latter, to free will. He also began to take account of "incursions" from the subliminal parts of the mind whenever a person is engaged in creative effort. In his earlier years, however, he was only prepared to say that individual activity, whether involving moral choices or creative endeavor, introduced novel elements into the universe; and the universe was "in so far forth" (to use a characteristic expression of his) undetermined and unpredictable.

## NOVELTY AND THE EXPERIENCE OF ACTIVITY

In the last decade of his life, James became absorbed in highly technical epistemological and metaphysical problems. He was eager to clarify and expand on several themes that had been implicit in his thinking from the very beginning of his career: pragmatism, which defined truth as a verification process leading satisfactorily from abstract ideas to concrete particulars; radical empiricism, which held that relations between things, conjunctive as well as disjunctive, were as much a part of our direct particular experience as the things themselves; and pluralism, which regarded the universe as loosely constructed, "strung-along," and unfinished, rather than as a consolidated unit.

One of James's chief concerns in all of this, however, was to make a systematic criticism of monistic determinism, whether of the idealistic or materialistic variety, and to present an alternative vision of the universe in which human freedom was at least a possibility. During this period, his tendency was to speak generally of "novelty" rather than of free will or chance. "Free-will pragmatically," he explained, "means *novelties in the world*, the right to expect that in its deepest elements as well as in its surface phenomena, the future may not identically repeat and imitate the past."[49]

James was not, it should be noted, contending for novelty in nature. In some respects he was less an indeterminist than his friend Charles S. Peirce. Peirce insisted that the presence of variety, growth, and increasing complexity in nature made it clear that chance and indeterminism as well as regularity and uniformity were essential features of the natural world. "Nature is not regular," he exclaimed. "No disorder would be less orderly than the existing arrangement." The more refined the scientist's measurements of natural events are, he observed, the less precise his findings. James, for his part, fully recognized (partly under Peirce's influence) that the laws of nature developed by the physical sciences were approximations, not absolute transcripts of reality, and that such concepts as matter, mass, inertia, and force were mental instruments or "artifacts," not facts of nature, which enabled scientists to deal fruitfully with natural processes. But his view of scientific laws as a man-made conceptual shorthand, "true so far as they are useful, but no farther," did not lead him to posit indeterminism in the natural world as Pierce did.[50] He accepted some form of determinism as a necessary presupposition of all scientific endeavor. "So far as physical nature goes," he said,

few of us experience any temptation to postulate real novelty. The notion of eternal elements (atoms, for example) and their mixture serves us in so many ways, that we adopt unhesitatingly the theory that primordial being is unalterable in its attributes as well as in its quantity, and that the laws by which we describe its habits are uniform in the strictest mathematical sense.

It is "when we come to human lives" that our point of view changes.[51] It was novelty in human experience, not in nature, that James sought to defend. In our direct, immediate perceptual experiences, as contrasted with our conceptual afterthoughts about them, we do, James argued, encounter real novelty. Concepts, he declared, being

thin extracts from perception, are always insufficient representatives thereof; and, although they yield wider information, must never be treated after the rationalistic fashion, as if they gave a deeper quality of truth. The deeper features of reality are found only in perceptual experience.[52]

Concepts are static extractions from experience (indispensable, of course, for human thought) from which change and novelty are, by definition, ruled out. But within our perceptual experiences, "phenomena come and go. There are novelties; there are losses. The world seems, on the concrete and proximate level at least, really to grow."[53] Conceptually, we do not see how Achilles can overtake the tortoise, since there is an infinite number of points for him to traverse. Perceptually, we see that Achilles does in fact overtake and pass the tortoise.

In speaking of novelty on the perceptual level of human experience, James liked to point out that reality as we know it immediately is Gothic in character: "a real jungle, where all things are provisional, half-fitted to each other, and untidy."[54] It was his thesis (originally put forward in *Principles of Psychology*) that human consciousness is a continuing flowing, ever changing stream whose elements never repeat themselves identically from moment to moment. Even if, for example, we recite the Gettysburg Address for the tenth time, our recitatory experience will be to some extent different from our nine previous experiences with it. Our memory of earlier renditions, our physical and emotional state on the tenth occasion, and the new environing conditions themselves will make our latest recitation in some degree a unique experience which had never occurred before and will never recur. And this is true of all of our concrete perceptual experiences: " 'the same returns not, save to bring the different.' Time keeps budding into new moments, every one of which presents a content which in its individuality never was before and will never be again. Of no concrete bit of experience was an exact duplicate ever framed."[55] Conceptual thinking minimizes these concrete novelties or regards them as "predetermined and necessary outgrowths of the being already there"; but radical empiricism, which insists on taking experience at face value, believes that what occurs in the perceptual flux suggests that "real novelties may be leaking into our universe all the time."[56] We may thus suppose "that some things at least are decided here and now, that the passing moment may contain some novelty, be an original starting-point of events, and not merely transmit a push from elsewhere. We imagine that in some respects at least the future may not be co-implicated with the past, but may be really addable to it, and indeed addable in one shape *or* another, so that the next turn in events can at any given moment genuinely be ambiguous, i.e., possibly this, but also possibly that.[57] To the qustion of *how* our concrete experiences come into being from moment to moment, James's response was:

Who can tell off-hand? The question of being is the darkest in all philosophy. All of us are beggars here, and no school can speak disdainfully of another or give itself superior airs. For all of us alike, Fact forms a datum, a gift, or *Vorgefundenes* ["find"], which we cannot burrow under, explain or get behind. It makes itself somehow, and our business is far more with its What than with its Whence or Why.[58]

And part of the What consists of the perceptual novelties which we experience all the time.

But James had something else in mind when he spoke of "novelty" in our perceptual experience. It was the "experience of activity," as he called it, with which all of us are familiar when we are striving inwardly to achieve a goal. The activity-experience in consciousness was the second factor which James wished to emphasize when speaking of novelty in the universe. Novelty in this sense had to do with the feeling of active effort (which he had first explored in *Principles of Psychology*) that we experience when a desire, sense of direction, or thought of purpose is present in our consciousness. If causal initiative on the part of the human will truly exists, it is to be found in this feeling of activity accompanying the idea of a result present in the consciousness. "As a matter of plain history," James declared, "the only 'free will' I have ever thought of defending is the character of novelty in fresh activity-situations."[59]

By this time, however, James had enlarged his earlier conception of free will—focusing on one idea rather than another and choosing between moral alternatives—to include all creative mental effort. As a typical example of a "fresh activity-situation," he proposed the following:

I am now eagerly striving . . . to get this truth which I seem half to perceive, into words which shall make it show more clearly. If the words come, it will seem as if the striving itself had drawn or pulled them into actuality out from the state of mere possible being in which they were. How is this feat performed? How does the pulling *pull*? How do I get my hold on words not yet existent, and when they come by what means have I *made* them come? Really it is the problem of creation; for in the end the question is: How do I make them *be*?[60]

In personal activity-situations like the above, we seem to experience "creation in its first intention . . . causality at work."[61] The doctrine of free will holds that the feeling of activity which we experience in such cases involves causal initiative on our part and that, consequently, "we ourselves may be authors of genuine novelty."[62]

With his usual candor, James admitted that what appears to be genuine novelty to the experiencer of an "activity-situation" may be nothing of the kind. The feeling of activity may not represent causal initiative; it may be "the consequences of older being," that is, an effect, not an original cause.[63] But James thought it represented novelty: "the grafting on to the past of something not involved therein."[64] He also thought that a person's conscious strivings let loose "subconscious allies behind the scene" and resulted in "uprushes" of energies originating in the subliminal or transmarginal part of the mind. "Our intuitions, hypotheses, fancies, superstitions, persuasions, convictions, and in general all our non-rational operations," he insisted, came from our subliminal consciousness.[65] Sometimes the "incursions" from the subconscious self came spontaneously; they were what he had once called "spontaneous variations in the functional activity of the excessively instable human brain." More often, though, he thought, the outbursts from the subconscious were responses to causal initiative on the part of the individual. Conscious effort, in short, stimulated subconscious activity and set deeper forces to work in the psyche. James did not link the subliminal consciousness to the Universal Spirit as Emerson did, though he did suggest that if religious experiences like conversion and mysticism had an objective basis in reality the encounter with what he somewhat fastidiously called the "More" took place at this level of consciousness. Freedom, however, did not require a "More" for James (especially not an omniscient More) as it did for Emerson. Freedom lay in the individual's exercise of causal initiative; and the incursions from the subconscious were responses to the individual's conscious efforts and not the major source of creativity as they were for Emerson.

To the very end, James insisted that the "concrete way of seeing"— the radical empiricist perspective—would yield new insights into the question of freedom.[66] He was understandably exasperated when George Stuart Fullerton, professor of philosophy at the University of Pennsylvania, undertook to reduce his position on free will to absurdity for the *Popular Science Monthly* by converting it into an abstract principle. Fullerton charged that James was contending for the causelessness of all human endeavor and presenting a world in which actions "must drop from a clear sky out of the void, for just in so far as they can be accounted for they are not 'free.'" But this meant "a reign of mere caprice," exclaimed Fullerton, in which the past was lawless, the present purposeless, and the future a "wall of darkness." By James's reasoning, according to Fullerton, a miser or a skinflint was just as likely to give money to a beggar, out of the blue, as a philanthropist or do-gooder. "It is a melancholy world, this world of 'freedom,'" he concluded.

In it no man can count upon himself and no man can persuade his neighbor. . . . It is a lonely world, in which each man is cut off from the great whole and given a lawless little world all to himself. And it is an uncertain world, a world in which a knowledge of the past casts no ray into the darkness of the future.[67]

James protested against the caricature Fullerton had made of his views and he attributed it to the "vicious abstractionism" which prevented antipragmatists like Fullerton from thinking of free will concretely.[68] In *The Meaning of Truth* (1909), his last book, James made a final effort to clarify his position. In saying that the will was free, James declared, the radical empiricist simply meant that

there are situations of bifurcation inside of his life in which two futures seem to him equally possible, for both have their roots equally planted in his present and his past. Either, if realized, will grow out of his previous motives, character and circumstances, and will continue uninterruptedly the pulsations of his personal life. But sometimes both at once are incompatible with physical nature, and then it seems to the naive observer as if he made a choice between them *now*, and that the question of which future is to be, instead of having been decided at the foundation of the world, were decided afresh at every passing moment in which fact seems livingly to grow, and possibility seems, in turning itself towards one act, to exclude all others.[69]

It was possible, James admitted, to mistake one's ignorance of what is predetermined for actual indeterminism. But the free-willer took his direct experience at face value; he felt that the choices he made between futures at critical junctures in his life were freely made and not predetermined. But this did not mean that there was a breach between his past and his future; it meant that he had redirected his past, just as a trainman, in throwing the switch, changes the direction of a train without altering the character of the train in any respect. A train was the same train, the passengers on it the same passengers, and the train's momentum the same momentum, no matter which way the switchman placed the switch fixing the train's direction. So with human choices: whatever future the individual chooses in moments of bifurcation will slide out of his past just as smoothly as the train slides by the switch.

The world, in short, was *"just as continuous with itself"* for believers in free will as for determinists."[70] "The moments of bifurcation, as the indeterminist seems to himself to experience them, are moments both of re-direction and of continuation."[71] To argue, as determinists do, that points of bifurcation and choice entail absolute disconnection between past and future was for James like saying that in the case of a train there was *"no* connection of any sort whatever, no continuous momentum, no identical passenger, no common aim or agent" on the two sides of a shunt or switch which had been moved.[72] What determinists did, James complained, was to abstract the "little element of discontinuity" which he was arguing for in concrete life from the "superabundant continuity of experience" and expand it into absolute disconnection and "raving chaos."[73]

James's final word on freedom was what it had always been: it was open to each person to decide for himself whether free will was an actuality or an illusion. Temperamentally (and James believed that personal temperament was decisive in issues of this kind) he of course preferred the free-will hypothesis to the postulate of universal determinism. He found closed systems of thought (what he called "block universes") personally distasteful. "I think it would have depressed him," George Santayana once wrote,

if he had had to confess that any important question was finally settled. He would still have hoped that something might turn up on the other side, and that just as the scientific hangman was about to dispatch the poor convicted prisoner, an unexpected witness would ride up in hot haste and prove him innocent.[74]

Where determinism was concerned, James was forever hoping to turn up something on the other side.

Santayana regarded James's treatment of the free-will question as "vague," but this is surely unfair.[75] It is true that James did not produce a systematic treatise on freedom and that he deliberately chose to ignore most of the classical arguments in the freedom-determinism debate (e.g., the problem of accountability) as either inconclusive or irrelevant to what he considered the vital issues at stake. It is also true that he was continually rethinking the problem, that his point of departure varied with his prime concern of the moment, and that what he said on one occasion sometimes seemed only loosely related to what he said on another. Yet James sought to illuminate, not pontificate; and if he offered no final answer to the question of freedom, this was because there were no final answers in his loose-jointed, strung-along, imperfectly unified metaphysical universe. Still, as a radical empiricist who insisted on taking direct, immediate experience seriously, James offered a fresh and lively approach to the old free-will question. He insisted on thinking of freedom, not as an abstract concept, but as a concrete, living, inner experience involving attention, effort, purpose, and choice on the part of the individual. As a radical empiricist, James departed considerably from the traditional concept of free will (which Edwards had attempted to demolish), but there was never any mistaking his own views: freedom must be felt to be known, and evidence for it lay in the experience of creative effort itself. James was irritated by the failure of rationalists to take seriously the existential freedom he was defending; but he never thought he had closed debate on the subject, and he was pondering it to the end.

It is a pity that James did not take the rationalist's view of freedom more seriously. The rationalist's freedom was not necessarily antithetical to the empiricist's. If James had linked his own existential freedom with rational insight (which Emerson thought was crucial to human freedom), he might have strengthened the case for the individual's causal initiative. Creative effort, it seems clear, depends to a large extent on knowledge and understanding. Without an awareness of the possibilities of experience there is little likelihood of innovative activity. From this point of view the rationalist is correct in associating knowledge with freedom and ignorance with slavery. James was quite right in rejecting the nineteenth-century rationalist's identification of knowledge with the discovery of immutable truths about a fixed reality. But he was wrong in refusing to make a place for knowledge of things in his account of creative action. It is surely possible to recognize the role of rational and moral insight in the development of freedom without in any way diminishing the creative role of individual effort. In a pluralistic universe like James's, the effort to understand experience produces creative insights that in turn generate new creative efforts. In such a universe not everyone is free, and none of us is free all of the time. We do, however, escape the monistic trap through intelligent effort. And what we accomplish remains to a large degree unpredictable.

Present-day indeterminists focus on the question of predictability more directly than James did. To ask whether the will is free, they say, really means asking whether human choices and actions are wholly predictable; and their own view is that they are not. The free act, they hold, is a creative act and by its very nature eludes prediction. ("Before the problem of the creative artist," acknowledged determinist Freud, "analysis must, alas, lay down its arms."[76]) It is easy to predict an eclipse or other astronomical event far in advance of its actual occurrence, but it is simply impossible to predict a creative human act (scientific, artistic, moral) at any time before its occurrence without actually performing the act of creation itself. The person who predicts the relativity theory would be an Einstein; the Apassionata Sonata, a Beethoven; the Sermon on the Mount, a Jesus; the telephone, an Alexander Graham Bell. The great French mathematician Jules Henri Poincaré perceived the solution to a mathematical problem that had bothered him for months the moment he set foot on the bus at Coutances; but, as William Barrett has pointed out, he could not have foreseen this event, for to do so "he would already have had to possess the solution to this problem, together with the psychological knowledge when, where, and how this solution would come to him—an obvious contradiction." The same is true of a line of poetry or a bar of music. It would have been impossible in principle (as well as in practice) for anyone to predict the second line of Emerson's "The Snow-Storm" or the third measure of Beethoven's Fifth Symphony, because not all the material necessary for the prediction would have been available to the forecaster until that very line or measure was actually being composed. To say that every line Emerson wrote or every bar Beethoven composed was determined by some combination of hereditary and environmental influences is "empirically entirely insignificant," to use Karl Popper's phrase, for it does not explain a single line of poetry or a single bar of music. Some of the factors it is necessary to know in order to predict occur simultaneously with the creative act itself.

With creativity, in short, prediction (which is closely related to explanation) can only be synchronous with emergence; human beings are always getting one jump ahead of the prevailing situation in creative endeavor. "Music history," according to Robert Craft, "not only backtracks and switches directions but in the persons of its greatest composers is remarkable chiefly for its unpredictability." In Craft's opinion, "causality and antecedents account for everything except the differences that matter most." This does not mean that the act of creation is a chance or random event; it always has an intelligible connection with (or "interdigitates with," as James put it) what precedes it. Yet it results in fresh and unpredictable being—that is, in what James called novelty.[77]

In summing up his "last word" as a philosopher shortly before his death in 1910, James quoted with hearty approval the words of his friend Benjamin Paul Blood: "There is no conclusion. What has concluded, that we might conclude in regard to it?"[78] But James had of course come to some tentative conclusions of his own. Rejecting the optimistic determinism of Spencer and the pessimistic determinism of Schopenhauer, he offered melioristic pluralism as a possible third way of conceiving the universe: "The world, it thinks, may be saved, on condition that its parts shall do their best. But shipwreck in detail, or even on the whole, is among the open possibilities."[79] James personally could do his best only in a universe in which the future was to some extent uncertain, ambiguous, challenging, even potentially hazardous, and in which the creative efforts of men and women made a real difference in history. The year before he died he told James Ward: "I think the center of my whole *Anschauung*, since years ago I read Renouvier, has been the belief that something is doing in the universe, and that *novelty* is real."[80]

# 8

# Mark Twain's
# Mechanistic Determinism

MARK TWAIN was what William James called a hard determinist. He came to believe that freedom was an illusion. And so was moral responsibility. When Joseph Twichell lent him a copy of Edwards's *Freedom of the Will* in 1902, he read it straight through at once and reported afterward that he felt as if he had been on a three-days' tear with a drunken lunatic. But in Edwards Twain thought he found confirmation for his own long-held views on man's subjection to necessity. "Jonathan," he wrote Twichell approvingly,

seems to hold . . . that the man (or his soul or his will) never *creates* an impulse itself, but is moved to action by an impulse back of it. That's sound!

Also, that of two or more things offered it, it infallibly chooses the one which for the moment is most *pleasing* to ITSELF. *Perfectly* correct! An immense admission for a man not otherwise sane.

But Twain balked at Edwards's reconciliation of determinism with moral accountability. Edwards correctly emphasized the role of necessity in human life, Twain said, but then he suddenly flew off "the logical track" and made man responsible to God for his thoughts, words, and deeds. And this was "frank insanity."

Twain thought *Freedom of the Will* botched the case for determin-

188

ism by its moralizing. Edwards's main trouble was that he confined his analysis to interior motives and overlooked the importance of exterior forces in shaping man's will. He did not seem to realize that "a man's mind is a mere machine—an *automatic machine* which is handled entirely from the *outside*, the man himself furnishing it absolutely nothing." If he had recognized the mechanical nature of the mind, he would have known that "the only rational & possible next station on *that* piece of road" was "the irresponsibility of man to God." But Jonathan "shirked," Twain told Twichell, and thus arrived at the following handsome piece of illogic:

Man is commanded to do so & so.
It has been ordained from the beginning of time that some men *sha'n't* & others *can't*.
*These are to blame; let them be damned.*[1]

But Twain shirked, too, in expounding his own brand of determinism. "I wish I could learn to remember that it is unjust and dishonorable to put blame on the human race for any of its acts," he wrote Twichell in November, 1904. "For it did not make itself, it did not make its nature, it is merely a machine, it is moved wholly by outside influences."[2] The letter was, nonetheless, filled with indignation and disgust over political corruption. No more than Edwards was Twain able to refrain from preaching to people, even though the rigorous determinism he espoused made human behavior practically a reflex act.

Twain loved to talk about free will and determinism. For years he argued with Twichell about the theological aspects of the free-will question. He also occasionally sat up half the night with William Dean Howells talking about freedom and fate. He did not, to be sure, spend all of his time pondering these questions. He was a humorist, satirist, social critic, and literary artist, not a philosopher or theologian, and his forays into the field of metaphysical speculation were sporadic and unsystematic. Still, he had a lifelong fascination with instances of luck, coincidence, accident, and turning points in his own and other people's lives, and he returned to the themes of chance and necessity time and again in his writings. And in his last dark years the question of freedom and determinism became a major preoccupation—one might almost say obsession—of his literary and intellectual life.

It used to be said that only a German philosopher was capable of thinking that the web of things was so tightly knit that the sneeze of a peasant in medieval Europe somehow affected the fate of Germany in the nineteenth century. But Twain came to believe exactly that. "Each event has its own place in the eternal chain of circumstances," he announced toward the end of his life, "and whether it be big or little it will infallibly cause the *next* event, whether the next event be the breaking of a child's toy or the destruction of a throne."[3] This way of looking at things meant that the present was co-implicated in the primal past. As Twain told his friend and biographer Albert Bigelow Paine:

When the first living atom found itself afloat in the great Laurentian sea the first act of that first atom led to the *second* act of that first atom, and so on down through the succeeding ages of all life, until, if the steps could be traced, it could be shown that the first act of that first atom has led inevitably to the act of my standing here in my dressing-gown at this instant talking to you.[4]

In such an iron network of causes and effects freedom was an illusion and the gift of life itself a gigantic fraud. "Life was not a valuable gift," Twain finally decided, "but death was"; and when man "could endure life no longer, death came and set him free."[5]

### Scientific and Religious Determinism

Twain's philosophy was shaped by both scientific and religious imperatives. He was tremendously impressed by the vast impersonal universe which modern science, especially astronomy, revealed. "He was always thrown into a sort of ecstasy by the unthinkable distances of space," according to Albert Paine.

The fact that Alpha Centauri was twenty-five trillions of miles away—two hundred and fifty thousand times the distance of our own remote sun, and that our solar system was traveling, as a whole, toward the bright star Vega, in the constellation of Lyra, at the rate of forty-five miles a second, yet would be thousands upon thousands of years reaching its destination, fairly enraptured him.[6]

Twain regarded the expression *light-year* as the most stupendous in the English language, and he was also awed by the enormous time-scale which geologists took for granted.[7] Most of all, though, he was struck by the implacability of the causal sequence in nature which he thought undergirded all scientific thinking in his day. Like most of his contemporaries, he thought of laws of nature as prescriptions, not descriptions, and to Paine he often spoke of

the immutable laws that hold the planets in exact course and bring the years and the seasons always exactly on schedule time. "The Great Law" was a phrase often on his lips. The exquisite foliage, the cloud shapes, the varieties of color everywhere; these were for him outward manifestations of the Great Law, whose principle I understood to be unity—exact relations throughout all nature.[8]

In *Letters from the Earth*, an uncompleted manuscript written toward the end of his life, Twain described how the Creator introduced "automatic, unsupervised, self-regulating law" into the universe and he made it clear that he regarded the law of nature and the law of God as interchangeable. But even the Almighty, he insisted, could not interrupt the inevitable sequence of cause and effect, beginning with the first act of the primal atom, which He had set in motion. Natural law was "exact and unvarying Law—requiring no watching, no correcting, no readjusting while the eternities endure!"[9] The new statistical view of scientific laws (as approximate rather than absolute regularities, operating with a high degree of probability, not invariantly) entirely escaped Twain's notice, though it was beginning to replace the old absolutist view during his lifetime. He probably would not have known what to make of British physicist Clerk Maxwell's remark that if the statistical approach based on the theory of probability (which shaped his treatment of the dynamic of gases) had come earlier in the history of science, "we might have considered the existence of a certain kind of contingency a self-evident truth, and treated the doctrine of philosophical necessity as a mere sophism."[10]

Twain was at times deeply moved by the colossal majesty of the universe which he thought modern science depicted: the immense tracks of space, the vast stretches of time, and the smoothly operating mechanism of cause and effect. At the same time he was overwhelmed by the thought of man's insignificance in such a universe. Man, he once wrote, was like "the microscopic trichina concealed in the blood of some vast creature's veins"; his life was but "the fleeting of a luminous mote through the thin ray of sunlight—and it is visible but a fraction of a second."[11] In buoyant moods, Twain took the eighteenth-century deist view of Thomas Paine: he saw beauty and use and benevolence in nature. But in moments of disillusion and despair—and these became

more frequent as he grew older—he could only scoff at the idea that
man lived in a friendly universe. There is "nothing kindly, nothing
beneficent, nothing friendly in Nature toward any creature, except by
capricious fits and starts," he wrote bitterly in his notebook in 1895.
"Nature's attitude toward all life is profoundly vicious, treacherous and
malignant."[12] In *Following the Equator* (1897), he described a lignified
caterpillar which he came across in New Zealand to demonstrate the
cruelty of nature. "Nature is always acting like this," he observed.

Nature cakes a fish's eyes over with parasites, so that it sha'n't be able to
avoid its enemies or find its food. She sends parasites into a starfish's system, which clog up its prongs and swell them and make them so uncomfortable that the poor creature delivers itself from the prong to ease its
misery; and presently it has to part with another prong for the sake of
comfort, and finally with a third. If it regrows the prongs, the parasite
returns and the same thing is repeated. And finally, when the ability to
reproduce prongs is lost through age, the poor old starfish can't get around
any more, and so it dies of starvation.[13]

As for man, let him remind himself of cholera, scarlet fever, sleeping
sickness, and the plague, whenever he commences to contemplate the
beauty and goodness of nature.

Twain's philosophy was formed by religion as well as by science.
His father was a freethinker, but his mother was a Presbyterian "of
that clean-cut strenuous kind," according to Paine, that regarded hell
and Satan as "necessary institutions."[14] Twain's mother saw to it that
her children attended Sunday School at the Presbyterian church in Hannibal regularly, were drilled in the Westminster catechism, recited Bible
verses, and kept the Sabbath. In a community of God-fearing, Bible-
reading fundamentalists the Clemens youngsters also learned that smoking, drinking, and sexual indulgence were devices of the devil to put
one's immortal soul in jeopardy.

While there is no reason to believe that Twain was ever a devout
believer like his mother, it is clear that the Calvinism which he imbibed
as a boy had lasting effects on his thinking. He read Paine's *Age of
Reason* as a young man; he also listened eagerly (so he claimed later
in life) to the evolutionary speculations of a Scotchman named Mac-
Farlane whom he met in a boardinghouse when he was working as a
printer in Cincinnati in 1856-57.[15] But though he early abandoned
whatever creedal beliefs he had once held, the Christian epic continued

to play a prominent role in the theater of his mind. The "religious folly you are born in you *die* in," Twain once lamented, "no matter what apparently reasonabler religious folly may seem to have taken its place meanwhile, & abolished & obliterated it."[16] Twain's wife Livy was a loyal churchgoer (like his mother) when he first met her, and after the marriage he consented for a time to family prayers, grace before meals, and daily Bible-readings; but he soon revolted against this regimen, and before long he had won Livy over to his own heterodox outlook. Twain regretted the part he had played in destroying his wife's Christian faith without giving her something else to replace it. But the cast of his own mind remained unmistakably Calvinistic.

It would be wrong to say that Twain's gospel of determinism was simply an adaptation of Calvin's *Institutes* to modern times. Still, his approach to the question of freedom and determinism was decisively shaped by Calvinist theology. And the rejections and negations of his final years centered around a passionate revolt against the Missouri Presbyterianism of his boyhood. Somewhat like Bellamy, Twain concluded in the end that the religion in which he and his countrymen were reared was an intolerable form of moral and intellectual slavery and that they must seek other and better ways of conceiving reality if life were ever to be made bearable.

Personally, Twain felt the bondage to religious imperatives acutely all his life. His Calvinist conscience (he called it the "Moral Sense" and heaped it with obloquy) was a lifelong torment to him. The remorse he felt as a boy over his father's death was reinforced when his mother took him into the room where his father lay and made him promise to be a better boy. He promised to be faithful, industrious, and upright, like his father, but he never felt that he had succeeded. Later on, he held himself personally responsible for a series of untimely deaths in his family: that of his younger brother Henry (who perished in a steamboat explosion), of his infant son Langdon (who died of diphtheria), and of his twenty-four-year-old daughter Susy (who succumbed to meningitis). Looking back on his childhood, he even blamed himself for the death of a drunken tramp in a fire because the matches he had given the tramp for his pipe started the fatal conflagration. "I am so worthless," he wrote home from New York on June 7, 1867, just before sailing on the *Quaker City* to the Holy Land, "that it seems to me I never do anything or accomplish anything that lingers in my mind as a pleasant memory. My mind is stored full of unworthy conduct . . .

towards you all, and an accusing conscience gives me peace only in excitement and restless moving from place to place."[17] To his friend Howells he once lamented:

But oh, hell, there is no hope for a person that is built like me, because there is no cure, no cure.

If I could only *know* when I have committed a crime: then I could conceal it, and not go stupidly dribbling it out, circumstance by circumstance, into the ears of a person who will give no sign till the confession is complete; and then the sudden damnation drops on a body like the released pile-driver, and he finds himself in the earth down to his chin.[18]

Twain felt like Huck Finn about it: "If I had a yaller dog that didn't know any more than a person's conscience does I would pisen him."[19] Or like the Connecticut Yankee: "I have noticed my conscience for many years, and I know it is more trouble and bother to me than anything else I started with."[20] "Now tell me," Twain exclaims in one story, "why *is* it that a conscience can't haul a man over the coals once, for an offense, and then let him alone?" And his conscience explains: "It is my *business*—and my joy—to make you repent of *every*thing you do." Twain's moral sense had nothing in common with Emerson's moral sentiment. "Rabies," he announced, "is an innocent disease, compared to the Moral Sense." But railing at the moral sense never really solaced him for long; what he needed was the help of Bellamy's Dr. Heidenhoff.[21]

Twain never succeeded, except in his art, in destroying what he called his "trained Presbyterian conscience." Conscience, he decided, was "the creature of *training*"; it was "whatever one's mother and Bible and comrades and laws and systems of government and habitat and heredities have made it," and it was inexpungeable.[22] But the deterministic philosophy which he worked out in his mature years probably helped lighten the unconscionable burden of guilt, remorse, and self-doubt that he carried always with him. If, Twain reasoned, whatever happens is simply one link in an unbroken sequence of mechanical causes and effects, one can scarcely hold himself accountable when things go wrong. At least so Twain kept telling himself.

But if determinism satisfied deep-seated needs in Twain's emotional life, it also accorded with what he believed to be true about the universe. Modern science, Twain was convinced, portrayed the world as a gigantic, impersonal, tightly knit network of causes and effects in which human beings played a wholly insignificant role. While frequently expressing reverence for the "great Master Mind" which "created this majestic universe and rules it," Twain insisted that the Creator had no interest in man and never interfered with the great unvarying laws governing the world.[23] When a Presbyterian paper in Chicago referred to man as "the most sublime existence in all the range of non-divine being—the chief love and delight of God," Twain reacted with fury and contempt.[24] He also ridiculed the belief that all that happened was for the best, and he regarded the doctrine of special providences (the belief that apparently accidental bits of good fortune were the result of divine intervention) as a special piece of foolishness. "Special Providence!" he once exclaimed. "The phrase nauseates me—with its implied importance of mankind and triviality of God."[25] There was no teleology in his determinism as there was in Emerson's.

Twain liked to think of his mechanistic philosophy as thoroughly modern, up-to-date, hard-boiled, and scientific. But in his belief that everything in the universe was welded into an iron block he was a monistic holist rather than a scientific determinist. Determinism, as a working assumption of scientists, does not insist on a perfectly coherent system; it simply assumes that every constituent in the universe is determined by some other constituent and that no event in it could have been different without at least one other event's having been different. Monistic holism, Twain's view, goes much farther than this; it holds that the universe is an absolute unity and that no event in it can be different without every other event in it also being different. Many scientists were beginning, even in Twain's lifetime, to dispense with determinism (the uniformity of nature and universal causation) as a necessary prerequisite for scientific explanation.[26]

## TRAINING, TEMPERAMENT, AND CIRCUMSTANCES

Twain did not attempt a full exposition of his philosophy of mechanistic determinism until late in life, and some critics regard it as a pessimistic response to the disasters that struck him in the 1890s: his bankruptcy in 1894 resulting from unwise investments, the sudden death of his beloved daughter Susy of spinal meningitis in 1896, the appearance of epileptic symptoms in his daughter Jean soon after, and the sinking of his wife Livy into hopeless invalidism in the years that followed. But it is a fact that Twain developed the main outlines of his philosophy during his years of greatest personal happiness and prosperity. He read W. E. H. Lecky's *History of European Morals* in the 1870s and responded with enthusiasm to the views of those moralists treated by Lecky who denied that man has intuitions of right and wrong and held, instead, that exterior forces shaped man's character and that selfish interests motivated his actions. To the Monday Evening Club in Hartford, Connecticut, he delivered an address in February, 1883, on "What Is Happiness?" which contained the major elements of the thesis he later presented at length in *What Is Man?* In it, he told the club members that man was an automatic machine getting all his inspiration from the outside and acting solely from the desire to please himself. Twain's audience protested that Twain was trying to deprive man of his dignity and that if his doctrine were accepted life would no longer be worth living. Recalling the occasion many years later, Twain remarked that the good people of Hartford, for all their intelligence, resisted his "simple and unassailable truths" because they were prisoners of "stupid misteachings handed down by stupid ancestors and docilely accepted without examination."[27]

In *A Connecticut Yankee in King Arthur's Court* (1889), Twain examined the effects of "stupid misteachings" on people living in Merrie England in the sixth century. "Training—training is everything," Hank Morgan, the Yankee from Connecticut, concludes resignedly after observing the absurd and at times lunatic behavior of King Arthur and his people for a while;

training is all there is *to* a person. We speak of nature; it is folly; there is no such thing as nature; what we call by that misleading name is merely heredity and training. We have no thoughts of our own, no opinions of our own; they are transmitted to us, trained into us. All that is original in us, and therefore fairly creditable or discreditable to us, can be covered up and hidden by the point of a cambric needle [later on Twain denied that a person possessed even this tiny bit of originality], all the rest being atoms contributed by, and inherited from, a procession of ancestors that stretches back a billion years to the Adam-clan or grasshopper or monkey from whom our race has been so tediously and ostentatiously and unprofitably developed.

When Morgan le Fay, sister of King Arthur, kills a young page for accidentally brushing against her knee, Hank despairs of making her understand the enormity of what she has done. "No, confound her," he reflects,

her intellect was good, she had brains enough, but her training made her an ass. . . . To kill the page was no crime—it was her right; and upon her right she stood, serenely and unconscious of offense. She was the result of generations of training in the unexamined and unassailed belief that the law which permitted her to kill a subject when she chose was a perfectly right and righteous one.

Similarly, when Sandy, the princess he befriends, mistakes a pigsty for an ogre's castle under enchantment and a bunch of hogs for ladies in captivity, Hank laments: "My land, the power of training! of influence! of education! It can bring a body to believe anything." Determined to free the people from subjection to the Church and the Nobility and to clear their minds of ignorance, prejudice, and superstition, Hank establishes "man factories" for teaching reading, writing, and modern technology. But the Church declares an interdict, the Nobility organizes an army to fight him, and most of the people he has been counting on go over to the forces of darkness. In the end all he has left are fifty-two young boys who have been under his own instruction long enough to resist the superstitions of the age. But his grand design for retraining the sixth-century feudal world ends in bloody failure, and it is Merlin the magician who has the last word.[28]

The power of training in shaping human behavior also forms the basis for the irony in *Pudd'nhead Wilson* (1894). "Training is everything," Twain reminds us in one of the book's chapter headings. "The peach was once a bitter almond; cauliflower is nothing but cabbage with a college education."[29] After the slave girl Roxana, who is only one-sixteenth black, secretly exchanges her baby ("thirty-one parts white") for her master's baby, the latter is brought up to be a humble slave in every respect while her own baby, in the role of the Driscoll heir Tom, is indulged and petted (especially by Roxana) and grows up to be an arrogant and vicious representative of the master class.[30] When Judge Driscoll, Tom's foster father, discovers what a scoundrel the young man has turned out to be, he blames himself. "He is worthless and unworthy," the Judge laments, "but it is largely my fault. He was entrusted to me by my brother on his dying bed, and I have indulged him to his hurt, instead of training him up severely, and making a man of him. I have violated my trust."[31] After the deception is discovered and the real Tom finds out that he is not a slave, his plight is pathetic.

He could neither read nor write, and his speech was the basest dialect of the negro quarter. His gait, his attitudes, his gestures, his bearing, his laugh

—all were vulgar and uncouth; his manners were the manners of a slave. Money and fine clothes could not mend these defects or cover them up, they could only make them more glaring and the more pathetic. The poor fellow could not endure the terror of the white man's parlour, and felt at home and at peace nowhere but in the kitchen. The family pew was a misery to him, yet he could nevermore enter into the solacing refuge of the "nigger gallery"—that was closed to him for good and all.[32]

Training, in short, made a pure white with 100 percent F.F.V. blood in his veins into a perfect slave.

But despite the *Pudd'nhead Wilson* chapter heading, Twain did not think that training was everything. He believed that temperament was just as crucial a factor as training in determining a person's character and behavior. He also believed what no psychologist would accept today: that temperament was acquired at birth. "Temperament," he said, "is the law of God written in the heart of every creature by God's own hand, and *must* be obeyed, and will be obeyed in spite of all restricting or forbidding statutes, let them emanate whence they may."[33] In a piece entitled "A Defense of General Funston" appearing in the *North American Review* in May, 1902, Twain announced that "the basis or moral skeleton" of a man is "inborn disposition—a thing which is as permanent as rock, and never undergoes any actual and genuine change between cradle and grave." Outside influences, including training, he added, help mold a man's character. But a man's disposition, he insisted, could not be changed; it was the basic skeleton around which all outside influences congealed.[34]

Throughout *Pudd'nhead Wilson*, Twain's belief that temperaments are born, not made, produces a basic ambiguity of intention. Though Twain makes it clear that Roxy's baby was spoiled by overindulgent adults, he also says that Tom was "a bad baby, from the very beginning of his usurpation" and he speaks of his "native viciousness."[35] When Roxy is driven by her son's monstrous behavior to tell him he was really born a slave, the young man is naturally thrown into a state of shock, and for a while he finds it difficult to continue associating freely and easily with white people. But "the main structure of his character was not changed" by the revelation, Twain tells us, "and could not be changed."[36] Tom gradually drops back into his old overbearing ways, and until Pudd'nhead Wilson exposes him publicly at the end no one suspects the deception.

Twain's belief that dispositions are inborn leads him dangerously

close to a belief in innate racial traits. Roxy, it is clear, thinks that her
son Tom's depravity is racially based. "It's de nigger in you, dat's what
it is," she rages when she learns he has refused a challenge to a duel.

Thirty-one parts o' you is white, en on'y one part nigger, en dat po' little
one part is yo' *soul*. Tain't wuth savin'; tain't wuth totin' out on a shovel
en throwin' in de gutter. You has disgraced yo' birth. What would yo' pa
think o' you. It's enough to make him turn in his grave.[37]

Roxy is amazed that the noble qualities of the distinguished ancestors
(both white and black) of whom she is so proud have not asserted
themselves in her son. "Whatever has come o' yo' Essex blood?" she asks
bewilderedly.

En it ain't on'y jist Essex blood dat's in you, not by a long sight—'deed it ain't!
My great-great-great-gran'father en yo' great-great-great-great-gran'father was
ole Cap'n John Smith, de highest blood dat Ole Virginny ever turned
out, en *his* great-great-gran'mother or somers along back dah, was Poca-
hontas de Injun queen, en her husban' was a nigger king outen Africa—en
yit here you is, a slinkin' outen a duel en disgracin' our whole line like a
ornery low-down hound! Yes, it's de nigger in you![38]

A little later she muses. "Ain't nigger enough in him to show in his
finger-nails, en dat takes mighty little—yit dey's enough to paint his
soul."[39]

But if Roxy is certain about it all, Twain wasn't. In Roxy's confused
account of her ancestry, Twain was surely poking fun at excessive concern with genealogy. He was also probably showing how thoroughly
Roxy had absorbed the racial views of her masters. The fact, moreover,
that one of the ancestors Roxy boasts is an African king adds to the
ambiguity of Twain's point. And so do other elements in the novel
which stress the power of training rather than inborn dispositions in
molding men. Twain tended to overemphasize whatever deterministic
factor (training or temperament) he happened to be thinking of at
the moment. And sometimes he forgot to mention that he believed that
a third factor, circumstances, was just as powerful in shaping human
behavior as training and temperament.

At times Twain regarded circumstances as all-powerful. Discussing
Tom Sawyer with Rudyard Kipling in the summer of 1889, he remarked that "neither religion, training nor education avails anything
against the force of circumstances that drive a man."[40] Twain talked

about circumstances where it is customary to speak of accidents. By circumstances he meant unanticipated incidents bringing about important changes in a person's life. He called them circumstances rather than accidents because he thought the latter word obscured the fact that the unforeseen conjuncture of two events redirecting the course of people's lives was just as causally determined as any other kind of happening. Circumstances were for Twain links in the inevitable series of incidents constituting one's life. "I am not able to conceive of such a thing as . . . an *accident*—that is to say, an event without a cause," he declared. "Each event has its own place in the eternal chain of circumstances."[41] When a young woman wrote him in 1906 to remark on the "happy accident" that had brought them together, Twain utilized the occasion to set her straight on the meaning of the word *accident*. He also discoursed at length on the power of circumstances, that is, on the way in which unexpected but causally determined conjunctures of events shaped human existence. In his own case, he said, a "series of accidents —that is to say, circumstances" took him from school upon his father's death and put him in a printing office, led him to meet by chance a pilot who taught him how to steer, took him to Nevada with his brother, made a reporter out of him and then a lecturer and author.[42]

Picking out the special circumstances making his life what it was became something of a game for Twain. Writing on "The Turning-Point of My Life" for *Harper's Bazaar* in 1910, the last year of his life, Twain singled out catching measles as a boy and finding a fifty-dollar bill on the street when he was a young man as crucial turning points in his own life. But he regarded neither of them (nor any of the other turning points mentioned in the article) as accidental. Turning points, he said, were simply conspicuous links in the long chain of turning points making up a person's life; each link takes its appointed place at its appointed time. "A person may *plan* as much as he wants to," he wrote, "but nothing of consequence is likely to come of it until the magician *Circumstance* steps in and takes the matter off his hands." Man thus lives under the "dictatorship of Circumstance"; circumstance is "man's master—and when Circumstance commands he must obey."[43]

But circumstance, though powerful, Twain added (suddenly recalling some of the other features of his philosophy) cannot work alone; it must have a partner. And the partner is temperament. Temperament directs what a person does with the circumstances coming his way. But since Twain believed that temperament was inborn, his conclusion was that an individual has no control whatsoever over the details of his life. "Circumstance, working in harness with my temperament, created them all and compelled them all." He admitted that this way of looking at the matter had diminished his regard for man.[44]

In ruling out chance (the fortuitous encounter of separate and unique events) as an explanation for what happens in the world, Twain made it clear that he was a fatalist rather than a necessitarian and that he was unaware of the crucial part that chance played in such scientific formulations as the kinetic theory of gases and Darwin's law of natural selection. What Twain would have made of twentieth-century physicist Werner Heisenberg's principle of uncertainty or indeterminacy (according to which it is possible to generalize about the average behavior of subatomic particles but impossible to measure the precise behavior of single particles) it is difficult to say.

While Twain was expounding his fatalistic philosophy, one of his contemporaries, Charles S. Pierce, mathematician, physicist, and philosopher who anticipated Heisenberg, was developing a system of thought in which chance, probability, novelty, and growth, as well as regularity and uniformity, were basic constituents of the universe. "Try to verify any law of nature," said Peirce, "and you will find that the more precise your observations, the more certain they will be to show irregular departures from the law." The facts of growth and increasing complexity in nature could not, in Peirce's opinion, be explained by mechanical forces; mechanical processes, he noted, were reversible, but evolutionary processes were not. "The endless variety in the world," he insisted,

has not been created by law. It is not of the nature of uniformity to originate variation, nor of law to beget circumstance. When we gaze upon the multifariousness of nature we are looking straight into the face of a living spontaneity. A day's ramble in the country ought to bring that home to us.[45]

On one level, of course, Twain subscribed to Peirce's view: he recognized the richness, variety, and seemingly endless novelties of life on the Mississippi, and he was also impressed by the chance encounters, accidental happenings, and surprising turning points in his own life. On another level, however, he found the idea of chance, novelty, and spontaneity intolerable, and when he came to philosophize he espoused a doctrine of mechanistic fatalism and moral nonresponsibility that necessitarians like Edwards and Emerson (and twentieth-century scientists) emphatically repudiated. Somehow, Twain felt better if he could believe that whatever happened (especially if things went wrong) was precisely fated to happen. He might not like it, but at least it wasn't his fault. The responsibility was training's, temperament's, or circumstance's, not Twain's. Years later, attorney Clarence Darrow used similar reasoning to get reduced sentences for convicted criminals.

## MAN AS A MACHINE

In *What Is Man?*, his most ambitious sustained exposition of his gospel of determinism, Twain stressed temperament and training rather than circumstances in accounting for man's fate. Written for the most part between 1898 and 1905, *What Is Man?* was a frontal attack on a number of beliefs that were popular among middle-class Americans in Twain's day: in freedom of the individual, in a fundamental moral law permeating the universe, in an innate moral sense that intuits right and wrong, in the doctrine of unselfish stewardship, and in the notion that man was "the chief love and delight of God." Twain called *What Is Man?* his "Bible," and he regarded it as potentially so explosive that instead of giving it to the general public he had it privately printed, unsigned, in a limited edition of 250 copies, in 1906, for distribution among friends.[46] It was of course far less shocking than he thought; indeed, his basic point had been made in Franklin's *Dissertation on Liberty and Necessity* in 1725. Still, the ideas Twain put forth in the book surely ran counter to much of the conventional wisdom in the United States at the turn of the century, and they would have been regarded as outrageous by respectable middle-class churchgoers and stuffy moralizers of all denominations.

*What Is Man?* is cast in the form of a dialogue between an old man and a young man, with the former instructing the latter in the elements of a mechanistic philosophy of life. A human being, the old man announces at the outset, is a machine; like a sewing machine or a coffee mill, he operates automatically in all of his thinking and acting. His behavior is shaped by two fundamental factors: by what the old man calls his "make" and by the impact of exterior influences on him. Man's make, that is, his temperament or disposition, is inborn (placed there by God), and it can never be altered. Individual temperaments vary a great deal; some people are naturally happy and others basically miserable, and nothing can ever change this. Bravery and cowardice are also inborn. But there is a "master impulse" that all men possess regardless of variations in individual temperament: the impulse to self-approval which is fundamentally a desire to content one's own spirit. "*From his cradle to his grave,*" declares the old man, "*a man never does a single thing which has any* FIRST AND FOREMOST *object but one— to secure peace of mind, spiritual comfort, for* HIMSELF."[47] Love, hate, kindness, charity, sympathy, and duty are all simply different ways in which people find outlets for this selfish impulse. Because of temperamental differences, the activities that satisfy the master impulse will vary from person to person. One man gets personal satisfaction from giving money to a beggar, another from being patriotic, and a third from doing missionary work in the slums. But there is no such thing as a conscience or moral sense at work in any of this. It is only the innate impulse to self-satisfaction finding expression for itself. "Whenever you read of a self-sacrificing act or hear of one," says the old man, "or of a duty done for *duty's sake*, take it to pieces and look for the *real* motive."[48] The real motive is self-approval: "It is our breath, our heart, our blood. It is our only spur, our whip, our goad, our only impelling power; we have no other."[49] Pious Christians are as self-regarding as anyone else. Good boys are motivated by self-interest just as bad boys are.

But exterior influences as well as inherent selfish impulses shape human behavior. Man is a chameleon, says the old man; "by a law of his nature he takes the color of his place of resort." Since this is so, training is important in molding character. When the young man asks for details, the old man responds:

Study, instruction, lectures, sermons? That is a part of it—but not a large part. I mean *all* the outside influences. There are a million of them. From the cradle to the grave, during all his waking hours, the human being is under training. In the very first rank of his trainers stands *association*. It is his human environment which influences his mind and his feelings, furnishes him his ideals, and sets him on his road and keeps him in it. . . . The influences about him create his preferences, his aversions, his politics, his tastes, his morals, his religion. He creates none of these things for himself. He *thinks* he does, but that is because he has not examined into the matter.[50]

Man, in other words, doesn't possess an iota of originality. "A man's brain is so constructed," says the old man, "that *it can originate nothing whatever*. . . . It is merely a machine; and it works automatically, not by will power."[51] This is just as true of geniuses like Shakespeare as it is of ordinary people. "Shakespeare created nothing. . . . *He was a machine, and machines do not create.*" Shakespeare, it is true, possessed "complex and admirable machinery" and was "a Gobelin loom," not "a sewing-machine, like you and me," but his mind, like everyone else's, worked mechanically in responding to outside influences.[52] The mind of every person, high and low, "works automatically and independent of his control—carries on thought on its own hook."[53] Free will is an illusion. "You cannot keep your mind from wandering, if it wants to," says the old man; "it is master, not you." The mind "is independent of the man. He has no control over it, it does as it pleases. It will take up a subject in spite of him; it will stick to it in spite of him; it will throw it aside in spite of him. It is entirely independent of him."[54] The old man concedes that there is such a thing as "free choice" (the ability to determine which of two things is "the nearest right and just"), but he insists that "free will" (the ability to act on the right suggestion and discard the wrong one) does not exist.[55] Knowledge, in other words, makes no difference; no matter how much we know we can never break out of the causal nexus. A person may know what is right and want to do it and yet act wrongly. His make and training determine what he does. And in the mechanical nature of this thinking and acting, he is really no better than a rat or an ant.

The old man even acknowledges that his own beloved Gospel of Self-Approval is a mechanical product, though he does not go on to say that if this is so there is no standard (except training and temperament) by which to estimate the validity of his gospel. Nor does he consider the possibility that awareness of the demands of the Master Impulse might make a difference in one's behavior. It occurs neither to him nor to Twain that in denying the reality of rational insight (on which Emerson based his transcendental freedom) they were making it impossible to regard the deterministic philosophy of *What Is Man?* as anything more than a mere mechanical result of a causal series of feelings and thoughts. In Emerson's philosophy, fate yielded to human knowledge and understanding; in Twain's, it reduced truth and falsehood, good and evil, and even freedom and necessity to meaningless distinctions.

Completely oblivious, however, to the logical dilemma into which he has argued himself, the old man goes on to draw two major conclusions from the philosophy he has been pressing on his young companion. For one thing, he points out that since man is a machine, he deserves neither praise nor blame for what he does. "You and I are but sewing-machines," he tells the young man. "We must turn out what we can; we must do our endeavor, and care nothing at all when the unthinking reproach us for not turning out Gobelins." "I suppose, then," rejoins the young man, "there is no more merit in being brave than in being a coward?" "*Personal* merit. No," agrees the old man. "A brave man does not *create* his bravery. He is entitled to no personal merit for possessing it. It is born to him."[56]

By emphasizing the fact that he is talking about *personal* merit, the old man (i.e., Twain) draws back from the absurd conclusion that we do not in fact judge some actions to be admirable and others to be despicable. The old man, moreover, goes on to recommend the cultivation of decent behavior in people, regardless of personal merit. Since training affects behavior so much, he says, it is worthwhile training people to be virtuous. This is the second major conclusion he draws from the philosophy he is expounding. The young man is puzzled. "Now then," he says, "I will ask you to tell me where there is any sense in training people to lead virtuous lives. What is gained by it?" The old man's answer:

The man himself gets large advantages out of it, and that is the main thing —to *him*. He is not a peril to his neighbors, he is not a damage to them— and so *they* get an advantage out of his virtues. That is the main thing to them. It can make this life comparatively comfortable to the parties concerned; the *neglect* of this training can make this life a constant peril and distress to the parties concerned.[57]

Having placed morality firmly on a social basis in this fashion, the old man goes on to give his companion the following advice: "Diligently train your ideals *upward* and *still upward* toward a summit where you will find your chiefest pleasure in conduct which, while contenting you, will be sure to confer benefits upon your neighbor and the community."[58]

By insisting that moral rules grow out of human experience, not out of the conscience's intuitions of right and wrong, and that they are to be judged by individual self-satisfaction and social utility, the old man has departed from traditional Christian views of morality. Still, all the great world religions, he tells the young man, including Christianity, have taught the kind of morality he is expounding: having regard for one's neighbors as well as for oneself. But there is a big difference. Traditional religion put the neighbor first, while the old man places the self ahead of neighbor and community. In so doing, he says, he is simply being more candid about human nature than the great religious leaders have been. He is telling it like it is: the Master Passion ("the supreme and absolute Monarch that resides in man") is the hunger for self-approval.[59] And so the rule should be, not love thy neighbor as thyself, but "Do right *for your own sake*, and be happy in knowing that your *neighbor* will certainly share in the benefits resulting.[60] Adam Smith's "invisible hand" would presumably harmonize private gain and social good.

Shortly after Twain's death, Paul Carus, editor of the *Monist*, published copious extracts from *What Is Man?* in his philosophical journal and accompanied them with a friendly commentary. Carus thought Twain's main point about the "machinelike operations" of the mind was quite sound, but he deplored the "gloom" which Twain cast over the facts he presented. In a long essay of his own on "the mechanistic principle" in the same issue of the *Monist*, Carus also tried to set Twain straight on the matter of freedom by distinguishing, somewhat as Jonathan Edwards had done, between necessity and compulsion. A man's will is determined by his character, he said, but that is far different from a man's actions being forced upon him against his will. A person is free, in short, if his actions are not compelled but are a general expression of his character. Carus then went on to take issue with Twain's contention that man's dignity as well as his freedom disappears if man is a machine and possesses no merit for what he does:

. . . what ground is there for dejection if man's actions really take place in accord with the mechanistic principle? Is man the worse that he is no exception to the common natural law, that his activity, like any other event in nature, is subject to the law of causation? Even though the means by which nature, with the help of mechanical laws, attains her ends to produce a rational creature be very simple, the fact of man's high standing in nature remains the same. . . . The laws of mechanics are the most general laws of the universe. Nothing moves, nothing stirs nor happens that does not act in agreement with the laws of motion, and there is no harm in it that man's activity takes place in perfect agreement with mechanical laws.[61]

Carus's views did not go unchallenged. In an essay on "Mechanism and the Problems of Freedom," philosopher Gertrude C. Bussey took sharp exception to the Twain-Carus philosophy of mechanism. She made three main points: that mechanical causation was a methodological postulate of science, not a necessary and universal principle of reality; that human beings construct machines and machines therefore embody purposes, and that even if mechanical causation were universal it would not rule out teleology in the world; and that mechanism fails to explain the existence of human values, purposes, ideals, and creativity. "The theory of mechanism itself," she concluded,

Is not . . . a purely natural product. It is due to the organizing activity of man's intelligence and could not exist without it. . . . This unifying of experience [which human intelligence achieves] demands . . . that man be able to separate himself from the chain of nature in order to combine and order the presentations that come to him. Hence the formulation of the theory of mechanism is a fact which mechanism itself fails to explain, and the very existence of the *theory* is evidence of its own inadequacy as a final explanation of all facts in the universe.

Carus responded to these criticisms much as Twain probably would have. Determinism, he reiterated, is a general feature of the world which expresses the truth that the law of causation remains unbroken. If we were omniscient, he added, we would be able to predict the history of the world from step to step, much as a person who has seen a moving picture once knows what is going to happen next when he sees it again. He confessed he simply did not understand Bussey's final point about rational transcendence.[62]

### LIFE AS BUT A DREAM

Carus overlooked one of Twain's main points: the selfishness of human nature. In *What Is Man?* Twain did more than present his mechanistic philosophy of life; he also placed great emphasis on the taint of self-interest in all that we do, and in this respect he was echoing Jonathan Edwards and anticipating Reinhold Niebuhr. In *The Mysterious Stranger*, however, he went even farther in his perception of "original sin" at work in the world, for he insisted that human beings are far worse when they act from self-transcending motives (the Moral Sense) than when they follow their self-regarding impulses.

*What Is Man?* has little artistic merit (though Clarence Darrow, who shared Twain's hard determinism and pessimistic bent, regarded it as a "remarkable little volume").[63] But *The Mysterious Stranger* possesses the beauty and power of Twain's best writing. It may be regarded as his last will and testament, for in it he had his last say on the subjects which had occupied his mind with such increasing urgency after the disasters of the 1890s. Twain made several attempts to write the story between 1897 and 1905, and the version published in 1916, six years after Twain's death, by Albert Paine, Twain's literary executor, represents one of three uncompleted versions (edited by Paine) plus a final chapter which Paine selected (and edited) as the intended ending from Twain's manuscripts.[64]

Where *What Is Man?* stressed temperament and training in explaining human behavior, *The Mysterious Stranger* emphasized what Twain called "circumstances." Unlike *What Is Man?*, it is almost totally devoid of hope. Twain's later years, especially after Livy's health broke, were increasingly wretched; and his determinism, by turns hopeful and gloomy when he was younger, became strongly pessimistic toward the end. In *The Mysterious Stranger* Twain did not bother to urge people to "train their ideals upward" as he had in *What Is Man?*; he had decided that it was an exercise in futility. It is significant, however, that Twain's spokesman in *The Mysterious Stranger* is a supernatural or transcendent being rather than an ordinary mortal. The exponent of metaphysical determinism, Twain seemed finally to realize, must be free even if no one else is, for he must assume, if he is to be taken seriously, that he has transcended his own deterministic framework and is voicing opinions reached by rational analysis and not simply mechanically generated. But the deterministic opinions which Twain expressed in his last important piece of writing utterly demolished all forms of human creativity, including the science from which he thought he had learned his determinism, and they must be regarded as revelations of his own despairing state of mind rather than as compelling insights into the nature of things.

The story Twain tells in *The Mysterious Stranger* is simple enough. A handsome young man strolls one afternoon into a sleepy little sixteenth-century Austrian town and makes himself known to Theodor, the boy narrator of the story, and his friends Nikolaus and Seppi. The stranger, Philip Traum, says he is the nephew of Satan, performs a series of breathtaking miracles for the boys, and also intercedes in astonishing ways in the lives of the villagers. Among other things, he arranges for Father Peter to find some gold coins for paying off the mortgage on his house; and when the kindly old man is charged with theft and thrown in jail, he arranges for his acquittal. But the bulk of the story has to do with the stranger's chats with the boys and with his revelations about the nature and destiny of man. In the stranger's conversations Twain brings together a number of themes that were much on his mind

in his later years: the paltriness of human nature, the idiocies of the
moral sense, the puerilities of orthodox Christianity, the forces of circumstances in shaping life, and the notion of death as a release from
life's intolerabilities. Twain's stranger, it quickly becomes clear, possesses
Twain's contradictions as well as his philosophy. He sneers at the moral
sense but passes judgment on people all the time. And he castigates
people for doing things they were mechanically fated to do. He is a
chronically indignant determinist.

Like Twain in his bitterest moments, the mysterious stranger regards
human beings as miserable slaves. They are the victims, he says contemptuously, of a variety of self-delusions; they live "a life of continuous and uninterrupted self-deception" and dupe themselves "from cradle
to grave with shams and delusions" which they mistake for realities.[65]
One of their greatest illusions is that they are superior and exalted beings, the highest form of life, and the center of the universe. In plain
fact, says Philip, human beings are weak and silly: "so dull and ignorant
and trivial and conceited, and so diseased and rickety, and such a shabby
poor worthless lot all around."[66] Most people are cowards; they act out
of fear of public opinion, and it is easy for determined minorities to
control them. "I know your race," Philip tells the boys.

It is made up of sheep. It is governed by minorities, seldom or never by
majorities. It suppresses its feelings and its beliefs and follows the handful
that makes the most noise. . . . The vast majority of the race, whether savage
or civilized, are secretly kind-hearted and shrink from inflicting pain; but in
the presence of the aggressive and pitiless minority they don't dare to assert
themselves.[67]

For a moment, Philip, in acknowledging the elements of kindness in
people, seems to be taking back the contemptuous things he has been
saying about human nature. But only for a moment. For he quickly
goes on to say that fear and cowardice completely blot out whatever
generous impulses people possess and lead them to engage in acts of
monstrous cruelty. Human beings enjoy torturing heretics and burning
witches, he reminds the boys, and they slaughter each other in ways
utterly unknown to the animal kingdom. And they do so largely because
vocal minorities manipulate them for self-advancing purposes of their
own and because they are afraid not to follow the crowd. Philip puts
on a little show for the boys about the history of the human race, and
it is an unrelieved story of wars, murders, and massacres. When Theodor

asks about the moral sense, which is supposed to distinguish humans from animals, Philip sets him straight on this too. The moral sense, he says, makes people act in ways that are simply inconceivable to dumb animals. When Theodor sees a young heretic being tortured and exclaims on the brutality of the act, Philip quickly reminds him:

No, it was a *human* thing. . . . No brute ever does a cruel thing—that is the monopoly of the snob with the Moral Sense. When a brute inflicts pain he does it innocently; it is not wrong; for him there is no such thing as wrong. And he does not inflict pain for the pleasure of inflicting it—only man does that. Inspired by that mongrel Moral Sense of his![68]

It is the moral sense, Philip explains, which leads factory owners to exploit their workers, the town loafer to abuse his faithful dog, and the villagers to burn girls at the stake for alleged witchcraft. Animals are incapable of such monstrosities because they are not "besmirched with the Moral Sense."[69] Compared to the Moral Sense, the selfish Master Impulse seems almost benign.

Having laid bare the ignorance, folly, cruelty, and superstition of the human race, Philip goes on to reveal that all of it is really inescapable. Man has no control over his destiny; everything he does is part of an inevitable series of acts that commenced with his first act. He is predestined, in short, to be damned; and there is no saving remnant among men and women in Twain's scheme as there was in Edwards's. Human beings are like dominoes. "Among you boys," young Satan explains,

you have a game: you stand a row of bricks on end a few inches apart; you push a brick, it knocks its neighbor over, the neighbor knocks over the next brick—and so on till all the row is prostrate. That is human life. A child's first act knocks over the initial brick, and the rest will follow inexorably. . . . Nothing can change the order of its life after the first event has determined it. That is, nothing *will* change it, because each act unfailingly begets *an* act, that act begets another, and so on to the end.[70]

So rigidly is each act bound to its predecessor in the chain of life that to change one act in a person's chain is to alter that person's career completely. All acts, moreover, are "of one size and importance"; to "snatch at an appointed fly is as big with fate for you as is any other appointed act." If Columbus as a boy had skipped "the triflingest little link" in the chain of acts set in motion by his first childish act, it would have altered his whole subsequent life. It would also have altered the

course of history, for he would not have become an explorer and discovered America. But no one ever does drop a link. Even when a person
is trying to make up his mind what to do, the deliberation is itself a
link in his life-chain. And if he decided to try to drop a link, "*that*
project would itself be an unavoidable link—a thought bound to occur
to him at that precise moment, and made certain by the first act of his
babyhood."

Theodore is profoundly disturbed by Philip's revelations about man's
fate. "He is a prisoner for life," he observes sadly, "and cannot get free."
"No," says Philip, "of himself he cannot get away from the consequences
of his first childish act. But," he adds, "I can free him."[71] The freedom
he bestows, however, turns out to involve death or insanity.

By using his miraculous powers Philip proceeds to change tiny links
in the life-chains of several of the villagers and thus completely alters
the course of their lives. Among others, he intervenes in the lives of
little Lisa Brandt and of Theodor's friend Nikolaus. Under the old chain
it was appointed that Nikolaus would save Lisa from drowning. But
by changing one seemingly trivial act in Nikolaus's life, Philip causes
the boy to arrive on the scene too late to save the girl. By the time he
arrives Lisa has struggled into deeper water, and in his efforts to rescue
her both are drowned. Theodor is horrified by what Philip has done.
But Philip explains that if the original chain of events had been unbroken and Nikolaus had saved Lisa, he would have caught cold afterward, contracted scarlet fever, and spent the rest of his life as "a paralytic
log, deaf, dumb, blind, and praying night and day for the blessed relief
of death."[72] As for Lisa, if she had survived, she would have gone on
to a life of crime ending in death at the hands of the executioner.
(Twain did not explain, because he could not, why the change Philip
made in Nikolaus's life-chart, which altered Lisa's destiny, did not also
change the lives of their parents and friends, including Theodor, and
then village, country, continent, and ultimately world history.) Overwhelmed by news of the drownings, Nikolaus's mother bitterly re-
proaches herself for the disaster. And Theodor reflects:

It shows how foolish people are when they blame themselves for anything
they have done. Satan knows, and he said nothing happens that your first act
hasn't *arranged* to happen and made inevitable; and so, of your own motion
you can't ever alter the scheme or do a thing that will break a link.[73]

When Lisa's mother hears of the tragedy, she goes mad with grief; and

at Theodor's pressing Philip agrees to alter the poor woman's future.
He makes a slight change in her life-chain and she ends by being burned
at the stake for uttering blasphemies. To the shocked Theodor Philip
patiently explains that the alteration saved the woman twenty-nine more
years of earthly misery.

Death, then, seems to be the only way to achieve freedom from the
heartbreaks and horrors making up human existence. There is one other
possibility: insanity. Father Peter is acquitted of the charge of theft, but
before he learns of his acquittal Philip visits him in jail and tells him
he was convicted as a thief and forever disgraced. The shock unseats
the old man's reason, and he develops delusions of grandeur and
imagines that he is the Emperor. Thereafter, he is, Philip tells Theodor,
"the one utterly happy person in this Empire." When Theodor protests,
Philip presses the point: "Are you so unobservant as not to have found
out that sanity and happiness are an impossible combination? No sane
man can be happy, for to him life is real, and he sees what a fearful
thing it is. Only the mad can be happy, and not many of those."[74]

But since not even many of the insane are happy, it is clear that the
chief means of release from the deterministic chain of sorrow and
misery that constitutes life is death. Twain makes this point time and
again in his story. Philip arranges death for Lisa, Nikolaus, and Lisa's
mother to save them from a future filled with misery. He compares the
fate of exploited workers in a French village with that of a heretic who
was tortured to death and points out that the heretic "is dead, now,
and free of your precious race; but these poor slaves here—why, they
have been dying for years, and some of them will not escape from life
for years to come."[75] When Gottfried Narr's grandmother is charged
with witchcraft and quickly confesses even though it means burning at
the stake, her (and Twain's) reasoning is: "If I hadn't, they might have
set me free. That would ruin me; for no one would forget that I had
been suspected of being a witch, and so I would get no more work, and
wherever I went they would set the dogs on me. In a little while I
would starve. The fire is best; it is soon over."[76] And death is absolutely
final. When Theodor tells Philip at the end of the story that he may see
him again in another life, the latter says quietly: "*There is no other.*"
Theodor's reaction at this point is one of relief and thankfulness.[77]

Is there any other road to freedom except through death? Would
it ever be possible to start a new chain of life going which would be
free of the intolerabilities of the old chain? At one point in *The Mys-*

*terious Stranger* Twain suggests another possible cure for the human predicament short of death: humor. But he is not sure that man's sense of humor is sufficiently developed to be of much help. "You have a bastard perception of humor," Philip tells Theodor,

nothing more; a multitude of you possess that. This multitude sees the comic side of a thousand low-grade and trivial things—broad incongruities, mainly; grotesqueries, absurdities, evokers of the horse-laugh. The ten thousand high-grade comicalities which exist in the world are sealed from their presence. The ten thousand are hid from the entire race.[78]

Asked to name some "high-grade comicalities," Philip singles out religion and politics for special scorn. "No religion exists," he exclaims, "which is not littered with engaging and delightful comicalities, but the race never perceives them." Hereditary royalties and aristocracies are also "deliciously comical," but so are republics and democracies. "All forms of government. . . ," Philip presses on, "are rich in funny shams and absurdities, but their supporters do not see it." But the chief comicality is religion, Papal or Presbyterian, and Philip returns to the church time and again to show his contempt for it. And at length he muses:

Will a day come when the race will detect the funniness of these juvenilities and laugh at them—and by laughing at them destroy them? For your race, in its poverty, has unquestionably one really effective weapon—laughter. Power, Money, Persuasion, Supplication, Persecution—these can lift at a colossal humbug,—push it a little—crowd it a little—weaken it a little, century by century: but only Laughter can blow it to rags and atoms at a blast. Against the assault of Laughter nothing can stand.[79]

In laughter, then, there does seem to be a glimmer of hope for humanity. But do people have the sense and courage to laugh their illusions out of existence? Perhaps not. Philip is not sanguine about the possibility. Still, he suggests, if human beings were to succeed in blowing their juvenile beliefs to pieces by a blast of laughter, perhaps they could at long last begin living as truly free beings, willing and able to face the hard demands of life honestly and courageously and without the deceptive solace of childish illusions.

Chiefest of the illusions incapacitating people for mature living, Twain had concluded, was the Christian religion, particularly in its fundamentalistic form. Christianity, with its anthropomorphic God, sickly conscience, Puritan moral code, special providences, heaven and hell, and

its belief that man was "the chief love and delight of God," had victimized people for centuries, Twain thought, and had kept them in
bondage to "pure and simple insanities." "Strange, indeed," Philip exclaims in his last communication to Theodor, "that you should not
have suspected that your universe and its contents were only dreams,
visions, fictions! Strange, because they are so frankly and hysterically
insane—like all dreams." Then comes a bitter blast at the anthropomorphic God of the Christian religion (who, Twain had decided, was
totally depraved):

a God who could make good children as easily as bad, yet preferred to make
bad ones; who could have made every one of them happy, yet never made
a single happy one; who made them prize their bitter life, yet stingily cut it
short; who gave his angels eternal happiness unearned, yet required his other
children to earn it; who gave his angels painless lives, yet cursed his other
children with biting miseries and maladies of mind and body; who mouths
justice and invented hell—mouths Golden Rules, and forgiveness multiplied
by seventy times seven, and invented hell; who mouths morals to other
people, and has none himself; who frowns upon crimes, yet commits them
all; who created man without invitation, then tries to shuffle the responsibility for man's acts upon man, instead of honorably placing it where it belongs, upon himself; and finally, with altogether divine obtuseness, invites
this poor, abused slave to worship him!

All of these things, Philip tells Theodor, are impossible except in a
dream; they are "the silly creations of an imagination that is not conscious of its freaks." At the same time he reveals that he himself has no
objective existence but is merely a part of Theodor's own consciousness:

I am but a dream—your dream, creature of your imagination. In a moment
you will have realized this, then you will banish me from your visions and
I shall dissolve into the nothingness out of which you made me. . . . But I
your poor servant have revealed you to yourself and set you free. Dream
other dreams, and better![80]

For Twain it was too late to dream other dreams. He never freed
himself from the spell of orthodox Christianity. To the end, the Christian
world view in its most fundamentalistic form shaped his view of reality.
Though he made fun of it, heaped scorn on it, and lashed out against it
in fury, he could never get it out of his mind for long. Both *What Is
Man?* and *The Mysterious Stranger*, for all their rebelliousness, discuss
life essentially in orthodox Christian terms; and *Letters from the Earth*,

though it is a sustained attack on the biblical view of the world and on
the Christian attitude toward sex, is also placed in a scriptural setting.
At times Adam and Eve and Jehovah and Satan seem to have been as
real for Twain as such friends as Twichell and Howells. When he
dictated his reflections on religion to Albert Paine in June, 1906, Twain
tried hard to distinguish between the vindictive God of the Old Testament, who brought sin into the world and then blamed man for it, and
the sublime God of modern deism who brought this stupendous universe
with its myriad wonders into being with one flash of thought and framed
its immutable laws with another. But almost immediately he finds himself blasting the Deist God as cruel and malicious, too, for creating a
world in which life preys on life and for foreordaining all the miseries
of man down to the tiniest details:

God has so contrived him that all his goings out and comings in are beset
by traps which he cannot possibly avoid and which compel him to commit
what are called sins—and God punishes him for doing these very things
which from the beginning of time He has always intended that he should
do.[81]

Thomas Paine would have been appalled by Twain's confusion of the
Deist God with the God of Calvinism.

Intellectually Twain had been chafing against the orthodox Christian
conception of things since early manhood; but emotionally he was never
able to emancipate himself (as Bellamy did) from the teachings of his
boyhood Calvinism. Freedom from the impossible demands of Christianity
on belief and conduct forever eluded him. He was born, it seemed to him,
with an ineradicable sense of guilt; he had Puritan morality inexpunge-
ably drilled into him as a child; and though he strove to do right in his
life and work, circumstances had a way of overpowering him at every
turn. Twain became increasingly bitter as he learned, in blow after blow,
that life simply didn't square with the religion he had learned in his
Hannibal Sunday School. The sudden loss of Susy while he was abroad
in 1896, Livy's long illness, decline, and death in 1904, and Jean's
epilepsy and abrupt death in 1909 were like swords thrust into his heart,
although he said he was "glad, for the sake of the dead, that they have
escaped."[82] But human suffering could not be reconciled with a benevolent
God. Nor could the vast implacable universe revealed by modern science
be harmonized with the notion that man was the chief delight of God.

Furthermore, the hypocrisy, sanctimoniousness, and stupid dishonesty of pious Americans and the intolerance and cruelty of organized religion through the ages belied the commonly accepted belief that Christianity elevated human nature. And the harsh Christian moral code, especially when it came to sex, ran counter to the vigorous life-force animating all creation.

But if the Christian universe was only a dream, was there anything but dreams? Was it all unreal, untrue? Was life itself an illusion? Shortly after Livy's death following a prolonged illness that Twain said almost killed him, his friend Twichell wrote to ask how things were going with him. In his reply, Twain expressed for a moment solipsistic sentiments similar to those appearing at the very end of *The Mysterious Stranger*:

. . . (a *part* of each day—or night) as they have been looking to me the past 7 years: as being NON-EXISTENT. That is, that there is *nothing*. That there is no God and no universe; and that there is only empty space, and in it a lost and homeless and wandering and companionless and indestructible *Thought*. And that I am that thought. And God, and the Universe, and Time, and Life, and Death, and Joy and Sorrow and Pain only a grotesque and brutal *dream*, evolved from the frantic imagination of that insane Thought.

"And so," he concluded, after another blast at the Old Testament God, "a part of each day Livy is a dream, and has never existed." But then he added soberly: "The rest of it she is real, and is gone. Then comes the ache and continues."[83]

# 9

# John Dewey's
# Organic Philosophy of Freedom

JOHN DEWEY took an organic view of freedom. He regarded it as a process, not a fixed state, and he thought its individual and social dimensions touched at every point. He also took an instrumentalist view. Freedom, he said, "has assumed various forms as needs have varied; its 'utility' has been its service in helping men deal with many predicaments."[1] Dewey wanted to put the idea of freedom to work in advancing science, democracy, and individuality in the modern industrial world, and he centered his hopes for a truly free society on the educational process. Where previous thinkers tended to emphasize either action or choice or insight in their definitions of freedom, Dewey regarded all three as essential to a proper understanding of the term. By combining intelligence, choice, and action in his concept of freedom and by associating them with continual growth on the part of the individual, Dewey departed markedly from the approach of earlier analysts, and he was able to cast new light on the perennial problem of freedom and determinism.

Dewey did not exactly solve the problem of freedom and determinism; he transformed it. The freedom-determinism problem, he thought, had become encumbered with "the refuse and debris of all kinds of other matters" which were "best 'solved' by letting alone."[2] Writing in 1909, he pointed out that the conviction persists—though history shows it to be a hallucination—that all the questions that the human mind has asked are questions that can be answered in terms of the alternatives that the questions themselves present. But in fact intellectual progress usually occurs through sheer abandonment of questions together with both of the alternatives they assume. . . . We do not solve them; we get over them.[3]

Dewey abandoned traditional approaches to the old free-will problem and proposed new perspectives from which to view the whole question of freedom and necessity. Influenced by Charles Darwin, G. W. F. Hegel, and the democracy of his boyhood Vermont community, he developed a philosophy of freedom that was hopeful and compassionate, as well as intellectually challenging, and which, in its efforts to put organic growth at the center of human experience, succeeded in illuminating all fields of thought and endeavor. Long before his death he was being called the "prophet and philosopher of freedom."[4]

## DARWIN, HEGEL, AND VERMONT

Darwinism (and modern science in general) played a major role in Dewey's experimental naturalism. Dewey was born in Vermont the year that *Origin of Species* was published, and it is customary to remark on the appropriateness of the coincidence. Dewey's outlook, like James's, was shaped by Darwinism, and in its mature form it was more radically Darwinian than James's. While vestiges of the fixities and finalities that shaped two thousand years of Western thought continued to linger even in James's open universe, Dewey's thinking came to be thoroughly informed by what he called "Darwinian genetic and experimental logic."[5] Dewey regarded *Origin of Species* as a milestone in the history of thought. In laying hands on "the sacred ark of absolute permanency" and in conquering "the phenomena of life for the principle of transition," Darwin, in Dewey's opinion, introduced a mode of thinking that was bound eventually to transform every field of knowledge.[6]

For Dewey, the Darwinian, process replaced permanency as the chief center of interest for the philosopher; and change, growth, and history became keys to understanding the universe. In Dewey's philosophy, nature was a system of interconnected changes and consisted of events rather than substances. This meant that process was universal and that so-called "objects" were really natural events with histories of movement and change to which human beings attached meanings for their own purposes. Some things, of course, changed more slowly than others in this ever moving universe. For some events, indeed, the rate of change was so slow and rhythmic that they seemed to possess stability and structure in comparison with more transitory and irregular happenings and could be taken as relatively permanent objects by which to measure the movements of the latter. Human thinking, especially scientific thinking, concerned itself with correlations among these changing events; and the knowledge which human beings accumulated about the orderly processes of change in nature facilitated their own processes of living. Man himself was for Dewey a mode of energy existing within nature and inseparably connected with other modes of energy; he was an organic part of the mutual interactions of changing things that made up the universe. Interaction was the key to both man and nature. There were interactions taking place within the human organism as well as interactions between the individual organism and its physical and social environment. The result was that the individual, society, and nature were continually transforming one another.[7]

Dewey was a Hegelian before he was a Darwinist, and although he eventually discarded German idealism for a thoroughgoing evolutionary naturalism, the Hegelianism of his early years left a lasting imprint on his mind. From George Sylvester Morris, dedicated Hegelian whom he encountered when he did graduate work at Johns Hopkins University in the early 1880s, Dewey learned like James to look with scorn on the passivistic *tabula-rasa* view of the mind expounded by British empiricists. Morris (and contemporary British idealistic philosophers like Thomas Hill Green whom Dewey also studied) taught that the mind was active, not passive, and that experience was an organic living whole. The organicism of the idealistic school of German and English thought had an enormous appeal for young Dewey, torn as he was by the split between the old values and the new science. Hegel's thought, he recalled many years later,

supplied a demand for unification that was doubtless an intense emotional craving, and yet was a hunger that only an intellectualized subject-matter could satisfy. It is more than difficult, it is impossible, to recover that early mood. But the sense of divisions and separations that were, I suppose, borne in upon me as a consequence of a heritage of New England culture, divisions by way of isolation of self from the world, of soul from body, of nature from God, brought a painful oppression—or, rather, they were an inward laceration. . . . Hegel's synthesis of subject and object, matter and spirit, the divine and the human, was, however, no mere intellectual formula; it operated as an immense release, a liberation. Hegel's treatment of human culture, of institutions and the arts, involved the same dissolution of hard-and-fast dividing walls, and had a special attraction for me.[8]

Dewey gradually Darwinized his thinking during the 1890s, partly under James's influence, but the Hegelian insistence on continuity of experience remained always with him. Continuity, like interaction, was a major concept in Dewey's mature philosophy; and in time he came to prefer the word *transaction* to the word *interaction*, because it was more in harmony with the concept of continuity. Dualism in any form—subject ond object, mind and body, man and nature, the individual and society, theory and practice, science and ethics, ends and means, cause and effect, stimulus and response—was intolerable to Dewey.

Dewey not only organicized philosophical thinking; he also democratized it. Implicit in the dualism of Western thought has been the belief that one of the two factors being isolated from experience for special attention is superior to the other: mind to body, theory to practice, ends to means, cause to effect. Dewey was fond of tracing these invidious distinctions to their social origin in classical times. In ancient Greece, especially Athens, where Western philosophy was born, society was divided into a laboring class which did all the "useful" work and a leisure class which was free to devote itself to intellectual pursuits. Dewey thought that the sharp division between knowing and doing embedded in Western thought plus the belief that the former was a "higher" category than the latter simply reflected Greek economic organization. But such a situation was pre-democratic, he insisted, and it had no place in modern thought. In Dewey's opinion, modern science and democracy logically required the elimination of such dichotomies, as well as of hierarchical thinking of any kind, from philosophical thought. "The observable world," he wrote in *Essays in Experimental Logic* (1916),

is a democracy. The difference which makes a fact what it is is not an exclusive distinction, but a matter of position and quantity, an affair of locality and aggregation, traits which place all facts upon the same level, since all other observable facts also possess them and are, indeed, conjointly responsible for them.[9]

Few philosophers have been as deeply democratic in their life and work as Dewey. His background was middle class. Son of a grocer in Burlington, Vermont, he mingled with youngsters coming from diverse

backgrounds (rich and poor as well as native American and immigrant)
in the local school before entering the University of Vermont. Life in
Burlington in Dewey's day was generally democratic—"not consciously,
but in that deeper sense in which equality and absence of class distinctions are taken for granted"—and young Dewey thoroughly absorbed
the democratic spirit.[10] His wife Alice, a talented woman with a strong
social concern and something of a feminist, encouraged his democratic
inclinations. And his association with the social work of Jane Addams
and Hull House while he was teaching at the University of Chicago in
the 1890s also reinforced his equalitarian outlook. To his thinking about
freedom Dewey brought a vital faith in democracy as well as an evolutionary point of view that insisted upon interaction and continuity in
nature and experience. Dewey was a professional: an immensely learned
man and a systematic thinker. His erudition made him a "philosopher's
philosopher," and his originality won him attention in philosophical
circles abroad as well as at home. But there was nothing self-conscious
or pedantic about his scholarship. He loved ideas, but he also loved
people, especially children, and he had a natural liking for lowly people
that made him unusual among people who devote themselves to the
life of the mind.[11]

Dewey's writings lack the verve and imagination of James's best
work He is not very quotable. Dewey's prose style tended to be abstract,
difficult, and at times obscure, mainly because he was trying to replace
the fixity and certitude contained in age-old ideas with process and inquiry and to organicize our thinking about all aspects of human experience. But there was nothing remote or abstract about Dewey himself.
Deeply committed to advancing freedom in the concrete, he marched
with pre-World War I suffragettes, supported Eugene Debs, Robert
LaFollette, and Norman Thomas for President, defended Sacco and Van-
zetti, headed a commission of inquiry into Stalinist charges against Leon
Trotsky, was associated with important academic-freedom cases in col-
leges and universities, lent his name to numerous civil-rights and civil-
liberties causes and organizations, and, perhaps most important of all,
wrote extensively about practical problems involved in primary and secondary school teaching. Dewey's ivory tower, like his own household,
was an enormously busy place. At times friends found him pecking diligently away at his typewriter with his children crawling noisily around
him.

During his Hegelian years, Dewey had little to say about freedom and what he said was extremely formalistic. In his first major work, *Psychology* (1887), his discussion of freedom was brief and perfunctory and lacked the excitement of the passages on freedom in James's *Principles of Psychology*. In the 1890s, however, while he was rapidly Darwinizing, he became seriously interested in the free-will question and in *Outlines of a Critical Theory of Ethics* (1891), *The Study of Ethics, A Syllabus* (1897), and essays for the *Monist* and the *Philosophical Review*, he began laying the groundwork for his organic and instrumentalist view of freedom. In 1908 he gave his first extended treatment of freedom from the new point of view in a series of chapters (entitled "The Theory of the Moral Life") which he contributed to *Ethics*, a college textbook written in collaboration with James H. Tufts of the University of Chicago. In *Ethics*, however, he dealt with only one aspect of freedom. But he returned time and again to the subject—in books like *Human Nature and Conduct* (1922), *Philosophy and Civilization* (1931), *Freedom and Culture* (1939), and in his treatises on education—and he invariably had something fresh and illuminating to say every time he discussed it. Though he never brought his scattered reflections on freedom into one grand system, there was an organic unity underlying everything he said about it. "Freedom," according to Dewey, "has too long been thought of as an indeterminate power operating in a closed and ended world." It was Dewey's purpose to show that in reality freedom consisted of "a resolute will operating in a world in some respects indeterminate, because open and moving toward a new future."[12]

Dewey saw freedom as taking three major forms: (1) in the choices we make; (2) in our power of action in carrying out these choices; and (3) in our ability to grow and develop in wisdom and foresight. While he frequently discussed these three kinds of freedom separately, he did not in fact think that one of them could be isolated from the other two except for purposes of analysis. He regarded them as inextricably intertwined. The "possibility of freedom is deeply grounded in our very beings," he declared. "It is one with our individuality, our being uniquely what we are and not imitators and parasites of others." But like all possibilities, he added, "this possibility has to be actualized; and, like all others, it can only be actualized through interaction with objective conditions." Social conditions, moreover, "interact with the preferences of an individual (that *are* his individuality) in a way favorable to actualizing freedom" only when the interaction develops "intelligence, not abstract knowledge and abstract thought, but power of vision and reflection."[13]

## FREEDOM AS REFLECTIVE CHOICE

Dewey saw a great deal of validity in the common notion that freedom involved choice. "There is an inexpungeable feeling that choice *is* freedom," he observed, "and that man without choice is a puppet" with "no acts which he can call his very own."[14] But he was extremely critical of the "libertarian" view that identified choice with an arbitrary freedom of the will. Like Jonathan Edwards, he rejected the idea that there was a special causal force or power in the mind which enabled a person to choose freely and without motivation if he so desired. A person who made choices without rime or reason, he said, would behave whimsically, capriciously and, in fact, imbecilically. He objected, moreover, to taking freedom out of the social world and cooping it up in some obscure region of the individual's mind, because he thought it isolated ethics from society. He also thought that advocates of free will, in their insistence on motiveless choice, had a false conception of the self; they regarded motive as an alien force, acting from the outside on the self, instead of being an intimate part of the self and expressing the self's very nature.[15]

The principle of continuity made it impossible for Dewey to accept the traditional concept of free will. His insistence on organic relations throughout experience led him to rule out flatly James's suggestion that the mind possesses independent causal initiative of its own (taking the form of intention and effort), because this kind of initiative seemed to come *ex nihilo* and sunder the organic connections between things. Dewey was not a causationist like Edwards; he disliked cause-effect dualism as much as any other kind of dualism. His predilection for continuity made him critical of all philosophical systems which split the experiential continuum up into arbitrary causes and effects and then tried to bring things back together by mechanical means. He repeatedly warned against substituting mechanical for organic relations and against eliminating, by artificial dualisms, the mutual transformations which he thought all natural events impinging on one another continually underwent. Causality, for Dewey, was simply another name for the sequential order of events itself, in which any event was both the beginning of one course of action and the end of another.[16] There was no place for a separate and independent human will in any of this.

What about the libertarian belief that free will and moral responsibility go hand in hand? Was it fair to hold people liable for what they do unless they have the power of contrary choice, that is, the power to

differently from the way they do in exactly the same circum-
~s? Dewey's answer was that libertarians confused the idea of free-
and responsibility by looking backward instead of forward. The
estion of responsibility, he said, rested on consequences, not on antecedents. Dewey thought the question of whether a person might have acted
differently from the way he did, in a precisely identical situation, was
irrelevant to the question of freedom. The important thing, he said, was
how a person behaved in the future; by commending or criticizing his
actions, we hope to have some effect on how he behaves the next time.
For Dewey, in short, praise and blame had a prospective rather than a
retrospective significance; they were concerned with the future consequences of holding a person accountable rather than with prior causal
conditions. We do not hold little babies, idiots, and psychotics accountable, because it has no effect on their future actions. But we do hold
young children liable for what they do, not necessarily because they acted
deliberately for the first time, but because we hope to shape their subsequent conduct. And we hold a child increasingly responsible as he gets
older, not because he has suddenly acquired free will, but because he is
capable of moral and intellectual growth and because the assumption of
responsibilities is an essential part of his development. We can't undo
the past, in short, but we can shape the future. "One is held responsible,"
said Dewey, "in order that he may *become* responsible, that is, responsive
to the needs and claims of others, to the obligations implicit in his position."[17] But would we excoriate a man like Hitler for his crimes as he
lay dying? Presumably not, on Dewey's reasoning, unless we thought our
verbal chastisement would have a beneficial effect on the future behavior
of other people. Dewey had nothing to say about "vicarious punishment"
(punishing all the members of a family for the misdeeds of one member) or about what might be called "preemptive punishment" (punishing innocent people in order to keep them and others in line), probably
because these were the practices of totalitarian societies and he was
thinking primarily of the democratic community.

Dewey's rejection of the case for free will did not mean that he
accepted the customary deterministic refutation of the libertarian position, namely, that acts of choice always have motives and are thus never
free. He thought that determinists (like Edwards) who argued this way
had just as faulty a conception of human nature as libertarians did. It
was a fallacy, Dewey insisted, to think of motive as an external force
which caused the self to do things. Such a view assumed that the self

was passive and needed to be stirred into action from the outside, and it also implied that the self was a fixed entity of some kind. Dewey regarded human nature as active and plastic, not passive and static, and he thought the idea that human beings possessed a group of ready-made powers like reason, will, and emotions, needing to be set into motion by exterior forces, was pure mythology. As biological organisms, human beings are born, he said, with a tremendous variety of tendencies or impulses (tendencies to respond in certain ways to changes in the environment and, in responding, to bring about other changes) which interweave with one another in all kinds of subtle ways. By interacting with the physical and social environment (with which the self is continuous), these instinctive modes of action develop into the desires, habits, purposes, and interests which make up the self. The self, in Dewey's view, was from the very beginning incessantly active. It needed no motives for action; it was naturally active and what it did defined what it was.

In Dewey's opinion, "motives" were really the active interests which formed the core of the self; they were ways in which the self acted or *moved* toward certain objects in which it was interested. To say that a person was motivated by greed (or benevolence) gave the impression that greed (or benevolence) was an independent power of some kind producing a certain type of behavior in people. But greed (or benevolence) was actually a kind of behavior in itself; it did not refer to something a person possessed but described a certain kind of activity. Greed (or benevolence) had to do with the quality of actions which were socially observed and disapproved (or approved). A person was not *moved* by greed, said Dewey; he *moved about* greedily and his activities revealed his character.[18]

Dewey's was an adverbial rather than adjectival universe. The identity of self and act was a central point in his ethics. And his view of motives as movements of the self toward objects in which it was interested enabled him to take a fresh look at the old question (which had concerned Twain so much) of egoism vs. altruism as springs of action. Dewey thought egoism and altruism were acquired dispositions, not inborn tendencies, and he insisted that they represented different degrees of interest in the world, not clashing contrarieties. Our native impulses, he said, are not actuated by a conscious regard for either one's own good or that of others; they are simply direct responses to situations. Gradually we learn to behave with regard for our own health and well-being and with consideration for the welfare of others; and the balance which we learn to strike between the two (both of which are necessary for fruitful living) defines our moral character. Dewey thought it was misleading to regard self-interest (as Twain did) as a universal motive determining all human behavior, including acts of generosity. In his opinion, "self" and "interest" were interchangeable concepts; interests really defined the self. Interests, he said, may be trivial or momentous, narrow or wide, transient or enduring, exclusive or inclusive. But an individual must be interested in what he is doing or he wouldn't do it. From this point of view, a "selfish" person is one with narrow interests, while an "unselfish" person has broad and generous interests. To be "disinterested" is not to lack interest in what you are doing; it is to take a fair and impartial view of what has engaged your interest.[19]

Dewey linked interests with individuality. Preferential action or selective behavior (growing out of individual interests) was, he thought, a universal trait, appearing not only in human beings but in all other living organisms as well. And even atoms and molecules, he said, are indifferent to some things and react energetically to others. Dewey thought that the "preferences" which a thing revealed by the way it responded to other things grew out of its very structure, and that differential responses of behavior were unmistakable evidence of a fundamental individuality or uniqueness in all things. He also thought they formed the basis for human choices. Unlike simpler forms of existence, human beings have many preferences. Because they are sensitive to a vast number of different conditions and undergo a tremendous variety of experiences (natural and social), they develop a large set of possible responses to things. Alternative preferences inevitably appear in every new situation, and people are drawn spontaneously in different directions. They hesitate, when confronted with puzzling situations, and their hesitation may develop into deliberation. At this point they begin to weigh the values of different courses of action, calculate the consequences of acting on the various competing preferences, and eventually form a new preference according to which they take action. And the choice they make both reveals their existing selves and helps shape their future selves. "In so far as a variable life-history and intelligent insight and foresight enter into it," said Dewey, "choice signifies a capacity for deliberately changing preferences."[20] And this activity of choosing represents a mode of freedom; it is an expression of the individual's unique life-history plus his intelligent foresight.

To the extent, then, that one possesses the habit of reflective intel-

ligence he is, according to Dewey, capable of acting in the light of a
foreseen future rather than being pushed into action from behind by
sheer impulse or mechanical routine. His thinking is therefore a genuine
"projection of the novel, deliberate variation and invention," and his
choice has transforming effects on himself and his environment.[21] Freedom, therefore, is percipient choice; it enables an individual to transcend
(but not make an absolute breach with) his environment and transform it.

## FREEDOM AS POWER TO ACT

Dewey realized that freedom as choice was meaningless without the
ability to act in accordance with choice. Another form of freedom (the
kind that reformers like Paine and Douglass cherished) was indispensable to freedom as choice: the power to carry desires and purposes into
operation unhampered by obstacles and restrictions. Historically, Dewey
noted, freedom defined as the power of effective action was at the heart
of the classic philosophy of liberalism. Liberals of the eighteenth and
nineteenth centuries stressed the natural rights of individuals to liberty,
and they fought courageously against despotic governments and oppressive laws which violated the individual's right to self-determination in
action. Moreover, they stressed natural wants as well as natural rights
and insisted that in a just society there would be no restrictions on the
power of individuals to carry their economic wants into effect by means
of free and unhindered enterprise, labor, and exchange. The upshot was
the philosophy of laissez-faire individualism which reduced governmental
action to a minimum and stressed freedom of individual behavior, particularly in the economic realm.

Dewey thought that the popular philosophy of "self-expression" was
similar in nature to laissez-faire liberalism, though it never formed a part
of the latter. According to the self-expression philosophy, freedom centered around the unrestricted expression of a person's basic impulses and
desires. The self-expressionist insisted that freedom would be a reality for
the individual only if law and custom refrained from interfering with
personal and domestic relations. Despite their basic differences, laissez-
faire individualism and self-expressionism had one thing in common:
they both stressed freedom as unhampered individual action.[22]

Dewey found much to praise in classic liberal individualism. Eighteenth-century liberalism, he acknowledged, succeeded in modifying institutions, laws, and social arrangements that were unquestionably oppres-

sive. By stressing the significance of the individual, moreover, laissez-faire liberals called attention to the unique and variable elements in human nature which Dewey regarded as the ultimate source of innovation and creativity. Their emphasis on equality of opportunity and on civil liberties (freedom of speech, press, worship, and association) was equally commendable. Dewey called freedom of thought, inquiry, and intercommunication the "vital nerve" of democratic institutions, though he justified them in terms of social benefits rather than as natural rights.[23] He was anxious to preserve the old-fashioned liberal tradition of civil liberty, individuality, and equality of opportunity in the modern world, but he regarded the underlying philosophy of classic liberalism as essentially fallacious. By viewing liberty as a natural right, he said, it tended to overlook its social dimension: the dependence of liberty, as the power to do things, on the distribution of power in society.

Historically, Dewey noted, the abolition of feudal restrictions and the liberalization of political institutions benefitted only a small group of people (mainly the rising industrial and trading classes) and not the mass of people as a whole. As the new commercial classes gained in power, moreover, they began subjecting large numbers of people to new modes of oppression of their own. Instead of being too individualistic, the liberal school, Dewey once remarked, was not individualistic enough: it helped emancipate individuals who possessed the means, economic and intellectual, to take advantage of the changed social conditions, but it did nothing to liberate the majority of individuals.[24]

Classic liberalism, moreover, was in Dewey's opinion too hostile to organization to have a realistic view of freedom. Excessive organization militated against freedom, he admitted, but freedom as the power to act effectively simply could not exist for long without some degree of organization. To achieve practical freedom, Dewey said, individuals had to agree to curtail some of their natural liberties and enter into association with other people "so that the activities of others may be permanently counted on to assure regularity of action and far-reaching scope of plans and courses of action."[25] Dewey did not think it was possible to draw up an abstract formula specifying the precise relation between individual freedom and social organization. The question was experimental in nature; it involved specific situations and concrete details, not abstract theory. The standard of judgment, he thought, was the balance of freedom and security achieved in any given instance as compared with practical alternatives.

But while Dewey deplored classic liberalism's excessive individualism and its hostility to organization, he reserved his sharpest criticism for its static view of human nature. Laissez-faire liberals seemed to think that individuals were born with ready-made natural rights and wants and that if external obstructions to their operation were removed, freedom would flourish and produce a harmonious society. Their views were somewhat like those of the free expressionists, who thought there was something intrinsically good about man's natural impulses and that freedom rested on their unrestricted operation. Both views, Dewey thought, overlooked the enormous role that interaction with the natural and social environment played in shaping man's impulses and desires.

Dewey did not deny the role of biological heredity in producing natural individual differences, but he did think it erroneous to conceive of the individual as an isolated entity existing apart from his surroundings. An individual's interrelations with nature and society, he pointed out repeatedly, were unremittingly active and energetic from the moment of birth. A person's native tendencies and impulses entered into ceaseless transactions with his environment, and the form they took was indelibly shaped by the social context in which they found expression. This is why Dewey thought it absurd to argue that men were equally free to act if only the same laws applied equally to everyone. Such a notion neglected the vast differences in individual capacities for action growing out of differences in economic and educational opportunities. "Since actual, that is, effective, rights and demands are products of interactions," he said,

and are not found in the original and isolated constitution of human nature, whether moral or psychological, mere elimination of obstructions is not enough. The latter merely liberates force and ability as that happens to be distributed by past accidents of history. This "free" action operates disastrously as far as the many are concerned.[26]

Dewey's conclusion was that freedom defined as the ability to act in accord with choice depended to a great extent on equitable social arrangements.

When it came to thinking about the social order, traditional liberals committed what was from Dewey's point of view another grave error. They made a sharp separation between the "sphere" of freedom and the "sphere" of authority and said that the great problem to be solved was fixing the proper boundaries between the two. Authority, they said, was the enemy of freedom; it had an inherent tendency to encroach on the sphere of liberty and establish despotism, and it must at all times be carefully watched and energetically opposed. Only when liberty exceeded its own boundaries and degenerated into license should authority be called upon to restore the balance. Dewey denied that freedom and authority could be split apart in this fashion; he thought there was an intimate union between the two. For Dewey, authority stood for the stability of social organization by means of which individuals received direction and support; individual freedom represented the forces of initiative, invention, and innovation which brought about changes in society. He thought both were essential to a viable society. The real problem was to ascertain the proper relationship between them.

Dewey, who was interested in the genesis of ideas, located the hostility of laissez-faire liberals to authority in historical experience. The old traditions and established organizations against which they fought in the eighteenth and nineteenth centuries were in fact rigid and oppressive and the liberals, as champions of innovation and change, did represent the creative force of individual freedom. By regarding existing institutions as necessary embodiments of the principle of authority, however, liberals began to think of authority as by its very nature external to individuality and inimical to freedom. But Dewey insisted that authority did not need to be either external to the individual or hostile to freedom. As a matter of fact, authority, he noted, was not ordinarily felt by the individual to be external; in the form of habits (which embodied society's traditions and customs), authority was built into the very constitution of individuals and shaped their deepest beliefs and purposes. Compared to the variable and innovating elements in human nature (the source of freedom and change), the conservative force of habit was overpowering. For most of history, in fact, people had preferred authority and stability to freedom and change. Only with the rise of science and technology in modern times did individuality, innovation, and change become significant factors in human affairs. But the exponents of laissez-faire liberty, who at first represented the forces of innovation and change, came in time to stand for conservatism and stability. While continuing to deprecate all authority in principle, they gradually set up a new authority—concentrated economic power—in place of the old authorities. And while they continued to glorify individual liberty and denounce social control, they came to be apologists for the new wealth and privilege and became just as resistant to social change as the old authorities they had once decried. Under the social institutions growing out of the new form of

economic power, the mass of economically underpowered and under-
privileged people were persistently denied effective freedom of action.[27]

Dewey wanted to discard, once for all, the old dualism of authority
and freedom which had produced so much confusion (and hypocrisy)
and to try to effect an interpenetration of the two. His own suggestion:
utilizing the methods of organized intelligence in social affairs. In the
field of science and technology, collective intelligence was the rule and
its achievements had been colossal. In Dewey's opinion, organized intelligence represented a remarkable organic union of individual freedom
and collective authority. Science had progressed, he said, by encouraging,
not suppressing, the variable and creative elements in human nature. Its
advances had been initiated by individuals who freed themselves from
the bonds of tradition and custom whenever they felt that the latter were
interfering with their own powers of observation and reflection. But
though science depended for its development on the freedom of individual
inquirers, its authority rested on the collective activity of the scientific
community as a whole. Every scientific researcher depended on methods
and conclusions that were common possessions; and his own discoveries
were publicly tested and developed and, if cooperatively confirmed, became part of "the common fund of the intellectual comonwealth."[28]
Dewey thought that the operation of cooperative intelligence displayed
in scientific enterprise was a model for the kind of organic union of freedom and authority which he sought. His deepest hope (though he realized it would be dismissed as romantic and utopian) was that the method
of collective and cooperative intelligence would eventually be applied
to all social relations. Only through this method did he think there was
any prospect that freedom in the form of power of action would ever
be extended from a favored few in any society to the bulk of citizens.

## FREEDOM AS GROWTH IN INTELLIGENCE

For Dewey, freedom as the power to act and freedom as choice were
inseparable. Choice would amount to nothing, he pointed out, if it did
not find expression in outward action and make a difference in objective
reality. And human action would be equally pointless if it only represented a power like an avalanche or an earthquake, with no choice behind it. But a choice growing out of blind impulse, even if allowed to
express itself freely, did not for Dewey represent genuine freedom. An
impulsive act might turn out all right, he admitted, but if it did so, it
was a matter of sheer luck. A person acting impulsively was not really

free; he was placing himself at the mercy of circumstances. And occasional good fortune actually narrowed his freedom of effective action in the long run by encouraging a foolhardy impulsiveness. Choice, to be free, must be intelligent; it must grow out of reflection on the range of possibilities open to the individual and a forecast of the consequences likely to follow from pursuing different courses of action.

Dewey thought that choice and action reinforced each other when intelligence was at work. Intelligent deliberation, he observed, led the individual to conceive of a wider field of action than would otherwise be open to him; and by acting in this wider field he gained greater knowledge and insight with which to handle future situations. Even in failure and defeat the reflective individual learned something, for he was continually developing the habit of intelligent choice. Freedom, said Dewey, "consists in a trend of conduct that causes choices to be more diversified and flexible, more plastic and more cognizant of their own meaning, while it enlarges their range of unimpeded operation."[29] Dewey, in short, linked freedom with the possibility of growth. "Potentiality of freedom," he said,

is a native gift or part of our constitution in that we have *capacity* for growth and for being actively concerned in the process and the direction it takes. Actual or positive freedom is not a native gift or endowment but is acquired. In the degree in which we become aware of possibilities of development and actively concerned to keep the avenues of growth open, in the degree in which we fight against induration and fixity, and thereby realize the possibilities of recreation of our selves, we are actually free.[30]

And again: "We are free not because of what we statically are, but in as far as we are becoming different from what we have been."[31] We increase in freedom, in other words, as we develop in character and wisdom and in the ability to choose and act intelligently.

Is freedom as capacity for growth a genuine possibility? How does it square with the idea that all events are governed by law—that is, are causally determined? If a person's every thought, word, and deed have prior causes, can it actually be said that he possesses freedom? Dewey's response to questions like these was that freedom need not reside in antecedents; it may lie in consequences. If, for example, one person's words influence another person, who is listening, to be more thoughtful and intelligent in his future choices and actions, the fact that the words spoken had antecedent causes subtracts nothing from the situation. Whatever their origin, the words uttered did have distinctive effects and made a real difference in the quality of the experience of the person hearing them. Dewey thought there was no worse superstition than the belief that "things are not what they are, and do not do what they are seen to do" simply because they have come into being in a "causal" way. Water, after all, *is* what it *does*, not what it is "caused" by; and the same is true of intelligent choice.[32] "It is assumed sometimes," said Dewey, "that if it can be shown that deliberation determines choice and deliberation is determined by character and conditions, there is no freedom. This is like saying that because a flower comes from root and stem it cannot bear fruit."[33]

In discussing the relation of freedom to scientific law, Dewey placed special emphasis on the fact that science deals with the relations among things, not with things in their uniqueness. Dewey, as we have seen, believed there was an irreducible individuality in all things and that even atoms and electrons displayed preferential behavior and selectivity in action. But a scientific law says nothing about an individual entity inherently; it is not concerned with the inner being of things. Scientific laws describe the uniform and regular relations of change among things, but they do not obliterate the elements of individuality and preference which all things possess. Dewey, like his fellow pragmatists James and Peirce, realized that modern scientists tended to think of laws as statistical in nature, not as universally and rigidly applicable to all existence, and that many of their laws were statements about an "average" found in the behavior of a tremendous number of things, no two of which were exactly alike. For this reason, he did not think that the uniformities and regularities among natural phenomena which were formulated in scientific laws eliminated choice as a distinctive fact having distinctive consequences.[34]

But if the individuality of all existences was as objectively real as the invariant relations among them, then the world was to some extent indeterminate. The world, said Dewey, was a "scene of risk; it is uncertain, unstable, uncannily unstable."[35] It displayed irregularities, as Peirce noted, as well as regularities. Dewey acknowledged that the traditional view that nature was fixed and settled once for all and that whatever uncertainty existed was in man's limited mind, not in nature, had compelling force. But to accept a dualistic partitioning of man and nature in this way was impossible for Dewey. He realized, moreover, that if the world were mechanically fixed for all time, freedom in the sense of intelligent choice and growth was an illusion. Only "*if* change is genuine, if accounts are still in process of making, and if objective uncertainty is the stimulus to reflection" would "variation in action, novelty and experiment" have a "true meaning." Dewey, like James, was convinced that from the empirical point of view "uncertainty, doubt, hesitation, contingency and novelty" and "genuine change which is not mere disguised repetition" were objective realities. He could not bring himself to believe that they occurred in human experience but not in the physical world, and in this respect he went beyond James in his indeterminism. Man, he emphasized, was continuous with nature, and surely the uncertainties in the life of man expressed "a culmination of facts in nature" as did other aspects of his existence. "Variability, initiative, innovation, departure from routine, experimentation," said Dewey,

are empirically the manifestation of a genuine nisus in things. At all events it is these things that are precious to us under the name of freedom. It is their elimination from the life of a slave which makes his life servile, intolerable to the freeman who has once been on his own, no matter what his animal comfort and security. A free man would rather take his chance in an open world than be guaranteed in a closed world.

It was this view of nature and experience which provided the metaphysical foundation for Dewey's pragmatic epistemology: instrumentalism (ideas as instruments for directing action), experimentalism (the necessity to try out ideas in action), and the doubt-inquiry view of the thinking process ( a process of inquiry touched off by the uncertainties encountered in experience). Dewey did not seem to think that his acceptance of a measure of indeterminism in nature and experience clashed with his beloved principle of continuity. And he did not, as an indeterminist, feel obliged, as James did, to make special efforts to account for the act of creation. His writings on aesthetics concentrated on the appreciative rather than the creative aspects of art, and his analysis of creative intelligence took for granted the appearance of new ideas in problematic situations. "Thoughts sprout and vegetate," he declared; "ideas proliferate. They come from deep unconscious sources. . . . Some suggestion surges from the unknown." It was in the thoughtful use people make of these suggestions "from the unknown" that Dewey located creativity and freedom.[36] His use of the word *unknown*, however, made it clear that he had come to regard human creativity as ultimately unanalyzable.

For Dewey the power of varied and flexible growth springing from intelligent choice was a fact. He did not think that the presence of uniform relations of change in the universe negated the reality of this kind of freedom. In fact, he said, these relations, when ascertained, can be a tremendous help to people in developing freedom as intelligent choice. To say, for example, that ideas have "causes" was to say that the origin and development of ideas (though not their quality) are changes connected with other changes. If, then, one determines what the connections are, he increases his mastery of ideas. Familiarity with the conditions under which choices arise, in other words, helps guide the intelligent formation of choices. It also increases the likelihood that they will be carried out effectively in action.[37]

The linking of freedom with knowledge was of course not new with Dewey. It was customary for philosophers in the rationalistic tradition, like Spinoza and Hegel, to define freedom as action emancipated by insight into necessity. Transcendentalists like Emerson also believed that insight into the nature of things freed one from fate. Leo Tolstoy once put it this way: the ox is a slave so long as he refuses to recognize the yoke and chafes under it; but if he identifies himself with its necessity and draws willingly instead of rebelliously, he is free. Dewey could not agree with this view of the matter. Insight into necessity by itself, he objected, provides no freedom. It is what one does with one's insights that counts. The foresight of possibilities was the important thing. Conscious submission to necessity was for Dewey fatalism, not freedom. Only if the ox "foresees the consequences of the use of the yoke, if he anticipates the possibility of harvest, and identifies himself not with the yoke but with the realization of its possibilities," does he act freely and voluntarily. Dewey acknowledged that perception of necessary laws played an important part in developing human freedom. But he did not think that insight into necessity by itself produced anything but awareness of necessity. "Freedom is the 'truth of necessity,'" he said, "only when we use one 'necessity' to alter another. When we use the law to foresee consequences and to consider how they may be averted or secured, then freedom begins." Intelligence, he insisted, "treats events as moving, as fraught with possibilities, not as ended, final."[38]

Dewey's philosophy of freedom was thoroughly evolutionary. He regarded human beings as well as natural events as ever developing and fraught with possibilities. For Dewey freedom (and virtue) did not rest on any specific achievement of an individual but resided in his increas-

ingly intelligent use of desire, deliberation, and choice. He thought the
free person was continually growing in his ability to cope with natural
and social forces, meet new situations wisely, and use foresight of the
future to refine and expand his present activity and enhance its quality.
"In the strictest sense," wrote Dewey,

> it is impossible for the self to stand still; it is becoming and becoming for
> the better or the worse. It is in the *quality* of becoming that virtue resides.
> We set up this and that end to be reached, but *the* end is growth itself. To
> make an end a final goal is but to arrest growth. Many a person gets morally
> discouraged because he has not attained the object upon which he set his
> resolution, but in fact his moral status is determined by his movement in
> that direction, not by his possession. If such a person would set his thought
> and desire upon the *process* of evolution instead of upon some ulterior goal,
> he would find a new freedom and happiness.[39]

There was nothing easy about the kind of freedom—the moral and
intellectual growth—which Dewey recommended. Freedom as growth,
he knew, continually runs up against habit. Habit is powerful because it
gives us facility in thinking and acting and there is a temptation to rest
on our oars and continue in the old ways, especially if they have brought
us success. But we cling to the old and avoid the challenge of the new
at the price of growth and freedom. The "growing, enlarging, liberated
self . . . ," said Dewey,

> goes forth to meet new demands and occasions, and readapts and remakes
> itself in the process. It welcomes untried situations. The necessity for choice
> between the interest of the old and of the forming, moving self is recur-
> rent. It is found at every stage of civilization and every period of life. . . .
> For everywhere there is an opportunity and a need to go beyond what one
> has been, beyond "himself," if the self is identified with the body of desires,
> affections, and habits which has been potent in the past. Indeed, we may say
> that the good person is precisely the one who is most conscious of the
> alternative, and is the most concerned to find openings for the newly form-
> ing or growing self; since no matter how "good" he has been, he becomes
> "bad" (even though acting upon a relatively high plane of attainment) as
> soon as he fails to respond to the demand for growth. Any other basis for
> judging the moral status of the self is conventional. In reality, direction of
> movement, not the plane of attainment and rest, determines moral quality.[40]

For Dewey the moral dichotomy was not between a lower and higher
(or carnal and spiritual) self, but between the attained, static self and

the moving, dynamic self. "If we state the moral law as the injunction to each self on every possible occasion to identify the self with a new growth that is possible," he said, "then obedience to law is one with moral freedom."[41] But he did not explain why some people sought to achieve this moral freedom and others did not. Emerson had the motions of the Universal Spirit to fall back on; James, the creative efforts of individuals. For Dewey there seemed to be only chance to account for the disparities between individuals when it came to moral quality. He did, however, place special emphasis on the development of social conditions which would encourage the intellectual and moral growth of individuals and narrow the role that chance played in these matters.

## FREEDOM AND THE SOCIAL ORDER

What conditions are necessary for the development of moral freedom? How is it possible to attain the freedom from blind impulse and dead habit which the power of reflective intelligence brings? Dewey regarded the problem of individual growth as essentially a social problem. He did not think that an individual could develop moral freedom by himself apart from interaction with other people. He gave considerable thought, therefore, to the kinds of social arrangements which he felt were required for the growth of intelligence in human beings. In his opinion, three conditions were indispensable: (1) guarantees of freedom of thought and communication; (2) a democratic social order; and (3) a proper educational system.

Like Paine, Dewey thought that freedom of thought was in some respects at the very heart of actual freedom. Without it, he said, the development of preferences into intelligent choices was impossible. But freedom of thought does not exist apart from freedom of speech, inquiry, and expression. Dewey was impatient with people who conceived of freedom as some kind of subjective state, residing comfortably in the mind of the individual, where it presumably could not be tampered with, unconnected with the individual's transactions with his surroundings. The mind simply did not exist as an isolated individual entity for Dewey; it was largely social in nature. He repeatedly called attention to the fact that the thoughts we think, even when we are alone, are shaped by language and that language is a product of social interactions.[42]

For Dewey, then, a continual interchange of ideas was a necessary condition for the development of free thinking. Ideas which are kept to oneself, he noted, either perish or become eccentric. Dewey thought public

;ion and debate were essential to the generation and development
as in the individual and to intellectual growth in general. But he
did not think that legal guarantees of free speech, press, religion, and
association by themselves guaranteed freedom of thought. He cherished
America's Bill of Rights freedoms, but he thought it was naïve to expect
that genuinely creative thinking by individuals would follow as a matter
of course from the removal of external impediments to its expression.
The mere absence of formal limitations on expression, he said, was more
likely to result in a proliferation of inept and silly ideas than in the
germination of worthwhile sentiments. Thinking, after all, was not an
inborn faculty requiring only opportunities for expression to function
properly. It was the most difficult activity in which men engaged and,
like every other human activity, it required favorable objective conditions
for its cultivation. Social conditions could either encourage the development of creative thinking or obstruct it. It was important to see to it that
they did the former. "A genuine energetic interest in the cause of human
freedom," said Dewey,

will manifest itself in a jealous and unremitting care for the influence of
social institutions upon the attitudes of curiosity, inquiry, weighing and testing of evidence. I shall begin to believe that we care more for freedom than
we do for imposing our own beliefs upon others in order to subject them to
our will, when I see that the main purpose of our schools and other institutions is to develop powers of unremitting and discriminating observation
and judgment.[43]

Dewey did not think American culture encouraged the growth of
creative intelligence. The United States, he said, was a "Great Society" in
its industrial and corporate form, but it was not a "Great Community"
possessing "an inclusive and fraternally associated public."[44] Although
modern science was essentially a cooperative enterprise, its technological
fruits had been harnessed to private gain and its benefits monopolized
by a minority of individuals with special talents in the acquisitive line.
But the majority of people were not only deprived of the economic benefits of modern technology; they were also shut off from the educational
and cultural opportunities that were rightfully theirs in a democratic
society. Dewey thought it was impossible for a society based on privilege
to achieve "widespread high excellence of mind."[45] He wanted all citizens
to share in the economic, educational, scientific, and artistic resources of
the nation, and he thought this would be possible only under some form

of socialism. In Dewey's Great Community (as in Bellamy's utopian commonwealth), the enduring values of the old individualism—initiative, individuality, innovation—would be joined with new values centering around cooperative endeavor, shared experience, and reciprocal solidarity. If the economic resources of the nation were cooperatively managed and shared, Dewey thought, there would be an "enormous liberation of mind, and the mind thus set free would have constant direction and nourishment. Desire for related knowledge, physical and social, would be created and rewarded; initiative and responsibility would be demanded and achieved."[46]

Dewey did not produce detailed specifications for his Great Community. He doubted, in fact, whether it was possible to develop "integrated individuality" by means of any all-embracing system or program.[47] He preferred to talk about a "planning society" rather than about a "planned society" because of the finalities implied in the more familiar phrase.[48] He was critical of Marxism because he thought its "monistic block theory of social causation" was unscientific, and he disapproved of the undemocratic methods favored by many of its exponents.[49] Since he thought that ends and means were closely related and were continually interacting and transforming one another, he was convinced that undemocratic means produced undemocratic consequences. Though he favored a high degree of social ownership, Dewey was basically a liberal pluralist. He regarded the political state as a secondary form of organization and thought that its main function was to promote and protect other more voluntary forms of organization in society. His emphasis was on local, face-to-face, neighborhood associations, and he hoped that interactions among local groups would offset the "dread impersonality" of modern technological society.[50] "Democracy," he wrote in *The Public and Its Problems* (1927), "must begin at home, and its home is the neighborly community." Unless "local communal life can be restored," he added, "the public cannot adequately resolve its most urgent problem: to find and identify itself. But if it be re-established, it will manifest a fullness, variety and freedom of possession and enjoyment of meanings and goods unknown in the contiguous associations of the past."[51] In a sense Dewey never left his boyhood community in Vermont.

Like Bellamy (whom he admired), Dewey called for a union of liberty and equality in the Great Community. He agreed with Bellamy in thinking that human beings do differ a great deal in their natural endowments; but, like Bellamy, he also believed that if they were to have the liberty to discover and nourish their individualities they must have equal opportunities for development and equal access to society's material and cultural resources. "The democratic ideal that unites equality and liberty," he said, "is . . . a recognition that actual and concrete liberty of opportunity and action is dependent upon equalization of the political and economic conditions under which individuals are alone free *in fact*, not *in some abstract metaphysical way*."[52]

If Dewey was vague about the precise economic shape the Great Community was to assume, he knew exactly what kind of values would pervade it: the values of modern democracy and modern science. The democratic methods of "consultation, persuasion, negotiation, communication, co-operative intelligence" were essential to his Great Community.[53] So was the scientific method: the method of free inquiry, cooperative testing, and shared communication. "Because the free working of mind is one of the greatest joys open to man," said Dewey, "the scientific attitude, incorporated in the individual mind, is something which adds enormously to one's enjoyment of existence."[54] Dewey thought science and democracy were firmly allied and that both were essential to developing the kind of freedom which he identified with intelligent growth.

To the school more than to any other social agency Dewey looked for the development of the democratic and scientific values he regarded as essential to the Great Community. Schools must not only be living models for the practice of freedom of inquiry, discussion, experimentation, and communication; they also had the responsibility of seeing to it that those leaving its walls had ideas worth thinking as well as the courage to express them. It was important to have freedom of expression; it was even more important that the ideas expressed be genuine, not sham, ideas and that they be the fruit of inquiry, observation, experimentation, and the careful weighing of evidence. What Dewey liked to call "free intelligence" was to pervade the organization, administration, methods, and curricula of educational establishments in the Great Community.[55] "Genuine freedom . . . is intellectual," wrote Dewey;

it rests in the trained *power of thought*, in ability to "turn things over," to look at matters deliberately, to judge whether the amount and kind of evidence requisite for decision is at hand, and if not, to tell where and how to seek such evidence. If a man's actions are not guided by thoughtful conclusions, then they are guided by inconsiderate impulse, unbalanced appetite, caprice, or the circumstances of the moment. To cultivate unhindered, unreflective external activity is to foster enslavement, for it leaves the person at the mercy of appetite, sense, and circumstance.[56]

Education came to occupy the primary position in Dewey's philosophy. He regarded *Democracy and Education* (1915) as in some respects his most important book because it made an organic connection between his conception of education and his broader philosophical views. Dewey thought it remarkable that professional philosophers had shown so little interest in education, and he was amused when his colleagues took him to task for giving too much attention to schools. Central to any democratic philosophy, he thought, was a philosophy of education. Dewey's major concepts—interaction, continuity, growth—converged in his educational philosophy. In the field of education as in all other fields Dewey emphatically rejected dualism of any kind: school and society, child and curriculum, individuality and cooperativeness, theory and practice, thinking and acting, learning and living. In Dewey's schools there was to be continuous interaction between education and experience, school and society, teacher and pupil, and between pupil and pupil. The ultimate objective was to nourish the kind of intellectual and moral growth in youngsters that conduced to freedom: *"freeing the life-process for its own most adequate fulfillment."*[57]

Dewey naturally rejected what he called the "straitjacket and chain-gang procedures" prevailing in American schooling in the late nineteenth century: concentration on memorizing a fixed (and presumably eternal) body of material, mechanical repetition of some exalted person's "thoughts," inculcation of discipline and obedience for their own sake, and emphasis on passivity on the part of the child. Dewey believed in learning by doing (i.e., by *thoughtful* doing), and he refused to make an arbitrary separation between vocational training and liberal arts. He also believed that students must learn to work together intelligently and that schools should be related to life as a whole. He insisted, furthermore, that subject matter have an organic relation to a student's developing needs, interests, and experiences. In *The Psychology of Number* (1895), which he wrote with James A. McLellan, he proposed a genetic method of teaching arithmetic based upon an explanation of how and why human beings developed numbers and upon a treatment of addition, subtraction, multiplication, and division as they come naturally in the child's experience.[58] He felt all studies should be presented in some such meaningful fashion and related to moral and intellectual growth.

In Dewey's educational philosophy, the emphasis was above all else on the child's individuality: on discovering and nourishing each child's special gifts and helping them to develop naturally and fruitfully. But it is a myth based on pure ignorance to say that Dewey recommended letting children express themselves spontaneously in school without guidance from teachers and without having to master any of the accumulated information of the past. Time and again he exposed the foolishness of the spontaneous-expression school of educational thought. Dewey simply did not believe there was any "spontaneous germination" in mental life.[59] Mind, he said on numerous occasions, was social in nature; it was formed by interactions between the individual's native tendencies and his social surroundings.

The only wise course of action following from Dewey's view of mind was to provide the child with the kind of educational environment most favorable to the development of constructive mental habits. Giving children certain materials and then leaving them alone to respond to the materials spontaneously, as some educationists proposed, seemed like utter nonsense to Dewey. He thought that their responses would be casual and sporadic, that efforts to use the materials would be clumsy and superficial, and that the children would probably end up by getting bored. Surely an experienced teacher, aware of the children's needs, experiences, and existing state of knowledge and skills, could make suggestions that would be more helpful to developing genuine freedom in the youngsters than a laissez-faire policy. "Freedom or individuality . . . is not an original possession or gift," said Dewey.

It is something to be achieved, to be wrought out. Suggestion as to things which may advantageously be taken, as to skill, as to methods of operation, are indispensable conditions of its achievement. These by the nature of the case must come from a sympathetic and discriminating knowledge of what has been done in the past and how it has been done.[60]

Dewey denied there was any inherent contradiction between freedom and discipline. He had nothing good to say, of course, for the harsh and restrictive view of discipline prevailing in the schools of his boyhood. But he insisted that, properly viewed, freedom and discipline were partners, not antagonists. Intelligent discipline was not mere drill; it was the kind of purposeful training that developed habits and skills which enabled people to perform their tasks effortlessly and imaginatively. Discipline, said Dewey, "represents original native endowment turned, through gradual exercise, into effective power." Without discipline, the mind could never achieve "independent intellectual initiative and control" over a subject. The aim of education was to develop a *"disciplined mind."*[61] But the disciplined mind was also a free mind, for freedom of the mind meant "mental power capable of independent exercise, emancipated from the leading strings of others."[62] The intelligently disciplined mind possessed "a freedom which is power: power to frame purposes, to judge wisely, to evaluate desires by the consequences which will result from acting upon them; power to select and order means to carry chosen ends into operation."[63]

The only freedom of enduring value, Dewey frequently said, was freedom of intelligence. But there was nothing static about freed intelligence. It involved ceaseless growth. And the "dominant vocation of all human beings at all times," Dewey said, should be intellectual and moral growth.[64] The test of all institutions was the extent to which they contributed to human growth. "Government, business, art, religion, all social institutions have a meaning, a purpose," declared Dewey.

That purpose is to set free and to develop the capacities of human individuals without respect to race, sex, class or economic status. And this is all one with saying that the test of their value is the extent to which they educate every individual into the full stature of his possibility. Democracy has many meanings, but if it has a moral meaning, it is found in resolving that the supreme test of all political institutions and industrial arrangements shall be the contribution they make to the all-around growth of every member of society.[65]

Dewey's idea of freedom, needless to say, required drastic social reconstruction for its realization.

## THE PROSPECTS FOR FREEDOM

Ideas were for Dewey plans of action and designations of operations to be performed. From this point of view, it is clear that he made heavy demands on the idea of freedom. The program contained in his definition of freedom called not simply for intelligent choice, or for the ability to act effectively, or for moral and intellectual growth; it demanded all three. Dewey would settle for nothing less, moreover, than the inclusion of all Americans—and, by implication, all human beings—in his program of freedom. He was, in short, a utopian like Bellamy. Though he was fully aware of the powerful social forces everywhere in the world militating against freedom in any form for more than a few people, he

never doubted that the quest for universal freedom was worth making
or that it would in time yield fruits. In the cool, clear, invigorating air of
Dewey's world, difficulties seem somehow always surmountable, doubts
resolvable, and problems solvable. Every teacher and every citizen, we
begin to think as we read Dewey, can eventually become a wholesome
organicist like Dewey himself.

Dewey's was a thoroughly healthy universe; integration, not conflict,
was at its heart. Contradictions between liberty and authority, individuality and social control, and freedom and determinism seemed un-
reasonable, unnecessary, and even unreal in Dewey's world. Dewey frequently inveighed against belief in a "higher" and more spiritual world
than the one we know empirically, because he thought it promised certainty where none existed and distracted people from the pressing tasks
of daily living. In a way, though, Dewey did not so much eliminate the
transcendent realm as merge it with the mundane world. The dualism
of ideal and real, like all other dualisms, was resolved into a harmonious
union in organic experience. Dewey moved with ease from description to
prescription and back again, and he managed to bring the abstract ideas
of the transcendent realm of Plato (his favorite philosopher) down to
earth and make them seem natural and familiar and part of our everyday
landscape. He extended the old Greek ideal to say: a sound mind in a
sound body in a sound environment. He proposed a new categorical im-
perative: "So act as to increase the meaning of present experience."[66]
Present experience, no matter how troubling, was bound to be rich in
constructive meanings. Future experiences would be even more meaningful. In an Age of Therapy, Dewey seems inordinately healthy-minded.
The tensions of the Marxist dialectic and the Freudian Trinity (id-ego-
superego) are not to be found in Dewey. And Dachau, Buchenwald,
Lubianka, Pearl Harbor, Hiroshima, and Vietnam seem remote in Dewey's
imperturbable pages.

Dewey denied charges of excessive optimism. His philosophy, he
insisted, recognized that the world was "precarious and perilous" and that
"suffering or undergoing" formed an important part of what we call
experience.[67] In his philosophy, it was the ubiquitous uncertainties and
ambiguities of experience, in fact, which generated the development of
intelligence. Thinking, he said, arises because of the appearance of incompatible factors in empirical situations. Dewey was no optimistic rationalist like Paine. He always spoke of "intelligence" rather than of "reason" because in the rationalist tradition reason represented a fixed entity

capable of intuiting universal and necessary truths. Basic to Dewey's philosophy, moreover, was the conviction that reflective thought was secondary and derivative and the "the universe of non-reflectional experience of our doings, sufferings, enjoyments of the world, and of one another" was primary." "The antecedents of thought," he said, "are our universe of life and love; of appreciation and struggle."[69] Knowing was only one kind of activity for Dewey; truth, only one kind of meaning. Art, which centered on consummatory enjoyment, was just as important as science, which centered on inquiry. The qualitative world of sound and colors, Dewey continually reminded his readers, was just as real and significant as the scientific world of abstract relations. Living for Dewey was the highest value, and it took many forms; thinking was not an end in itself but a means to living fruitfully.

Dewey thought that pessimism (like Twain's) was a paralyzing doctrine. "In declaring that the world is evil wholesale," he said, "it makes futile all efforts to discover the remediable causes of specific evils and thereby destroys at the root every attempt to make the world better and happier."[70] Dewey thought the world could be made better and happier, but he rejected wholesale optimism. Referring to the notion that this is the best of all possible worlds, he once asked wryly: "If this is the best possible, what would a world which was fundamentally bad be like?"[71] Dewey never denied that we live in "a fearful, an awful world" (though he never talked about its "ultimate cruelty" the way James did). "Our magical safeguard against the uncertain character of the world," he once wrote,

is to deny the existence of chance, to mumble universal and necessary law, the ubiquity of cause and effect, the uniformity of nature, universal progress, and the inherent rationality of the universe. . . . Through science we have secured a degree of power of prediction and control; through tools, machinery and an accompanying technique we have made the world more conformable to our needs, a more secure abode. . . . But when all is said and done, the fundamentally hazardous character of the world is not seriously modified, much less eliminated.[72]

Still, the world was not so hopelessly bad but that it could be made better. Dewey, like James, regarded himself as a meliorist. "Meliorism," he said, "is the belief that the specific conditions which exist at one moment, be they comparatively bad or comparatively good, in any event may be bettered."[73] But each generation had to achieve freedom and democracy for itself, Dewey pointed out, for goals like these had to be "worked out in terms of needs, problems, and conditions of the social life" which was itself "changing with extreme rapidity from year to year."[74] Dewey had great hopes for humanity, but the demands he made on it were even greater.

In the late 1940s, when Dewey was in his eighties, he lost the manuscript of a just-completed book while he was traveling. The book contained a summary of his philosophical views and represented several years of hard work. The loss crushed him for a few days. Then he snapped back into action and began rewriting his book. "You know," he told friends, "in a way this has given me new ideas starting over fresh again. I think I have better ideas now."[75] Even losses could become gains in Dewey's philosophy; one learns from, not bemoans, the past. A year before his death in 1952 at the age of ninety-two, Dewey addressed a group of graduate students at Columbia University. During the discussion Dewey acknowledged that it was a discouraging time to be a philosopher. Then he said: "But now I am talking to the young and I am afraid I have sounded discouraging. In a very important sense it is a time to be a philosopher. The old slogans, the old formulas are obviously not working. It is a challenge to new and creative hypothesis, some bold and imaginative venture in thought." And he added: "All it requires is some ideas, imagination, and, I warn you, guts."[76]

# Epilogue

IN THE LATTER PART of the twentieth century there was more willingness among professional philosophers to take the question of free will seriously than there had been in William James's day and less inclination to take universal causal determinism for granted. Richard Taylor argued persuasively for the idea that human beings are free agents who possess causal initiative and can make thoughtful decisions and perform meaningful actions that transcend the conditioning circumstances in which they find themselves.[1] Corliss Lamont insisted on an individual's freedom of choice, that is, his power to decide between two or more genuine alternatives without being completely determined by his heredity, education, economic circumstances, and past history as an individual; and he noted that an increasing number of American philosophers were beginning to accept some form of free will.[2]

There were, in addition, two new arguments, centering on the fundamental unpredictability of human decisions, which challenged the doctrine of universal determinism. One line of thought emphasized the fact that predictions have a way of interfering with the event predicted where human beings (as opposed to natural events) are concerned. The other stressed the fact that human decisions (and, for that matter, all creative acts) are inherently unpredictable, since not all the knowledge necessary for making the predictions is available until the very moment of decision. In order to predict what we are going to do in the future, in other words, we need to know what knowledge we will possess when that time comes; but knowledge of our own future knowledge is logically impossible.[3]

The renewed interest in free will among American intellectuals did not of course mean the demise of determinism. Deterministic assumptions continued to be powerful with many, perhaps most, thinkers in America in the last part of the twentieth century. In science, it is true, the fact that no causes can be assigned for the emission of alpha particles by radioactive material led some people to question the principle of universal determinism. Werner Heisenberg's Principle of Uncertainty, formulated in the 1920s, also led some physicists to abandon determinism as a postulate for their work and even to dispense with the concept of cause as a useful heuristic principle for studying natural processes. Heisenberg's principle (still accepted as valid in the scientific community) asserts the impossibility of predicting both the future position and the future velocity of a subatomic particle at the same time. While some scientists took the line that the uncertainty lies in our knowledge rather than in nature itself (epistemological indeterminism), there were others who held that the uncertainty is inherent in the natural world itself and not simply in our knowledge about it (ontological indeterminism). In the social and behavioral sciences, however, there was no uncertainty principle, and determinism seemed to be practically fixed dogma. "I can predict the will and choices of men," claimed one social scientist, "by exactly the same technique I use to predict other natural phenomena."[4] Every event was causally necessitated, American behaviorists insisted, and that meant human actions as well as natural processes.

Psychologist B. F. Skinner was probably the most influential determinist among the behavioral scientists. Skinner not only dismissed with impatience the kind of freedom that Taylor and Lamont defended; in *Beyond Freedom and Dignity* (1971), a popular summary of his views that won much attention, he also presented the thesis that individual autonomy, freedom, dignity, and responsibility were sentimental, illusory, and prescientific notions and that Americans should get rid of them and face squarely the fact that an individual consists of no more than his genetic endowment (anatomical and physiological characteristics) plus a repertoire of behavior resulting from overt responses to the stimuli (contingencies of reinforcement) impinging on him from his environment. "There is no place in the scientific position," said Skinner, "for a self as a true orginator or initiator of action."

Skinner, like most of his colleagues in the behavioral sciences, was an optimistic determinist, somewhat like Mark Twain when he wrote *What Is Man?*. He thought that if we planned our controls carefully and redesigned human behavior properly we could not only clean up the mess that foolish notions coming from the "literature of freedom" had produced, but also achieve in time a kind of Heavenly Behavioral City on Earth. He called his planned-reinforcement utopia "Walden Two," but it would have repelled Thoreau and discomfited Bellamy.[5] Skinner sincerely believed that denial of freedom (in the sense of individual autonomy) was essential to scientific psychology. But he failed to explain how it was possible to judge objectively between two environmentally produced opinions or why his own reasoning processes should, on the behavioristic assumptions he made, carry any more weight than anyone else's. Nor could he claim any special validity (i.e., survival value) for his behavioristic philosophy. The most he could say was that environmental contingencies made it more reinforcing for some people than for others.

Despite Skinner, the belief in free agency continued to be powerful in the late twentieth century. Many Americans took for granted a certain amount of individual autonomy without getting into the technicalities of the free-will question, and they thought of people as in some sense free agents. Commenting on Skinner, Noam Chomsky had this to say:

Perhaps, as the classical literature of freedom and dignity sometimes suggests, there is an intrinsic human inclination toward free creative inquiry and productive work, and humans are not merely dull mechanisms formed by a history of reinforcement and behaving predictably with no intrinsic needs apart from the need for physiological satiation. Then humans are not fit subjects for manipulation, and we will seek to design a social order accordingly.[6]

Nevertheless, the strain of hard determinism, always lurking in the background in the history of American thought, became increasingly pronounced and began to take a fatalistic turn in the 1960s and 1970s. Discussing the meaning of the Vietnam War for the United States, Sheldon S. Wolin concluded grimly in the summer of 1975 that the nation had reached a "dramatic and qualitative break" in its history:

We have moved from a society of free choice and opportunity to a society shaped by necessity. Instead of being the showcase refutation of Marxian determinism, we have become an instance of it. . . . [W]e have learned that the nation does have a fate, and concentrations of power in the name of welfare are easily transmuted into power to suppress liberty and promote empire. . . . [B]y some terrible irony, we have been forced to enter history a second time, in this our bicentennial year. The first time we entered proclaiming our independence and liberty, the second time frantically trying to conceal our dependence and servitude.[7]

Wolin's pessimism was by no means exceptional. There was no question but that in the 1970s the American people were experiencing a serious crisis in self-confidence. As attachment to such time-honored institutions as church, school, and family weakened markedly and as the old certainties associated with these institutions declined in influence, questions about fundamentals became insistent in the United States. A series of catastrophes—the ghastly Vietnam War, the assassination of several beloved popular leaders, bitter racial strife, outbursts of violence on college campuses, revelations of unprecedented dishonesty and corruption in high office, and prolonged economic crisis—converged in the 1960s and 1970s to force Americans to question their own wisdom and virtue and the uses they were making of their freedom at home and in the world at large. For the first time in American history, a considerable number of Americans were beginning to doubt themselves and their ways of living. Some people, in fact, were beginning to wonder not only whether the nation could ever actually solve the problems facing it but also whether the effort to do so was really worth the trouble.

The average citizen, it is true, continued to assert his fierce confidence in the rectitude of his country and its institutions. Most liberals and radicals, moreover, for all their criticisms of American life, continued in the main to assert their faith in melioristic endeavor. Nevertheless, an ennervating fatalism, new for America, was beginning in the late 1960s to spread in popular cultural circles carrying great weight with young people. Pauline Kael was struck by the convictionless atmosphere, absence of shared values, brutalities taken for granted, and glorification of loser-heroes appearing in American films (produced mainly for a youthful audience) in the 1970s. "In the movies now," she reported, "people don't talk about the future; they don't make plans; they don't expect much." A little later she added: "The nihilistic coarse-grained movies are telling us that nothing matters to us, that we're all a bad joke."[8] At Harvard University Richard Hunt was shocked by the "depressingly fatalistic conclusions about major moral dilemmas" he encountered in an undergraduate class on Nazi Germany, and he concluded that many young people "nowadays hold to a despairingly deterministic view of the past and present."[9]

Among scholars, too, there was increasing gloom and considerable talk about the inevitable decline of freedom everywhere. The late Hannah Arendt thought that American institutions of liberty, for all their ups and downs during the past two centuries, had earned their "due meed of glory," but she was uncertain about their future and noted that free institutions had always been an exception in history.[10] Hans Morgenthau noted the decline of democratic government throughout the world, and Robert Heilbroner was convinced that the world's problems (especially the population explosion, the deterioration of the environment, and the danger of war with obliterative weaponry) were practically insoluble or, at best, manageable only by a drastic curtailment of political and economic freedom.[11] Christopher Lasch was struck by the "sense of cultural disintegration" and the decay of critical thought in the United States, George Kennan pronounced American civilization a failure, and Michael Novak began to wonder in the summer of 1975 whether "forty years from now there will exist a free, independent, and democratic United States of America." The "disaffection with freedom in America," Alfred Kazin observed in July, 1976, "is furtive, ashamed and confused. But it certainly exists on a wide scale."[12]

As the United States entered the third century of its existence as a national state, the prevailing mood was one of anxiety, bewilderment, frustration, and self-doubt rather than of elation, triumph, pride, and self-confidence. Many Americans seem to have learned for the first time in the 1960s and 1970s that their country was not perfect; next, apparently, they had to learn that it was not totally depraved. The founders of the American republic would have been astonished at the situation. "Posterity!" exclaimed John Adams in a letter to Abigail on April 26, 1777, "You will never know, how much it cost the present Generation, to preserve your Freedom! I hope you will make good Use of it. If you do not, I shall repent in Heaven, that I ever took half the Pains to preserve it."[13]

The crisis of the 1970s was in its deepest reaches a spiritual one, and it involved the very morale of the American republic. The future of America, it appeared, rested on a Jamesian act of faith on the part of the American people: faith in freedom as rational insight and moral effort and in the possibility of acting intelligently and courageously, but not self-righteously, on that faith amid the ruins of ancient teleologies. It was a utopian faith, doubtless, like all idealistic affirmations; whether it was also an illusion, as Twain thought, remained to be seen. There was no determinist on the scene prepared to forecast the future with assurance.

# Notes

CHAPTER ONE

1. "Miscellanies," No. gg., Harvey G. Townsend, *The Philosophy of Jonathan Edwards from His Private Notebooks* (Eugene, Ore., 1955), p. 237.

2. "Extracts from His Diary," *The Works of President Edwards*, 4 vols. (New York, 1844), 1:12.

3. Edwards, "Personal Narrative," in Clarence H. Faust and Thomas H. Johnson, eds., *Jonathan Edwards: Representative Selections* (New York, 1935), p. 64.

4. "Dissertation Concerning the End for Which God Created the World," *Works of President Edwards*, 2:255.

5. "Miscellaneous Observations," *The Works of Jonathan Edwards*, 2 vols. (London, 1835), 2:481.

6. *Original Sin*, ed. Clyde A. Holbrook (New Haven, 1970), p. 423.

7. A Farewell Sermon, Preached at Northampton, June 22, 1750, *Works of President Edwards*, 8 vols. (Worcester, 1808), 1:139.

8. Townsend, *Philosophy of Edwards*, p. 155.

9. Faust and Johnson, *Edwards*, p. xl.

10. Jonathan Edwards, *Freedom of the Will*, ed. Paul Ramsey (New Haven, 1957), p. 273.

11. Ibid., pp. 255-56.

12. Whitby accepted moral causes of the will's choices and insisted only on the "Freedom of the Will from Necessity, or a Determination to one, *i.e.*, either to Good or Evil only." It was difficult, he thought, but not impossible for the will to act in accord with good rather than evil inducements. See *A Discourse Concerning {Five Points}*, 2d. ed. (London, 1735), p. 344. Clarke, similarly, thought the will acted in accord with moral motives (the last judgment of the understanding) which he carefully distinguished from physical efficients, for, he said, "Moral Necessity, is evidently consistent with the most perfect Natural Liberty." See *A Discourse Concerning the Being and Attributes of God*, 5th ed. (London, 1719), pp. 98-99.

13. Thomas Chubb, *A Collection of Tracts on Various Subjects* (London, 1730), pp. 386, 377. See also T. L. Bushell, *The Sage of Salisbury: Thomas Chubb, 1679-1747* (New York, 1967), and Conrad Wright, "Edwards and the Arminians on the Freedom of the Will," *Harvard Theological Review* 35 (October 1942): 241-61.

14. Isaac Watts, *An Essay on the Freedom of the Will in God and in Creatures* (London, 1732), pp. 14, 19, 32, 50.

15. Conrad Wright, *The Beginnings of Unitarianism in America* (Boston, 1955), p. 101.

16. Edwards, *Freedom of the Will*, p. 181.

17. See James E. White, "Avowed Reasons and Causal Explanations," *Mind* 80 (April 1971): 238-45, who argues that avowed reasons are not causal explanations, while W. D. Gean, "Reasons and Causes," *Review of Metaphysics* 19 (1966): 667-88, believes that reason-explanations are a type of causal explanation. See also "Reasons and Causes," *Encyclopedia of Philosophy*.

18. Edwards, *Freedom of the Will*, p. 248.

19. Ibid., p. 143.

20. Ibid., p. 144. Italics added.

21. Ibid., p. 348.

22. Ibid., pp. 348-49.

23. Ibid., p. 163.

24. Ibid., p. 164.

25. John Calvin, *Institutes of the Christian Religion*, trans. John Allen, 2 vols. (Philadelphia, 1921), 1:239; James Kendall Hosmer, ed., *Winthrop's Journal*, 2 vols. (New York, 1908), 2:637-39.

26. Edwards, *Freedom of the Will*, p. 379n.

27. Carl G. Jung, *Synchronicity* (Princeton, N.J., 1973).

28. Edwards, *Freedom of the Will*, p. 207.

29. Ibid., p. 224.

30. Ibid., p. 332.

31. Ibid., p. 427.

32. Ibid., p. 310.

33. Ibid., p. 349.

34. Ibid., p. 266.

35. Ibid., p. 399.

36. James Dana, *An Examination of the Late Reverend President Edwards's 'Enquiry on Freedom of the Will'* . . . (Boston, 1770), p. 75.

37. Edwards, *Freedom of the Will*, p. 405.

38. Dana, *Examination*, p. 75. I have modernized Dana's spelling.

39. Edwards, *Freedom of the Will*, p. 410.

40. Ibid., p. 369.

41. Ibid., p. 370.

42. Ibid., p. 374.

43. Ibid., p. 370.

44. Wright, *Beginnings of Unitarianism*, p. 104.

45. Gay, *Natural Religion, as Distinguish'd from Revealed* (Boston, 1759), p. 12.

46. William B. Sprague, *Annals of the American Pulpit* (New York, 1865), 8:60.

47. Frank Hugh Foster, *A Genetic History of the New England Theology* (Chicago, 1907, pp. 224-69; Joseph Haroutunian, *Piety versus Moralism: The Passing of the New England Theology* (New York, 1932), pp. 220-57.

48. *The English Works of Thomas Hobbes*, ed. Sir William Molesworth (London, 1840), 4:247, 273.

49. Ibid., 5:19.

50. Locke, *Essay Concerning Human Understanding*, 2 vols. (New York: Dover Publications, 1959), 1:308-80.

51. Mortimer Taube, *Causation, Freedom and Determinism* (London, 1936).
52. Dana, *Examination*, pp. 83, 120.
53. Beach Newtoun, *A Preservative against the Doctrine of Fate . . . Proposed to the Consideration of Young Students in Divinity* (n.p., 1770), p. 10.
54. Henry Philip Tappan, *A Review of Edwards's "Inquiry into the Freedom of the Will"* (New York, 1839), p. 129.
55. Franklin, *A Dissertation on Liberty and Necessity*, in Leonard Labaree et al., eds., *The Papers of Benjamin Franklin* (New Haven, 1959-      ), 1:63.
56. Ibid., pp. 62-63.
57. Ibid., p. 62.
58. "On the Providence of God in the Government of the World," *Papers of Franklin*, 1:264.
59. Edwards, *Freedom of the Will*, pp. 370-71, 430-31.
60. Dana, *Examination*, p. v.
61. Samuel West, *Essays on Liberty and Necessity* (New Bedford, Mass., 1795), Part First, p. 18; Jonathan Edwards, Jr., *A Dissertation Concerning Liberty and Necessity* (Worcester, 1797), p. 95.
62. Tappan, *Review of Edwards*, p. 191. See Charles M. Perry, *Henry Philip Tappan, Philosopher and Educator* (Ann Arbor, 1933) for Tappan's Calvinist background and the development of his Platonism under the influence of Victor Cousin. On the subject of free will, Albert T. Bledsoe's views were similar to Tappan's. See his *An Examination of President Edwards' Inquiry into the Freedom of the Will* (Philadelphia, 1845).
63. Rowland G. Hazard, *Freedom of the Mind in Willing* (Boston and New York, 1889). See also *Man a Creative First Cause* (Boston, 1884) and *Two Letters on Causation and Freedom in Willing, Addressed to John Stuart Mill* (Boston, 1869).
64. Ibid., p. 395.
65. *Works of President Edwards*, 8 vols. (Leeds, 1807), 2:82.

## CHAPTER TWO

1. "Predestination, Remarks on Romans, IX, 18-21 . . . ," in Philip Foner, ed., *The Complete Writings of Thomas Paine*, 2 vols. (New York, 1945), (hereafter cited as *Writings*), 2:894-97.
2. "A Serious Address to the People of Pennsylvania on the Present Situation of Their Affairs," from the *Pennsylvania Packet*, December 1, 1778 (hereafter cited as "Serious Address"), in *Writings*, 2:287; "Plan of a Declaration of the Natural, Civil and Political Rights of Man," probably drawn up in January, 1793, in ibid., p. 558; "Dissertation on First Principles of Government," July, 1795 (hereafter cited as "First Principles"), in ibid., p. 579.
3. "The Rights of Man," in ibid., 1:299 (hereafter cited as "Rights of Man").
4. "The Age of Reason," in ibid., p. 498 (hereafter cited as "Age of Reason").
5. F. R. Tennant, "Natural Law," *Encyclopedia of Religion*, ed. James Hastings, 12 vols. (New York, 1908-1922), 9:200.
6. "The American Crisis," 2, January 13, 1777, in *Writings*, 1:72.
7. "The Forester's Letters," 3, April 24, 1776, in ibid., 2:78.
8. "The Forester's Letters," 4, May 8, 1776, in ibid., p. 83.
9. Paine to Henry Laurens, Spring, 1778, in ibid., p. 1143.
10. "Age of Reason," p. 496.
11. Paine to a Committee of the Continental Congress, October, 1783, in *Writings*, 2:1228.
12. "Rights of Man," p. 275; "Candid and Critical Remarks on a Letter Signed Ludlow," from *Pennsylvania Journal*, June 4, 1777, in *Writings*, 2:275.
13. Ibid., p. 274; "Public Good," December 30, 1780, in ibid., p. 306; "Address and Declaration of the Friends of Universal Peace and Liberty" (August, 1791), in ibid., p. 534.

14. "Rights of Man," p. 273.
15. Ibid., pp. 251-52.
16. "Common Sense," in *Writings*, 1:5 (hereafter cited as "Common Sense); C. B. Macpherson, *The Political Theory of Possessive Individualism: Hobbes to Locke* (London, 1962).
17. Paine to Thomas Jefferson (1789), *Writings*, 2:1298.
18. "Rights of Man," p. 359.
19. "Common Sense," p. 4.
20. "Rights of Man," p. 359.
21. "Common Sense," p. 5.
22. Ibid., pp. 4-6.
23. "Rights of Man," p. 278.
24. Ibid., p. 276.
25. Paine to Jefferson, p. 1298.
26. Ibid., p. 1299.
27. "Remarks on a Letter Signed Ludlow," *Writings*, 2:274-75.
28. "Rights of Man," p. 276.
29. "Remarks on a Letter Signed Ludlow," p. 275.
30. "First Principles," pp. 583-84.
31. "Reflections on Titles," from *Pennsylvania Magazine* (May 1775), in *Writings*, 2:33.
32. "Age of Reason," p. 463; W. H. G. Armytage, "Thomas Paine and the Walkers: An Early Episode in Anglo-American Co-operation," *Pennsylvania History* 18 (January 1951): 25.
33. "Prosecution of 'The Age of Reason'" (September, 1797), in *Writings*, 2:743.
34. "Age of Reason," p. 465.
35. "Prosecution of 'The Age of Reason,'" p. 728.
36. "Age of Reason," p. 464.
37. "Rights of Man," p. 291.
38. "Serious Address," p. 285.
39. "Rights of Man," p. 291.
40. "Thoughts on Defensive War," from *Pennsylvania Magazine* (July 1775), in *Writings*, 2:54.
41. "Rights of Man," p. 295.
42. Ibid., p. 414, n. 34.
43. Ibid., p. 341.
44. Letter from *National Intelligencer*, November 29, 1802, in *Writings*, 2:918; "A Dialogue between General Wolfe and General Gage in a Wood near Boston," from *Pennsylvania Journal*, January 4, 1775, in ibid., p. 48.
45. "First Principles," p. 584.
46. "Dissertion on Government; the Affairs of the Bank; and Paper Money" (1786), in *Writings*, 2:370.
47. "Agrarian Justice" (1795-96), in ibid., 1:607.
48. "Serious Address," pp. 284-89.
49. "First Principles," pp. 579, 581, 583.
50. "Rights of Man," pp. 374, 367.
51. "Answer to Four Questions on the Legislative and Executive Powers" (1782), in *Writings*, 2:531.
52. "Letter to the Abbé Raynal, on the Affairs of North America . . ." (1782), in ibid., 2:211-63.
53. "Common Sense," p. 19.
54. "The American Crisis," 5, 1, 13, in *Writings*, 1:120, 123, 232.
55. "Common Sense," p. 39; George Washington to Joseph Reed, Cambridge, January 31, 1776, in John C. Fitzpatrick, ed., *The Writings of George Wash-*

*ington*, 39 vols. (Washington, D.C., 1931-44), 4:297; April 1, 1776, ibid., p. 455.

56. "To Mr. Hulburt, of Sheffield, One of the Mortified Federal Members of the Massachusetts Legislature," from *Aurora*, March 12, 1805, in *Writings*, 2:977.

57. "African Slavery in America," from *Pennsylvania Journal and the Weekly Advertiser*, March 8, 1775, in ibid., p. 18.

58. "A Serious Thought," from *Pennsylvania Journal*, October 18, 1775, in ibid., p. 20.

59. Ibid., 1:xix.

60. Paine to Jefferson, New York, January 25, 1805, in ibid., 2:1462.

61. "Reflections on Unhappy Marriages," from *Pennsylvania Magazine* (June 1775) and "An Occasional Letter on the Female Sex," from ibid. (August 1775), in *Writings*, 2:34-38, 1118-20. See also Audrey Williamson, *Thomas Paine, His Life, Work and Times* (New York, 1973), pp. 31, 56, 58, 68, 168. June Sochen, *Herstory: Women in American History* (New York, 1974), pp. 79-81, portrays Paine as a feminist advocate.

62. Paine to Georges Jacques Danton, Paris (1793), in *Writings*, 2:1335.

63. "Address to the People of France," September 25, 1792, in ibid., p. 539.

64. Paine to Messieurs Condorcet, Nicolas de Bonneville and Lanthenas, Paris, June, 1791, in *Writings*, 2:1318; "Agrarian Justice," in ibid., 1:608.

65. "Address and Declaration of the Friends of Universal Peace and Liberty," August, 1791, in ibid., 2:534; "Age of Reason," p. 516.

66. Crane Brinton, "Thomas Paine," *Dictionary of American Biography*, 20 vols. (New York, 1928-36), 14:161.

67. Edmund Burke, *The Writings and Speeches of Edmund Burke*, 12 vols. (New York, 1901), vol. 3, *Reflections on the Revolution in France*, p. 242.

68. Ibid., pp. 240-41, 559.

69. Paine to Mr. Secretary Dundas, London, June 6, 1792, in *Writings*, 2:451.

70. "Common Sense," p. 43.

71. "Serious Address," p. 284.

72. "Rights of Man," pp. 266-67.

73. "Shall Louis XVI Be Respited?" Address read by Bancal to French National Convention, January 19, 1793, in *Writings*, 2:556; Paine to Georges Jacques Danton, May 6, 1793, in ibid., p. 1337; "First Principles," p. 588; "To the Citizens of the United States," from *National Intelligencer*, November 15, 1802, in ibid., p. 911.

74. "The American Crisis," 1, 4, in ibid., 1:50, 102.

75. "To the French Inhabitants of Louisiana," September 22, 1804, in ibid., 2:964-65.

76. "Address to the People of Pennsylvania," *Pennsylvania Packet*, December 10, 1778, in ibid., p. 293.

77. "Rights of Man," pp. 388, 439-40, 449.

78. "Agrarian Justice," in *Writings*, 1:620.

79. Charles Hawtrey, *Various Opinions of the Philosophical Reformers Considered; Particularly Pain's Rights of Man* (London, 1792), p. 80; John Bowles, *Protest against T. Paine's "Rights of Man"* (London, 1792), pp. 13, 30; *A Letter from a Magistrate to Mr. William Rose, of Whitehall, on Mr. Paine's Rights of Men* (London, 1791); John Quincy Adams, "Letters of Publicola," in *The Writings of John Quincy Adams*, ed. Worthington C. Ford, 7 vols. (New York, 1913-1917), 1:65-110.

80. William Graham Sumner, *Earth Hunger and Other Essays* (New Haven, 1913), pp. 79-83, 107-203; Henry Hayden Clark, *Thomas Paine: Representative Selections* (New York, 1944, 1961), pp. lviii-lxxii.

81. Stewart H. Benedict, ed., *Blacklash: Black Protest in Our Time* (New York, 1970), pp. 287-90; Staughton Lynd, *Intellectual Origins of American Radicalism* (New York, 1968).

82. Carl Becker, *The Declaration of Independence* (New York, 1922), pp. 277-

79; Clinton Rossiger, *Seedtime of the Republic* (New York, 1953), pp. 437-49; Charles Beard, *The Republic* (New York, 1943), pp. 38-40.

83. John Dewey, *Human Nature and Conduct* (New York, 1922), pp. 306-7.

84. Richard Taylor, *Freedom, Anarchy, and the Law* (Englewood Cliffs, N.J., 1973), p. 118.

85. "To the Citizens of the United States," from *National Intelligencer*, November 15, 1802, in *Writings*, 2:910.

86. Paine to Kitty Nicholson Few, London, January 6, 1789, in ibid., p. 1276.

CHAPTER THREE

1. William H. Gilman et al., eds., *The Journals and Miscellaneous Notebooks of Ralph Waldo Emerson* (1960-     ), 2:52 (hereafter cited as *Journals and Notebooks*).

2. Ibid., 6:210.

3. See Arthur C. McGiffert, *Young Emerson Speaks* (Boston, 1938), pp. 263-71, for a list of Emerson's sermons, published and unpublished. Some of the titles: "Self-Direction and Self-Command," "True Freedom," "Freedom and Dependence," "The Power of the Soul," and "The Limits of Self-Reliance."

4. Sermon no. 53, "Freedom and Dependence," October 24, 1829, Emerson Papers, Houghton Library, Harvard University, Cambridge, Mass.

5. Perry Miller, ed., *The Transcendentalists* (Cambridge, Mass., 1950), p. 8.

6. *Journals and Notebooks*, 7:40.

7. "The Lord's Supper," Sermon delivered before the Second Church in Boston, September 9, 1832, *The Complete Works of Ralph Waldo Emerson*, Concord edition, 12 vols. (Boston and New York, 1903-4), 11:24 (hereafter cited as *Works*).

8. Emerson to William Emerson, Boston, November 19, 1832, in *The Letters of Ralph Waldo Emerson*, ed. Ralph L. Rusk, 6 vols. (New York, 1939), 1:357-58 (hereafter cited as *Letters*).

9. Ralph Waldo Emerson to Edward Bliss Emerson, Newton, Mass., May 31, 1834, in ibid., 1:412-13. Punctuation marks added.

10. October 2, 1832, *Journals and Notebooks*, 4:46.

11. "The American Scholar" (1837), *Works*, 1:104.

12. April 10, 1843, E. W. Emerson and W. E. Forbes, eds., *The Journals of Ralph Waldo Emerson*, 12 vols. (New York, 1909-14), 6:380 (hereafter cited as *Journals*).

13. "Self-Reliance" (1841), *Works*, 2:49.

14. March 18, 1838, *Journals*, 4:414.

15. "Character" (1844), *Works*, 3:100.

16. "Self-Reliance," p. 50.

17. "The Transcendentalist" (1842), *Works*, 1:334, 347-48.

18. December 22, 1839, *Journals*, 5:359; "The American Scholar," p. 91.

19. "Friendship" (1841), *Works*, 2:214-15.

20. "Self-Reliance," pp. 73-74; ibid., 49, uses "neutrality" instead of "godlike independence," which appears in *Essays by Ralph Waldo Emerson*, First and Second Series Complete in One Volume with Introduction by Irwin Edman (New York, Thomas Y. Crowell, 1926, 1951), p. 35.

21. "Self-Reliance," p. 89.

22. November 7, 1838, *Journals*, 5:120.

23. "Self-Reliance," p. 76; "The Natural History of the Intellect," *Works*, 12:29; "Self-Reliance," p. 46.

24. "Spiritual Laws" (1841), *Works*, 2:140-41. The Concord edition uses "deepening channel" instead of "God's depths." The latter phrase, which I am using, appears in the Crowell edition of Emerson's essays (n. 20 above), p. 100.

25. "Self-Reliance," p. 70, uses "obedience" for "soul," which appears in the Crowell edition, and also uses "work" on p. 54 instead of "thing" which appears in

the latter volume on p. 38. I am following the text of the Crowell edition here.

26. *Journals*, 7:255; *Works*, 7:399; *Journals*, 3:423.

27. "Voluntaries," *Works*, 9:207.

28. *Journals and Notebooks*, 2:320.

29. Ibid., 2:33.

30. Ibid., 7:98.

31. J. G. Crowther, *Men of Science* (New York, 1936), p. 321.

32. *Journals and Notebooks*, 2:65; "Fate" (1860) *Works*, 6:48-49.

33. *Journals*, 7:101.

34. "Illusions" (1860), *Works*, 6:325.

35. "Power" (1860), ibid., 6:54.

36. "Montaigne" (1850), ibid., 4:170.

37. "Power," p. 54.

38. "Thoughts on Modern Literature," *Works*, 12:33.

39. "The Over-Soul," ibid., 2:268.

40. *Journals and Notebooks*, 4:309-10. See Martin Wolfson, "A Note on 'Insight,'" *Journal of Philosophy* 44 (1947): 684-85.

41. "Literary Ethics" (1838), *Works*, 1:182; "The Method of Nature" (1841), ibid., 1:210.

42. "The Over-Soul," pp. 267-97.

43. October 15, 1835, *Journals*, 3:555.

44. Howard E. Gruber et al., eds., *Contemporary Approaches to Creative Thinking* (New York, 1962), pp. 39-42. See also A. M. Taylor, *Imagination and the Growth of Science* (New York, 1970), pp. 8-9.

45. "The Method of Nature," pp. 204, 221-22.

46. "The Tragic," *Works*, 12:406-7; "Modern Literature," ibid., p. 331.

47. Merrill D. Peterson, *The Jefferson Image in the American Mind* (New York, 1962), p. 201.

48. *Journals*, 10:361.

49. *Works*, 1:142; 3:142; 2:262; 5:51; 12:272.

50. *Journals and Notebooks*, 2:44, 57, 58.

51. "Spiritual Laws," p. 141.

52. "New England Reformers" (1844), *Works*, 3:284-85.

53. "The Young American" (1844), ibid., 1:390.

54. "The Transcendentalist," p. 349.

55. "Character," pp. 97-98; "Lecture on the Times (1841), *Works*, 1:281.

56. "Fate," p. 23.

57. "Character," p. 94; "Walter Savage Landor," *Works*, 12:342.

58. "Lecture on the Times," *Works*, 1:276, 280-81.

59. "The Young American," p. 390; "The Transcendentalist," p. 351; June 22, 1838, *Journals*, 4:491.

60. *Works*, 5:144; James K. Hosmer, ed., *Winthrop's Journal*, 2 vols. (New York, 1908), 2:637-39.

61. Sermon no. 24, "Self-Direction and Self-Command" (1828), Emerson Papers.

62. Sermon no. 42, "True Freedom" (1829), Emerson Papers.

63. Sermon no. 124, "Freedom," August 13, 1831; Sermon no. 42, "True Freedom," July 4, 1829, Emerson Papers.

64. "Self-Reliance," p. 69.

65. "Worship," *Works*, 6:240; "Nature," ibid., 3:195; "The Fugitive Slave Law," ibid., 11:240.

66. 1859, *Journals*, 9: 247.

67. "The Fugitive Slave Law," p. 236.

68. Irwin H. Polishook, *Roger Williams, John Cotton and Religious Freedom* (Englewood Cliffs, N.J., 1967), pp. 29, 71; Jonathan Boucher, *A View of the Causes and Consequences of the American Revolution* (New York, 1797, 1967), p. 509.

69. "The Transcendentalist," p. 334.

70. "Self-Reliance," p. 51.

71. "Spiritual Laws," p. 141.

72. *Nature*, in *The Collected Works of Ralph Waldo Emerson* (Cambridge, Mass., 1971), 1:25.

73. "Fate," p. 22.

74. Ibid., p. 15.

75. Ibid., pp. 3-4.

76. Ralph Waldo Emerson to Caroline Sturgis Tappan, July 22, 1853, *Letters*, 4:376.

77. "Fate," pp. 19, 5.

78. Ibid., pp. 6-8.

79. Ibid., p. 20.

80. Ibid., pp. 23, 25, 31-32.

81. "Beauty," *Works*, 6:288.

82. "Fate," pp. 22, 27.

83. Ibid., pp. 33, 27, 32-33.

84. Ibid., pp. 28, 25, 29.

85. *Nature*, in *The Collected Works*, 1:33, 41-42.

86. *Winthrop's Journal*, 2:637-39; Sidney Hook, *The Metaphysics of Pragmatism* (Chicago, 1927), pp. 138-41.

87. "Fate," p. 27.

88. "Worship," p. 240.

89. "Fate," pp. 48-49.

90. Ibid., p. 35.

91. *Letters*, 4:376.

92. Louis Ruchames, "Two Forgotten Addresses by Ralph Waldo Emerson," *American Literature* 28 (January 1957): 425-33; July, 1851, *Journals*, 8:236.

93. "The Fugitive Slave Law," p. 183.

94. 1851, *Journals*, 8:182, 194, 111.

95. "The Fugitive Slave Law," pp. 219, 229, 232.

96. "John Brown," *Works*, 11:277; "Theodore Parker," ibid., p. 290.

97. *Journals*, 9:336, 572.

98. Ibid., 8:316.

99. "The Celebration of the Intellect," *Works*, 12:113.

100. November 13, 1839, *Journals*, 5:323; "Civilization," *Society and Solitude* (1870), *Works*, 7:25.

101. "Milton," *Works*, 12:250.

## CHAPTER FOUR

1. James Parton, *Life of Andrew Jackson*, 3 vols. (Boston, 1887-88), 3:283-84.

2. Arthur Stryon, *The Cast-Iron Man: John C. Calhoun and American Democracy* (New York, 1935), p. 360.

3. G. Gordon Post, ed., *A Disquisition on Government and Selections from the Discourse* (Indianapolis, 1953), p. vii; Charles M. Wiltse, *John C. Calhoun, Nationalist, 1782-1828* (New York, 1944), p. 2; Ralph Henry Gabriel, *The Course of American Democratic Thought* (New York, 1956), p. 112.

4. Speech on Resolutions in Reference to the War with Mexico, January 4, 1848, *The Works of John C. Calhoun*, 6 vols. (New York, 1854), 4:420 (hereafter cited as *Works*).

5. *Life of Calhoun, Presenting a Condensed History of Political Events from 1811 to 1843* (New York, 1843), p. 5.

6. Remarks on Presenting His Resolutions on the Slave Question, February 19, 1847, *Works*, 4:345-46. Italics added.

7. Speech on His Resolutions in Reference to the War with Mexico, January 4, 1848, ibid., p. 417.

8. Report on the Causes and Reasons for War, June 3, 1812, *The Papers of John C. Calhoun* (Columbia, S.C., 1959), 1:122 (hereafter cited as *Papers*).

9. Speech on the Albany Petition for Repeal of the Embargo, May 6, 1812, ibid., p. 64.

10. Speech on Suspension of Non-Importation, June 24, 1812, ibid., pp. 131-32.

11. Speech on the Military Situation, October 25, 1814, ibid., p. 259.

12. Speech on the Bill to Repeal the Restrictive System, April 6, 1814, ibid., pp. 243, 246.

13. Speech in Defense of the Republican Foreign Policy, April 6, 1814, ibid., p. 250; Speech on the Bill for an Additional Military Force, January 14, 1813, ibid., p. 154.

14. Report on Relations with Great Britain, November 29, 1811, ibid., p. 67; Speech on the Loan Bill, February 25, 1814, ibid., p. 212.

15. Report on Relations with Great Britain, November 29, 1811, ibid., p. 66; Report on the Causes and Reasons for War, June 3, 1812, ibid., p. 116; Speech on Loan Bill, February 25, 1811, ibid., pp. 214. 219.

16. Speech on the Dangers of "Factious Opposition," January 15, 1814, ibid., pp. 189-201, 195; Speech on the Bill for an Additional Military Force, January 14, 1813, ibid., pp. 160-61.

17. Speech on the Dangers of "Factious Opposition," ibid., p. 199.

18. First Speech on the Military Academies Bill, January 2, 1816, ibid., pp. 288-89.

19. Speech on the Revenue Bill, January 31, 1816, ibid., p. 325.

20. Speech on the Tariff Bill, April 4, 1816, ibid., p. 356.

21. Speech on Internal Improvements, February 4, 1817, ibid., pp. 401-2, 403.

22. Allan Nevins, ed., *The Diary of John Quincy Adams, 1794-1845* (New York, 1951), p. 265; Charles Francis Adams, ed., *Memoirs of John Quincy Adams*, 12 vols. (Philadelphia, 1875), 6:75.

23. Onslow to Patrick Henry on the Powers of the Vice-President, as President of the Senate, *Works*, 6:334-35, 337.

24. Gerald Capers, *John C. Calhoun—Opportunist: A Reappraisal* (Gainesville, 1960).

25. From *South Carolina Exposition*, December, 1828, in *Works*, 6:2, 40.

26. Speech in Reply to Webster, on the Resolutions regarding the Rights of the States, February 26, 1833, ibid., 2:308.

27. Speech on the Removal of Public Deposits, January 13, 1834, ibid., p. 338.

28. Speech on Bill to Regulate the Deposits of the Public Money, May 28, 1836, ibid., p. 547.

29. *A Discourse on the Constitution and Government of the United States*, ibid., 1:199.

30. Speech on the Bill to Prevent the Interference of Certain Federal Officers in Elections, February 22, 1838, ibid., 3:390, 399.

31. Speech on Passage of the Tariff Bill, August 5, 1842, ibid., 4:201.

32. Calhoun quoted this phrase on several occasions. See ibid., 4:245, 286; 6:143.

33. Speech on the Bill to Prohibit Deputy-Postmasters from Receiving & Transmitting . . . Certain Papers . . . , April 12, 1836, ibid., 2:529.

34. Cincinnatus [pseud.], *Freedom's Defence; or, a Candid Examination of Mr. Calhoun's Report on the Freedom of the Press* (Worcester, 1836), p. 23.

35. Speech on Abolition Petitions, March 9, 1836, *Works*, 2:466; Remarks on the Right of Petition, February 13, 1840, ibid., 3:440.

36. Speech on Reception of Abolition Petitions, February 6, 1837, ibid., 2:631, 630.

37. Remarks . . . on His Resolutions in Respect to the Right of the States, and the Abolition of Slavery, December 27, 1837, ibid., 3:147.

38. Speech on the Motion to Repeal the Direct Tax, January 31, 1816, ibid., 2:144.

39. Speech on the Bill for Making Further Appropriations to Bring the . . . War with Mexico to a Speedy . . . Conclusion, February 9, 1847, ibid., 4:325.

40. William M. Meigs, *The Life of John Caldwell Calhoun*, 2 vols. (New York, 1917), 2:448.

41. Margaret Coit, *John C. Calhoun* (Boston, 1950), p. 513.

42. Mill called it "a posthumous work of great ability" in *Considerations on Representative Government* (New York: 1958), p. 244.

43. Address to People of South Carolina, 1831, *Works*, 6:138.

44. Speech on the Oregon Bill, June 27, 1848, ibid., 4:507.

45. Ibid., p. 512.

46. *Disquisition on Government*, ibid., 1:1, 8, 12.

47. Ibid., p. 8.

48. Speech on the Compensation Bill, January 17, 1817, ibid., 2:176.

49. *Disquisition*, ibid., 1:56.

50. Ibid., pp. 53-54.

51. Ibid., p. 55.

52. Calhoun to Pakenham, April 18, 1844, ibid., 5:337.

53. Calhoun to William R. King, August 12, 1844, ibid., p. 391.

54. Speech in Reply to Mr. Webster, February 26, 1833, ibid., 2:285.

55. See Coit, *Calhoun*, pp. 518-32; Wiltse, *Calhoun, Nationalist*, p. 398, and Wiltse, *John C. Calhoun, Sectionalist, 1840-1850* (Indianapolis, 1951), p. 484.

56. *Disquisition, Works*, 1:18, 49-50.

57. Speech on His Amendment to Bill Authorizing Issue of Treasury Notes, October 3, 1837, ibid., 3:114. For strictures on Hamilton's favoritism toward "the most powerful classes of society," see Speech on Bill to Prevent the Interference of Certain Federal Officers in Elections, February 22, 1839, ibid., pp. 390 ff.

58. February 25, 1814, ibid., 2:100.

59. Speech on the Force Bill, February 15-16, 1833, ibid., p. 245.

60. Speech on His Resolutions in Reference to the War with Mexico, January 4, 1848, ibid., 4:416.

61. *Disquisition*, ibid., 1:46.

62. Speech on Force Bill, February 15-16, 1833, ibid., 2:252.

63. Ibid., p. 229.

64. Ibid., p. 237.

65. "Notes on Nullification," in Gaillard Hunt, ed., *The Writings of James Madison*, 9 vols. (New York, 1900-1910), 9:588.

66. For his answer to this charge, see Speech on the Independent Treasury Bill, March 10, 1838, *Works*, 3:274.

67. Speech on the Commercial Treaty with Great Britain, January 9, 1816, *Papers*, 1:312.

68. See, for example, *Works*, 1:168 and 3:639.

69. Speech on the Reception of Abolition Petitions, February 6, 1837, ibid., 2:631.

70. George Fitzhugh, *Cannibals All! Or Slaves without Masters* (Cambridge, Mass., 1960), p. 78.

71. Address at Sanitary Fair, Baltimore, April 18, 1864, *The Collected Works of Abraham Lincoln*, 9 vols. (New Brunswick, N.J., 1953-55), 7:301-2.

72. Speech, Independence Hall, Philadelphia, February 22, 1861, ibid., p. 240; Speech at a Republican Banquet, Chicago, December 10, 1856, ibid., 2:385.

73. William E. Dodd, *Statesmen of the Old South* (New York, 1929), p. 167.

## CHAPTER FIVE

1. "An Appeal to the British People," May 12, 1846, in Philip S. Foner, *The Life and Writings of Frederick Douglass*, 4 vols. (New York, 1950), 1:154-55 (hereafter cited as *Life and Writings*); "The Decision of the Hour," June 16, 1861, ibid., 3:121.

2. "The Claims of the Negro Ethnologically Considered," ibid., 2:308; *Life and Times of Frederick Douglass* (London, 1962), pp. 187, 87, 156 (hereafter cited as *Life and Times*).

3. Robert William Fogel and Stanley L. Engerman, *Time on the Cross*, 2 vols. (Boston, 1974).

4. "The Republican Party," from *Douglass' Monthly*. August, 1860. *Life and Writings*, 2:491-92.

5. *Life and Times*, pp. 202-3.

6. Ibid., p. 204.

7. Frederick Douglass, *My Bondage and My Freedom* (New York, 1969), p. 333.

8. Gilbert Osofsky, ed., *Puttin' on Ole Massa: The Slave Narratives of Henry Bibb, William Wells Brown, and Solomon Northrup* (New York, 1969), pp. 379, 63.

9. *Life and Times*, pp. 50, 51.

10. Ibid., pp. 79-80.

11. Caleb Bingham, ed., *The Columbian Orator: Containing A Variety of Original and Selected Pieces, Together with Rules Calculated to Improve Youth and Others in the Ornamental and Useful Art of Eloquence* (Boston, 1832), pp. 241-42, 112; *Life and Times*, p. 85.

12. *Life and Times*, p. 86.

13. Ibid., pp. 124, 143.

14. Ibid., p. 150; "An Appeal to the British People," *Life and Writings*, 1:157.

15. Benjamin Quarles, *Frederick Douglass* (New York, 1948), p. 15.

16. Frederick Douglass to William Lloyd Garrison, Dublin, September 16, 1845, *Life and Writings*, 1:120.

17. Douglass to Garrison, Belfast, January 1, 1846, ibid., p. 127.

18. Douglass to Garrison, London, May 23, 1846, ibid., p. 172.

19. Douglass to Garrison, Perth, January 27, 1846, ibid., p. 133.

20. "Farewell Speech to the British People," London, March 30, 1847, ibid., p. 229.

21. Ibid., pp. 230, 212.

22. Ibid., p. 230.

23. *My Bondage and My Freedom*, p. xxiii; *Life and Times*, p. 257; "The Anti-Slavery Movement," January, 1855, *Life and Writings*, 2:360; "The Do-Nothing Policy," from *Frederick Douglass' Paper*, September 12, 1851, in ibid., p. 405.

24. "Lecture on Slavery, No. 2," December 8, 1850, ibid., p. 140.

25. Frederick Douglass to Horace Greeley, Glasgow, April 14, 1846, ibid., 1:148.

26. Benjamin Quarles, *Black Abolitionists* (Oxford, 1969), pp. 122-23.

27. "The Meaning of July Fourth for the Negro," July 5, 1852, *Life and Writings*, 2:189, 192.

28. Ibid., p. 200.

29. "The Slaveholders' Rebellion," July 4, 1862, ibid., 3:248.

30. "The Claims of the Negro Ethnologically Considered," July 12, 1854, ibid., pp. 292, 293; James C. Prichard, *The Natural History of Man* (London, 1843), p. 546. In later years, Douglass cited Ethiopia and Carthage as well as Egypt as evidence that civilization flourished in northern Africa at a time when Europe was still floundering in ignorance and barbarism. See "Address of Frederick Douglass at the Inauguration of the Douglass Institute, Baltimore, October 1, 1865," *Journal of Negro History* 54 (April 1969): 174-83.

31. *Life and Times*, p. 45.

32. "The Claims of the Negro Ethnologically Considered," pp. 304-5.

33. "What the Black Man Wants," April, 1865, *Life and Writings*, 4:161.

34. "The Future of the Negro People of the Slave States," February 12, 1862, ibid., 3:218-19.

35. "The Claims of the Negro," ibid., 2:305.

36. "What the Black Man Wants," p. 161; "Is It Right and Wise to Kill a Kidnapper?" from *Frederick Douglass' Paper*, June 2, 1854, in *Life and Writings*, 2:285; "Second Proclamation," from *Niles' Register*, December 3, 1854, in ibid., p. 267.

37. "A Few Words to Our Own People," from *North Star*, January 19, 1849, in ibid., 1:347.

38. "Pumpkins," from *North Star*, October 19, 1849, in ibid., p. 408.

39. "Prejudice against Color," from *North Star*, June 13, 1850, in ibid., 2:130.

40. "Henry Clay and Slavery," from *North Star*, February 8, 1850, in ibid., p. 107; *Life and Times*, p. 85.

41. *My Bondage and My Freedom*, p. 90; "Danger to the Abolition Cause," from *Douglass' Monthly*, June, 1861, in *Life and Writings*, 3:112-13; *My Bondage and My Freedom*, p. 139; "Danger to the Abolition Cause," p. 112; "The Proclamation and a Negro Army," from *Douglass' Monthly*, March, 1863, in *Life and Writings*, 3:323.

42. "The Address of Southern Delegates to Their Constituents," from *North Star*, February 9, 1849, in *Life and Writings*, 1:359.

43. "A Plea for Free Speech in Boston," from *Liberator*, December 14, 1860, in ibid., 2:539.

44. Ibid.

45. "The Proclamation and a Negro Army," p. 325.

46. Douglass to Garrison, February 26, 1846, ibid., 1:141.

47. Douglass to Garrison, September 28, 1845, ibid., p. 121.

48. "Farewell Speech to British People," London, March 30, 1847, ibid., p. 209.

49. Douglass to Thomas Van Rensselaer, Lynn, Mass., May 18, 1847, ibid., p. 245; "American Slavery," New York City, October 22, 1847, ibid., p. 270.

50. Ibid., p. 275.

51. For his views on the U.S. Constitution, see ibid., 1:208-9, 245, 270, 261-67, 274-75, 352-53; 2:115-19, 152-53, 155-56, 369, 380-82, 419-24, 467-80.

52. Quarles, *Douglass*, pp. 141-68.

53. *Life and Times*, p. 275.

54. "To the Rochester *Democrat and American*," October 31, 1859, *Life and Writings*, 2:462.

55. "How to End the War," from *Douglass' Monthly*, May, 1861, in ibid., 3:94.

56. "The National Unity," from *Douglass' Monthly*, July, 1862, in ibid., p. 241.

57. "The Proclamation and a Negro Army," New York City, February, 1863, ibid., p. 322.

58. Douglass to Montgomery Blair, Rochester, September 16, 1862, ibid., p. 286.

59. "Why Is the Negro Lynched?" from *The Lesson of the Hour* (1894), in ibid., 4:513.

60. Quarles, *Douglass*, p. 124.

61. Douglass to Montgomery Blair, Rochester, September 16, 1862, *Life and Writings*, 3:286.

62. "The President and His Speeches," from *Douglass' Monthly*, September, 1862, in ibid., pp. 266-70.

63. "Oration in Memory of Abraham Lincoln," April 14, 1876, ibid., 4:312.

64. Ibid., p. 314.

65. *Life and Times*, p. 359.

66. Allen T. Rice, *Reminiscences of Abraham Lincoln* (New York, 1886), p. 193.

67. What Shall Be Done with the Slaves if Emancipated?" from *Douglass'* ber 5, 1872, in *Life and Writings*, 4:299.

68. *Life and Times*, pp. 379, 396.

69. Ibid., p. 378.
70. Douglass to W. J. Wilson, Rochester, August 8, 1865, *Life and Writings,* 4:172-73.
71. *Life and Times,* pp. 450, 451, 479.
72. Ibid., pp. 539, 536.
73. "Give Us the Freedom Intended for Us," from the *New National Era,* December 5, 1872, in *Life and Writings,* 4:299.
74. "The Color Line," from *North American Review,* June 1881, in ibid., pp. 342-52.
75. *Life and Times,* p. 551.
76. Ibid., p. 537.
77. Ibid., p. 373.
78. Ibid., p. 462.
79. Ibid., p. 546.
80. *Life and Writings,* 4:109-10.
81. "Why Is the Negro Lynched?" from *The Lesson of the Hour,* in ibid., pp. 491-523.
82. Ibid., p. 149.
83. *Life and Times,* p. 388.
84. Ibid., p. 535.
85. Ibid., p. 546.

## CHAPTER SIX

1. "Concerning the Founding of Nationalist Colonies," *New Nation* 3 (September 23, 1893) : 434.
2. Arthur E. Morgan, *Edward Bellamy* (New York, 1944), p. 3.
3. Sylvia E. Bowman, *The Year 2000: A Critical Biography of Edward Bellamy* (New York, 1958), p. 51; Morgan, *Bellamy,* p. 192.
4. Bowman, *The Year 2000,* pp. 22, 98.
5. Morgan, *Bellamy,* p. 226.
6. Thomas A. Sancton, "Looking Inward: Edward Bellamy's Spiritual Crisis," *American Quarterly* 25 (December 1973) : 538-57; Morgan, *Bellamy,* p. 198; Edward Bellamy, *Equality* (New York, 1897), p. 265.
7. Sylvia E. Bowman, *Edward Bellamy Abroad: An American Prophet's Influence* (New York, 1962), p. 287.
8. Edward Bellamy, *The Blindman's World and Other Stories* (Boston and New York, 1898), p. 61.
9. Ibid., p. 64.
10. Ibid., p. 334.
11. Edward Bellamy, *Dr. Heidenhoff's Process* (New York, 1880), p. 117.
12. Ibid., p. 123.
13. Ibid., p. 170.
14. Ibid., p. 83.
15. Ibid., p. 86.
16. Ibid., p. 107.
17. Ibid., p. 121.
18. Ibid., p. 105.
19. Ibid., p. 139.
20. Bowman, *Bellamy Abroad,* p. 278.
21. Edward Bellamy, *Miss Ludington's Sister: A Romance of Immortality* (Boston, 1884), p. 252.
22. Ibid., p. 256.
23. *Blindman's World,* p. 16.
24. Ibid., p. 29.

25. Bertrand Russell, *Our Knowledge of the External World* (New York, 1929), p. 182.

26. Edward Bellamy, "Why I Wrote 'Looking Backward,'" from *Nationalist* (May 1980), in *Edward Bellamy Speaks Again!* (Kansas City, Mo., 1937), p. 199.

27. Bowman, *The Year 2000*, p. 44.

28. William Graham Sumner, *The Challenge of Facts and Other Essays* (New Haven, 1914), p. 25.

29. *Bellamy Speaks Again*, pp. 82-83.

30. Edward Bellamy, *Looking Backward, 2000-1887* (Modern Library, New York, 1917), p. 234.

31. Ibid., p. 92.

32. *Bellamy Speaks Again*, p. 44.

33. *Looking Backward*, p. 159.

34. Ibid., pp. 136-37.

35. *Bellamy Speaks Again*, pp. 121-22.

36. *Looking Backward*, p. 47.

37. Ibid.

38. Ibid., p. 234.

39. Ibid., p. 92.

40. J. W. Roberts, *Looking Within: The Mischievous Tendencies of 'Looking Backward' Made Manifest* (New York, 1893), p. 211.

41. Ibid., p. 221.

42. Conrad Wilbrandt, *Mr. East's Experiences in Mr. Bellamy's World: Records of the Years 2001 and 2002* (New York, 1891), p. 188.

43. Richard Michaelis, *A Sequel to Looking Backward, or Looking Further Forward* (London, 1891), p. 35.

44. Ibid., p. 48.

45. Edward Bellamy, "Some Misconceptions of Nationalism," from *Christian Union*, November 13, 1890, in *Bellamy Speaks Again*, p. 124.

46. "Talks on Nationalism," from *New Nation* (Boston), 1891, in Bowman, *Bellamy Abroad*, pp. 420-21.

47. Bellamy, *Equality*, p. 80.

48. Ibid., p. 9.

49. Ibid., p. 5.

50. Ibid., p. 17.

51. Ibid., p. 80.

52. Ibid., pp. 81-82.

53. Ibid., pp. 82-83.

54. Ibid., p. 101.

55. Ibid., p. 86.

56. Everett W. MacNair, *Edward Bellamy and the Nationalist Movement, 1889-1894* (Milwaukee, 1957), p. 35.

57. J. Foster Biscoe, "Attitude of the Press," *Nationalist* 1 (October 1889): 22.

58. "Work for Women," *Springfield Union*, March, 1873, quoted by Sylvia E. Bowman, "Bellamy's Missing Chapter," *New England Quarterly* 31 (March 1958): 56.

59. *Equality*, p. 392.

60. Ibid., p. 61.

61. Ibid., p. 400.

62. Ibid., p. 262.

63. Ibid., p. 136.

64. *Looking Backward*, pp. 211-12.

65. Ibid., pp. 214-15.

66. *Equality*, pp. 132-33.

67. Ibid., p. 410.

68. *Looking Backward*, p. 216.

69. Ibid., pp. 212, 217.

70. Edward Bellamy, *Talks on Nationalism* (Chicago, 1938), p. 122.

71. Ibid., p. 85.

72. *Equality*, p. 138.

73. "Mr. Bellamy and Christianity," *Andover Review* 15 (April 1891): 418.

74. *Looking Backward*, pp. 237-38.

75. *Equality*, p. 265; see also Bowman, *The Year 2000*, p. 28.

76. Morgan, *Bellamy*, pp. 260-75.

77. Robert C. Tucker, ed., *The Marx-Engels Reader* (New York, 1972), p. 353; *Equality*, pp. 344-45.

78. *Talks on Nationalism*, p. 166.

79. *Equality*, p. 344.

80. Morgan, *Bellamy*, pp. 80-81.

81. *The Federalist Papers* no. 34 (New York: Mentor Books, New American Library, 1961), p. 208.

82. Sancton, "Looking Inward," p. 540; Morgan, *Bellamy*, p. 150. See also E. F. Schumacher, *Small Is Beautiful: Economics As If People Mattered* (New York, 1974).

83. R. H. Tawney, *Equality* (New York, 1931, 1961), p. 268.

84. *New Nation* 1 (November 22, 1891): 695.

85. R. E. Bisbee, "Some Characteristics of Edward Bellamy," *Coming Age* 1 (February 1899), p. 185.

## CHAPTER SEVEN

1. William James, *The Principles of Psychology*, 2 vols. (New York, 1950), 2:513, 576.

2. James, "The Dilemma of Determinism," *The Will to Believe and Other Essays* (New York, 1956), p. 149.

3. Thomas H. Huxley, *Method and Results* (New York, 1896), pp. 192-93.

4. James, "On Some Hegelisms," *Will to Believe*, p. 271. I'm assuming that James's reference to the "ridiculous 'freedom to do right'" is a response to the Huxley passage.

5. *Principles of Psychology*, 1:440.

6. Max C. Otto et al., *William James: The Man and the Thinker* (Madison, Wisc., 1942), p. 43.

7. James, *The Varieties of Religious Experience* (New York, 1902), p. 158.

8. Ralph Barton Perry, *The Thought and Character of William James*, 2 vols. (Boston, 1935), 1:472.

9. *Varieties of Religious Experience*, p. 157.

10. *Letters of William James*, 2 vols. (Boston, 1920), 1:147-48.

11. Perry, *James*, 1:339-40.

12. *Principles of Psychology*, 1:132.

13. Ibid., p. 136.

14. Ibid., pp. 138-39.

15. Ibid., p. 139.

16. Ibid., pp. 288-89.

17. Max Eastman, *Heroes I Have Known* (New York, 1942), p. 266.

18. *Principles of Psychology*, 1:402.

19. Ibid., p. 452.

20. Ibid., pp. 453-54.

21. Ibid., 2:562.

22. Ibid., p. 561.

23. Ibid., p. 548.

24. Ibid., pp. 573-74.

25. James, *Essays in Radical Empiricism* (New York, 1909), pp. 183-84.

26. "Dilemma of Determinism," pp. 147, 150-51.

27. Ibid., p. 164.
28. Ibid., p. 165.
29. Ibid., p. 178.
30. Ibid., pp. 172-73.
31. Ibid., p. 174.
32. Ibid., pp. 175-76.
33. Ibid., p. 157.
34. *Principles of Psychology*, 2:576-77.
35. *Will to Believe*, p. 157n.
36. "Great Men and Their Environment," *Will to Believe*, p. 218.
37. Ibid., p. 233.
38. Ibid., p. 219.
39. Ibid., p. 226.
40. Ibid., p. 229.
41. Ibid., p. 244.
42. Ibid., p. 227.
43. Ibid., p. 230.
44. Ibid., p. 226n.
45. Ibid., p. 246.
46. Ibid., pp. 247-49.
47. "The Importance of Individuals," *Will to Believe*, pp. 256-57, 261.
48. Grant Allen, "The Genesis of Genius," *Atlantic Monthly* 47 (March 1881):
374; John William Draper, *Thoughts on the Future Civil Polity of America* (New York, 1865), p. iv; Robert Stover, "Great Man Theory of History," *Encyclopedia of Philosophy*, 8 vols. (New York, 1967), 3:378-82; Sidney Hook, *The Hero in History* (Boston, 1943), p. xi.
49. "Some Metaphysical Problems Pragmatically Considered," *Pragmatism and Four Essays from the Meaning of Truth* (New York, 1955), p. 84.
50. *Papers of Charles Sanders Peirce*, 8 vols. (Cambridge, Mass. 1965), 6:46, 553; James, *The Meaning of Truth* (New York, 1909), p. 58.
51. James, *Some Problems of Philosophy* (London, 1911), pp. 150-51.
52. Ibid., p. 97.
53. Ibid., p. 46.
54. "Frederic Myer's Service to Psychology" (1901), in Gardner Murphy and Robert O. Ballou, *William James on Psychical Research* (New York, 1960), p. 223.
55. *Some Problems of Philosophy*, p. 148.
56. Ibid., pp. 147, 132.
57. Ibid., pp. 139-40.
58. Ibid., p. 46.
59. James, *Essays in Radical Empiricism*, p. 185.
60. Ibid. pp. 181-82.
61. Ibid., p. 184.
62. *Some Problems of Philosophy*, p. 145.
63. Ibid.
64. *Pragmatism and Four Essays*, p. 83.
65. *Varieties of Religious Experience*, pp. 206, 229, 473.
66. *Meaning of Truth*, p. 216.
67. George Stuart Fullerton, "Freedom and 'Free-Will,'" *Popular Science Monthly* 18 (December 1900): 189-90, 191.
68. *Meaning of Truth*, p. 254. John M. E. McTaggart's discussion of free will in chap. 5 of *Some Dogmas of Religion* (London, 1906) was also James's target.
69. Ibid., pp. 250-51.
70. Ibid., p. 252.
71. Ibid., p. 254.
72. Ibid., p. 252.

73. Ibid., p. 254.

74. George Santayana, *Character and Opinion in the United States* (London, 1921), p. 82.

75. Ibid., p. 81.

76. "Dostoevski and Parricide," *The Standard Edition of the Complete Psychological Works of Sigmund Freud*, ed. James Strachey (London, 1961), 21:177.

77. William Barrett, "Determinism and Novelty," in Sidney Hook, ed., *Determinism and Freedom in the Age of Modern Science* (New York, 1958), p. 36; Karl Popper, *The Open Society*, 2 vols. (Princeton, N.J., 1971), 2:210; Robert Craft, *Prejudices in Disguise* (New York, 1974), p. 101.

78. James, "A Pluralistic Mystic," *Memories and Studies* (New York, 1912), p. 411.

79. *Some Problems of Philosophy*, p. 142.

80. Perry, *Thought and Character of James*, 2:656.

CHAPTER EIGHT

1. Albert Bigelow Paine, *Mark Twain: A Biography*, Stormfield ed., 3 vols. (New York, 1929), 3:1156-58.

2. Mark Twain to Joseph Twichell, November 4, 1904, *Mark Twain's Letters*, ed. Albert Bigelow Paine, Stormfield ed., 2 vols. (New York, 1929), 2:763-64.

3. Bernard DeVoto, ed., *Mark Twain in Eruption* (New York and London, 1940), p. 386.

4. Paine, *Mark Twain*, 1:397.

5. Bernard DeVoto, ed., *Letters from the Earth* (New York, 1962), p. 46.

6. Paine, *Twain*, 3:1509.

7. DeVoto, *Twain in Eruption*, p. 247n.

8. Paine, *Twain*, 3:1469.

9. *Letters from the Earth*, p. 12.

10. Arthur Koestler, *The Act of Creation* (New York, 1964), p. 690.

11. Albert Bigelow Paine, ed., *Mark Twain's Notebook* (New York, 1935), pp. 170, 323.

12. Ibid., pp. 255-56.

13. *Following the Equator*, Stormfield ed., 2 vols. (New York, 1929), 1:271-72.

14. Paine, *Twain*, 1:36.

15. There is some doubt as to whether Twain's recollections about MacFarlane can be taken literally. See Paul Baender, "Alias Macfarlane: A Revision of Mark Twain's Biography," *American Literature* 38 (1966-67), pp. 187-97.

16. Mark Twain to William Dean Howells, Hartford, January 7, 1884, in Henry Nash Smith and William M. Gibson, eds., *Mark Twain–Howells Letters: The Correspondence of Samuel L. Clemens and William Dean Howells, 1872-1910*, 2 vols. (Cambridge, Mass., 1960), 2:461.

17. Paine, *Twain*, 1:322-23.

18. Ibid., 2:735.

19. *The Adventures of Huckleberry Finn*, Stormfield ed. (New York, 1929), p. 321.

20. *A Connecticut Yankee in King Arthur's Court*, Stormfield ed. (New York, 1929), pp. 152-53.

21. "The Facts Concerning the Recent Carnival of Crime in Connecticut," in *The Mysterious Stranger and Other Stories*, Signet ed. (New York, 1962), pp. 33-34; *Letters from the Earth*, p. 181.

22. *Mark Twain's Autobiography*, 2 vols., introd. by Albert Bigelow Paine (New York and London, 1924), 1:131; *Twain's Notebook*, pp. 348-49.

23. Paine, *Twain*, 3:1353; *Twain's Notebook*, p. 361.

24. *Twain in Eruption*, pp. 383-84.

25. *Twain's Notebook*, p. 190.

26. For monistic holism, see William H. Hay, "Free-Will and Possibilities," *Philosophy of Science* 24 (July 1957): 207-14. For changing scientific thought, see Karl Pearson, *The Grammar of Science* (New York, 1957); Karl Popper, *The Open Society*, 2 vols. (Princeton, N.J., 1962), 2:85, and William Werkmeister, *A Philosophy of Science* (New York, 1940), pp. 454-55.

27. William E. H. Lecky, *History of European Morals from Augustus to Charlemagne*, 2 vols. (New York, 1876), chap. 1, "The Natural History of Morals," pp. 1-160; *Twain in Eruption*, p. 241. For date, see *Twain-Howells Letters*, 2:693n.

28. *Connecticut Yankee*, pp. 150, 150-51, 177.

29. *Pudd'nhead Wilson*, Hillcrest ed. (New York, 1904), p. 49.

30. Ibid., p. 23.

31. Ibid., p. 133.

32. Ibid., p. 224.

33. *Letters from the Earth*, p. 40.

34. Charles Neider, ed., *Life As I Find It {by} Mark Twain* (Garden City, N.Y., 1961), p. 241; "A Defense of General Funston," *North American Review* 174 (May 1902): 613.

35. *Pudd'nhead Wilson*, pp. 38, 43.

36. Ibid., p. 92.

37. Ibid., p. 139.

38. Ibid.

39. Ibid., p. 140.

40. DeLancey Ferguson, *Mark Twain: Man and Legend* (Indianapolis and New York, 1943), p. 241; Neider, *Twain, Life As I Find It*, p. 316.

41. *Twain in Eruption*, p. 386.

42. Ibid., pp. 384-93.

43. Charles Neider, *The Complete Essays of Mark Twain* (Garden City, N.Y., 1963), pp. 480-81.

44. Ibid., p. 484.

45. Charles Hartshorne and Paul Weiss, eds., *Collected Papers of Charles Sanders Peirce*, 8 vols. (Cambridge, Mass., 1965), 6:46, 553. See also Frances M. Hamblin, "A Comment on Peirce's 'Tychism,'" *Journal of Philosophy* 42 (1945): 378-83.

46. Mark Twain to William Dean Howells, April 2, 1899, *Twain-Howells Letters*, 2:689.

47. *What Is Man? and Other Philosophical Writings*, ed. Paul Baender (Berkeley, Calif., 1973), p. 136.

48. Ibid., p. 151.

49. Ibid., p. 147.

50. Ibid., p. 161.

51. Ibid., p. 130.

52. Ibid.

53. Ibid., p. 176.

54. Ibid., p. 177.

55. Ibid., p. 200.

56. Ibid., p. 131.

57. Ibid., p. 165.

58. Ibid., p. 169.

59. Ibid., p. 170.

60. Ibid., p. 173.

61. "Mark Twain's Philosophy," *Monist* 23 (April 1913): 181-223; "The Mechanistic Principle and the Non-Mechanical," ibid., pp. 224-76.

62. "Mechanism and the Problem of Freedom," *Monist* 27 (April 1917): 295-306; "Determinism and Free Will," ibid., pp. 306-11.

63. Clarence Darrow, *Verdicts Out of Court*, ed. Arthur and Lila Weinberg (Chicago, 1963), pp. 281-82.

18. Ibid., pp. 151-56; *Human Nature and Conduct*, pp. 118-22.
19. *Theory of Moral Life*, pp. 156-63; *Democracy and Education* (New York, 1916), pp. 350-54.
20. *Philosophy and Civilization*, p. 276.
21. John Dewey et al., *Creative Intelligence: Essays in the Pragmatic Attitude* (New York, 1917), p. 28.
22. *Philosophy and Civilization*, pp. 276-82.
23. *Philosophy of Education*, originally pub. as *Problems of Men* (New York, 1946, 1958), p. 121.
24. *Philosophy and Civilization*, p. 281.
25. *Human Nature and Conduct*, pp. 306-7.
26. *Philosophy and Civilization*, pp. 281-82.
27. Joseph Ratner, ed., *Intelligence in the Modern World: John Dewey's Philosophy* (New York, 1939), pp. 343-63.
28. Ibid., p. 359.
29. *Philosophy and Civilization*, p. 291.
30. *Theory of Moral Life*, p. 172.
31. *Philosophy and Civilization*, p. 291.
32. Ibid., pp. 292-93.
33. *Human Nature and Conduct*, p. 311.
34. Ibid., pp. 293-95.
35. *Experience and Nature*, p. 41.
36. *Human Nature and Conduct*, pp. 310-11, 314.
37. *Philosophy and Civilization*, p. 295.
38. *Human Nature and Conduct*, pp. 312-13.
39. *Theory of Moral Life*, pp. 172-73.
40. Ibid., pp. 173-74.
41. Ibid., p. 174.
42. *The Public and Its Problems* (New York, 1927), pp. 166-70; *Philosophy and Civilization*, p. 314; *Philosophy of Education*, p. 267.
43. *Philosophy and Civilization*, p. 297.
44. *The Public and Its Problems*, p. 109.
45. *Individualism Old and New* (New York, 1929), p. 133.
46. Ibid., pp. 132-33.
47. Ibid., p. 167.
48. *Intelligence in the Modern World*, p. 431.
49. *Freedom and Culture* (New York, 1963), p. 88.
50. Ibid., p. 159.
51. *The Public and Its Problems*, pp. 213, 216.
52. *Philosophy of Education*, p. 116.
53. *Freedom and Culture*, p. 175.
54. *Individualism*, p. 161.
55. *Intelligence in the Modern World*, p. 724.
56. *How We Think* (New York, 1909), pp. 66-67.
57. *The Child and the Curriculum* (Chicago, 1902), p. 17.
58. James A. McLellan and John Dewey, *The Psychology of Number and Its Application to Methods of Teaching Arithmetic* (New York, 1895).
59. *Intelligence in the Modern World*, p. 624.
60. Ibid., p. 627.
61. *How We Think*, p. 63.
62. Ibid., p. 64.
63. *Experience and Education* (New York, 1938), p. 64.
64. *Democracy and Education*, p. 310.
65. *Reconstruction in Philosophy*, p. 186.
66. *Human Nature and Conduct*, p. 283.

64. John S. Tuckey, *Mark Twain and Little Satan* (West Lafayette, Ind.,
65. William M. Gibson, ed., *The Mysterious Stranger* (Berkeley, 1969),
66. Ibid., p. 51.
67. Ibid., p. 154.
68. Ibid., p. 72.
69. Ibid., p. 80.
70. Ibid., p. 115.
71. Ibid., pp. 115-16.
72. Ibid., p. 118.
73. Ibid., p. 128.
74. Ibid., pp. 163-64.
75. Ibid., p. 73.
76. Ibid., pp. 79-80.
77. Ibid., p. 403.
78. Ibid., p. 164.
79. Ibid., pp. 164-66.
80. Ibid., pp. 404-5.
81. Charles Neider, "Mark Twain: Reflections on Religion," *Hudson Review* (August 1963): 352.
82. Paine, *Twain*, 3:1459.
83. Gibson, ed., *Mysterious Stranger*, Introduction, pp. 30-31.

## CHAPTER NINE

1. *Philosophy and Civilization* (New York, 1931), p. 271.
2. "Freedom of the Will," in Paul Monroe, ed., *A Cyclopedia of Education*, vols. (New York, 1911), 2:705.
3. *The Influence of Darwin on Philosophy and Other Essays in Contempora Thought* (New York, 1910), p. 19.
4. Horace M. Kallen, "Freedom and Education," *The Philosopher of the Common Man: Essays in Honor of John Dewey to Celebrate His Eightieth Birthday* (New York, 1940), p. 15.
5. *Influence of Darwin*, p. 18.
6. Ibid., pp. 1, 8-9.
7. For Dewey's philosophy of nature, see *Reconstruction in Philosophy* (New York, 1920), *Experience and Nature* (New York, 1925), and *The Quest for Certainty* (New York, 1929).
8. Dewey, "From Absolutism to Experimentalism," in George P. Adams and William Pepperell Montague, eds., *Contemporary American Philosophy*, 2 vols. (New York, 1930), 2:19.
9. *Essays in Experimental Logic* (New York, 1916), p. 214.
10. Paul A. Schilpp, *The Philosophy of John Dewey* (New York, 1939), p. 3.
11. For biographical material on Dewey, see George Dykhuizen, *The Life and Mind of John Dewey* (Carbondale, Ill., 1973); Neil Coughlan, *Young John Dewey: An Essay in American Intellectual History* (Chicago, 1975); Max Eastman, *Great Companions* (New York, 1942); and Schilpp, *Philosophy of Dewey*.
12. *Philosophy and Civilization*, p. 298.
13. Ibid., pp. 297-98.
14. Ibid., p. 271.
15. For Dewey's discussion of free will, see his pieces on "Freedom of the Will" and "Determinism" in Monroe, *Cyclopedia of Education*, 2:705-6, 318; *Theory of the Moral Life* (New York, 1960), pp. 147-76; *Human Nature and Conduct* (New York, 1922), pp. 8-11; *Philosophy and Civilization*, pp. 272-74.
16. *Experience and Nature*, pp. 99-100.
17. *Theory of Moral Life*, p. 170.

67. *Experience and Nature*, p. 42; *Reconstruction in Philosophy*, p. 86.
68. *Essays in Experimental Logic*, p. 9.
69. Ibid., p. 75.
70. *Reconstruction in Philosophy*, p. 178.
71. Ibid.
72. William James, *A Pluralistic Universe* (Cambridge, Mass., 1977), p. 45; Dewey, *Experience and Nature*, pp. 42, 44.
73. *Reconstruction in Philosophy*, p. 178.
74. *Philosophy of Education*, pp. 39-40.
75. *New York Times*, October 19, 1949, p. 31.
76. Irwin Edman, "America's Philosopher Attains an Alert 90," *New York Times Magazine*, October 16, 1949, pp. 17, 74-75.

## EPILOGUE

1. Richard Taylor, *Action and Purpose* (Englewood Cliffs, N.J., 1966); see also Taylor, *Metaphysics* (Englewood Cliffs, N.J., 1963), pp. 44-53, 68-69.
2. Corliss Lamont, *Freedom of Choice Affirmed* (Boston, 1967).
3. Andrew Oldenquist, "Self-Prediction," *Encyclopedia of Philosophy*, 8 vols. (New York, 1967), 7:345-46.
4. Rollin W. Workman, "Is Indeterminism Supported by Quantum Theory?" *Philosophy of Science* 26 (1959): 251-59, discusses the problem; George A. Lundberg, *Can Science Save Us?* (New York, 1947), p. 107.
5. B. F. Skinner, *Beyond Freedom and Dignity* (New York, 1971); *About Behaviorism* (New York, 1974), p. 248; *Walden Two* (New York, 1948).
6. Noam Chomsky, "The Case against B. F. Skinner," *New York Review of Books*, December 30, 1971, p. 23.
7. Sheldon S. Wolin, *New York Review of Books*, June 12, 1975, p. 23.
8. Pauline Kael, "After Innocence," *New Yorker*, October 1, 1973, pp. 113-18; "Onward and Upward with the Arts," ibid., August 5, 1974, p. 44.
9. Richard M. Hunt, "No-Fault Guilt-Free History," *New York Times*, February 16, 1976.
10. *New York Review of Books*, June 26, 1975, p. 3.
11. Hans Morgenthau, "Decline of Democratic Government," *New Republic*, November 9, 1974, pp. 13-18; Robert Heilbroner, *An Inquiry into the Human Prospect* (New York, 1974).
12. *Partisan Review* 42 (1975): 368; for Kennan, see Elie Kedourie, "Is Democracy Doomed?" *Commentary* 62 (November 1976): 40; Michael Novak, *Commentary* 61 (July 1975): 71; Alfred Kazin, "Every Man His Own Revolution," *New Republic*, July 3 & 10, 1976, p. 24.
13. L. H. Butterfield et al., *The Book of Abigail and John: Selected Letters of the Adams Family, 1762-1784* (Cambridge, Mass., 1975), p. 173.

# Bibliographical Essay

IN PREPARING THIS BOOK, I immersed myself in the writings of all of the major thinkers treated here, on the assumption that what they said about freedom was integrally related to their general philosophy. It became clear as I proceeded not only that their views on freedom grew naturally out of their deepest metaphysical assumptions, but also that what they thought about freedom was the best clue to grasping their systems as a whole. In the discussion of sources which follows I have not included every book and essay that helped shape my interpretation of the various figures appearing in this book, but only those that seemed crucial for an understanding of their thinking about freedom. (For example, Dewey's *How We Think*, a marvelous introduction to Dewey's philosophy in brief form, does not appear among the books mentioned here, while *Freedom and Culture* does.) I have included secondary as well as primary sources in my recommendations, and of course interpretations of the men I have analyzed which differ from my own point of view. I have also listed some general books and essays on freedom and necessity which helped to clarify my own thinking about the subject before I launched my studies of particular individuals. I have included only a few of the many biographies and special studies which I read while familiarizing myself with the opinions of the thinkers treated here, and I have not repeated in this essay all of the references contained in the footnotes to the nine chapters and epilogue of the book.

### FREEDOM AND DETERMINISM

Mortimer J. Adler, *The Idea of Freedom* (2 vols., New York, 1958-61), is a useful introduction to definitions of freedom by Western thinkers from the Greeks onward, although it is somewhat overschematized, and Ruth Nanda Anshen, *Freedom: Its Meaning* (New York, 1940) contains essays on the subject by Charles Beard, John Dewey, Raphael Demos, Ralph Barton Perry, Herbert Schneider, and other Americans as well as by Europeans (Croce, Whitehead, Bergson, Russell, et al.), while Horace M. Kallen, ed., *Freedom in the Modern World* (New York, 1928) concentrates on the views of Americans: John Dewey, Zachariah Chafee, Jr., Clarence Darrow, Max Eastman, and others. Kallen's *A Study of Liberty* (Yellow Springs, Ohio, 1959) presents a philosophy of freedom much like Dewey's and includes an informative philological analysis of the words *free* and *liberty*. In a chapter entitled "Of Human Freedom" in *The Metaphysics of Pragmatism* (Chicago, 1927), Sidney Hook discusses the subject with the lucidity for which he was to become famous.

D. J. O'Connor's *Free Will* (New York: Anchor Books, 1971) is an excellent brief presentation of the issues at stake in the free-will controversy, and John Wild presents an existential view of freedom similar to William James's in *Existence and the World of Freedom* (Englewood Cliffs, N.J., 1963). In *Free Will and Four English Philosophers* (London, 1906), Joseph Rickaby criticizes Hobbes, Locke, Hume, and Mill from the free-will point of view. Bernard J. Berofsky, ed., *Free Will and Determinism* (New York, 1966), Gerald Dworkin, ed., *Determinism, Free Will, and Moral Responsibility* (Englewood Cliffs, N.J., 1970), and Sidney Morgenbesser and James Walsh, eds., *Free Will* (Englewood Cliffs, N.J., 1962) contain essays, ancient and modern, on the free-will question; and Sidney Hook, ed., *Determinism and Freedom in the Age of Modern Science* (New York, 1958) deals with the freedom-determinism question largely from the point of view of contemporary science. Christian Bay, *The Structure of Freedom* (Stanford, 1958) and Felix E. Oppenheim, *Dimensions of Freedom* (New York, 1961) take a generally analytical approach.

In *What Is Liberty?* (New York, 1939), Dorothy Fosdick emphasizes circumstantial freedom and warns against authoritarianism disguised as liberty. In *Four Essays on Liberty* (New York, 1969), Isaiah Berlin makes the important point that if social and psychological determinism were established as an accepted truth, our very modes of speech and thought would be utterly transformed. Like Dorothy Fosdick, he also defends "negative" liberty from external restraint and criticizes the notion of "positive" freedom as obedience to a higher law. But C. B. Macpherson has an excellent criticism of Berlin's point of view in *Democratic Theory: Essays in Retrieval* (London, 1973), pp. 95-119, and proposes transforming negative liberty into counterextractive liberty (immunity from the extractive power of others) and positive liberty into developmental liberty. Walter Berns links freedom and virtue (a common theme in this book) in *Freedom, Virtue, and the First Amendment* (Baton Rouge, 1957) and argues that freedom must be subordinate to justice and morality.

For discussions of freedom as creativity and its relation to predictability, see Ninian Smart, *Philosophers and Religious Truth* (New York, 1964, 1969), pp. 45-74; Maurice Cranston, *Freedom* (New York, 1953); and William Barrett, "Determinism and Novelty," in Sidney Hook, ed., *Determinism and Freedom*, pp. 30-39. J. W. T. Mason's *Creative Freedom* (New York, 1926) is disappointing. Influenced by Bergson, Mason explains creativeness as self-development and emphasizes the spontaneity of what is creatively new, but he has little to say about the dynamics of creation. Milton C. Nahm's *The Artist as Creator: An Essay of Human Freedom* (Baltimore, 1956), a systematic examination of originality and intelligibility in the arts, stresses the "great analogy" of the artist to God, as creator and maker, in Western thought, but ends by endorsing Erich Frank's view that "even the finest accomplishment of the human spirit is not real creation, for all human creation presupposes as its matter the world which man has not created himself."

Karl Popper makes a convincing case against determinism in "Indeterminism in Quantum Physics and in Classical Physics," *British Journal for the Philosophy of Science* 1 (August and November 1950): 117-33 and 173-95, and Daniel Lerner has assembled some essays taking different views of causality by specialists in philosophy, biology, political science, sociology, and economics in *Cause and Effect* (New York, 1965). In *The Dimensions of Liberty* (Cambridge, Mass., 1961), Oscar and Mary Handlin show how Americans have looked upon liberty as the proper use of power and discuss the ways in which people have attempted to limit and control it. And in *Chance and Destiny* (Boston, 1954), Oscar Handlin discusses eight turning-points in American history (which would have fascinated Twain) growing out of the momentary convergence of a myriad of personal and social factors. He adopts James's rather than Twain's view of the matter: that chance within the limits of a given situation is always a possibility, and that there is therefore always scope for the assertion of an individual's influence in history.

On the liberty-equality question, T. V. Smith's two books, *The American Philosophy of Equality* (Chicago, 1927) and *The Democratic Way of Life* (Chicago, 1926), and R. H. Tawney's *Equality* (Capricorn Books, New York, 1961) are enormously illuminating. Jerome Frank, *Fate and Freedom* (New York, 1945), a book which should be reprinted in paperback, is a zestful defense of Jamesian freedom and an irreverent demolition of historical and psychological determinism and of inevitabilism of any brand. Frank likes (as I do) Justice Holmes's remark that "the mode in which the inevitable comes to pass is through effort."

## JONATHAN EDWARDS

Jonathan Edwards's position appears at length in *Freedom of the Will* (New Haven, 1957), with a fine introductory essay by Paul Ramsey, and in an abbreviated version in *Freedom of the Will* (Library of the Liberal Arts, Indianapolis and New York, 1969), with a thoughtful introduction by Arnold S. Kaufman and William K. Frankena. But it is also worthwhile to consult the following pieces by Edwards: "Concerning the Divine Decrees in General, and Election in Particular," *The Works of President Edwards* (8 vols., ed. Edward Williams and Edward Parsons, Leeds, 1806-1811), 8:384-423; "Concerning Efficacious Grace," 8:424-73; "Concerning the Perseverance of the Saints," 8:474-99; "A Divine and Supernatural Light," 8:3-21; "God Glorified in Man's Dependence," 6:469-84; *The Great Christian Doctrine of Original Sin Defended*, 2:79-387; "The Justice of God in the Damnation of Sinners," 6:391-430; "The Sole Consideration that God is God, Sufficient to Still All Objections to His Sovereignty," 6:513-24.

For interpretations of Edwards's views on freedom, see Alfred Owen Aldridge, *Jonathan Edwards* (New York, 1964), pp. 80-100, 108-19; Frank H. Foster, *A Genetic History of the New England Theology* (Chicago, 1907), chapters 3 and 9; Joseph Haroutunian, *Piety versus Moralism* (New York, 1932), chapter 9; Clyde A. Holbrook, *The Ethics of Jonathan Edwards* (Ann Arbor, 1973), pp. 38-47; Holbrook, "Editor's Introduction," in Jonathan Edwards, *Original Sin* (New Haven, 1970), pp. 1-101; Holbrook, "Edwards Re-Examined," *Review of Metaphysics* 13 (June 1960): 623-41; Perry Miller, *Jonahan Edwards* (New York, 1949), pp. 110-26, 251-63; Arthur E. Murphy, "Jonathan Edwards on Free Will and Moral Agency," *Philosophical Review* 68 (May 1959): 181-202; Harvey G. Townsend, "The Will and the Understanding in the Philosophy of Edwards," *Church History* 16 (December 1947): 210-20; and Conrad Wright, "Edwards and the Arminians on the Freedom of the Will," *Harvard Theological Review* 35 (October 1942): 241-61.

Harvey G. Townsend, *The Philosophy of Jonathan Edwards from His Private Notebooks* (Eugene, Oregon, 1955) contains passages illuminating Edwards's views on predestination and free grace. For an interesting discussion of Edwards's views on causality, see A. N. Prior, "Limited Determinism," *Review of Metaphysics* 16 (September 1962): 55-61, and two responses to Prior: Mary Mothersill, "Professor Prior and Jonathan Edwards," ibid. (December 1962), pp. 366-73, and J. B. Schneewind, "Comments on Prior's Paper," ibid., pp. 374-79. In an essay for the *American Philosophical Quar-*

*terly* 4 (January 1967): 72-78, "Is Choice Determined by the 'Strongest Motive'?" Rem B. Edwards argues that the chief function of choice is to decide between conflicting motives by concentrating attention on one of them, increasing its intensity, and thus causing it to prevail.

The following essays discuss influences on Edwards: Edward H. Davidson, "From Locke to Edwards," *Journal of the History of Ideas* 24 (July-September 1963): 355-72; Paul Helm, "John Locke and Jonathan Edwards: A Reconsideration," *Journal of the History of Philosophy* 7 (January 1969): 51-61; and James H. Tufts, "Edwards and Newton," *Philosophical Review* 49 (November 1940): 609-22.

Rufus Suter, "The Problem of Evil in the Philosophy of Jonathan Edwards," *Monist* 44 (1934): 280-95, analyzes Edwards's five solutions to the problem of evil. Peter H. Hare, "Rowland G. Hazard (1801-88) on Freedom in Willing," *Journal of the History of Ideas* 33 (January-March 1972): 155-64, is the first scholarly study of Hazard's views.

## THOMAS PAINE AND NATURAL RIGHTS

Thomas Paine's thinking about freedom is scattered throughout his essays, pamphlets, books, and letters (though especially in *Common Sense* and *The Rights of Man*), and it is worth one's while to read *The Complete Writings of Thomas Paine* (2 vols., ed. Philip S. Foner, New York, 1945) in order to acquaint oneself with his natural-rights views. David Freeman Hawke's *Paine* (New York, 1974) is a fine analysis of both Paine's life and his thought. In a chapter on Paine in *Damaged Souls* (Boston and New York, 1923), Gamaliel Bradford says Paine taught people the value of liberty "even if he was not a very sure guide as to the use of it."

For the natural rights and social contract theory in general, J. G. Gough, *The Social Contract* (Oxford, 1936), David G. Ritchie, *Natural Rights* (London, 1894), and Leo Strauss, *Natural Right and History* (Chicago, 1950) are standard, while C. B. Macpherson, *The Political Theory of Possessive Individualism* (Oxford, 1962) is a provocative newer critical study. Paul K. Conkin, *Self-Evident Truths* (Bloomington, Indiana, 1970) and Gilman Ostrander, *The Rights of Man in America, 1606-1861* (Columbia, Missouri, 1960) deal with American attitudes toward natural rights; and Bernard Bailyn's *The Ideological Origins of the American Revolution* (Cambridge, Mass., 1967) has an illuminating analysis of the relation between the American Revolution and liberty in chapters 3 and 6. The first chapter of Albert K. Weinberg, *Manifest Destiny* (Baltimore, 1935) discusses the expansionists' use of natural-rights doctrine.

For Paine's political and social thought, see Henry Collins's fine introduction to Paine's *Rights of Man* (Penguin Books ed., 1969); Robert B. Dishman, *Burke and Paine on Revolution and the Rights of Man* (New York,

1971); Joseph Dorfman, "The Economic Philosophy of Thomas Paine," *Political Science Quarterly* 53 (September 1938): 372-86, which stresses Paine's conservatism; Winthrop Jordan, "Familial Politics: Thomas Paine and the Killing of the King, 1776," an interesting new reading of familiar old material, appearing in the *Journal of American History* 60 (September 1973): 294-309; Cecilia Kenyon's critical essay, "Where Paine Went Wrong," *American Political Science Review* 45 (December 1951): 1086-99; Charles E. Merriam, Jr., "The Political Theories of Thomas Paine," *Political Science Quarterly* 14 (September 1899): 389-404; R. R. Palmer, "Tom Paine: Victim of the Rights of Man," *Pennsylvania Magazine of History and Biography* 46 (April 1942): 161-75; Howard Penniman, "Thomas Paine—Democrat," *American Political Science Review* 37 (April 1943): 244-62; C. E. Persinger, "The Political Philosophy of Thomas Paine," *University of Nebraska Graduate Bulletin* 100, series 6, no. 3 (July 1901): 54-74; and Strother B. Purdy, "A Note on the Burke-Paine Controversy," *American Literature* 39 (November 1967): 373-75.

Eric Foner's *Tom Paine and Revolutionary America* (New York, 1976) is a painstaking and penetrating analysis of the origin and development of Paine's ideas and their relation to eighteenth-century radicalism in America and Europe. R. R. Fennessy contrasts Burke and Paine in *Burke, Paine and the Rights of Man* (The Hague, 1963); and Thomas Copeland, who calls the Burke-Paine controversy "the most crucial ideological debate ever carried on in English," corrects the inaccuracies of previous writers about Paine's relations with Burke in *Our Eminent Friend Edmund Burke: Six Essays* (New Haven, 1949), pp. 146-89. In *Edmund Burke and the Natural Law* (Ann Arbor, 1958), Peter J. Stanlis shows how Burke's philosophy was shaped by classical and scholastic natural law and explains how his view of human rights differed from that of Paine.

For recent discussions of natural rights, see the following: Henry D. Aiken, "Rights, Human or Otherwise," *Monist* 52 (1958): 502-20; Peter L. Berger, "Are Human Rights Universal?" *Commentary*, September, 1977, pp. 60-63; Ralph M. Blake, "On Natural Rights," *Ethics* 36 (1925): 86-96; Stuart M. Brown, Jr., "Inalienable Rights," *Philosophical Review* 44 (April 1955): 192-211; William K. Frankena, "Natural and Inalienable Rights," ibid., pp. 212-32; H. L. A. Hart, "Are There Any Natural Rights?" ibid., pp. 175-91; Margaret Macdonald, "Natural Rights," in Peter Laslett, ed., *Philosophy, Politics and Society* (Oxford, 1956), pp. 35-55; George H. Mead, "Natural Rights and the Theory of Political Institution," *Journal of Philosophy, Psychology, and Scientific Methods* 12 (March 18, 1915): 141-55; Joseph Margolis, "That All Men Are Created Equal," *Journal of Philosophy* 52 (June 23, 1955): 337-46; D. D. Raphael, *Problems of Political Philosophy* (New York, 1970), pp. 102-6; B. A. Richards, "Inalienable Rights:

Recent Criticism and Old Doctrine," *Philosophy and Phenomenological Research* 29 (March 1969): 391-404; Marvin Schiller, "Are There Any Natural Rights?" *Ethics* 79 (July 1969): 309-15; and William J. Wainwright, "Natural Rights," *American Philosophical Quarterly* 4 (January 1967): 79-84.

### RALPH WALDO EMERSON

Emerson's ideas about freedom, like Paine's, are scattered throughout his writings, including his journals, but they appear in a more concentrated form in *Nature* (1836) and in such essays as "Self-Reliance," "Spiritual Laws," "The Over-Soul" (*Essays First Series*), "Experience," "Character," "Nature" (*Essays Second Series*), "Fate," "Power," and "Illusions" (*The Conduct of Life*). There are many editions of these works, but the standard edition is *The Complete Works of Ralph Waldo Emerson* (12 vols., Boston and New York, 1903-4). The older edition of the journals, edited by E. W. Emerson and W. E. Forbes, is *The Journals of Ralph Waldo Emerson* (12 vols., New York, 1909-14), and the new edition, still in process, is William H. Gilman et al., eds., *The Journals and Miscellaneous Notebooks of Ralph Waldo Emerson* (Harvard, 1960-    ).

The essay, "Fate," perhaps Emerson's most brilliant and surely one of the finest ever written by an American, is Emerson's only sustained examination of the freedom-necessity question. George Willis Cooke has a perceptive analysis of the essay in chapter 24 of *Ralph Waldo Emerson: His Life, Writings and Philosophy* (Boston, 1881), pp. 331-50, in which he links it to the other themes in Emerson's thought. Clinton F. Oliver examines "Emerson's Concept of Freedom" briefly in *Journal of Human Relations* (Winter 1953): 50-62, and Stephen Whicher does so at greater length in *Freedom and Fate: An Inner Life of Ralph Waldo Emerson* (Philadelphia, 1953). Whicher's study casts searching new light on Emerson, but as the subtitle indicates it concentrates on Emerson's personal development rather than on his objective philosophy of freedom.

The following books devoted to Emerson's thought have something to say in passing about his conception of freedom: Jonathan Bishop, *Emerson on the Soul* (Cambridge, Mass., 1964); Oscar W. Firkins, *Ralph Waldo Emerson* (Boston and New York, 1915); Edwin D. Mead, *The Influence of Emerson* (Boston, 1903); and Sherman Paul, *Emerson's Angle of Vision* (Cambridge, Mass., 1952). My own study, *American Transcendentalism, 1830-60: An Intellectual Inquiry* (New York, 1974) places Emerson's thought in the context of the Transcendental movement as a whole. I found the following books helpful in thinking about intuition and creativity: Mario Bunge, *Intuition and Science* (Englewood Cliffs, N.J., 1962); Howard E. Gruber et al., eds., *Contemporary Approaches to Creative Thinking* (New York,

1962); Arthur Koestler, *The Act of Creation* (New York, 1964); and
A. M. Taylor, *Imagination and the Growth of Science* (New York, 1970).

## JOHN C. CALHOUN

John C. Calhoun's ideas on liberty and government appear in *Disquisition on Government* and *Discourse on the Constitution of the United States*,
both of which may be found in volume 1 of *The Works of John C. Calhoun*,
R. C. Crallé, ed. (6 vols., New York, 1854-56), and in "South Carolina Exposition," *Works*, 6:1-59. For his views on free speech, see his "Speech on
the Dangers of 'Factious Opposition,'" January 15, 1814, in *The Papers of
John C. Calhoun* (Columbia, S.C., 1959), 1:189-201, and "Onslow to Patrick
Henry on the Powers of the Vice-President as President of the Senate,"
*Works*, 6:322-48. He discusses liberty and union, during his nationalist days,
in "Speech on the Repeal of the Direct Tax," January 31, 1816, *Works*,
2:135-53, "Speech on the Tariff Bill," April 6, 1816, ibid., pp. 163-73, and,
during his nullificationist days, in "Speech on the Force Bill," February 15-16,
1833, ibid., pp. 197-262, and "Speech on His Resolutions in Support of State
Rights," February 26, 1833, ibid., pp. 262-309.

For discussions of freedom and slavery, see "Speech on the Reception of
Abolition Petitions," February 6, 1837, *Works*, 2:625-33, "Remarks on the
States' Rights Resolutions in Regard to Abolition," December 27, 1837, ibid.,
3:140-202, "Remarks on Presenting His Resolutions on the Slave Question,"
February 19, 1847, ibid., 4:339-49, "Speech on His Resolutions in Reference
to the War with Mexico," January 4, 1848, ibid., pp. 396-424, and "Speech
on the Oregon Bill," June 27, 1848, ibid., pp. 479-512.

For his general political and social philosophy, see Richard N. Current,
*John C. Calhoun* (New York, 1963); Ralph Lerner, "John C. Calhoun," in
Martin J. Frisch and Richard G. Stevens, eds., *American Political Thought:
The Philosophic Dimensions of American Statesmanship* (New York, 1971),
pp. 99-124; and August O. Spain, *The Political Theory of John C. Calhoun*
(New York, 1951). John L. Thomas, ed., *John C. Calhoun: A Profile* (New
York, 1968) contains essays on various aspects of Calhoun's life and thought
by Ralph H. Gabriel, Charles Wiltse, Gerald Capers, Margaret Coit, Richard
Current, and other scholars. Christopher Hollis's chapter on Calhoun in *The
American Heresy* (London, 1927), is an Englishman's defense of Calhoun's
ideas on liberty and slavery and remains a curiosity. Nathaniel W. Stephenson
makes a more restrained defense in "Calhoun and the Divine Right of the
Majority" in *Scripps College Papers*, no. 3 (Claremont, Calif., March, 1930),
pp. 21-38; and George Kateb, in "The Majority Principle: Calhoun and His
Antecedents," *Political Science Quarterly* 84 (1969): 583-605, discusses Calhoun's concurrent majority as a theory of the permanent minority.

The following are also of interest: William H. Freehling, "Spoilsmen and Interests in the Thought and Career of John C. Calhoun," *Journal of American History* 53 (June 1965): 25-42; chapter 4, "John C. Calhoun: The Marx of the Master Class," in Richard Hofstadter, *The American Political Tradition* (New York, 1948), Theodore R. Marmor, "Anti-Industrialism and the Old South: The Agrarian Perspective of John C. Calhoun," *Comparative Studies in Society and History* 9 (July 1967): 377-406; Charles E. Merriam, "The Political Philosophy of John C. Calhoun," *Studies in Southern History and Politics* (New York, 1914), pp. 317-38; and "John C. Calhoun, Realist," in Vernon L. Parrington, *Main Currents in American Thought* (3 vols., New York, 1927, 1930), 2:69-82.

## Frederick Douglass

For Frederick Douglass's thought on freedom and slavery, the three autobiographies are fundamental: *Narrative of the Life of Frederick Douglass* (Cambridge, Mass., 1960), with an introduction by Benjamin Quarles; *My Bondage and My Freedom* (New York, 1969); and *The Life and Times of Frederick Douglass* (London, 1962). The following speeches and essays, all to be found in *The Life and Writings of Frederick Douglass* (4 vols., ed. Philip S. Foner, New York, 1950), are of special interest: "An Appeal to the British People," May 12, 1846, 1:154-65; "American Slavery," October 22, 1847, 1:269-78; "The Constitution and Slavery," March 16, 1849, 1:361-67; Lecture on Slavery, December 1, 1850, 1:132-39; Lecture on Slavery, December 5, 1850, 2:139-49; "The Meaning of July Fourth for the Negro," July 5, 1852, 2:181-204; "The Claims of the Negro Ethnologically Considered," July 12, 1854, 2:289-309; "The Anti-Slavery Movement," January, 1855, 2:333-59; "The Constitution and Slavery," March 26, 1860, 2:467-80; "A Plea for Free Speech in Boston," December 14, 1860, 2:538-40; "How to End the War," May, 1861, 3:94-96; "The Decision of the Hour," June 16, 1861, 3:118-25; "What Shall Be Done with the Slaves if Emancipated?" January, 1862, 3:188-91; "The Future of the Negro People of the Slave States," February 12, 1862, 3:210-25; "The Proclamation and a Negro Army," February, 1863, 3:321-37; "The Present and Future of the Colored Race in America," May, 1863, 3:347-59; "What the Black Man Wants," April, 1865, 4:157-65; "Give Us the Freedom Intended for Us," December 5, 1872, 4:298-300; Oration in Memory of Abraham Lincoln, April 14, 1876, 4:309-19; and "The Color Line," June, 1881, 4:342-52.

Benjamin Quarles has written a good biography, *Frederick Douglass* (New York, 1948), and in *Frederick Douglass* (Englewood Cliffs, N.J., 1968) has assembled essays by and about Douglass. Two of Quarles's essays for the *Journal of Negro History* are helpful: "The Breach between Douglass and Garrison," 23 (April 1938): 144-54, and "Frederick Douglass and the Woman's Rights Movement," 25 (January 1940): 35-44. "Freedom is and has always been America's root concern," according to Quarles, and in *Black Abolitionists* (New York, 1969), he deals with what he calls abolition's "different drummers." J. W. Cooke, "Freedom in the Thought of Frederick Douglass, 1845-1860," *Negro History Bulletin* (February 1969), pp. 6-10, is a good brief summary of how Douglass thought of freedom. August Meier, "Frederick Douglass' Vision for America: A Case Study in Nineteenth-Century Negro Protest," in Harold M. Hyman and Leonard W. Levy, eds., *Freedom and Reform: Essays in Honor of Henry Steele Commager* (New York, 1967), pp. 127-48, stresses the moral nature of Douglass's thinking about reform, and a popular biography, Booker T. Washington, *Frederick Douglass* (Philadelphia, 1907), says Douglass "was for liberty, at all times, and in all shapes." Herbert J. Storing, "Frederick Douglass," in Martin J. Frisch and Richard G. Stevens, eds., *American Political Thought* (New York, 1971), pp. 145-66, scans his life as a whole. Ronald T. Takaki shows his ambivalence toward violence in "Not Afraid to Die: Frederick Douglass and Violence," in *Violence in the Black Imagination* (New York, 1972).

It is a good idea to examine some of the other slave narratives in order to put Douglass's experiences in perspective. John F. Bayliss, ed., *Black Slave Narratives* (New York, 1970); Arna Bontemps's two collections, *Five Black Lives* (Middletown, Conn., 1971) and *Great Slave Narratives* (Boston, 1969); and Gilbert Osofsky, ed., *Puttin' on Ole Massa* (New York, 1969) are immensely useful, as are such studies of slavery as John W. Blassingame, *The Slave Community* (New York, 1972); William F. Cheek, ed., *Black Resistance before the Civil War* (Beverly Hills, Calif., 1970); David Brion Davis, *The Problem of Slavery in Western Culture* (Ithaca, N.Y., 1966); Eugene D. Genovese, *Roll, Jordan, Roll: The World the Slaves Made* (New York, 1974); Leon F. Litwack, *North of Slavery: The Negro in the Free States, 1790-1860* (Chicago, 1961); and Richard C. Wade, *Slavery in the Cities: The South, 1820-1860* (London and New York, 1964). One wonders why a major film has never been made of one of the great slave narratives like Gustavus Vasa's or Douglass's.

## EDWARD BELLAMY

Edward Bellamy's discussion of psychological freedom may be found in *The Blindman's World and Other Stories* (Boston and New York, 1898) and in such novels as *Dr. Heidenhoff's Process* (New York, 1880) and *Miss Ludington's Sister: A Romance of Immortality* (Boston, 1884). His philosophy of collective freedom appears in *Looking Backward, 2000-1887* (Modern Library, New York, 1917), *Equality* (New York, 1897), *The Religion of Solidarity*, ed. Arthur E. Morgan (Yellow Springs, Ohio, 1940), and in Joseph Schiffman, ed., *Selected Writings on Religion and Society* (New York, 1955).

For Bellamy's response to the charge that Nationalism was inimical to freedom, see such essays as "Declaration of Principles," "Nationalism—Principles, Purposes," "What Nationalism Means," "Some Misconceptions of Nationalism," and "'Looking Backward' Again" in *Edward Bellamy Speaks Again!* (Kansas City, Mo., 1937); "To A Lover of Freedom," "To an Opponent to Paternalism," "To a Woman's Rights Advocate," and "To a Lover of Variety" in *Talks on Nationalism* (Chicago, 1938); and editorials and articles in *The Nationalist* (3 vols., Boston, 1889-91) and *The New Nation* (4 vols., Boston, 1891-94), which he edited.

Arthur E. Morgan's biography, *Edward Bellamy* (New York, 1944), contains important Bellamy material published nowhere else, as does his *Philosophy of Edward Bellamy* (New York, 1945). Sylvia E. Bowman's two studies, *Edward Bellamy Abroad: An American Prophet's Influence* (New York, 1962) and *The Year 2000: A Critical Biography of Edward Bellamy* (New York, 1958), also contain material pertinent to a grasp of Bellamy's concept of freedom. Bowman's essay, "Bellamy's Missing Chapter," *New England Quarterly* 31 (March 1958): 47-65, discusses his attitude toward women. For commentaries on Bellamy, see Daniel Aaron, "Edward Bellamy: Village Utopian," in *Men of Good Hope* (New York, 1951), pp. 92-132; George J. Becker, "Edward Bellamy: Utopia, American Plan," *Antioch Review* 14 (Summer 1954): 181-94; David Bleich, "Eros and Bellamy," *American Quarterly* 16 (Fall 1964): 445-59; Louis Filler, "Edward Bellamy and the Spiritual Unrest," *American Journal of Economics and Sociology* 8 (April 1949): 239-49; John Hope Franklin, "Edward Bellamy and the Nationalist Movement," *New England Quarterly* 11 (December 1938): 739-72; Albert William Levi, "Edward Bellamy: Utopian," *Ethics* 55 (January 1945): 131-44; Charles Madison, *Critics and Crusaders* (New York, 1947), pp. 134-54; Lewis Mumford, *The Story of Utopias* (New York, 1922), pp. 159-69; Vernon L. Parrington, Jr., *American Dreams: A Study of American Utopias* (New York, 1947), pp. 69-97; J. Elliot Ross, "On Rereading Bellamy," *Commonweal* 23 (February 14, 1936): 432-34; Elizabeth Sadler, "One Book's Influence: Edward Bellamy's 'Looking Backward,'" *New England Quarterly* 17 (December 1944): 530-55; Thomas A. Sancton, "Looking Inward: Edward Bellamy's Spiritual Crisis," *American Quarterly* 25 (December 1973): 538-57; Joseph Schiffman, "Edward Bellamy's Altruistic Man," *American Quarterly* 6 (Fall 1954): 195-209; Schiffman, "Edward Bellamy's Religious Thoughts," *Publications of the Modern Language Association* 68 (September 1953): 716-32; and John L. Thomas, "Utopia for an Urban Age: Henry George, Henry Demarest Lloyd, Edward Bellamy," *Perspectives in American History* 6 (Cambridge, Mass., 1972): 135-63. John L. Thomas's lengthy introduction to *Looking Backward* (Cambridge, Mass., 1967), pp. 1-88, is extremely perceptive and cites unpublished Bellamy material. In "Experience and Utopia: The Making of Edward Bellamy's *Looking Backward*," *Journal of American Studies* 11 (April 1977): 54-60, R. Jackson Wilson insists that Bellamy really was backward-looking: he feared industrialism and workingmen, and his utopian dream was basically preindustrial.

For William Graham Sumner's antithetical views on liberty and equality, see *Earth-Hunger and Other Essays* (New Haven, 1913). It is entertaining for a while (and then tiresome) to scan some of the responses (usually in the form of novels) to *Looking Backward*. A couple of them are friendly: Thomas Reynolds, *Prefaces and Notes, Illustrative, Explanatory, Demonstrative, Argumentative, and Expostulatory to Mr. Edward Bellamy's Famous Book, "Looking Backward"* (London, 1890) and Solomon Schindler, *Young West: A Sequel to Edward Bellamy's Celebrated Novel, Looking Backward* (Boston, 1894). Most of them are hostile: Richard Michaelis, *A Sequel to Looking Backward; or, "Looking Further Forward"* (London, ca. 1890); J. W. Roberts, *Looking Within* (New York, 1893); George Sanders, *Reality; or, Law and Order vs. Anarchy and Socialism* (Cleveland, 1898); W. W. Satterlee, *Looking Backward and What I Saw* (New York, 1890); Mrs. John B. Shipley, *The True Author of Looking Backward* (New York, 1890), which falsely accused Bellamy of plagiarism; Arthur D. Vinton, *Looking Further Backward* (Albany, 1890); and Conrad Wilbrandt, *Mr. East's Experiences in Mr. Bellamy's World* (New York, 1891).

## WILLIAM JAMES

William James's famous essay, "The Dilemma of Determinism," appears in *The Will to Believe and Other Essays* (Dover, N.Y., 1956), and in the same volume appear three other essays relevant to the freedom-determinism question: "Great Men and Their Environment," "The Importance of Individuals," and "On Some Hegelisms." James's essay, "Great Men and Their Environment," was in part a response to two essays by Grant Allen arguing that culture was determined by physical circumstances: "Hellas and Civilization," *Popular Science Monthly Supplement,* September, 1878, pp. 398-406, and "Nation-Making," *Popular Science Monthly Supplement*, December, 1878, pp. 121-27. Allen replied to James's essay in "The Genesis of Genius," *Atlantic Monthly* 42 (March 1881): 371-81. John Fiske also replied to James but was critical of Allen in "Sociology and Hero-Worship," ibid., pp. 75-84.

In James's *Principles of Psychology* (2 vols., Dover, N.Y., 1950), the sections on The Automaton Theory, Attention, and Will are especially pertinent to the free-will question, and in *Pragmatism and Four Essays from the Meaning of Truth* (Meridian Books, New York, 1955), the following four essays are of interest: "Some Metaphysical Problems Pragmatically Considered," "The One and the Many," "Pragmatism and Common Sense," and

"Pragmatism and Religion." The essays on "The Types of Philosophic Thinking" and "Monistic Idealism" in *A Pluralistic Universe* (New York, 1909); on "Humanism and Truth" and "Abstractionism and Relativismus" in *The Meaning of Truth* (New York, 1909); chapters 9 through 13 on novelty in *Some Problems of Philosophy* (London, 1911); the essay on "The Experience of Activity" in *Essays in Radical Empiricism* (New York, 1912); and the one on "The Feeling of Effort," later rewritten for inclusion in *Principles of Psychology*, in *Collected Essays and Reviews* (New York, 1920), pp. 151-219, are all important for understanding James's thinking about freedom. One should also examine his wonderful letters, *Letters of William James* (2 vols., ed. Henry James, Boston, 1920) and Ralph Barton Perry's superb intellectual portrait, *The Thought and Character of William James* (2 vols., Boston, 1935), a work which contains previously unpublished material by James.

In *The Origins of Pragmatism* (London, 1968), A. J. Ayer has excellent discussions of Charles Peirce on chance (pp. 103-11) and of James on free will (pp. 212-19). Gay Wilson Allen, who has written a good biography of James, has an essay on Jamesian freedom in Sydney J. Krause, ed., *Essays on Determinism in American Literature* (Kent, Ohio, 1964). Gertrude A. Bussey, *Typical Recent Conceptions of Freedom* (Greenfield, Mass., 1917), discusses James. John K. Roth, *Freedom and the Moral Life* (Philadelphia, 1969), a study of James's ethics, devotes chapter 3 to James's views on freedom. Edward L. Thorndike, "A Pragmatic Substitute for Free Will," in *Essays Philosophical and Psychological in Honor of William James* (New York, 1908), makes James's meliorism consistent with determinism. And John Wild, *The Radical Empiricism of William James* (New York, 1969), discerns existential elements in James's views on freedom.

For recent discussions of James's essay, "The Dilemma of Determinism," see Robert W. Beard, "James and the Rationality of Determinism," *Journal of the History of Philosophy* 5 (1967): 149-56; William H. Hay, "Free-Will and Possibilities," *Philosophy of Science* 24 (July 1957): 207-14; Douglas Clyde Mcintosh, "Responsibility, Freedom, and Causality: Or, The Dilemma of Determinism or Indeterminism," *Journal of Philosophy* 37 (1940): 42-51; and Clarence Shute, "The Dilemma of Determinism after Seventy-Five Years," *Mind* 70 (1961): 331-50.

James M. Edie, "Notes on the Philosophical Anthropology of William James," in Edie, ed., *An Invitation to Phenomenology* (Chicago, 1965), pp. 110-32, says that action for James was another word for freedom. S. P. Fullinwider, "William James's 'Spiritual Crisis,'" *The Historian* 38 (November 1975): 39-59, and Cushing Strout, "William James and the Twice-Born Sick Soul," *Daedalus* 97 (Summer 1968): 1062-82, stress psychological factors in James's search for freedom. William Barrett sees James as very much of our own times: "Our Contemporary, William James," *Commentary*, December, 1975, pp. 55-61.

## MARK TWAIN

Mark Twain presents his "Gospel of Determinism" at length in *What Is Man?* and *The Mysterious Stranger*, and the editions of these works published by the University of California Press contain valuable introductory analyses plus related Twain material: *What Is Man? And Other Philosophical Writings* (ed. Paul Baender, Berkeley, 1970) and *The Mysterious Stranger* (ed. William M. Gibson, Berkeley, 1970). John S. Tuckey's edition of *Mark Twain's Which Was the Dream?* (Berkeley, 1967) contains deterministic musings of Twain's, and his edition of *Mark Twain's Fables of Man* (Berkeley, 1972) is filled with hitherto unpublished material by Twain on "The Myth of Providence," "The Dream of Brotherhood," and "The Nightmare of History."

Twain's determinism also appears in *The Autobiography of Mark Twain* (ed. Charles Neider, New York, 1961); in essays on "The Turning-Point of My Life" and on "Corn-Pone Opinions" in *The Complete Essays of Mark Twain* (ed. Charles Neider, Garden City, N.Y., 1963); in *The Connecticut Yankee in King Arthur's Court* (many editions); in "A Defense of General Funston" and "Rudyard Kipling on Mark Twain" in Charles Neider, ed., *Mark Twain: Life as I Find It* (Garden City, N.Y., 1961); in *Letters from the Earth* (New York, 1962); in *Pudd'nhead Wilson* (Grove Press edition, New York, 1955); in "What Is Man?" in *Mark Twain in Eruption* (ed. Bernard DeVoto, New York, 1940); and in "The Symbols of Despair" in *Mark Twain at Work* (ed. Bernard DeVoto, Cambridge, Mass., 1942). Charles Neider presents Twain's religious views, as dictated by Twain in June, 1906, in "Mark Twain: Reflections on Religion," *Hudson Review* 16 (August 1963): 329-52. Albert B. Paine's biography, *Mark Twain* (3 vols., New York, 1929) and his edition of *Mark Twain's Letters* (2 vols., New York, 1929) and *Mark Twain's Notebooks* (New York, 1935) are also valuable for tracking down Twain's philosophy.

There are a prodigious number of books and essays on various aspects of Twain's life and work, many of them of a high order indeed; but when it comes to determinism, the most pertinent books are the following: Gladys Bellamy, *Mark Twain as a Literary Artist* (Norman, Okla., 1950); Van Wyck Brooks, *The Ordeal of Mark Twain* (New York, 1920), a book which still sets many Twain scholars' teeth on edge; Pascal Covici, Jr., *Mark Twain's Humor* (Dallas, 1962), chapter 9; and John S. Tuckey, *Mark Twain and Little Satan* (Lafayette, Ind., 1963). The following essays also touch on Twain's mechanistic determinism in one way or another: Sir John Adams, "Mark Twain, Psychologist," *Dalhousie Review* 13 (January 1934): 417-26;

Charles A. Allen, "Mark Twain and Conscience," *Literature and Psychology* 7 (May 1975): 17-21; Richard Altick, "Mark Twain's Despair," *South Atlantic Quarterly* 34 (October 1935): 359-67; Stanley Brodwin, "Mark Twain's Masks of Satire: The Final Phase," *American Literature* 45 (May 1973): 206-27; Clinton S. Burhans, Jr., "The Sober Affirmation of Mark Twain's Hadleyburg," *American Literature* 34 (November 1962): 375-84; Paul Carus, "Mark Twain's Philosophy," *Monist* 23 (April 1913): 181-223; James M. Cox, "Pudd'nhead Wilson: The End of Mark Twain's American Dream," *South Atlantic Quarterly* 58 (Summer 1959): 351-63; Sherwood Cummings, "*What is Man?*: The Scientific Sources," in Sydney J. Krause, ed., *Essays on Determinism in American Literature* (Kent, Ohio, 1964); Ellwood Johnson, "Mark Twain's Dream Self in the Nightmare of History," *Mark Twain Journal* 15 (Winter 1970): 6-12; Alexander E. Jones, "Mark Twain and the Determinism of *What Is Man?*," *American Literature* 29 (1957): 1-17; Coleman O. Parsons, "The Devil and Samuel Clemens," *Virginia Quarterly Review* 23 (Autumn 1947): 582-605; Parsons, "The Background of *The Mysterious Stranger*," *American Literature* 32 (March 1960): 55-74; Robert A. Rees and Richard Dilworth Rust, "Mark Twain's 'The Turning Point of My Life,'" *American Literature* 40 (January 1969): 524-35; Stuart P. Sherman, "The Misanthropy of Mark Twain," *Nation* 13 (December 21, 1916): 588-89; John S. Tuckey, "Mark Twain's Later Dialogue: The 'Me' and the Machine," *American Literature* 41 (1969-70): 532-42; and Hyatt Howe Waggoner, "Science in the Thought of Mark Twain," *American Literature* 8 (1936-37): 357-70.

Hamlin Hill, *Mark Twain, God's Fool* (New York, 1973), illuminates Twain's last, sad years. John Tuckey has assembled essays and extracts from books discussing *The Mysterious Stranger* in *Mark Twain's The Mysterious Stranger and the Critics* (Belmont, Calif., 1968). W. H. Roberts, "Are We Machines? And What of It?" *Journal of Philosophy* 28 (1931): 347-56, discusses the machine metaphor amusingly and points out that it would be easy to prove that pretty girls were peaches if one took liberties with the concept of peaches the way mechanists do with the concept of machine. A good discussion of Charles S. Peirce's criticism of determinism appears in Frances Murphy Hamblin's "A Comment on Peirce's 'Tychism,'" *Journal of Philosophy* 42 (1945): 378-83. Sholom J. Kahn's *Mark Twain's Mysterious Stranger: A Study of the Mysterious Stranger Texts* (Columbia, Mo., 1978), which appeared too late for discussion in this chapter, rejects the 1916 Paine-Duneka edition of *The Mysterious Stranger* and considers the true text to be among Twain's best work.

## JOHN DEWEY

The best single introduction to John Dewey's philosophy of freedom is the essay on "Philosophies of Freedom" appearing in *Philosophy and Civilization* (New York, 1931), pp. 271-98, which covers a wide range of questions regarding the concept. In a less ambitious essay, "The Problem of Freedom," in Ruth Nanda Anshen, ed., *Freedom: Its Meaning* (New York, 1940), pp. 359-74, Dewey examines the freedom of "co-operative individualities." For the rest, Dewey's treatment of freedom in its different aspects appears in a wide variety of books and essays. For discussions of free will and determinism, see the essays on "Determinism" and "Freedom of the Will" in Paul Monroe, ed., *A Cyclopedia of Education* (5 vols., New York, 1911): 2:318, 705-6; *Human Nature and Conduct* (New York, 1922), pp. 8-11; the essays on "The Superstition of Necessity," "The Ego as Cause," and "The Psychology of Effort" in *Philosophy, Psychology, and Social Practice* (ed. Joseph Ratner, New York, 1963); "Self-Realization as the Moral Ideal," *Philosophical Review* 2 (November 1893): 652-64; and *Theory of the Moral Life* (with an introduction by Arnold Isenberg, New York, 1960), pp. 147-76. Such books as *Creative Intelligence: Essays in the Pragmatic Attitude* (New York, 1917), containing an essay by Dewey on "The Need for a Recovery of Philosophy" (pp. 3-69); *Democracy and Education* (New York, 1916); *Experience and Nature* (New York, 1925); *Intelligence in the Modern World* (ed. Joseph Ratner, New York, 1939); and *The Quest for Certainty* (New York, 1929) place Dewey's views on freedom in the context of his instrumental and experimental naturalism, and they make exciting reading despite Dewey's placid style.

For Dewey's social philosophy as it relates to freedom, see *Freedom and Culture* (New York, 1939); "Freedom of Thought and Work," *New Republic* 22 (May 5, 1920): 316-17; *Individualism, Old and New* (New York, 1929); *Liberalism and Social Action* (New York, 1935); "Liberty and Social Control," *Social Frontier* 2 (November 1935): 41-42; and *The Public and Its Problems* (New York, 1927). The following books and articles contain material on education and freedom: "Academic Freedom," *Educational Theory* 23 (January 1902): 1-14; *Dewey on Education* (ed. Reginald D. Archambault, New York, 1966); the one-volume edition of *The Child and the Curriculum* and *The School and Society* published by the University of Chicago (Phoenix Books, n.d.); *Experience and Education* (New York, 1938); *John Dewey on Education: Selected Writings* (ed. Reginald Archambault, New York, 1964); *Philosophy of Education*, originally published as *Problems of Men* in 1946 (Totowa, N.J., 1966); and *Schools of Tomorrow* (New York, 1915), written with Evelyn Dewey. Dewey's essay on "Mediocrity and Individuality" for the *New Republic* 33 (December 6, 1922): 35-37, associates freedom with individuality and criticizes the classificatory submergence of individuals in the averaged aggregates of intelligence tests.

For discussions of Dewey's philosophy of freedom, see John R. Arscott,

"Two Philosophies of Freedom," *School and Society* 74 (November 3, 1951): 276-79; Kenneth Benne, "The Human Individual: John Dewey," *University Review* 7 (October 1940): 48-56; Richard J. Bernstein, "Knowledge, Value, and Freedom," in Charles W. Hendel, ed., *John Dewey and the Experimental Spirit in Philosophy* (New York, 1959), pp. 63-92; Denton L. Geyer, "Three Types of Education for Freedom," *School and Society* 46 (November 29, 1947): 406-9; William Hay, "John Dewey on Freedom and Choice," *Monist* 48 (July 1964): 346-55; Sidney Hook, "John Dewey—Philosopher of Growth," *Journal of Philosophy* 56 (December 3, 1959): 1010-18; Horace Kallen, "Freedom and Education," in *The Philosopher of the Common Man: Essays in Honor of John Dewey to Celebrate His Eightieth Birthday* (New York, 1940), pp. 15-32; Kallen, "Individuality, Individualism, and John Dewey," *Antioch Review* 19 (Fall 1959): 299-314; Gail Kennedy, "Dewey's Concept of Experience: Determinate, Indeterminate, and Problematic," *Journal of Philosophy* 56 (October 8, 1959): 801-14; Bella K. Milmed, "Dewey's Treatment of Causality," *Journal of Philosophy* 54 (January 3, 1957): 5-19; and Lloyd P. Williams, "The Experimentalist's Conception of Freedom," *Educational Theory* 4 (April 1954): 105-12.

### RECENT DISCUSSIONS OF FREE WILL AND DETERMINISM

For a good summary, with critical comments, of recent discussions of free will, see Harald Ostad, "Recent Work on the Free-Will Problem," *American Philosophical Quarterly* 4 (July 1967): 179-207. John G. Gill's essay, "The Definition of Freedom," *Ethics* 82 (October 1972): 1-20, is a bit eccentric but makes some illuminating points. Two older essays which take an anti-deterministic point of view are A. D. Lindsay's fascinating piece, "Moral Causation and Artistic Production," *International Journal of Ethics* 15 (July 1905): 399-417, and A. A. Merrill's enlightening analysis of a spontaneous act, "Prediction and Spontaneity," *Journal of Philosophy, Psychology, and Scientific Methods* 16 (1919): 161-62.

Recent defenses of some form of free will appear in the following: Douglas Browning, "Creativity, Correspondence, and Statements about the Future," *Philosophy and Phenomenological Research* 28 (1967-68): 514-36; Frederick Ferré, "Self-Determinism," *American Philosophical Quarterly* 10 (July 1973): 165-76; Carl Ginet, "Can the Will Be Caused?" *Philosophical Review* 71 (1962): 49-55; and Keith Lehrer, "Can We Know That We Have Free Will by Introspection?" *Journal of Philosophy* 57 (March 3, 1960): 145-57. Robert C. Neville, *The Cosmology of Freedom* (New Haven, 1974), argues that sometimes we choose what motivation we will allow to be determinative, and he links free choice with other personal and social freedoms. Andrew Oldenquist summarizes the arguments against determinism associated with unpredictability in "Self-Prediction," *Encyclopedia of Philoso-*

*phy* (8 vols., 1967), 7:345-48; and Michael Scriven, "An Essential Unpredictability in Human Behavior," in Benjamin B. Wolman, ed., *Scientific Psychology* (New York, 1965), pp. 411-25, argues the case for unpredictability. A. Aaron Snyder, "The Paradox of Determinism," *American Philosophical Quarterly* 9 (October 1972): 353-56, insists that it is self-refuting to suppose there can be a proof of the doctrine of universal causal determinism. But H. W. Hintz, "Causation, Will, and Creativity," *Journal of Philosophy* 55 (1958): 514-20, thinks that neither libertarianism nor determinism is empirically proven; David L. Perry, "Prediction, Explanation, and Freedom," *Monist* 49 (1965): 234-84, thinks freedom is compatible with prediction and explanation in human affairs; and A. J. Stenner, "On Predicting Our Future," *Journal of Philosophy* 61 (1964): 415-28, argues that our inability to predict the future course of history accurately is due to lack of empirical knowledge and should be viewed as a difficulty to be overcome. In "Determinism in History," *Philosophy and Phenomenological Research* 20 (March 1960): 291-317, Ernest Nagel dissociates prediction from determinism and upholds the latter.

For Richard Taylor's defense of free agency, see his *Action and Purposes* (Englewood Cliffs, N.J., 1966) and his *Metaphysics* (Englewood Cliffs, N.J., 1963), pp. 44-53. Corliss Lamont defends somewhat similar views in *Freedom of Choice Affirmed* (Boston, 1967) and presents a good summary of recent opinions on the subject. For a scientist's view, see Arthur Compton's two books, *The Freedom of Man* (New Haven, 1935) and *The Human Meaning of Science* (Chapel Hill, 1940). B. F. Skinner has presented popular expositions of his determinism in *Beyond Freedom and Dignity* (New York, 1971), *About Behaviorism* (New York, 1974), and *Walden Two* (New York, 1948). Thoughtful criticisms of Skinner appear in Finley Carpenter, *The Skinner Primer: Behind Freedom and Dignity* (New York, 1974); Noam Chomsky, "The Case against B. F. Skinner," *New York Review of Books*, December 30, 1971, pp. 18-24; and Anne E. Freedman, *The Planned Society: An Analysis of Skinner's Proposals* (Behaviordelia, 1972). Willard E. Enteman has a lucid discussion of the implications for free will of Heisenberg's Principle of Uncertainty in "Microphysics and Free Will," in Enteman, ed., *The Problem of Free Will* (New York, 1967), pp. 281-99.

# Index